For Joan Scott,
from whom I have
learned so much
about conceptualizing

gender,

Caroline Bynum

Gender and Religion

Gender and Religion: On the Complexity of Symbols

Edited by

Caroline Walker Bynum
Stevan Harrell
and Paula Richman

Beacon Press   Boston

Beacon Press
25 Beacon Street
Boston, Massachusetts 02108

Beacon Press books are published under the auspices
of the Unitarian Universalist Association
of Congregations in North America.

92 91 90 89 88 87 86   8 7 6 5 4 3 2 1

Library of Congress Cataloging-in-Publication Data
Gender and religion.
  Includes index.
  1. Sex—Religious aspects.   2. Sex role—Religious
aspects.   I. Bynum, Caroline Walker.   II. Harrell,
Stevan.   III. Richman, Paula.
BL65.S4G46   1986   291.1′78343   86-47552
ISBN 0-8070-1008-1

Contents

Contents

Preface

This book is the second in a series written by the faculty of the Comparative Religion Program at the University of Washington. In 1976 the University of Washington received a grant from the National Endowment for the Humanities to foster research and teaching in the humanities, particularly in interdisciplinary programs. Part of this grant went to the Comparative Religion Program, which had been founded in 1974. Comparative Religion set aside a portion of its share to fund release time for faculty members so they could participate in a two-year research seminar under the leadership of program member Charles F. Keyes. During the second year of the seminar its members, working on a number of different religious traditions, produced a group of essays united by their focus on the nature of charisma and the genre of sacred biography. These essays were published as *Charisma and Sacred Biography* (Journal of the American Academy of Religion Thematic Series 48:3–4, Scholars Press), edited by Michael A. Williams.

In 1981 the Comparative Religion faculty decided to launch a second series of discussions. They chose the topic religion and gender and asked program member Caroline Bynum to chair the group. Fifteen faculty members and advanced graduate students of the University of Washington then began common reading and discussion on the religious roles of men and women and the uses of gender-related symbols in various religious traditions. We were joined by several visitors, most important among them Margaret Mills, now at the University of Pennsylvania, and Paula Richman, then of Colby College. This book has grown out of those discussions. We would like to acknowledge here the important contributions made to the formulation of the topic by seminar members who did not contribute chapters to this book: Pamela Amoss, Frank Conlon, E. Valentine Daniel, Christine Greenway, Arthur Kleinman, Mary O'Neil, and Eugene Webb.

The chapters in this book were produced by true collaboration. Members of the religion and gender seminar spent a full year reading together, arguing, and exchanging ideas before any individual began to write. If the chapters seem to ring changes upon the same themes, to reflect a common approach, and to build upon similar questions to reach cross-cultural conclusions, that is because, in the course of two years of talking together, we really learned from each other. All of us attempt to show, in various ways, the complexity of gender as a symbolic system—in its relationships to the social order, in its polysemic meanings, and in its variation with the perspective of the perceiver. Chapter 1, the introduction, provides a theoretical discussion of this kind of complexity.

In illustrating this theme our authors discuss a wide variety of religious traditions—Buddhism, Hinduism, Islam, Zoroastrianism, Christianity of several kinds, Neo-Confucianism, Chinese folk religion, and modern psychoanalysis, treated as an evolving myth. They also examine a spectrum of religious phenomena, from folk practices and ritual to theological arguments, and use many types of sources: myths and folktales, poetry and devotional epics, literature, theological and philosophical texts, oral traditions, ethnographic material, psychoanalytic tracts and case studies, journalistic accounts and pamphlets.

Using these materials, our authors have produced three different, but closely related, kinds of chapters. Those in part 1 are concerned with gender as culturally constructed meaning. In chapter 2 Laal Jamzadeh and Margaret Mills use food rituals to describe the differences in gender constructions between Zoroastrian and Muslim women in Iran. In chapter 3 Charles F. Keyes describes how Buddhist initiation ritual defines maleness for the Northern Thai. Stevan Harrell's chapter 4 shows how concepts of gender are related to the way Taiwanese villagers perceive and interact with ghosts. And in chapter 5 Carolyn M. Wallace shows us the differences between official ideal and actual practice in the gender ideology of The Church of Jesus Christ of Latter-day Saints.

Part 2 concentrates on the multivocality or polysemy of gender symbols. In chapter 6 Paula Richman examines the Tamil Buddhist text *Maṇimēkalai,* showing how the author skillfully creates two different messages about world renunciation in the same text—one closely connected with gender in the real world and one using gender as a more generally applicable symbol. Alison H. Black in chapter 7 pursues a similar line of reasoning for a broader tradition, demonstrating that Chinese philosophical discourse over the last two millennia has used gender in a series of different but interconnected ways. The final chapter in this section, chapter 8, is by Michael A. Williams; in it he examines in detail three texts of ancient gnosticism, finding in each of them a different use of gender symbolism.

Part 3 emphasizes the different perspectives that men and women in the same tradition bring to the perception of gender symbolism. In chapter 9 John Stratton Hawley finds a gender-linked contrast in the devotional poetry of Krishna attributed to two major Hindi poets: Sūr Dās (a male) and Mīrā Bāī (a female). Caroline Walker Bynum, in chapter 10, discusses the spiritual writing of the late Middle Ages, finding a similar contrast between the dichotomous symbols used by male writers and the more unified, continuous symbols preferred by women. And in chapter 11, John E. Toews looks at gender-linked perspectives in psychoanalysis, showing that Melanie Klein's interpretation of the Oedipus story and its cultural meaning differs from that of Sigmund Freud in ways closely parallel to those found by Bynum and Hawley in examining very different traditions.

The three editors of this volume have worked closely together. Caroline Bynum led the seminar, worked with the individual authors as they formulated topics and approach, and wrote the introduction. Stevan Harrell supervised the assembling of the papers into a volume during the academic year 1983–1984. Paula Richman has been the real "editor" in this project; although all of us have spent time working with many of the authors in revising and refining their papers, she has done the most, and the most-detailed work. The fact that several of the authors have acknowledged her by name in their footnotes indicates that her assistance has gone well beyond what is ordinarily provided to authors of articles.

The editors would like to thank all the authors for their willingness to rewrite and refine their contributions in order to achieve coherence in the volume. We would also like to thank Michael H. Fisher, Sheila Levine, Frank Reynolds, Lorna Rhodes, Guenther Roth, and Judith Van Herik for their suggestions. We have been fortunate that Sarah Abigail Smith, under the auspices of a Graduate Opportunity Research Assistantship from the Graduate School at the University of Washington, was available to us as research assistant, typist, and additional voice in copyediting. Amanda Udis-Kessler has contributed greatly to copyediting and proofreading as well. We are also grateful to Liesel Rombouts of the University of Washington Comparative Religion Program and to Pauline Wing and Dorothy Evertsen of Colby College for secretarial assistance. In addition, we wish to thank Eugene Webb, chairperson of the Comparative Religion Program from its inception until 1985, and Michael A. Williams, present chairperson, for using limited departmental funds to underwrite certain of our initial costs. We thank Kenneth Pyle, director of the Jackson School of International Studies at the University of Washington, for a grant that helped defray editorial expenses. Finally, we express our appreciation to Kathryn Gohl and to Caroline Birdsall and Pam Pokorney of Beacon Press for the efficiency and enthusiasm with which they handled our manuscript at every step on the way to publication.

CAROLINE WALKER BYNUM
STEVAN HARRELL
PAULA RICHMAN

Seattle, Washington, 1985

x

One

Introduction: The Complexity of Symbols
Caroline Walker Bynum

Until recently the field of comparative religion dealt with *homo religiosus*—the religious experience of man. The fact that religious man often worshiped Mother Nature was considered an oddity, a stage he outgrew as he moved on to more transcendent (and frequently male) deities. When, under the impetus of feminist theory, "religious woman" began to be considered, scholars noted that she often worshiped a Father God or found the transcendent revealed in a male figure. Since societies in which women worshiped male deities tended to be societies in which men were dominant and since indeed the lack of interest in woman's religious experience seemed most acute among male scholars who studied patriarchal societies and patriarchal religions, some radical reformers began to suggest that male deities themselves were the problem. Recent feminist critiques of both Western and non-Western religious traditions have agreed that men gain authority from the fact that the source of ultimate value is often described in anthropomorphic images as Father or King.[1] But feminist activists have been sharply divided between those who would respond by discarding male symbols in religion—often discarding much of the theological tradition in question as well—and those who would rewrite liturgies and reform language to insert female symbols and pronouns among male ones.[2]

However the debate about current religious language and practice is finally resolved, the questions of feminists have changed the course of scholarship. It is no longer possible to study religious practice or religious symbols without taking gender—that is, the

1

cultural experience of being male or female—into account. And we are just beginning to understand how complex the relationship between religion and gender is. This volume of essays is intended to respond to the present situation of scholarship by explaining what it means to take gender seriously in studying religion and what it means to take religion seriously when asking questions about gender. This book is about both gender *and* religion.

Our Approach

In exploring the relationship between gender and religion, the authors of this volume insist upon two fundamental insights. First, they insist upon the feminist insight that all human beings are "gendered"—that is, that there is no such thing as generic *homo religiosus*.[3] No scholar studying religion, no participant in ritual, is ever neuter. Religious experience is the experience of men and women, and in no known society is this experience the same. Second, this volume assumes the phenomenological insight that religious symbols point men and women beyond their ordinary lives. As Paul Ricoeur explains it, there is no such thing as a religious symbol that is merely a sign of or statement about social structure.[4] However religious symbols "mean," they never simply prescribe or transcribe social status. Rather they transmute it, even while referring to it. Religious symbols are, as the anthropologist Victor Turner puts it, "polysemic"; they have the quality of possessing manifold meanings.[5]

The basic contribution of our collection of essays is to elaborate a theory of religious symbol as "polysemic" and a theory of experience as "gendered," and to elaborate these in such a way that each insight informs the other more fully than has previously been the case in American scholarship. It is to suggest that gender-related symbols—symbols that, at one level, signify maleness or femaleness (and symbols never merely signify)—do not simply determine the self-awareness of men and women as gendered nor do they simply reflect cultural assumptions about what it is to be male or female. Gender-related symbols, in their full complexity, may refer to gender in ways that affirm or reverse it, support or question it; or they may, in their basic meaning, have little at all to do with male and female roles. Thus our analysis admits that gender-related symbols are sometimes "about" values other than gender.

2

But our analysis also assumes that all people are "gendered." It therefore suggests, at another level, that not only gender-related symbols but all symbols arise out of the experience of "gendered" users. It is not possible ever to ask How does a symbol—any symbol—mean? without asking For whom does it mean?

Some examples may make our method clearer. Let us take three cases of gender-related images from the chapters that follow. The Church of the Latter-day Saints, sometimes known as the Mormons, teaches that all spirits are created by a Heavenly Father and a Heavenly Mother and progress toward perfection in this life and beyond as members of human families. To Mormon adherents, the individual self has gender for all eternity, and this gender reflects a male/female division lodged at the heart of ultimate reality. To Christians in medieval Europe, on the other hand, God was sometimes seen as a bridegroom to whom all souls, no matter what sort of sexual body they inhabited, related as brides. But the "otherness" of God from creation meant that this God could also be seen as a whirlwind, a circle whose center is everywhere, or a nursing mother; it meant that all such epithets were finally valueless for evoking or explaining the essence of the divine. If we turn to the Chinese tradition, we find yet a third way in which gender symbols refer to the ultimately real. A beloved document of Confucianism says: "Heaven [Ch'ien] is my father and Earth [K'un] is my mother." But the Confucian tradition also teaches that wholeness is a feminine image and that wholeness transcends diversity. The ultimate, to a Chinese philosopher, is clearly not father or masculine; but if it is feminine, it is so only with an expanded meaning of feminine that leaves its referent in social experience far behind. Self and cosmos are thus not male and female for a Chinese philosopher or a Christian mystic in the same sense in which they are male and female for a Mormon. But do they have gender at all? And, if so, what does it mean to attribute gender to that ultimate Wholeness or Oneness that is beyond distinction or definition?

These three cases raise questions about the meaning of religious symbols. How do such symbols refer to and make use of gender? But the questions we ought to ask do not stop here. For it is also unclear, in the three cases described above, *whose* meaning we are analyzing. Neo-Confucian theories, which may be understood as feminizing the cosmos, were produced by men. Male mystics in medieval Europe venerated the Virgin Mary and wrote of Jesus as

3

mother. Mormon theologians (all male by theological prescription) prohibit the priesthood to women because fatherhood means leadership. But what is the significance of Chinese men elaborating the idea of wholeness as feminine? Do female mystics in Christian Europe see God as mother and mean by *mother* what their male counterparts mean? Do Mormon women experience in the same way as Mormon men their church's theories of male and female roles lasting for all eternity? The purpose of our volume is to address these sorts of questions.

Some Recent Scholarship

Although our approach has been influenced by the large amount of recent theoretical literature both on feminism and on symbol, as well as by current work on women done by cultural anthropologists, it is important to point out several recognized genres of discussion to which our book does not belong. First, our book does not belong to that group of works (among which the most distinguished recent example is Falk and Gross, *Unspoken Worlds*) that seeks to remedy the earlier scholarly neglect of women by examining and comparing women's religious experiences across cultures.[6] Although we agree that women have been ignored and that ignorance about their religious roles badly needs rectifying, our goal is not to contribute to the body of information either about sex roles generally or about women's religious roles in particular. Some of the essays presented here (especially that of Jamzadeh and Mills but also those by Bynum, Keyes, and Harrell) do contribute new information about women's religious experiences. But the goal of our volume is to explore how religious symbols relate to "genderedness"—to people's experiences as males and females—and not, or at least not primarily, to further knowledge of women's religious behavior.

Second, our book is not about male dominance. We do not here join the current discussion (of which Peggy Reeves Sanday's *Female Power and Male Dominance* is a sophisticated example) about the extent of male dominance in religious traditions or about the explanations for it.[7] Most of the religious traditions explored in our book have articulated theories of male primacy; some of the chapters (for example, the one by John E. Toews) help us to understand why. But our volume does not enter the debate about domi-

4

nance at either the empirical or the causal level. We do not seek to compare male-dominant traditions with other traditions, such as certain native American ones, characterized by sharp role differentiation and complementarity.[8] Nor are we interested in finding a cause—either in biology, or in economic relations, or in symbols themselves—for the presence or absence of male dominance.[9]

Third, our book is not primarily about the cultural and sociological conditions for gender ideologies. Although our approach has certain elements in common with a recent example of this genre, Ortner and Whitehead's *Sexual Meanings,* our agenda is different from theirs. Symbolic anthropologists, like Ortner, Whitehead, Rosaldo, and others, have devoted their attention to what they call the "hegemonic (male-biased) ideology" and have avoided the question of women's perspective. They defend their assumption that a dominant cultural conception of gender effectively masks differences arising from women's experiences by arguing that "some form of asymmetry favoring men is present in all cultures and that women's perspectives are to a great extent constrained and conditioned by the dominant ideology."[10] We feel that the extent to which this is true is a matter to be decided empirically not programmatically, and we suspect that, even where there is no hint of an alternative ideology to counter a dominant one, subordinate and dominant individuals will experience the accepted ideology in different ways. The chapters that follow devote their primary attention to unmasking differences in perspectives rather than to delineating the features of the mask.

Moreover, anthropologists such as Ortner have sometimes— either implicitly or explicitly—presented their exploration of symbol as an argument for cultural as opposed to biological causation.[11] Indeed the challenge of sociobiology has made such argument necessary. But we do not intend to enter the debate over whether biology or cultural experience "causes" gender. Our concern is with religion, not more generally with culture, and our approach to religious symbols, both in themselves and as expanded into ritual and myth, is more phenomenological than determinist. Our question is How do symbols mean? not What produces them? or How do they function? Some of the essays presented here, especially those by Harrell, Keyes, Jamzadeh and Mills, and Wallace, suggest the sociological setting of certain symbols—that certain symbols tend to emerge in the presence of certain configurations of society. Other essays, especially those by Richman, Black, Bynum, and Toews, suggest the cultural setting of specific symbols—that certain symbols tend to be associated with specific symbol clusters and with identifiable cultural values. But it is not our agenda to isolate sociological or cultural causes of gender-related symbols or to see these symbols in turn as causes.

Fourth, our book is not a contribution to the debate between reformist and radical feminists on "the goddess" or to the related debate between feminists and antifeminists on the same topic.[12] In the past decade, American feminists have argued about the advisability and practicability of resurrecting or inventing female deities and symbols. In response to the radical feminist spiritualists who argue for the so-called goddess solution, certain writers, both feminist and antifeminist, have suggested that this agenda is based on a misunderstanding of the nature of symbol and tradition. The debate has generated polemical writing on both sides, as well as scholarly efforts to explore the complex of meanings associated with goddesses or other anthropomorphic female symbols in the religious traditions of the world.[13] Some of the chapters in this volume, especially those by Williams and Black, contribute to this debate by arguing that female symbols are so polysemic as to be accessible to both male and female ritual participants; some chapters (for example, those by Bynum and Toews) even suggest that, on occasion, men may be more attracted than women to symbols that refer to the female. But we do not see our collection of essays as focusing primarily on goddesses, on female-referring symbols, or on symbols used by women.

The Three Groups of Essays and Their Context

In exploring religion and gender, our essays fall into three groups. The first group, which treats symbol primarily as it is expanded into ritual, focuses on gender as culturally constructed. The second group, which treats specific gender symbols primarily in the context of other symbols as they appear in texts, focuses on the ways in which symbols mean. The third group, which also focuses on texts, includes the questions of the first two groups but adds a focus on the genderedness of author and audience. The coherence of each group of essays will become clearer if we examine their scholarly contexts.

Part 1—those chapters by Jamzadeh and Mills, Keyes, Harrell, and Wallace—is composed by anthropologists and folklorists on the basis of ethnographic research. It comes closest in method to the cultural anthropology of Ortner, Whitehead, Rosaldo, and others discussed above. Indeed all the chapters in this volume share with cultural anthropology and with recent feminist psychology an emphasis on the distinction between gender and sex.[14]

Sex is the term scholars use to designate the differences between men and women that can be attributed to biology. All human beings, whatever their sexual preference and cultural setting, have a sex. *Gender* is the term used to refer to those differences between male and female human beings that are created through psychological and social development within a familial, social, and cultural setting. All human beings have gender as well as sex, and this gender is culturally constructed. In other words, what people understand themselves to be qua male and female is learned and shaped within culture, and religious symbols are one of the ways in which such meanings are taught and appropriated.

The fields of psychology and cultural anthropology—especially as written by Americans—have recently begun detailed exploration of this process of cultural construction of gender; some of this work lies in the background of our first set of chapters, all of which explore both the ways in which messages about gender are conveyed by symbols and the ways in which social values shape the meaning of gender symbols. Thus Harrell suggests in his chapter that the complex fears that Chinese men feel about women influence the kind of ghosts these men see; Jamzadeh and Mills argue that differences in the food rituals of Zoroastrian and Shi'a Muslim women in Iran are shaped by the relative differences in the constraints imposed on women by the two societies.

None of the chapters in this volume simply follows the anthropological method of Ortner and Whitehead, however. Although the authors of *Sexual Meanings* are deeply concerned with the complexity of symbols and the cultural experiences of both men and women, we have tried to work out an understanding of symbol as polysemic and of experience as gendered that differs from theirs. Even in part 1, whose chapters are the most anthropological in method, we are not concerned primarily either with the question of cause—that is, with the exact distribution of biology and culture responsible for the male/female distinction—or with the way in which a culture develops a dominant ideology about gender. As I shall explain below, we take our stand with French feminism, which focuses on the fact and experience of genderedness, rather than with American feminism, which focuses on cause. We also take our stand with the more phenomenological approach to symbol characteristic of Ricoeur, rather than with the somewhat more functionalist approach characteristic of much recent anthropology. The authors of the first four chapters are thus concerned less with symbols as a model of culture than with symbols in the context of gendered experience. And they see symbols as not merely reflecting and shaping but also inverting, questioning, rejecting, and transcending gender as it is constructed in the individual's psychological development and sociological setting. Thus Wallace's chapter examines how men and women experience the gender symbols of Mormonism differently, although men and women receive the same theological and social messages encoded in the symbols. Harrell looks not merely at the gender of the ghosts seen by Taiwanese but also at the relationship between the gender of the seer and the gender of what is seen. Keyes discusses ways in which the messages of Thai society about maleness are not simply reinforced by Buddhist initiation ritual but also inverted and questioned.

The chapters in part 2—those by Richman, Black, and Williams—are composed by scholars trained in either comparative religion or intellectual history. Each of these essays has at its heart a text or set of texts. Yet, despite the very different material employed by these authors and the fact that the societies they study are not amenable to the kind of ethnographic exploration possible in the first group of essays, the method in the second group has similarities to that in the first. This second set of authors also focuses on religion, not on culture generally, and on religious symbols as polysemic.

Recent scholarship in the field of religion has been characterized by intensive and sophisticated discussion of the nature of symbol. I cannot enter here into the complexities of such discussion, but by treating three major theorists—Clifford Geertz (especially in his early writings), Victor Turner, and Paul Ricoeur—I can explain why we have opted for Ricoeur's more phenomenological approach. All three theorists see religious symbol as that which gives meaning to ordinary experience, not merely as a sign that points to it. All three are concerned with the believer or ritual participant as the one who receives or appropriates meaning. But of the three, Geertz relates symbol most closely to what it signifies. For this reason Geertz has been explicitly used (and misused) by some theorists who argue that female-referring symbols are especially attractive to women.[15]

In his now-classic essay "Religion as a Cultural System," Geertz argues that symbol provides "model of" and "model for."[16] In other words, to Geertz, religious symbols, which he defines as "historically created vehicles of reasoning, perception, feeling, and understanding,"[17] give meaning to existence by providing a model of the world as it is and a model for the world as it ought to be—a template that shapes ordinary experience by reflecting it and, in the process, imparts value from beyond it. In contrast to Geertz's concept of model, we might place Ricoeur's theory that symbols are opaque, oblique, and analogical.[18] To Ricoeur, it is not the case that the symbol points out a meaning, that the meaning exists and the symbol names it. Rather the symbol itself in some sense precedes meaning; it "gives rise to thought." Water may signify (i.e., point to) cleanliness, but it will never "mean" cleanliness. For cleanliness itself will point to absence of or freedom from something else, something palpable and real but not communicable in a single word; it may even point beyond absence of whatever is "soiling" to another state of "purity" that not only transcends the opposites of clean/dirty, pure/sinful, good/evil but also expresses the subjective, human experience of such freedom. To Ricoeur, symbols point beyond ordinary experience, and *beyond* has a different meaning from Geertz's *beyond*. Although neither theorist thinks that symbol merely transcribes social structure, the beyond, for Geertz, is a set of ultimate values that, in a complicated but discoverable way, mirror the world. It is this "mirroring" that imparts meaning. For Ricoeur, in contrast, the beyond is open-ended—not really discoverable except by analogy. And meaning is not so much imparted as appropriated in a dialectical process whereby it becomes subjective reality for the one who uses the symbol.[19] Therefore Ricoeur's model at least allows for the possibility that those with different gender experiences will appropriate symbols in different ways, whereas Geertz tends to suggest that *the* symbol system is *the* framework for all, no matter how complex its mirroring of reality may be. Moreover, Geertz's idea of "model of and for" inevitably suggests that gender-related symbols in some sense reinforce the experiences of men and women qua men and women.

The anthropologist Victor Turner does not really understand symbol in the same way as Ricoeur, but there are several similarities between them. Both see symbol as reflecting not just a multiplicity of meanings but a multiplicity of relationships between meanings. Both see symbol using as a process of appropriating meaning. To Turner, symbols reflect in some deep way a "likeness" between the orectic (sensory) and the abstract or normative poles of meaning; symbols unify or "condense" natural physiological facts (e.g., milk, food, breasts) and normative or social values (e.g., nurture, matriliny, etc.). The using of symbol takes the ritual participant through a process, from social integration through crisis to some sort of reversal or redress and finally to reintegration.[20] Although Turner's approach is more functionalist than Ricoeur's, the two theorists agree in emphasizing two aspects of symbols: their capacity to refer simultaneously to many levels of human experience and their capacity to bring users to appropriate that to which the symbol points. Because of this agreement, we have adopted Turner's term *polysemic symbol* to signify an emphasis, first, on the multivalent quality of images and, second, on symbol using as an active process of appropriation.

Despite the deep indebtedness of many of our authors to the example of Geertz's scholarship, the essays in our volume come closer to the understanding of symbol found in Turner and Ricoeur. And the chapters in part 2 in particular are directed toward an exploration of gender symbols as polysemic. Richman opens the question of how specific gender symbols convey meaning by asking in what ways a particular female figure in a particular text can be read. She discovers that the figure can be read in two ways: in one, her gender is crucial to the religious meaning of the text; in the other, gender is largely irrelevant. It is impossible to determine how the text means without asking both how it refers outside itself to other texts and to society and for whom (what audience as well as what author) it has meaning. But, because symbols (and their expansion into narrative) are polysemic, the two readings of the text are not mutually exclusive. Building on this insight, Black and Williams consider a series of texts and discover, once again, that they both do and do not refer to culturally constructed gender. Gnostic and Chinese notions of wholeness/oneness and diversity/ multiplicity perhaps spring from men's and women's experience of gender and sexuality, and they are communicated in images of gender and of sexual activity. But the experiences they come to "mean"—the experiences of simplicity and fragmentation—are far from the experience of social maleness and femaleness. In other words, Geertz's idea that symbol is model of and model for—even in its most complex sense—proves inadequate to the texts we consider here. Gender symbols seem sometimes to function as Geertz suggests. But when they are found at the heart of a religious tradition, they seem not so much to communicate information about gender—expressing its meaning for the society or even rejecting that meaning—as to conjure up the basic human fact, both glorious and painful, of multiplicity and fragmentation itself.

The third set of essays in this volume builds on the first two sets. Like the second set, these chapters are written by scholars trained in the history of religions and intellectual history. They focus on texts. The texts considered are, however, even more diverse than those in the second group. Indeed at first glance the final paper, by Toews, may not seem to belong at all. The psychoanalytic tradition it explores is not, one might argue, a religion. In answering this argument, we leave aside the suggestion that has sometimes been made that, in our postmodern, secularized world, psychoanalysis has functioned as a kind of religion. We merely point out that Toews treats the psychoanalytic use of the Oedipus story as a myth, subject to interpretation and reinterpretation by various tellers of the tale, and that (according to Ricoeur's model) myth is "a species of symbol, a symbol developed into narrative form, articulated within a time and space that cannot be coordinated with critical history and geography."[21] Thus, according to our model, Toews, like Bynum and Hawley, considers gender symbols and their expansion in ritual and narrative. More important, however, Toews not only asks the same questions as Bynum and Hawley about the genderedness of the users of symbols; he also finds answers that coincide in intriguing ways with the conclusions of the other two authors.

The final three chapters share with those in part 1 an understanding of gender as culturally constructed. The authors conclude from their analyses that gender symbols sometimes serve to express and reinforce cultural notions of gender. Bynum and Toews find the gender asymmetry characteristic of both Western European social arrangements and European social and theological theory reflected in certain aspects of the gender symbols of medieval mystics and modern psychologists. The final set of essays also shares with those of Richman, Williams, and Black a notion of religious symbol as polysemic. Hawley and Bynum, like Richman, stress the ways in which a female-referring symbol may or may not in its meaning reflect or invert the social experience of its user. Toews and Bynum, like Black, are interested in whether or not symbols convey meaning through evoking opposition or through reconciling opposites in either paradox or synthesis. What this final group of essays adds to the analysis developed in the first two sets is an awareness of the genderedness of authors and ritual participants.

Like the idea of gender as culturally constructed and the idea of religious symbol as polysemic, the idea of genderedness has a scholarly context. It is a feminist insight, but feminist in a particular sense. For feminism is no more monolithic than is the recent discussion of symbol by anthropologists and students of comparative religion. Certain schools or emphases within feminism can, however, be identified, and two are relevant here. While all feminism arises from concern with the asymmetrical treatment of women in modern scholarship and modern life, it is safe to say very generally that American feminism in the early 1970s tended to emphasize the similarity of men and women; by the early 1980s it had begun to stress the differences between them. It is also safe to say that American feminism has tended to be empirical, inductive, and concerned with causal analysis, wrestling repeatedly with the question Why is the condition of women as it is today? whereas French feminism has been more literary and phenomenological, wrestling with the question How can we talk about women's experience?[22] The chapters in this volume reflect the recent concern of American feminism with difference. They also come closer to French than to American feminism because they avoid causal questions as—at least at this stage of scholarship—unanswerable and focus rather on devising ways of understanding and talking about the differing experiences of women and men. They attempt to deal with the difficult question of understanding women's perspectives even within traditions where explicit social and theological theories express male dominance and where most of the texts are produced by men.

Thus, to the insight that gender is culturally constructed and the insight that all religious symbols are polysemic, the chapters in part 3 add the conviction that experience is gendered. In other words, not only do gender symbols invert or reject as well as reinforce the gender values and gender structures of society, they also may be experienced differently by the different genders. For example, Bynum argues that all Christians in medieval Europe tended to see God as male and soul as female. But, she argues, these concepts did not mean the same thing for women and men. To religious women, such images of self continued social experience; to religious men, such images were inversions and reversals of the power and status normally attributed to them. Not only did it mean a different thing for a man to see himself as a "bride of Christ," but such use of symbol involved a different mode of symbolic operation, one grounded in contradiction rather than continuity.

In adding a concern for the genderedness of experience, the final essays in this volume all ask the same question. What is striking is that their answers are parallel. Bynum, Hawley, and Toews do not, of course, find that medieval mystics, Hindi poets, and twentieth-century psychoanalysts have the same concepts of gender or reflect (or reject) the same social conditions. They do however find that the men and women of a single tradition—when working with the same symbols and myths, writing in the same genre, and living in the same religious or professional circumstances—display certain consistent male/female differences in using symbols. Women's symbols and myths tend to build from social and biological experiences; men's symbols and myths tend to invert them. Women's mode of using symbols seems given to the muting of opposition, whether through paradox or through synthesis; men's mode seems characterized by emphasis on opposition, contradiction, inversion, and conversion. Women's myths and rituals tend to explore a state of being; men's tend to build elaborate and discrete stages between self and other.[23]

13

Implications of Our Analysis

The agreement in part 3 casts new light on the chapters in parts 1 and 2. For example, when read in light of the suggestions about genderedness found in Bynum, Toews, and Hawley, the conclusions of Keyes about male initiation take on new significance. Keyes finds that male initiation reflects a sharp break with the world, whereas female rituals in Thai society express a greater continuity between the religious and the social experience of women. Similarly, Jamzadeh and Mills suggest that women's food rituals in Iran express and give meaning to, rather than reverse or reject, women's marginalized and domestic lives and the female social networks that characterize them. Such conclusions appear to reflect in ritual the kind of gendered experience Bynum, Toews, and Hawley find in texts. To take a more problematic example, the tendency noted by the authors of part 3 for men to use woman as a symbol of "the other" and to stress oppositions or reversals may be reflected both in the emphasis of (male) Chinese philosophers on correlative thinking and in their choice of holistic images associated with the feminine as a means of naming what is of ultimate value.[24]

Indeed, if the conclusions of these final chapters are correct, the phenomenological theory of symbol I discussed above may need modification. While retaining Turner's notion of symbol as polysemic and Ricoeur's idea that symbol is never merely sign, we may need to adapt for women the processual or dialectical elements in Turner and Ricoeur. That is, we may need to modify their models of how symbols mean by incorporating women's tendency to emphasize reconciliation and continuity. The symbolic reversals so important to Turner as a component of ritual may be less crucial for women than for men.[25] The synthesis of objective referent and subjective meaning, which Ricoeur thinks is achieved in the user by the symbol, may be for women less a dialectical process than an acceptance of, a continuous living with, paradox. Thus attention to gender in the study of religion would lead not only to a questioning of Clifford Geertz's theory of symbol as "model of and model for" but also to an adjustment of even those more phenomenological insights that seem to allow for a greater complexity of relationship between social facts and symbolic meanings. In other words, the phenomenological emphasis of Ricoeur on the process by which

14

the symbol is appropriated may need to be expanded by the phenomenological emphasis of French feminism on genderedness until we have a more varied and richer notion of the experiences of symbol users. By taking female symbol-users seriously, we might evolve an understanding of symbol itself in which paradox and synthesis take an important place beside dialectic, contradiction, and reversal.[26]

Such suggestions remain suggestions. Much more research would be necessary to elevate them to the level of generalizations, and the careful work of Black and Williams warns of the dangers of premature theorizing. As Toews points out in chapter 11, the only way to determine how men and women reinterpret their myths is to look at what particular groups of men and women say. It will not do to return to the essentialist and ethnocentric notions of female nature or of the "eternal feminine" that animated early twentieth-century research. The basic conclusion of our volume is that gender symbols are complex in their relationship to other symbols, to authors and ritual participants, and to society. We suggest here no single model of male or female symbol-using. But we do insist that gender in any society is a cultural fact (not reducible to biological sex), that religious symbols are never merely a model of the cultural fact of gender, and that no theory of symbol can be adequate unless it incorporates women's experience and discourse as well as men's.

In conclusion, then, we make no arguments about the nature of "religious woman" or "religious man." We put forward no theory of the cross-cultural meaning of female or male symbols. We lend support to no current schemes of religious reform that involve the creation of new symbols or the exclusion of old ones. While sympathetic to the intention of those who would reshape the palpable inequities in society by providing new images, we find the meaning of symbols, myths, and rituals too multilayered, too complex in its relationship to social structure and social values, to feel confident either that new rituals are easily created or that radical excisions of traditional symbols will have predictable results.

And yet, radical suggestions lurk behind our cautious, academic conclusion that our subject is a complex one. One such radical conclusion has been drawn before:[27] even traditional symbols can have revolutionary consequences. For, if symbols can invert as well as reinforce social values (as Black, Keyes, and Hawley suggest), if traditional rituals can evolve to meet the needs of new participants (as Harrell, Jamzadeh, and Mills suggest), then old symbols can acquire new meanings, and these new meanings might suggest a new society. If the images we explore in such detail in the chapters that follow—images of men becoming female cowherds for Krishna, for example, or of the marriage of Gnostic soul and spirit as escape from defilement—have not in the societies that produced them brought about the equality of the sexes, it is not, so to speak, the fault of the images.

A second radical conclusion lies behind our method as well. It is simply this: if we turn our attention not to what gender symbols signify (for they never merely signify) but rather to how men and women use them, we may find that the varied experiences of men and women have been there all along. To say this is in no way to suggest that we should maintain the religious status quo, for, as things are, women's voices in all their multiplicity are very hard to hear. But it is to argue that those who wish to effect the sort of changes that will let women's experiences speak may need to work, not to substitute female-referring symbols for male-referring symbols, but to open new symbolic modes. If we take as women's rituals and women's symbols the rituals and symbols women actually use, and ask how these symbols mean, we may discover that women have all along had certain modes of symbolic discourse different from those of men. Even where men and women have used the same symbols and rituals, they may have invested them with different meanings and different ways of meaning. To hear women's voices more clearly will be to see more fully the complexity of symbols. If this is so, an awareness of the genderedness of symbol users will enrich our understanding of both symbol and humanity.

Notes

1. Carol P. Christ and Judith Plaskow, eds., *Womanspirit Rising: A Feminist Reader in Religion* (San Francisco and New York: Harper and Row, 1979); Charlene Spretnak, ed., *The Politics of Women's Spirituality: Essays in the Rise of Spiritual Power within the Feminist Movement* (New York: Doubleday-Anchor, 1982). In working out the ideas in this introduction, I am particularly indebted to Stephen Greenblatt, Frank Reynolds,

Joan W. Scott, John Toews, Judith Van Herik, and my fellow editors for assistance. In what follows, I have used the first-person pronoun to express my own opinions but have referred to myself in the third person when summarizing my chapter.

2. On this debate see Rosemary Radford Ruether, "Goddesses and Witches: Liberation and Countercultural Feminism," *Christian Century*, Sept. 10–17, 1980, pp. 842–47; idem, "The Feminist Critique in Religious Studies," *Soundings* 64.4 (1981):388–402; and Larry D. Shinn, "The Goddess: Theological Sign or Religious Symbol?" *Numen: International Review for the History of Religions* 31.2 (1984):175–98.

3. On the ways in which the so-called generic *homo* is not really generic, see Judith Shapiro, "Anthropology and the Study of Gender," in *Soundings* 64.4 (1981):446–65; Edwin Ardener, "Belief and the Problem of Women" and "The 'Problem' Revisited," in *Perceiving Women*, ed. Shirley Ardener (New York: John Wiley and Sons, 1975), pp. 1–27.

4. See Paul Ricoeur, "The Symbol Gives Rise to Thought," in *Ways of Understanding Religion*, ed. Walter H. Capps (New York: Macmillan, 1972), pp. 309–17; and idem, *The Symbolism of Evil*, trans. E. Buchanan (Boston: Beacon, 1967). This formulation depends upon Ricoeur's understanding of sign. Recent work in semiotics would use *sign* differently.

5. See Victor Turner, *The Forest of Symbols: Aspects of Ndembu Ritual* (Ithaca: Cornell University Press, 1967).

6. Nancy Auer Falk and Rita M. Gross, eds., *Unspoken Worlds: Women's Religious Lives in Non-Western Cultures* (San Francisco and New York: Harper and Row, 1980). For other examples of this genre, see Judith Hoch-Smith and Anita Spring, eds., *Women in Ritual and Symbolic Roles* (New York and London: Plenum Press, 1978); Rita M. Gross, ed., *Beyond Androcentrism: New Essays on Women and Religion* (Missoula, Mont.: Scholars Press for the American Academy of Religion, 1977); and Bruce Lincoln, *Emerging from the Chrysalis: Studies in Rituals of Women's Initiation* (Cambridge: Harvard University Press, 1981).

7. Peggy Reeves Sanday, *Female Power and Male Dominance: On the Origins of Sexual Inequality* (Cambridge: Cambridge University Press, 1981). See also the helpful remarks on this issue in Sherry Ortner and Harriet Whitehead, "Introduction: Accounting for Sexual Meanings," in *Sexual Meanings: The Cultural Construction of Gender and Sexuality*, ed. Ortner and Whitehead (Cambridge: Cambridge University Press, 1981), pp. 2–6.

8. For examples of such traditions, see Annemarie Shimony, "Women of Influence and Prestige among the Native American Iroquois," and Joseph W. Bastien, "Rosinta, Rats, and the River: Bad Luck Is Banished in Andean Bolivia," in Falk and Gross, *Unspoken Worlds*, pp. 243–74.

9. We also avoid the vexed question of the "status" of women. Fortu-

17

nately much recent anthropological and historical discussion is critical of this way of posing the question. See Martin King Whyte, *The Status of Women in Preindustrial Societies* (Princeton: Princeton University Press, 1978), esp. pp. 116–17; Michelle Zimbalist Rosaldo, "The Use and Abuse of Anthropology: Reflections on Feminism and Cross-cultural Understanding," *Signs: Journal of Women in Culture and Society* 5 (1980):401; Naomi Quinn, "Anthropological Studies on Women's Status," *Annual Review of Anthropology* 6 (1977):181–83; and Penny Schine Gold, "Preface," in *The Lady and the Virgin: Image, Attitude, and Experience in Twelfth-Century France* (Chicago: University of Chicago Press, 1985).

10. Ortner and Whitehead, *Sexual Meanings,* p. x.

11. See Ortner and Whitehead, *Sexual Meanings.* See also Sherry Ortner, "Is Female to Male as Nature Is to Culture?" and Michelle Z. Rosaldo, "Women, Culture, and Society: A Theoretical Overview," in *Women, Culture, and Society,* ed. Michelle Z. Rosaldo and Louise Lamphere (Stanford: Stanford University Press, 1974), pp. 67–87, 1–42.

12. See the works cited in nn. 1 and 2 above.

13. See, for example, James J. Preston, ed., *Mother Worship: Theme and Variations* (Chapel Hill: University of North Carolina Press, 1982); Elaine Pagels, "What Became of God the Mother? Conflicting Images of God in Early Christianity," *Signs: Journal of Women in Culture and Society* 2 (1976):293–303; Judith Ochshorn, *The Female Experience and the Nature of the Divine* (Bloomington: Indiana University Press, 1981); and Cheever Mackenzie Brown, *God as Mother: A Feminine Theology in India: An Historical and Theological Study of the Brahmavaivarta Purāna* (Hartford, Vt.: Claude Stark, 1974).

14. See Judith Van Herik, "The Feminist Critique of Classical Psychoanalysis," in *The Challenge of Psychology to Faith,* ed. David Tracy and Steven Kepnes [*Concilium: Revue internationale de théologie* 156] (Edinburgh: T. and T. Clark, 1982), pp. 83–86.

15. See Carol P. Christ, "Why Women Need the Goddess: Phenomenological, Psychological, and Political Reflections," in Christ and Plaskow, *Womanspirit,* pp. 274–75. While Geertz should not be held responsible for misinterpretation of his theory (and I think Christ's position is a partial misinterpretation), it is nonetheless true that his famous formulation suggests too close a relationship between symbol and social condition. It is also hard to see how it really allows adequately for the genderedness of symbol users.

16. Clifford Geertz, "Religion as a Cultural System," in *Anthropological Approaches to the Study of Religion,* ed. Michael Banton (London and New York: Tavistock Publications, 1966), pp. 1–46.

17. Clifford Geertz, *Islam Observed* (New Haven: Yale University Press, 1968), p. 95. See also ibid., p. 97: "Religious patterns . . . have a double

aspect: they are frames of perception, symbolic screens through which experience is interpreted; and they are guides for action, blueprints for conduct."

18. See the works referred to in nn. 4 and 5 above.

19. Stephen N. Dunning, "History and Phenomenology: Dialectical Structure in Ricoeur's *The Symbolism of Evil*," *Harvard Theological Review* 76.3 (July 1983):1–21.

20. See Victor Turner, "Social Dramas and Stories about Them," in *On Narrative*, ed. W. J. T. Mitchell (Chicago: University of Chicago Press, 1981), pp. 137–64; and idem, *Forest of Symbols*. On this point see also Shinn, "Goddess."

21. Ricoeur, "Symbol Gives Rise to Thought," p. 316.

22. Elaine Marks and Isabelle de Courtivron, eds., *New French Feminisms: An Anthology* (Amherst: University of Massachusetts Press, 1980), pp. ix–xiii, 1–9.

23. The agreement of these final three papers in conclusion as well as method finds certain suggestive parallels in recent theories about both women's psychology and women's discourse. See Carol Gilligan, *In a Different Voice: Psychological Theory and Women's Development* (Cambridge: Harvard University Press, 1982); Nancy Chodorow, *The Reproduction of Mothering: Psychoanalysis and the Sociology of Gender* (Berkeley: University of California Press, 1978); Sandra Harding and Merrill B. Hintikka, eds., *Discovering Reality: Feminist Perspectives on Epistemology, Metaphysics, Methodology, and Philosophy of Science* (Dordrecht, Boston, and London: D. Reidel, 1983); and the selections by Irigaray, Kristeva, and Cixous in Marks and de Courtivron, *New French Feminisms*. There has, however, been much criticism of the essentialist overtones of such work, especially Gilligan's. See Judy Auerbach et al., "Commentary on Gilligan's *In a Different Voice*," *Feminist Studies* 11.1 (Spring 1985):149–61; Debra Nails et al., eds., *Women and Morality, Social Research* 50.3 (Autumn 1983); and Joan W. Scott, "Is Gender a Useful Category of Historical Analysis?" paper delivered at the American Historical Association meeting, December 1985.

24. To say this is not to undercut Alison Black's partial disagreement with recent feminist philosophy when she argues that the holistic values made ultimately important by Chinese male philosophers are understood by them and by many Western feminists as feminine both in substance and in method.

25. On this point see Caroline Walker Bynum, "Women's Stories, Women's Symbols: A Critique of Victor Turner's Theory of Liminality," in *Anthropology and the Study of Religion*, ed. Frank Reynolds and Robert Moore (Chicago: Center for the Scientific Study of Religion, 1984), pp. 105–25.

26. I note with amusement that my move in this paragraph—to suggest that previous insights be expanded by mine into a new synthesis—might be called a "feminine" proposal.

27. Natalie Zemon Davis, drawing on the work of anthropologists such as Turner, has made this point in *Society and Culture in Early Modern France* (Stanford: Stanford University Press, 1975), pp. 124–51, and in "Anthropology and History in the 1980's," *Journal of Interdisciplinary History* 12.2 (1981):267–75.

Part 1

Gender as Culturally Constructed Meaning

Two

Iranian *Sofreh:* From Collective to Female Ritual

Laal Jamzadeh and Margaret Mills

Introduction

This chapter examines differences in the social organization and symbolic interpretation of a ritual display shared by Zoroastrian and Shi'a Muslim communities in Iran. Differences in the ideology and ritual process attached to the display in the two communities suggest broader differences in the concept of community operating in the two groups, particularly with regard to gender and religious participation. *Sofreh* in orthodox Zoroastrian contexts developed neither the themes of female exclusiveness nor the emphasis on votive and patron-dependent relationships that characterize the ritual among Muslims.[1]

The Iranian ritual *sofreh,* a cloth on which is displayed a pre-scribed selection of foodstuffs and other objects, plays a part in a variety of calendrical and votive ceremonies. *Sofreh* are displayed by both Muslims and Zoroastrians, whose faith was the state

The authors wish to thank the members of the University of Washington's interdepartmental seminar on religion and gender and earlier audiences at the American Folklore Society and Middle East Studies Association annual meetings in 1981 who commented on versions of this chapter. Special thanks are due to the editors of this volume for patient assistance in preparing the manuscript, and most especially to Anne Betteridge and Sabra Webber for critical readings of it.

A very pertinent and challenging reading of this essay, together with important supplementary information, was received by Margaret Mills from Michael M.J. Fischer, but unfortunately was solicited too late to be religion of Iran prior to the Muslim conquest in 642 C.E. In both groups, the *sofreh* display is essential to the religious consecration of foodstuffs that are ritually consumed as the culmination of certain rites. An examination of available ethnographies reveals, however, that current uses of *sofreh* by Muslims differ substantially in emphasis and ritual setting from those of Zoroastrians.

Zoroastrians dedicate and display *sofreh* in practically all religious ritual contexts, especially in the cyclical *gæhambar* feasts—communal thanksgiving gatherings that take place every two months. Participation in *gæhambar* feasts is prescribed for all members of the community, both men and women.[2] Votive use of *sofreh* among Zoroastrians is deemphasized and remains marginal to the general significance of the rite, in the interpretations of practitioners.

Among Muslims, however, the term *sofreh* has come to designate primarily a votive rite dominated by women, according to ethnographies of both rural and urban communities. In the rural

incorporated in the body of the text (Fischer, personal communications, October 2 and October 24, 1985). An attempt has been made to take account of Fischer's observations in the notes. On the basis of his own field work in Yazd and Qum in the 1970s, Fischer concluded (contrary to Boyce and to our findings here), that Zoroastrians are as involved with votive procedures as are Muslims, with in many instances virtually identical ritual procedures and texts. If this is the case, then the burden of the argument here shifts to accounting for the relative emphasis (in Fischer's portrayal as well as here) on female management in votive procedures in each group (whereas non-votive ritual is managed predominantly by men); on the manner, degree, and circumstances of the integration of male and female worship activities in the two groups; and on how the distribution of worship patterns is affected by urbanization, development, and most recently, by the emergence of a Muslim theocracy in Iran. The Zoroastrian votive *sofreh* conducted by women, described late in this essay, would be read as more prominent in popular piety than Boyce considered them to be. The differences here described between Zoroastrians and Muslims in the symbolic interpretations of *sofreh* display components persist, and invite comparisons between the two communities at the level of the meanings of actions, that is, of cosmology and the signification and symbolic interpretation of some highly similar ritual practices.

Remaining errors are of course the authors' own. Mills gratefully acknowledges financial support from the NEH Translation Grant program during part of the preparation of this chapter.

tradition especially, not only the enactment process but the symbolic interpretation of *sofreh* as well becomes dominated by images of the female, as suppliant or supernatural patron or both. Religious use of *sofreh* among Muslins is limited to these votive rites; where *sofreh* rituals survive in nonvotive contexts, Muslims do not consider that they address sacred personages. Whereas male attendance and even occasional male sponsorship are reported from urban contexts,[3] a number of descriptions report that rural *sofreh* explicitly prohibit male attendance.

As part of the *gæhambar* feasts, Zoroastrian *sofreh* express the unconditional membership of all believers in a unified, good cosmic order. As Muslim votive rituals, *sofreh* create a personal, hierarchical relationship between a human suppliant, usually female, and a supernatural benefactor, either female or male. The striking elaboration of the votive *sofreh* in the hands of Muslim women contrasts with women's relative exclusion from leadership in other group devotional activities. Among present-day Iranian Zoroastrians, women participate in a wide variety of personal and calendrical rituals. Although Zoroastrian women occasionally resort to votive *sofreh* in situations of personal need, votive rituals seem to play a minor devotional role, compared to their popularity with Muslim women.

Zoroastrian *Sofreh:* Foodways, Cosmology, and Community

The Zoroastrians of Iran numbered twenty-five to thirty thousand before the Islamic Revolution of 1978.[4] Along with the Parsis of India, who emigrated from Iran after the Islamic conquest of 642 C.E., they comprise the surviving followers of the ancient prophet of Iran, Zarathushtra (Greek: Zoroaster). Rich in complex rituals, Zoroastrianism survived in Iran despite discrimination and harassment by the dominant Muslim population. Frequent communal religious feasts (*gæhambar*) constituted an important expression of solidarity for the minority community as well as a mechanism for the redistribution of resources during periods of hardship.

Certain themes, expressed in the *gæhambar* feasts through the choice and treatment of foodstuffs and other ritual materials for the *sofreh* and other phases of the rite, can best be understood as part of the community's general ideology pertaining to foodstuffs. Beliefs and practices regarding food can be shown to follow

25

Zoroastrian cosmology minutely. Nevertheless, while Zoroastrian foodways form an internally coherent system, this system does not exist in isolation. In the Muslim era, this system has been formed and maintained not only with reference to Zoroastrian cosmology, but also through interaction with the dominant Muslim community.

Some Zoroastrian practices and attitudes are shared by the surrounding Muslim population and can be understood as direct inheritances of older custom by the Muslim population. Certain striking contrasts in food behavior and belief also occur, marking ideological divergences between the two groups and serving as boundary markers, reinforcing the groups' separateness in the eyes of their members. Some Zoroastrians see certain food customs, particularly the votive *sofreh*, as ideologically alien borrowings from Islam. In order most effectively to describe the Zoroastrian *sofreh* in the context of *gæhambar* feasts, we will first consider certain aspects of general Zoroastrian foodways that both provide a context for understanding the Zoroastrian idea of *sofreh* and help illuminate the relations between the two religious communities.

Zoroastrian Foodways: Sacredness and Community Boundaries

Certain Zoroastrian foodways are shared by Iranian Muslims. Similar practices may or may not receive the same interpretation in the two groups, however. One attitude shared among all ethnic and religious groups in Iran is the great respect for bread as God's bestowal (*ne'mæt-e xoda*). Wasting or soiling bread is considered a grave sin all over Iran. As will be demonstrated below, a special veneration for bread and other wheat products, over other grains and foodstuffs, is visible in a number of *sofreh* rituals. Another practice common to both communities, as Donaldson noted, is a "notable lack of conversation at an ordinary Iranian meal."[5] This reticence at meals has its roots in ancient Iranian practices. Zoroastrians traditionally begin and end each meal with a silent prayer of praise and should not "break" the prayer during the meal.[6] Thus in orthodox theory at least, every meal is a consecrated one. Contemporary Zoroastrians add that this practice was prescribed to avoid excitement or anger during meals.

Alongside such common attitudes and tendencies are extreme differences between Zoroastrian and Muslim foodways. For example, pork and wine are proscribed for all Muslims. In contrast, moderate drinking of wine was in fact encouraged among Zoroastrians. It is asserted in Zoroastrian wisdom literature that the use of wine in moderation helps digestion, increases vitality and vigor of mind and body, augments memory, improves eyesight, hearing, and speech, and induces pleasant sleep and freshness of spirit.[7] Drinking to excess and intoxication, however, were regarded as sinful and harmful to body and mind.[8] In the *Dadestan-i Dinig,* a Middle Persian catechism,[9] giving or selling wine to those who are prone to abuse it is regarded as a grievous sin and an evil occupation. As for the proscription of pork, surviving artifacts (such as decorations on eating and drinking vessels and the magnificent bas reliefs at the royal hunting retreat of Taq-i Bustan) as well as folklore and literature of the pre-Islamic period refer widely to boar hunting and the consumption of pork.

A striking difference between Zoroastrian and Muslim Iranian eating habits is the attitude toward fasting. Muslims value the annual month of daylight fasting, Ramadan, as one of the five pillars of the faith, an act of obedience to divine decree pleasing to God, and a ward against evil. In addition to the required month of fasting, there are various supererogatory and recommended fast days distributed through the liturgical calendar.[10] Fasting for Muslims is an act of purification that trains one to control one's needs and desires and deepens spiritual life.[11] Muslims believe that the self-restraint of fasting improves behavior, mood, and personality. Muslims also regard fasting as therapeutic and favorable to health, if not undertaken during illness. Fasting is also prescribed for atonement of sins.[12] In contrast, all claims for abstinence and self-mortification as sources of spiritual merit and physical benefit are foreign to Zoroastrianism. In Zoroastrian thinking it is sinful to harm one's body and so to cause needless suffering. Grief, poverty, and ill health strengthen the forces of evil in this world and should be avoided. It is religious duty to be happy, healthy, strong, and rich. Dastur Dhalla, a twentieth-century Zoroastrian priest, writes that the human soul requires a healthy, strong body in order to live its strenuous life on earth. Wholesome food is the first essential to prevent the body from languishing and to give it necessary strength; thus it is a sin to fast from food. He adds that the only fast enjoined by the Prophet is the fast from sin.[13]

Zoroastrian Cosmology and the Duty of Celebration

Zoroastrian cosmology postulates an ongoing struggle being played out in this world between the Good Creation of Ahura Mazda and the Evil Creation of Ahriman. Care for the health and strength of the body as well as the mind is tied to this cosmology, for human beings were created to take part in the struggle of Good against Evil, by the proper exercise of their free will. The manifestations of evil in this world, against which righteous humans are expected to struggle, range from pollution, sickness, misery, and poverty to falsehood, injustice, and treachery. Zoroastrians are encouraged to pursue physical and mental health and to practice the doctrine of Good Thoughts, Good Words, and Good Deeds, to produce, till the earth, erect houses, and raise cattle. In so doing, they advance the cause of Good and weaken the Evil principle, bringing about the eventual downfall of Evil and the creation of Heaven on Earth. Zoroaster did not preach life on earth for the purpose of gaining heaven, but "a joyful orientation to bodily life [and] a robust faith in living."[14]

In keeping with this general emphasis on worldly well-being and the preservation of the community's health and vigor, the Zoroastrian religious calendar provides an abundant variety of joyous occasions for food sharing. Even in the oppressive times of the seventeenth century, Tavernier records the Zoroastrians' general love of feasting and of eating and drinking well.[15] These feasts, still celebrated today, are of several overlapping types, including shrine pilgrimages with animal sacrifices or other food bestowals, the bimonthly communal *gæhambar* feasts of thanksgiving, and personal rites such as initiation, marriage, and death memorials. The personal feasts are often held jointly with the seasonal holidays. All varieties of feast involve the consecration and distribution of foods to the community. Some of these ritual distributions of food, along with the *sofreh* which serves to consecrate the food, passed over into Shi'a Muslim practice. However, there they were combined with very un-Zoroastrian themes of abstention (such as partial fasting) and mourning for religious martyrs. The unambiguously celebratory tone of Zoroastrian religious feasts (including death memorials) contrasts strongly with the characteristic Shi'a Muslim devotional spirit, which combines mourning, sacrifice, and world denial with themes of communal celebration.[16]

Zoroastrian Cosmology and the Composition of Sofreh

If cosmological doctrine thus dictates the joyful tone of Zoroastrian religious feasts, it further shapes specific aspects of ritual as well. Most Zoroastrian ritual occasions require the formal display of the *sofreh* cloth, with certain religiously significant objects placed upon it. After the blessing and consecration of the food on the *sofreh* through group prayer and liturgical recitation led by a priest, the whole congregation partakes of the food to share the merit of participation in the celebration. All food is for human consumption: no food is wasted or burned. Shares of the consecrated food of the *gœhambar* are sent to the homes of all those who were not able to attend the ceremony, reinforcing the pancommunal nature of the feast.

The particular objects placed on the *sofreh* have specific symbolic values, though the selection of items varies in local practice. Dastur M. Homji, the learned high priest of the Fasli Zoroastrians of Bombay, explained that in all the rituals of the Parsis, five "da's" or *d*'s are essential items for the table:[17] (1) *darak*, grapes, (2) *divo*, light, (3) *dood*, milk, (4) *daisy*, flowers,[18] and (5) *dadam*, pomegranate. For Iranian Zoroastrians, essential items for the *sofreh* include a mirror, a small fire for incense (especially for burning the seeds of wild rue, whose Persian name, *esfand*, also means holy), fresh warm bread, fresh water, greens and fruits, and a tray with a combination of seven kinds of dried fruits and nuts called *lork*. If the ceremony is a death memorial, a portrait of the deceased is present; on a nonfunerary *sofreh*, a portrait of Zoroaster may appear. *Sofreh* relating to initiation and wedding ceremonies have additional, special constituents. For instance, a pair of scissors displayed is said to ward off evil, sugar molded in the shape of a cone stands for sweetness of life, a green scarf symbolizes good fortune and stability, and a needle and green thread are emblems of the mending and solving of problems. Thyme leaves mixed with rice are placed on the wedding *sofreh* for the priest to scatter over the couple for blessing. The color green, reiterated in this array, has retained a general connotation of auspiciousness in arid Iran, as in the expression *sæbzbæxti,* "green" or good fortune.

Despite regional variations in both the items included and details of interpretation, the centrality of the spread-out cloth and its display of objects in almost all Zoroastrian rituals as well as the general congruity of the selection of objects suggest that the displayed objects represent the basic seven categories of Ahura Mazda's Good Creation. Ahura Mazda, the Creator of Good, is believed to have six separate aspects or entities, which in later tradition have come to be personified as archangels. The objects on the *sofreh* represent physical manifestations of these seven Holy Immortals (*Amesha Spentas*). Each Immortal has a physical aspect as well as a spiritual one. These physical aspects correspond to the major categories of creation, over which the Amesha Spentas have protective power. The six Amesha Spentas are (1) *Vohu Manah,* Good Thought, who in this world protects and is represented by cattle; (2) *Asha Vahishta,* Best Righteousness, who has as physical aspect in this world fire and heat energy; (3) *Xshathra Vairyo,* Desirable Kingdom or Power, represented by metals; (4) *Spenta Armaiti,* Holy Devotion, represented by earth; (5) *Haurvatat,* Wholeness and Health, "who cares for the waters"; and (6) her twin sister *Amertat,* Immortality, the guardian of plants. The seventh, Ahura Mazda, the Wise Lord who encompasses all the six aspects and embodies wisdom, is the protector of humankind.

All these creations are represented on the *sofreh.* Milk, eggs, and meat dishes represent domesticated animals. Light from a lamp and fragrant fire on a metallic pedestal, as well as coins and/or a mirror represent the second and third creations, respectively. Water is usually present in a bowl, with green leaves such as thyme floating on it representing plants, just as the twin sisters Haurvatat and Amertat appear together in Iranian mythology and literature. The picture of the deceased or of the Prophet would, in this interpretation, represent the seventh creation, humankind. Contemporary Zoroastrians see the earth as represented by the clay floor surface upon which the priest sits to consecrate the *sofreh.* They furthermore see the seventh creation, humankind, as represented by the priest himself, present in the act of consecration.[19] Keeping all these blessings of God before the assembly reminds them to appreciate and enjoy all parts of the good creation, to reconfirm the faith, and to strengthen communal ties through sharing these blessings.

Although this array of items survives in certain Muslim *sofreh,* the holistic cosmological doctrine that informs it does not. While ethnographers of Muslim communities, such as Honari,[20] recognize an echo of Zoroastrian cosmology in the general patterns of seven items, neither they nor the Muslims who dedicate *sofreh* seem aware of the particular cosmological inventory just described, a cosmological representation explicitly acknowledged by present-day Zoroastrians.[21]

Gæhambar *Feasts: The Cycle of Unification*

The cycles of Zoroastrian ritual feasts and the manner in which they are celebrated further reiterate the cosmological themes of the unity of the good creation and the place of all believers in that unity. The *gæhambar* feasts, five-day festivals occuring bi-monthly, are thought to derive from rites connected with several different agricultural cycles, an interpretation that has caused several scholars to designate them thanksgiving ceremonies.[22] Popularly, and according to later religious documents, the six feasts are connected with the six stages of creation, in the following order: sky (believed to be mineral or metallic in composition), waters, earth, vegetation, animals, and humankind. Boyce believes that the seventh creation, fire, was honored on New Year's Day, which followed immediately upon and became connected with the sixth *gæhambar.* She therefore sees the New Year's festival at the vernal equinox, which survives both in Zoroastrian practice and also as a secular holiday among Iranian Muslims, as originating in a seventh or annual *gæhambar.*[23] It is among Zoroastrians, however, that calendrical rituals involving *sofreh* are most elaborated.

It is obligatory for those who can afford it to sponsor a feast as part of the calendrical cycle, preferably in perpetuity by permanent endowment.[24] "Personal" *gæhambar,* including communal distributions of consecrated food, are also celebrated for death memorials or in thanksgiving to commemorate a healing or other resolution of difficulty. The merit derived from the act of charity either accrues to the originator of the endowment or adds to the good deeds of the deceased, to be weighed against his or her evil deeds in determining whether he or she goes to heaven or hell.

Endowments to commemorate deliverance from difficulties come closest to duplicating the spirit and motives of votive *sofreh,* but these expressions of personal gratitude are subsumed in Zoroastrian context by the celebration of general communal well-being, which is the overarching purpose and spirit of *gæhambar.*

It is meritorious, even obligatory, for all community members to participate in the feast by sharing the dedicated food. Celebrating *gæhambar* is designated meritorious; not celebrating them is sinful, according to the tenth-century (C.E.) *Dinkard* (Deeds of religion) and elsewhere.[25] Attendance at the *gæhambar* is therefore mandatory, not invitational. Jamzadeh was told that in the city of Yazd, one of the main population centers of Zoroastrians remaining in Iran, on the night before a *gæhambar,* some white paint or a light is placed at the house door to guide and remind everyone, including the soul of the deceased, to attend the feast.[26] Those Muslim poor whose poverty does not allow them to consider non-Muslims' food unclean, as some wealthier devout do, partake of the food distribution as well. Since participation is a religious duty, Zoroastrian poor do not regard themselves as objects of charity in receiving *gæhambar* food. These events are the principal occasion for the community to gather and are mandatory for all, rich and poor, friendly or not. Social harmony and the patching up of rifts in the community are an overt purpose of *gæhambar,* directly connected with Zoroastrians' religious goals on earth.

These themes of generalized solidarity are explicit in *gæhambar* ideology.[27] Although they are communal, most *gæhambar* feasts take place in private homes. Endowed *gæhambar* should continue to be celebrated in the homes of their founders (or of the deceased, in the case of death memorials), with the result, as Mary Boyce reports, that Zoroastrians are reluctant to sell a family house even after the departure of the entire family from the community. If there is a *gæhambar* attached to a particular dwelling, family members may return from distant cities to celebrate the feast in an otherwise deserted house, or may delegate responsibility for the celebration and for the management of its endowment to nonrelatives still resident in the community.[28] More immediately, the custom of celebrating each *gæhambar* service at the house of its founder means that on a day when several endowments are sponsoring feasts, the priest and the congregation move steadily from one *gæhambar* to another around the village or neighborhood.

These are times of both worship and joy, attended by the entire community. The only exception to this participation is young adult women, who attend only *gæhambar* sponsored by their own families. According to Boyce's informants, restrictions on their participation stem from social modesty rather than from religious prescription.[29] In their physical setting and manner of institutionalization, *gæhambar* ceremonies unite the believing community across time and space.

The immense task of cooking bread and other foodstuffs for the *gæhambar,* mostly completed during the night and morning before the ceremony, is shared by both male and female members of the sponsoring family and invited helpers. In the Zoroastrian village of Sharifabad near Yazd, Boyce observed a preparation process in which male and female tasks were intricately coordinated.[30] The men kneaded the large quantities of bread dough and tended the ovens, while women shaped the loaves and stacked the cooked bread.

The next day, during the consecration ceremony, the priest recites a liturgy from the sacred book, the Avesta, over the *sofreh,* upon which the bread and other foodstuffs are arrayed together with the ritual inventory described above. Male laity simultaneously accompany him with recited prayers. The women of the sponsoring family cook additional foodstuffs, and during the recitation they bring them, steaming and fragrant, to the *sofreh,* where their fragrance is said to please the sacred personage or the departed soul who is being honored. While male priests and laymen take the lead in verbal consecration, women's food preparation activities become a part of the worship, complementing the sacred words of the men in receiving and honoring the sacred guests.

In the village of Sharifabad, at the meal following the dedication and ritual food distribution, women and men sit apart, and men are served first. But in urban *gæhambar,* men and women sit and eat together. Despite some hierarchical tendencies, however, sexual segregation is not as pronounced in Zoroastrian *gæhambar* as it is in Muslim *sofreh* meals, as will be seen. At the *gæhambar* feasts the male host waits upon both male and female guests, and Boyce observed that only the priest and the ritual corpse-bearers, men as professionally impure as the priest is pure, refrained from speech during the meal (see earlier note 5). The rest of the guests chatted merrily together.

In one further statement of solidarity, at the conclusion of the *gæhambar*'s liturgy recitation the fragrant fire is carried around the entire assembly, each person wafting the smoke into his or her face and repeating *"hamazurbim"* ("may we be united in strength").[31] Among the Parsis of India, the *hamazurbim* formula is recited with the congregation holding hands. Thus, the cyclical and the personal *gæhambar,* key ceremonies among Zoroastrians, combine the sharing of a rich abundance of foodstuffs with an invocation, through the *sofreh,* of the particular terms of the ancient cosmology. The communal enactment of the *gæhambar,* together with the symbols invoked in its *sofreh,* is a strong statement of the ideology of unification—both cosmic and social—implicit in Zoroastrian cosmology. The integration of male and female roles as expressed in the celebration of *gæhambar* feasts is a striking aspect of this cosmology of unification.

The Muslim Development of *Sofreh:* Foodways, Negotiated Relationships, and Gender

Sofreh display as a dedicatory ceremony forming part of a religious feast occurs among Shi'a Muslims in Iran primarily as a votive ritual. *Sofreh* that comprise only the display of objects on a cloth, not connected with a ritual meal, also occur at the secular New Year's ceremony (a holiday retained from the Zoroastrian calendar) and at weddings, where their function is nondevotional.[32] As votive rituals, Muslim *sofreh* meals are sponsored and staged predominantly by women, and several votive *sofreh* reported from rural communities explicitly forbid male participation.

There is a striking similarity between Muslim and Zoroastrian *sofreh* in the inventory of objects and foodstuffs placed on the cloth, while the process and participation rules for the ritual meal differ greatly between Muslims and Zoroastrians. When Muslims attach specific symbolic values to the objects on the *sofreh,* they do so with reference to a larger Muslim ideology rather than to pre-Islamic traditions. The intricate integration of personal, memorial, and calendrical celebrations as part of the Zoroastrian cosmology of unification is replaced by an emphasis on personal supplication and sacred patronage. Appeals for special intervention by saints and other supernatural personages through votive *sofreh* are not approved by the Muslim orthodoxy, but are devoutly undertaken by many Shi'a women. Whereas *gæhambar sofreh* is an essential component of the central ritual cycle of the whole Zoroastrian community, in Muslim context *sofreh* becomes a marginal rite, but one highly developed in the hands of women. *Sofreh* sponsorship and attendance offer Muslim women opportunities for both individual initiative and communal participation in religious observance. Such opportunities are otherwise attenuated for women in the central communal rituals of Shi'a Islam, such as Friday prayer, because of limitations on women's public appearances and self-expression in mixed-gender groups.

Muslim *sofreh* for which detailed scenarios have been published are primarily from rural village contexts,[33] although an urban tradition flourishes as well. Besides detailed inventories of the items required on the *sofreh* and descriptions of the prescribed manner of preparing and serving the ritual meal, some of these reports include synopses of verbal texts recited by women over the *sofreh* prior to the meal. These recitations in the presence of the *sofreh* guests correspond structurally to Avestan verses and prayers recited by the Zoroastrian priest and his congregation to consecrate the *gæhambar sofreh*. The content of these recitations, however, differs vastly from the highly ritualized, colloquially unintelligible Avestan, for it addresses in the most colloquial language the specific concerns of the women dedicants.

Some rural *sofreh* in particular make ritual use of oral narratives that in nonritual contexts are performed and regarded as fictional folktales (*æfsaneh*). In the context of votive *sofreh,* they are treated as sacred origin legends, told in conjunction with or in place of narratives that the orthodox clergy also regard as sanctified. Besides their dual status in a tradition that otherwise sharply distinguishes sacred fact from secular fiction, these stories' other striking feature is their female centeredness. They develop themes and dramatic configurations with direct relevance to women's everyday lives and to the quandaries they attempt to resolve through votive *sofreh.*

Sofreh gatherings are criticized, especially by the urban Muslim orthodoxy, as a perversion of charity, a pseudoreligious excuse for a party.[34] The Muslim votive *sofreh* combines devotional and social activities in a way not unlike the Zoroastrian *gæhambar,* but orthodox Muslims, far from seeing the integration of devotional and social activities as desirable, see this combination as irreligious.

In the Muslim context, everything about *sofreh* becomes marginal, problematical, and (not coincidentally) female centered. The very fact of their votive purpose makes the rituals suspect in the eyes of the orthodox. The objects placed on the *sofreh* cloth include both the paraphernalia of orthodox Muslim prayer and a number of items borrowed from the Zoroastrian cosmological array. In some *sofreh* the dedicatory texts also combine orthodox Muslim liturgy with nonorthodox narratives. Finally, the appropriateness of women's *sofreh* sponsorship is questioned by religious authorities. Wherein, then, lies the appeal of votive *sofreh* for Muslim women?

Muslim Foodways: Hospitality and Reciprocity

The Iranian ethic of reciprocity in hospitality and food sharing is an informing concept of Muslim votive rites. A proverb in Persian runs, "The bread of the manly remains in the stomach of the unmanly," (*Nan-e mærd dær sheæm-e namærd mimaneh*), to the effect that those who do not reciprocate hospitality are ignoble. By inviting a powerful supernatural or sacred personage to attend a ritual meal, the human *sofreh* sponsor invites the supernatural to enter into a relationship of reciprocity. If the supernatural accepts the invitation, he or she accepts also the responsibility to help the hostess with her problem. A woman may stage two ritual meals: one invites the supernatural's help, and a second is "held in trust" and staged after the sought-for resolution of difficulties has occurred. Or she may simply vow to a named supernatural that she will stage a *sofreh* on the successful conclusion of her difficulties, and perhaps as an annual commemorative event thereafter. In either case, the relationship sought is personal, special, and reciprocal.

The *sofreh* prestation, unlike other types of votive offering, takes the form of a formal meal attended by other members of the sponsor's social group, and so becomes not only an act of worship but a complex social event. Women who attend another woman's *sofreh* are further invited to use that ritual as a setting for making *sofreh* pledges of their own concerning some personal need. One *sofreh* vow thus may generate a chain of vows and prestations to a given personage. As a meal of formal invitation to a supernatural, *sofreh* forms part of the general ethic of hospitality. As effective a tactic as hospitality may be to initiate patron-client or other useful social connections in the everyday world, it is precisely this resemblance to mundane social negotiations that makes *sofreh* suspect in the eyes of the religious orthodoxy. From the orthodox viewpoint, such an invitation addressed to a sacred personage amounts to bargaining for blessings.

Sofreh *Displays: Religious and Secular Forms*

While religious *sofreh* are substantially limited to votive rites among Iranian Muslims, two forms of nonvotive *sofreh* also regularly occur. Muslims do not conceive of these *sofreh* as religious, however. Nor do these two uses of *sofreh,* in the secular New Year's ceremonies and at weddings, involve a ritual meal, but they do preserve, in attenuated form, themes of community prominent in Zoroastrian *gæhambar.* Yet even the communal ties they celebrate are more limited networks of personal ties rather than the pancommunal unity celebrated in the *gæhambar* cycle. The New Year's *sofreh* emphasizes the celebration and preservation of existing family ties and themes of physical prosperity, while customs connected with *sofreh* at weddings celebrate the formation of new family bonds through marriage and promote the good fortune of the bride in her new family setting, in particular. The secular New Year, celebrated at the vernal equinox, is a survival of the Zoroastrian ritual calendar celebrated entirely independently of the Muslim lunar year. The New Year's *sofreh* is widely displayed in both rural and urban homes and shares with Muslim votive *sofreh* many physical elements borrowed from the Zoroastrian *gæhambar* ritual. The Muslim interpretation of the inventory of ritual objects, however, does not reflect Zoroastrian cosmology. One of the best known forms of the New Year's *sofreh* is called the *sofreh* of seven *s*'s. Its components must include seven objects with names beginning with initial *sin* or *s* (*sofreh-e haft sin*).

Commentators on the Muslim New Year's *sofreh* (Massé, Honari, Betteridge) have described this display as summing up, in a general way, life's goods and necessities.[35] Honari notices in repetitions of the number seven (those items designated by the initial letter *sin,* the seven dried fruits) a reflection of Zoroastrian numerology and, in general, veneration of the seven Amesha Spentas. Honari does not see any deep significance to the choice of the letter *sin* to circumscribe the choice of objects. He points out that other versions of the New Year's *sofreh* stipulate seven *shin* or *chin* and concludes that the eclecticism of such lists precludes any basis in organized religious belief. Ordinary Muslims who display the New Year's *sofreh* are in all likelihood less aware of its specific Zoroastrian cosmological basis than are folklorists such as Honari. Honari does point out in his discussion of the pervasive occurrence of seven as a sacred number that in general Iranian astrological belief wishes and their fulfillment are connected with the seventh house—an association that links manipulations of seven symbolism at New Year and in other settings with more explicitly votive rites.

It is in certain aspects of Muslim New Year's *sofreh* ritual procedures, rather than in their symbolic interpretation, that *gæhambar* themes are most closely replicated. The items for the *sofreh* display are assembled in the days prior to New Year's Day. At the precise moment when the sun enters Aries, the beginning of the New Year by ancient Iranian calculations, custom stipulates that the entire family, including any servants living in the household, should be gathered around the *sofreh.* If the gathering is incomplete, the survival of the family intact for the coming year is jeopardized. Honari reports an occasional custom of reading, over the *sofreh,* seven verses from the Qor'an that begin with the letter *sin,* an apparent structural equivalent to Zoroastrian Avesta recitation over the *gæhambar sofreh.*

Muslims also visit the New Year's *sofreh* of family and neighbors in a manner reminiscent of the round of *gæhambar* attendance in Zoroastrian communities. In cities, after the household assembly, family groups move about the neighborhood or the city to visit friends and family. These visits are, however, selective rather than pancommunal.[36] Even in rural communities, where visitation is sometimes comprehensive, gender segregation is practiced. Mary Martin observed a pancommunal visitation pattern in the village of Baghestan, in eastern Iran, in the early 1970s.[37] Everyone in the village visited each household's *sofreh* in succession, in a formal procession. In contrast to the serial visitation of *gæhambar,* however, the men's and women's processions were totally separate and sequential; gender divisions thus condition this expression of community solidarity. Nevertheless it appears, not surprisingly, that the communal, collective aspects of *sofreh* ritual are better preserved among Muslim villagers than in the towns. Our information suggests that among urban Zoroastrians in Yazd, *gæhambar* as well were increasingly attended only by family members in recent years.[38] It appears that in both Muslim and Zoroastrian communities, collectivity persists more strongly in village celebrations, while family and personal ties predominate in urban contexts. Most notably, our available data suggest that the segregation of male and female visitants of New Year's *sofreh* in some Muslim villages is more stringent than in Zoroastrian *gæhambar* processions on similar occasions. This segregation becomes more extreme in Muslim votive *sofreh* reported from rural areas.

In wedding *sofreh* (called *sofreh-e 'æqd*) as well as New Year's displays, the particular ties celebrated and promoted are those of the extended family: in the case of the wedding, the new relationship constituted by the marriage contract, at the reading of which the *sofreh* is displayed. The *sofreh* is assembled in the bride's home, by her female relations. In Muslim as in Zoroastrian custom, the wedding *sofreh* commonly includes such items as a mirror, a pair of scissors, molded cones of sugar, a green silk kerchief or other green silk, and a needle and thread. These items have already been glossed in Zoroastrian context. They are somewhat differently interpreted in Muslim context, where they are tied to the personal fortunes of the bride. The kerchief is an item of feminine apparel connected with female modesty and seclusion. The needle and thread are key items of feminine technology. Together, the three suggest to the outside observer the virtues of chastity and industry that the bride should bring to her new family. In Herat, in Persian-speaking Afghanistan, a kerchief, needle, and thread are explicit symbols of the exchange by which a bride is given from one family to another in return for a bride-price. These items are the formal gifts given by the bride's family to the groom's, through which the bride's family acknowledges their acceptance of the marriage offer. The gifts are kept by the groom's mother and displayed to friends and family as tokens of the oral contract, prior to the actual wedding. The needle and thread in Shiraz and elsewhere in Iran more specifically affect the welfare of the bride: while the marriage contract is being read, a female friend of the bride should sew a small piece of green silk with a needle and thread (the latter often of seven colors) in order to "sew up the lips of the mother-in-law" and prevent her from criticizing the bride.[39]

Scissors are connected in some communities with the bride's assumption of married status: one component of traditional preparation of the bride in some communities is the cutting of her fore- and sidelocks into bangs in the hairstyle that identifies married women.[40] The cones of sugar are crushed and scattered over the heads of the couple to "sweeten" their relationship and the bride's life in her new home. For good fortune, the bridal couple should view each other for the first time in the mirror, placed before them during the contract reading. Thus, personal connections and personal fortune are highlighted in these manipulations of the *sofreh*'s symbolic array; general cosmology is not. Furthermore, in the case of wedding *sofreh,* there is a feminization of the symbolic interpretation of the ritual objects. This feminization becomes even more apparent in the Muslim elaboration of votive *sofreh.*

Muslim Votive Sofreh

Sofreh are offered by Muslim women to a variety of individual, named spiritual intercessors, mostly deceased holy personages of Islam. Some of those to whom *sofreh* are offered are not identifiable in Muslim hagiography, and some are explicitly identified as nonsacred supernatural beings, called *pæri* (the word is cognate to English *fairy*). This is not the *pars pro toto* address to individual aspects of a cosmic whole implied by *gæhambar* dedications. Whereas Zoroastrian *gæhambar* essentially address the total benign supernatural community on behalf of the total human community, participation in Muslim *sofreh,* though a group effort, is private, optional, and publicized by word of mouth through women's personal networks. The main thrust of votive *sofreh* sponsorship is to establish a personal relationship with a particular supernatural being for particular purposes. Common purposes for votive *sofreh* include healing the sick, solving sterility problems, achieving a desired marriage, bringing a traveling family member home safely, or more rarely, on behalf of a larger community, relieving a drought or other affliction. Some of the supernaturals addressed are "specialists" in the handling of one or more types of problem; others are considered effective intercessors for any need.

While differences in purpose and participatory rules between

Muslim and Zoroastrian *sofreh* are clear from examination of existing ethnographic literature, ritual preparation is another matter. From the rural ethnographies it appears that Muslim votive *sofreh* require more preparatory ritual manipulation of the *sofreh*'s components to be carried out by the sponsor, acting alone, than do Zoroastrian *gæhambar sofreh*. A number of significant ritual activities in Muslim votive *sofreh* are therefore solitary. Comparatively speaking, less attention is paid in the literature to the preparatory phases of Zoroastrian *gæhambar sofreh,* presumably because these phases are not core parts of the event as they are in Muslim votive *sofreh.* While Zoroastrian women pay close attention to ritual cleansing of the cooking area prior to the cooking, both the purification process and the actual food preparations, as described by Boyce, are cheerfully communal and the cooking is not highly ritualized.[41]

In the emphasis placed on the special ways the woman sponsor must assemble and prepare votive *sofreh* foods (as contrasted with everyday food-handling), women's domestic activities are foregrounded and sacralized in Muslim votice *sofreh* in a more detailed way than in Zoroastrian *gæhambar*. In some Muslim votive *sofreh,* preparatory phases include a consecration liturgy performed by the sponsor alone on the evening prior to the group consecration at the actual meal. The visit of the supernatural is thought to occur overnight, in private, between these two consecratory phases, not during the communal meal as in the case of *gæhambar*. Important aspects of the Muslim votive relationship are negotiated not only at the meal, but in the ceremonies of preparation leading up to it.

A detailed analysis of a rural votive *sofreh* reveals to an even greater degree those feminizing and personalizing tendencies already traced in nonvotive Muslim uses of *sofreh*. The urban votive *sofreh* are no less personalized than the rural ones, but some of them may be less feminized in that men may attend and even sponsor *sofreh* on occasion. Anne Betteridge described a prerevolutionary *sofreh* sponsored by an urban elite woman that was attended by both men and women and included singing and dancing.[42] An informant from Tehran told Mills of a *sofreh* dedicated to Abol Fazl, one of the Shi'a martyrs, sponsored in Tehran in 1984 as a weekly open house by a woman who invited anyone, male or female, with a need or problem to attend and contribute to the event. Many participants came to petition for the safety of family members on the Iraqi battle front. The sponsor's house was open to the poor so that any who were hungry might come and eat the dedicated meal.[43] Before the revolution, the occurrence of sexually integrated invitational *sofreh* in urban contexts might have been interpreted as reflecting secularizing tendencies under Western influence. In the wake of the revolution and the suffering attendant on the war with Iraq, popular piety is high, and joint male and female participation in *sofreh* partakes of a more sober spirit. The feminization of the ritual should therefore be regarded as contingent on local and temporal conditions, more fully realized in some Muslim contexts than others, but manifest overall when the spectrum of Muslim uses of *sofreh* is compared to Zoroastrian *sofreh*'s place in orthodox practice. Sexual segregation in the Muslim *sofreh* is by no means a simple function of religious orthodoxy: some of the most sexually exclusive rural *sofreh* are also the most unorthodox, as will be illustrated later. Moreover, the copresence of men and women at urban *sofreh* takes on different significance under different historical circumstances.

There appears to be a systematic variation in the degree of heterodoxy of votive *sofreh*. The dedication of *sofreh* to nonsacred supernaturals and the use of folktales in their liturgy are reported only by the rural ethnographers. From Betteridge's description and Mills's interview with the Tehran resident who has sponsored and attended *sofreh* in Tehran both before and since the Islamic revolution, urban *sofreh* appear to be more "Islamic" in content.[44] Urban informants reject the dedication of *sofreh* to *pæri,* and the texts in urban *sofreh,* at least at those attended by middle- and upper-class women, also tend to be texts accepted as religious by the orthodoxy. Nevertheless, the women's contention that these *sofreh* are good Muslim practice does not seem to convince the clergy. Whether rural *sofreh* are by and large more heterodox than urban *sofreh* remains uncertain, however. The Iranian ethnographers of the rural scene were particularly interested in documenting "folk" practices of all kinds and may have selected for description *sofreh* that featured the most colorful departures from the orthodoxy familiar to their urban readers.[45] The attribution of greater heterodoxy to rural women's religion, as expressed in *sofreh,* therefore must remain provisional pending directly comparative research. Questions of class and education level also figure in what may appear to be urban/rural distinctions.

In summary, feminization, personalization, and heterodoxy all appear to be more developed in Muslim than in Zoroastrian *sofreh* rituals. It may be possible to attribute the personalization and heterodox tendencies of the ritual partly to the social and religious position and needs of Muslim women, but the positions of women in rural and urban contexts differ significantly. Economic class has also significantly affected gender relations in Iran in recent decades. Bearing in mind that Muslim votive *sofreh* present a spectrum of possibilities and that available data may not represent the full range of those possibilities or their relative frequency in various socioeconomic settings, a rural *sofreh* that manifests the more extreme degrees of heterodoxy, feminization, and personalization is presented below.

A Case Study: The *Sofreh* for Lady Tuesday in Khorassan

The *sofreh* dedicated to three female supernaturals, the Ladies *Hur* (Houri), *Nur* (Light), and *Sehshænbeh* (Tuesday), is described by Shokurzadeh as a village form common all over Iran.[46] The three women to whom it is dedicated are dubiously identified by Shokurzadeh's informants as two daughters of the Prophet (*Hur* and *Nur*), and a "virtuous woman associate of theirs, who was called 'Lady Tuesday' (*Bibi Sehshænbeh*) because she was born, married, and died on that day." Monday night, or "Tuesday eve" as it would be designated in Persian, is specifically identified as auspicious for contact with *pæri* or fairies. Despite the Muslim lineages supplied for Ladies Hur and Nur, performance of this *sofreh* is prohibited during the months of Safar and Moharram, two of the holiest months in Islam because of the holidays they contain. Thus, far from being assimilated to the Muslim liturgical calendar, this, like some other *sofreh*, is defined in opposition to it. Nonetheless, Shokurzadeh's informants regarded this *sofreh* as efficacious for all needs.

Beginning her preparations for the *sofreh* on a Monday, the sponsor must beg ingredients for the ritual meal from at least three households that contain at least one member named Fatimeh (namesakes of the Prophet's daughter and Ali's wife, the most revered woman in Shi'a Islam). Begging from households with female members named after the Prophet's family is a frequently reported feature of rural Muslim *sofreh*. While communal "pot-luck" *gæhambar* (*gæhambar-e toji*) are reported from some Zoroastrian communities,[47] begging is a major departure from the spirit of Zoroastrian feasts. In *gæhambar* the sponsor distributes food to express gratitude for plenty and self-sufficiency and to share that plenty with the community. In the Muslim case, begging may be seen as an expression of the sponsor's personal helplessness and her reliance on divine grace, manifested by the generosity of others, in times of difficulty. One does not, however, beg *sofreh* ingredients from strangers: while the beggar is sometimes instructed to go heavily veiled or after dark so as to be unrecognized, she visits neighborhood households whose female members are known to her by name and, in a small community, most likely already know of her intention to hold a *sofreh*. This contrasts with ordinary Muslim charity, which is anonymous. In Muslim votive *sofreh,* charity is made circular within the local community by the sponsor's begging: the sponsor solicits food from the very households whose members she invites to the *sofreh*. She thus becomes both suppliant and host to them, just as she does to her supernatural guest. The intentional assumption of a posture of poverty and dependency in Muslim votive *sofreh* is a striking reversal of Zoroastrian ideology, which univocally rejects poverty and self-denial, even denying that poor Zoroastrians attending *gæhambar* are objects of charity.

Invitation to Muslim women's votive *sofreh* is informal, spread by word of mouth, rather than public and general as *gæhambar* or the mosque prayer announced daily by the muezzin's call. Under circumstances Betteridge describes,[48] invitation may be not only personal but competitive. Betteridge reports a case in which two sisters-in-law offered rival *sofreh* at the same hour of the same day to see who could command the presence of which of their mutual friends and family. Thus personal networks may be strengthened in votive *sofreh* at the expense of a general solidarity such as that achieved by serial attendance at clusters of *gæhambar*.

In Shokurzadeh's description, once the sponsor has announced her intention to hold a *sofreh,* by invitation or begging or both, she purchases or assembles other supplies for the ritual meal and lays them out on a clean *sofreh* cloth in a closed and locked room overnight. The materials assembled in the room are the following: sugar; salt; chick-peas and raisins mixed together; a kohl bottle and applicator; a glass of *sekænjebin,* a sweet-sour vinegar drink; a mirror; a clean prayer rug or mat, a rosary, and a prayer seal (*mohr*), the paraphernalia of Shi'a prayer; a volume of the Qor'an; knives and other equipment and all the ingredients for the *ash* or soup that is the main food of the communal meal (these include both the begged and the other materials); two lighted candles, one on either side of the *sofreh;* and a lighted lamp, in addition to the candles, so that the *sofreh* will never be in darkness.

Parallels between this votive array and both Zoroastrian *gæhambar* and Muslim New Year's *sofreh* are evident, with some differences in interpretation. Sugar is for social harmony and prosperity, as elsewhere. Salt, along with bread, is the archetypal hospitality item. To have "eaten the salt" of another person means one has accepted hospitality and the obligation of reciprocity. The sanctity of wheat products has already been noted. When the supernatural visits the *sofreh* during the night, he or she is believed to leave finger marks in the dishes of salt and flour in particular, to indicate acceptance of the feast. The chick-peas and raisins are a variation on the dried fruit mixtures noted elsewhere. Kohl, besides being a female cosmetic item, is connected with other-worldly vision in folktales. *Sekænjebin,* like the vinegar on the New Year's *sofreh,* is fermented but nonalcoholic, possibly a substitute for wine used in Zoroastrian contexts. The mirror is familiar from wedding *sofreh.* The prayer equipment acts as an invitation to the supernatural to consecrate the *sofreh* with prayer. The prayer seal or *mohr* is a round of baked clay from the shrine of the Shi'a martyrs Hussein at Kerbela or Imam Reza in Mashhad. It is used to rest the forehead upon while bowing in prayer, so that one's head may touch holy earth. The notion of earth's holiness is particularized and personalized in Shi'a *sofreh,* in contrast to the generalized notion of the holiness of earth expressed in Zoroastrian *sofreh* symbolism. The substitution of the Qor'an for a human image is in keeping with Muslim rejection of human representations in religious contexts: God's Word to man takes the place of the physical image of His Messenger.[49] The consecration of the tools of food preparation along with the meal ingredients supports the interpretation that women's work in particular receives sanctification through votive *sofreh.*

Once all the items are laid out, the sponsor of the ceremony recites the petitionary prayer, then locks the room from the outside. All the liturgy of this rural Muslim votive *sofreh,* both solitary and collective, is conducted by women, in contrast to the *gæhambar.* Males are totally excluded from participation in this and in some other Muslim votive *sofreh* and are said to risk blindness if they approach the *sofreh* display. According to Shokurzadeh, pregnant women are also excluded lest they endanger a male fetus. The seclusion of the *sofreh* display in a locked, inner room during the period when the supernatural is expected to visit it, together with the exclusion of male participants, places the supernatural visit squarely in the private, female domain. Most rural *sofreh* invoke, in various ways, the power and status available to women through pious and circumspect behavior, particularly by the manipulation of seclusion rules. These restrictions form part of a complex of concepts about male and female, visibility and invisibility, exposure and enclosure, veiling and the protective seclusion of women. Some *sofreh* procedures stipulate that *sofreh* components must never be exposed to the open sky while in preparation or use, but must be prepared indoors, in lighted surroundings, the indoor world being the world of pious women. The danger to men's vision, should they catch sight of this enclosed, female ritual world, is an extreme assertion of the power of women embodied in *sofreh,* one of the few female-controlled rites in Islam.

After her prayer, the sponsor fasts until the next day. Such behavior accords with Muslim views on piety and dedication, but contrasts with Zoroastrian *sofreh* practice as described by Boyce in which the gregarious women preparing the ritual food lighten their late-night labors by sampling their product. Next morning, the Muslim sponsor examines the surface of the salt and flour for marks of the supernaturals' touch.

Using the flour consecrated by the saints' touch, the sponsor prepares a special bread called *komaj,* containing oil and sugar as well as the usual water and salt. Two loaves are made; one small one is first given to a child as charity, and a larger one is later broken above the sponsor's head at the *sofreh* and distributed to the guests as part of the dedicatory meal. The sponsor and her helpers also prepare the noodle soup called *ash,* using consecrated flour and other ingredients. While the soup simmers in a covered kettle, lighted candles are placed atop it and more prayers are recited over it.

The general gathering begins around noon. To begin the *sofreh* meal, a prepubescent girl breaks the large loaf of bread above the head of the sponsor, thereby putting her under the protective influence of its consecration. The virgin status of the young girl who performs this and subsequent ritual acts reiterates the theme of female power through purity and enclosure. Next, the girl spoons some of the soup from one bowl to another during a recitation of texts, including a religious narrative and the tale synopsized below. An *atu* or female religious teacher first recites a chapter of the Qor'an (*Surah al-Rahman,* "The Merciful"). As in *gæhambar,* liturgical recitation is directly juxtaposed with the manipulation of prepared foods. After the recitation, spoonfuls of the soup thus consecrated are given to each guest.

After the Qor'anic verses, the *atu* recites a *rowzeh.* *Rowzeh* in general are formal martyrdom narratives, published in books but orally interpreted and sermonized by specialists. In the first ten days of the month of Muharram, during which the martyrdom of the family of Hussein, the Prophet's grandson, occurred, both men and women gather, either separately or in segregated congregations, to hear *rowzeh* reciters in formal religious services. In this *sofreh,* however, the term *rowzeh* is applied to the origin legend of this particular votive rite, a narrative that has no place in the orthodox canon of Shi'a religious narratives. A full translation of Shokurzadeh's text of this narrative appears in the appendix to this chapter. Briefly, the story is as follows:

> A young girl is abandoned in the wilderness by her father at the behest of her jealous stepmother. Wandering and weeping, she comes upon three beautiful women, houris of Paradise, in a white tent in a wood by a spring. They are cooking an *ash* or soup. The women, Hur, Nur, and Sehshænbeh by name, hear her tell her story and tell her that if she is rescued, she should make a vow to cook an *ash* dedicated to them. They direct her to beg from seven Fatimehs the flour and various dried legumes for the soup and distribute the cooked soup to the women of the neighborhood. They teach her further details of preparing the *sofreh* and then disappear.
>
> The girl is rescued by a prince on a hunting trip. He is impressed by her good sense and kindness and marries her against his mother's

wishes. The girl, in seclusion and unable to leave the palace, undertakes her vow by arranging food in seven niches around her room, veiling herself as if to go out, and "begging" the food from the niches. Her mother-in-law sees this activity and denounces the girl to her son as an inveterate beggar. The prince, enraged, tips over her soup pot, and she curses him.

As a result of the curse, the prince is falsely accused of the murder of two of his courtiers. His father imprisons him. His bride sends a message to him, through his mother, to repent and honor her vow. The prince orders his mother to prepare the soup. The courtiers are found alive, and the prince is freed and his bride vindicated. The prince avows his belief in the power of Ladies Hur, Nur, and Sehshænbeh.

Following this narrative, the attending women light a piece of oil-soaked rag atop a brick "in the name of the twelve imams,"[50] reinvoking orthodox Shi'a religious authority. When the rag has burned out, they share the soup and other items in a communal meal. After the *ash* is eaten, the dishes are washed "in a clean spot,"[51] and the wash water is disposed of where it will not be stepped upon because the water is considered purified by contact with the consecrated food. The brick and rag are cast into running water, which is always considered pure.

There are obvious messages for women of all ages in this *sofreh* legend. First, there is the promise of solidarity with powerful female supernaturals who see and understand women's predicaments, especially those resulting from uneasy affinal relationships. The young heroine is rewarded for humility, circumspection, loyalty, and piety. Although her devotions are solitary and private, their purpose is to solidify corporate family relationships (i.e., to preserve her miraculously achieved marriage). The tension between her and her mother-in-law is resolved by an ironic reversal of normal power relationships. In ordinary circumstances, a young bride is totally under her mother-in-law's thumb. In the story, the mother-in-law's contempt for the girl and her attempt to break up the marriage are punished through the misfortune of her son. The woman's rejection of her daughter-in-law jeopardizes the lineage by putting her own son in mortal danger. Her action demonstrates the power, for good or ill, that women perceive themselves to have over the welfare of their male relatives, particularly their sons, through appropriate or inappropriate action. For the harm to be undone, the mother-in-law and her son must admit their fault and recognize the legitimacy and power of the humble young girl's relation with the sacred. Yet this power is nonetheless rooted in respect for senior women (the houris and Fatimeh, the Prophet's daughter) and obedience to them. These themes together address the need for negotiated respect and solidarity among women within the coresidential extended family. These relationships are the focal tension points in traditional women's lives. Furthermore, because the prince bears the punishment for interfering with the girl's *sofreh,* the story constitutes a warning to men not to interfere with devotional activities special to women.

All of the folktale-type narratives associated with votive *sofreh* in the existing ethnographic literature present in various ways the issue of how female social behavior directly affects the welfare of their families. While the messages are socially conservative, they nonetheless emphasize the power of individual women to affect the well-being of the family and of society as a whole, through manipulations of personal relations with the supernatural and with family members—especially in-laws.[52] Both kinds of relationships require negotiation and diplomacy. For adult women, married out of their natal households into those of strangers, successful family relationships are, like relationships with the supernatural, achieved, not merely bestowed. Women, in their own view, determine the success of such relationships by individual action.

Common Themes in *Sofreh:* Diphasic Structure

While the content of this story is consistent with other rural *sofreh* narratives, in the contemporary urban tradition reported by Betteridge recitation texts appear limited to *rowzeh* proper, which are not so dominated by themes of female socialization. Mills's informant from Tehran also insisted that only *sofreh* dedicated to the recognized martyrs of Shi'a Islam are offered in the city, accompanied by orthodox *rowzeh* recitations; she considered other types of dedications and narratives to be superstitious. Nonetheless, in the urban tradition, themes of negotiated female solidarity are expressed in the interactive process of *sofreh,* if not in its narratives.

The urban votive *sofreh* described by Betteridge displayed a sharply defined diphasic structure in which the initial atmosphere of devotion and mourning gave way to joyful celebration, ribaldry,

49

feasting, singing, and social dancing. The celebratory tone of the second phase of Muslim votive *sofreh* echoes the gaiety of Zoroastrian *gæhambar* feasts and further highlights that gaiety through juxtaposition with somber Shi'a themes of mourning. While this juxtaposition is strongly condemned as irreligious by Shi'a clergy as well as by some pious women, it can be seen as a powerful expression of the votive *sofreh* sponsor's emotional predicament, poised in faith between affliction and grateful celebration.

Descriptions of rural votive *sofreh* given to Shokurzadeh and other male researchers also imply a diphasic structure. The two recitative sections are pivotal, dividing the dedicatory phase of the ritual from the general feast. In some of the rural *sofreh*, orthodox martyrdom narratives and folktales are juxtaposed and performed in the same ceremony. The arrangement of the narratives mediates the transition between the more sober and the lighter phases of the ritual, with the more orthodox religious text standing first, as does the Qor'anic recitation in the *sofreh* described above. Male ethnographers do not mention any equivalent of the women's parties that formed a lively sequel to the dedicatory activities in *sofreh* Betteridge attended. These male researchers were not able to attend rural *sofreh* and relied instead upon descriptions by female informants. Probably their women informants suppressed details concerning this phase of the proceedings, out of either social modesty or fear of religious censure, or both.

The Shi'a clergy and some lay people criticize votive *sofreh* on three major grounds. First, *sofreh* improperly juxtapose devotion and social celebration. Second, they are a perversion of charity because those who share the *sofreh* food are not the truly needy. Third, votive appeals to saints are a perversion of faith and reliance on Divine grace: they amount to bargaining for blessings and verge on *shirk*, the heresy of attributing divine powers to individuals other than God. Women who are devoted to *sofreh* reject these criticisms, saying in their own defense that they distribute food to the poor at shrines simultaneously with celebrating *sofreh* at home and that their devotion to the saints of Islam, as intercessors with God only, is sincere and unconditional. In this debate, the original dual purpose of Zoroastrian *gæhambar*—the redistribution of surplus resources in an egalitarian fashion throughout the community and the assertion of communal solidarity through group devotions—is split apart and criticized on separate grounds in Muslim ideological contexts. The gathering of women is censured as frivolous, a mischievous exploitation of the pretext of worship. The redistribution of goods is rejected as false charity. It is not as the legacy of a despised minority religion that the *sofreh*'s hybrid nature is criticized, however, but as a female misperception of piety.

A comparison to those charitable institutions approved by the Muslim clergy gives insight into the "un-Islamic" aspects of *sofreh*. The critical rejection of female-controlled, domestically centered commensalism and charity stands in strong contrast to the orthodox approval of the public, male-controlled *væqf* or charitable endowments. *Væqf* are donations (by either men or women) of income-producing durable property, often lands or buildings, to a shrine, mosque, school, or other religious institution. The clergy attached to that institution manage the trust, sometimes in consultation with the donor family, using the proceeds for endowed *rowzeh* or charitable distributions or for the upkeep of the institution. Both *væqf* and votive *sofreh* have their historical roots in Zoroastrian *gæhambar* endowments. The *væqf* became a major mechanism for the consolidation of economic and political power in the hands of the Shi'a clergy who administered them, to such an extent that Reza, the first Pahlavi shah, acted in the 1920s to nationalize the *væqf* as part of his basic strategy to consolidate an effective central government.

Unlike *væqf,* but like Zoroastrian *gæhambar* endowments, the Muslim votive *sofreh* remain in the homes and under the control of their original donors, generally female. Domestic votive *sofreh* often become annual commemorative events during the lifetime of the donor or beneficiary. Participants stoutly defend *sofreh* as devotional behavior and frankly enjoy its social aspects. This mixture of group devotions and social networking, controlled by women and orchestrated to their personal and life-cycle needs, serves social purposes of women in a wide cross-section of Iranian society. The quantity of resources redistributed through *sofreh* is not large; it is unlikely that *sofreh* constitute a significant diversion of alms from *væqf* and other forms of male-controlled charity. What Muslim women achieve in votive *sofreh* is a measure of devotional autonomy for themselves and an occasion for extending social networks beyond the family.

Completing the Circle: Zoroastrian Votive *Sofreh*

One further development of *sofreh* requires mention in order to elucidate fully the relationship between the Muslim votive rite and its Zoroastrian antecedents. Votive *sofreh* is in fact practiced among Zoroastrians, chiefly among women. Rostam Belivani, Boyce's expert informant in the village of Sharifabad, condemned the votive *sofreh* practiced by women alone as a borrowing from folk Islam, not a proper expression of Zoroastrian piety.[53] Like the Muslim clergy, Belivani viewed votive *sofreh* as a misapprehension of the nature of divine grace. In any case, Zoroastrian votive *sofreh* appear to be far less numerous than the *gæhambar* feasts and remain peripheral to the major cycle of benefactions.

The purposes for votive *sofreh* appear similar among Zoroastrian and Muslim women. Data are scanty concerning individual motivation in either population. Of particular interest is the Zoroastrian votive *sofreh* reported by Boyce, which includes a detailed discussion of its purpose. A Sharifabadi woman undertook a particular, solitary form of *sofreh* as a last resort for relief from illness and distress that she suffered after she unwittingly polluted a sacred space: her menses had begun unexpectedly while she was present at a shrine. Through this event, which polluted the shrine, the woman found herself involuntarily at odds with the forces of Good. When other cures failed, she finally had recourse to the *Sopra-e Sabzi* (in literary Persian, *sofreh-e sæbz, Sofreh* of the Green One), one of the *sofreh* that is most strikingly at odds with orthodox religious practice, either Zoroastrian or Muslim. This particular *sofreh* is reported, in almost identical form, by Sadeq Hedayat in Muslim context and by Boyce from her Sharifabadi informant.[54]

The *sofreh* is staged out of doors, by the lone woman petitioner, with help from one older woman assistant. Hedayat stipulates that, for Muslims, it is efficacious if this woman be an unbeliever, preferably a Zoroastrian. There are no human guests, and the petitioner is required to sleep out alone overnight in the open air, beside the *sofreh*—a highly inappropriate action for a proper woman. In folk belief, virtuous women do not find refuge in the wilderness, but seek to escape from it, as the story analyzed earlier illustrates. Religious recitations, either of Avesta or Qor'an respectively, are forbidden for this *sofreh*. The name of God must not be invoked. The personage appealed to is generally identified as the princess of the *pæri*. According to Hedayat, the princess is likely to visit the *sofreh* in animal form, as a cat or a pigeon. In the Zoroastrian case, at the conclusion of the *sofreh*, the petitioner is advised that on returning home she should bring the priest to pray in her home, to make sure that the supernatural who has been invoked does not follow her home and capriciously invade the domestic space.

This *sofreh* contradicts most of the communal, religious, and domestic themes of both Muslim and Zoroastrian *sofreh* tradition. Only in its selection of objects and foods does it retain the shape of the more familiar votive *sofreh*. So systematically does it invert the procedures and the implied communal and religious values of *sofreh* and its *gæhambar* antecedents that this rite might be designated anti-*sofreh*. Yet in the case reported by Boyce, the rite was considered effective to redress a separation from the sacred and to repair physical damage done to a religious believer by involuntary ritual pollution. For repair of a breach with the sacred, this recourse to nonsacred, female supernatural power entails a further, voluntary withdrawal from religiously "safe" locales and practices.

Conclusion

The ambiguous religious status of votive *sofreh*, for both Muslim and Zoroastrian women, multiplies its expressive and effective possibilities for its practitioners, who are themselves to varying degree cut off from direct access to the sources of legitimate religious power. Present-day Zoroastrian women have a more active role in the central religious rites of *gæhambar* than do Shi'a women in the main public devotional activities of Islam. Zoroastrian development of *sofreh* as a woman's rite is correspondingly less pervasive and less visible.

Zoroastrian *gæhambar* feasts, the main locus of *sofreh* in Zoroastrianism, are nonvotive, ideally pancommunal, and require intense cooperation by men and women together. Men's or women's personal rituals of thanksgiving or commemoration are assimilated to the cyclical celebration of the total community by being held during one of the *gæhambar* feast periods. The departed soul or divine principle being honored gives no physical evidence of his or her presence. The male group recitation of Avestan

53

prayers and the group closing statement of the *gœhambar,* *"Hamazurbim"* ("May we all be united in strength"), reiterate themes of communal solidarity under the aegis of religious liturgy.

By contrast, Muslim *sofreh* in its most elaborated form is votive, personal, predominantly female, invitational-communal, occasional, and centered around individual needs and goals and negotiated personal relationships. In rural examples especially, the invited supernatural is expected to leave physical evidence of his or her presence. Participation by ordinary males is either marginal or forbidden. The narrative texts embedded in Muslim *sofreh* (whether orthodox martyrdom narratives or folk legends centered on helpless individuals) portray serious rents in the social fabric that can only be mended by the personal intervention of the supernatural. Furthermore, the particular folktale texts that figure in Muslim votive *sofreh* specifically address issues of personal solidarity among women, through the reciprocal balancing of acts of generosity and respect, of rejection and punishment. The world of Muslim women's votive *sofreh* is personal, physical, and negotiated at all levels, mirroring their experience of achieved membership in the marital family.

Those types of votive *sofreh* reportedly practiced by Zoroastrian women are visibly less social and pancommunal than *gœhambar sofreh* ceremonies. An extreme example of the solitary form is the *sofreh-e sœbz,* described earlier. In other Zoroastrian votive *sofreh* Boyce describes, the minimal definition of a proper distribution of food among Zoroastrian women (as contrasted with a *gœhambar*) stipulates that food must be sent to households within at least a three-door radius of the sponsors.[55] There is no obligation to include the whole community: only a certain minimal dispersal of alms is prescribed. Votive *sofreh* thus constitute a minor form of Zoroastrian *sofreh* ceremonies, in part because they are less than pancommunal. On the contrary, Muslim votive *sofreh,* especially the urban variety, offend Shi'a orthodoxy by being too social.

Significantly, then, it is Shi'a Muslim women, who are relatively excluded from the public communal activities of religious orthodoxy, who have adapted the symbolic repertoire of the scorned minority Zoroastrian religion as a medium of communal religious expression for themselves. *Sofreh* gatherings, like pilgrimages and public *rowzeh* recitations commemorating the Shi'a martyrs, are a main arena for women to express their membership in the religious community. Of these three activities, *sofreh* is the ritual most firmly situated in women's sphere, in the domestic space, and the only one over which women exercise complete organizational control. In *sofreh*, the less enfranchised (Muslim women) unconsciously borrow the symbolic idiom of the disenfranchised non-Muslim minority. They also reinterpret its symbolic content to develop statements about the problem of powerlessness within their community and to articulate their conviction that their needs and desires do merit divine recognition and support, that the weak do have means to influence the strong.

In the Zoroastrian case, the forces of discrimination and a dwindling population threaten the survival of the entire community. Correspondingly, rituals bring to the forefront statements of faith in the combined strength of the community. Paradoxically, such difficulties as the shortage of priests in small communities have caused women to take an increased share of ritual responsibility for activities, including the care of temples and shrines. These duties formerly belonged to lay males, who in turn have assumed ritual duties such as the tending of sacred fires, formerly reserved for the clergy.[56] The intensity and frequency of ritual activities in the *gæhambar* cycle also necessitate the active participation of both sexes. Drawn more fully into cooperative ritual practice with men by the adverse pressures on their whole community, Zoroastrian women appear to have a less gender-segregated religious life than do Muslims. Yet they too retain, in what Boyce calls "semi-secret" rituals, the female spiritual resource of the votive *sofreh*.

An examination of votive *sofreh* as it now exists in the two communities does not yield clear conclusions about the origin of the practice, but does invite comparison of the relations between each community's women and its religious institutions. With the present state of available data, it is not possible to say whether votive *sofreh* developed as a women's rite in popular Zoroastrianism, before the arrival of Islam, or whether it developed among Muslim women and was reintroduced into Zoroastrianism, as Belivani believes. We can say, however, that in each case, votive *sofreh* is viewed as a marginal, heterodox practice by the religious establishment. The terms under which it is criticized underline differences in the concepts of community operating in the two groups, particularly basic oppositions in the expectations for communal religious participation with respect to gender. The common ground between Zoroastrian and Muslim votive *sofreh* cannot be ignored, however. In both cases, a predominantly male orthodoxy criticizes women's attempts to initiate an individual, personal relationship with the sacred, on the analogy of earthly personal relationships. An examination of differences returns, inevitably, to a sense of a common need underlying women's devotional activities. The difference in degree of attention paid to votive *sofreh* in the two traditions may reflect a difference in the degree to which women's participation in the main religious tradition is marginalized under current social conditions. Yet the sharing of the ritual and its immediate goals, even in a limited degree, suggests a congruency of needs between Zoroastrian and Muslim women.

Appendix
The Story of the Sofreh of Bibi Hur, Bibi Nur, and Bibi Sehshœnbeh

This appendix is a full translation of the narrative included in the description of the rite, in Ibrahim Shokurzadeh's *'Æqayed o Rosum-e 'Ameh-ye Mærdom-e Khorassan* (Tehran, 1346 A.H.), pp. 29–32. Shokurzadeh does not quote any single informant, nor does he specify to what extent the text he gives has been edited from one or more oral performances. Lack of information as to the exact provenance and status of the text discourages fine-grained analysis of its contents; nonetheless it is presented in its entirety for the sake of details that contribute further to the themes discussed in general terms in the body of this chapter.

Once there was, once there was not.[57] Long ago there was a man with one daughter. His wife died, and the girl was motherless. In order not to be alone, the man took another wife. His new wife was very cruel and mean toward the girl and had no interest in her, and because the woman was of bad character, she thought about getting rid of her. In order to do this, one day she pretended to be sick and said to her husband, "Your daughter is very inauspicious, her presence in this house has no felicity or good omen for me. If you want me to recover from this illness, and be healthy, you must go as soon as possible and abandon her in the desert for the wolves to eat." This ignorant man, who was very partial to his second wife, saw no alternative to obedience. He put the girl on a horse and took her to a spot very far off in the desert. There he put her down, asleep, under a tree, and returned to the city. Some hours later the girl awoke and called her father, and heard no answer. Solitary and alone she ran in all directions. In a panic, she sought her father, not knowing that her ignoble father had left her in the desert and gone, to let her feed the wolves. Little by little night came on. The girl, out of fear of predatory animals, climbed a tree and stayed there till morning. At dawn she climbed down, put her faith in God, and set out. Tearfully she wandered in all directions, begging God and his Prophet for her deliverance. She walked and walked, till she arrived at a wood, and there she suddenly spied a white tent. She went up to it and saw three very beautiful women (houris) there, sitting beside a spring, cooking soup, and they had also set a bowl of water down beside the soup pot. She stepped forward and greeted them. The women, who were Bibi Hur, Bibi Nur, and the third, Bibi Sehshænbeh, politely returned her greeting and asked about her condition. The girl explained her situation to them. After the three holy houris heard her story, they said to her, "If you wish to see repose and reach your goal, make a vow that you will cook the soup of Bibi Hur and Bibi Nur and Bibi Sehshænbeh." The girl said, "How is this soup cooked?" The houris answered, "Thus, that if you gain your wish, you go and beg from seven Fatimehs a little flour and chick-peas and dried beans and lentils and mung beans, and cook a soup from that, and distribute it to the women of the quarter." Then they taught the girl the manner of cooking the soup and the customs for laying the *sofreh* and the other customs for that vow, and then suddenly disappeared from view. The girl was cheered and vowed to herself that if she were delivered from this wood and free of her stepmother's grip, and gained a comfortable existence, she would lay a *sofreh* for Bibi Hur and Bibi Nur, and with this in mind she said to herself,

"Oh, Lord, grant my plea,
From my stepmother's trap set me free."

She had not even finished the verse when she suddenly saw three riders appear from afar, approaching her. One of them was the son of the king of that country, and the other two were the sons of the vizier and the chief justice. As soon as the prince's glance fell on the girl, he fell in love with her, not with one heart but with a hundred. He came forward and said to the girl, "Oh, girl, have you any water that we could drink? We have come far and are thirsty." The girl said "Yes," and took the bowl of water from beside the soup pot and gave it to the prince. When the bowl was empty, she filled it with cold water from the spring and gave that to the prince. The prince asked, "What is the wisdom in this, that you first gave us warm water, then cold?" The girl said, "At first you were freshly arrived from the road and your bodies were hot. I gave you warm water to quench your thirst somewhat, and then I gave you cold, to completely remove your heat and thirst." The prince was very pleased by the ready retort and understanding and accomplishment of the girl. He set her up behind him on the horse and took her to the palace and married her according to custom, and thus the girl's fortune turned.

One day the girl recalled her vow, that whenever she achieved comfort and wealth, she would cook the soup for Bibi Sehshænbeh. She fell to thinking how she could fulfill her vow as soon as possible. But because she was the daughter-in-law of the king and could not go and beg from seven Fatimehs the flour and the rest of the ingredients, of necessity she put a little flour and chick-peas and lentils in seven of the niches around the room, then put on a *chador* and went "begging" from one niche to the next. At this moment the queen saw her, and went directly and gave the information to her son, and said, "Dear boy, if you want me to hold my milk lawful to you,[58] throw this beggarly girl out! See how lowly she is, that even now she cannot renounce her old beggarly ways!"

The prince came to the girl immediately, to see if this was true. When he came in, he saw that the girl had put a pot on to boil and was making soup. He was very annoyed and gave the pot a good kick, and tipped over the soup. The girl wept and cursed him. The next day the prince went hunting with the vizier's son and the judge's son. The vizier's son and the judge's son carelessly got lost. However much the prince searched for them, he could not find them. Of necessity he finally turned his horse back toward the city. As he rode along, lost in thought, suddenly he heard a voice from behind him. He turned around, but there was no one there. First he was afraid, then he said to himself, "I must have been mistaken." When he had gone a few more steps, the same sound came to his ears. Again he turned his head and again no one was there. At this moment his glance fell on the rear of the horse, and he saw the severed heads of the vizier's son and the judge's son tied on behind him, one on each side. In a panic he whipped up the horse and raced back to the city with all possible speed. The king assumed that he had killed the vizier's son and the judge's son and ordered him imprisoned. Some days later the queen wanted to go to see her son, and the girl said, "Tell your son, 'If you had not kicked my soup pot, you would not have suffered this affliction. Now if you can find the faith to make a vow to prepare the soup of Bibi Sehshænbeh, be assured that you will be released from prison.'" The moment the prince heard this from his mother, he knew that this unjust accusation was on account of the girl's curse, and he ordered his mother to go immediately and prepare the pot of soup. The soup was not even ready when the news came that the vizier's son and the judge's son had been found.

Everyone was happy and rejoiced, and the prince was released from prison and vowed to himself that after this he would have perfect faith in the soup of Bibi Hur and Bibi Nur and Bibi Sehshænbeh.

Notes

1. *Sofreh* designates the cloth on which meals in general are served as well as the ritual display here described. The indefinite singular is used in many Persian constructions where English would use indefinite plural. Persian usage has been retained for Persian terms in the text to avoid attaching an English plural to a Persian stem. The transliteration system used employs English spelling conventions for consonants, except for *kh*, which is equivalent to German *ch*, *q* and ', for voiced and unvoiced glottal stops respectively (Arabic *qaf* and *'ain*), and *gh*, which represents the Arabic letter *ghayn*, a velar trill akin to French *r*. The vowels *a* and *u* have close to their long values in English (as in *hall* and *rude*); *i* is pronounced like *ee* in English *beet*. Corresponding short vowel values are represented by *æ, e,* and *o* (as in *hat, pen,* and *tote*).

2. *Nírangestán* 119:20, in *Aérpatestán and Nírangestán*, ed. and trans. S. J. Bulsara (New York: AMS Press, 1977); *Dinkard* 8:20, 23, 26, in *The Dinkard*, trans. Peshotan dastur Behramjee Sanjana (Bombay: Duftur Ashkara Press for the Sir Jamshedji Jeejeebhai Translation Fund, 1874–1876); *Saddar Bundehesh*, chap. 50, in *Saddar Nasr and Saddar Bundehesh: Persian Texts Relating to Zoroastrianism*, trans. B. N. Dabhar (Bombay: Trustees of the Parsee Punchayat Funds and Properties, 1909).

3. Anne Betteridge, personal communication to Mills, Oct. 4, 1984. Mills interview with N.V., Philadelphia, July 14, 1984. Women informants who preferred anonymity are designated by initials only in these notes.

4. The population has probably declined further since the Islamic Revolution, but exact figures are unavailable.

5. Bess Allen Donaldson, *The Wild Rue* (London: Luzac and Co., 1938), p. 190

6. E. W. West, trans., *Pahlavi Texts, Pt. II: The Dadistan-i Dinik and the Epistles of Manuskihar* (Delhi: Motilal Banarsidass, 1965), chap. 40.7–12, pp. 135–36; reprint of *Sacred Books of the East,* ed. F. Max Müller, vol. 18 (Oxford: Oxford University Press, 1882). The state of silent reverence between prayers is called *baj*.

7. *Minuxerad* 16:37–48, in *Pahlavi Texts, Pt. III: Dina-i Mainog-i Khirad*, trans. E. W. West (Delhi: Motilal Banarsidass, 1967), pp. 47–48; reprint of *Sacred Books of the East,* ed. F. Max Müller, vol. 24 (Oxford: Oxford University Press, 1885), pp. 47–48.

8. *Minuxerad* 16:49–63 in West, *Pahlavi Texts, Pt. III; Nírangestán* bk. 1, chap. 9.2, in Bulsara, *Aérpatestán and Nírangestán,* p. 106.

9. West, *Pahlavi Texts, Pt. II,* chap. 50.4, p. 177.

10. *Qor'an* 2:183–87; A. H. Sakr, "Fasting in Islam," *Journal of the American Dietetic Association* 67:1 (1975):18.

11. Ibid.

12. *Qor'an* 5:92. Cf. Sakr, "Fasting," p. 19.

13. M. N. Dhalla, *Zoroastrian Civilization from the Earliest Times to the Downfall of the Last Zoroastrian Empire, 651 A.D.* (New York: Oxford University Press, 1922), p. 187.

14. Ibid., p. 75.

15. Jean Baptiste Tavernier, *Les six voyages . . . en Turquie, en Perse, et aux Indes* (Paris, 1692), pt. 1, bk. 4, chap. 8.

16. Anne Betteridge, in personal communication to Mills, Oct. 4, 1984, points out that many Shi'a religious occasions are anticipated with cheerful excitement by ordinary believers, despite the somber themes expressed in the events.

17. Personal communication to Jamzadeh, 1980.

18. Dastur Homji used *daisy,* a loanword from English, to designate flowers in general. The inclusion of a recent loanword in such a list is an indication of the local variation and eclecticism of such symbolic assemblages: the symbolic set can be completed satisfactorily in many ways, and the initial-letter mnemonic seems to be a flexible convenience. In J. J. Modi's description of the Parsi initiation ceremony, in *The Religious Ceremonies and Customs of the Parsees,* 2d ed. (Bombay: Jehangir B. Karani's Sons, 1937), pp. 181–82, requisites included show Indian influence, such as the red *kunkun* powder used by Hindus for marking the forehead, as well as the necessary substitution of different fruits in the display for those Iranian fruits not found in India.

19. Mary Boyce, *A Persian Stronghold of Zoroastrianism* (Oxford: Oxford University Press, 1977), p. 51. The metallic receptacle for the fire came into use in Iran in the nineteenth century under the influence of the Parsis; prior to that, a brazier that held earth was used, and the brazier itself was often of clay, either of which could reinforce representation of the fourth creation. Mirrors were originally metallic, part of the third creation.

20. Morteza Honæri, *A'inha-ye Noruzi* (New Year's customs) (Tehran: Entesharat-e Vezaræt-e Færhæng o Honær, Mærkæz-e Mærdom Shenasi-e Iran, Publication No. 1, 1353), pp. 35 ff., 60. Cf. Henri Massé, *Persian Beliefs and Customs* (New Haven: Human Relations Area Files, 1954), p. 152.

21. Boyce, *Persian Stronghold,* pp. 50–51.

22. M. N. Dhalla, *History of Zoroastrianism* (New York: Oxford University Press, 1938), p. 73.
23. Boyce, *Persian Stronghold*, p. 31. Because the secular New Year's celebration includes one of the few nonvotive uses of *sofreh* surviving among Muslims, New Year's *sofreh* will be briefly discussed later in the chapter.
24. Boyce, *Persian Stronghold*, pp. 32, 35. Fischer ("Zoroastrians," pp. 179–84) discusses in some detail food distributions made from fire temples in connection with vows. Unlike Boyce, Fischer portrays charitable meals for fulfillment of vows or other personal thanksgivings as separate from the *gæhambar* cycle, but says they are "confused" with one another (p. 180). Our interpretation would favor conflation or integration rather than confusion of the two domains.
25. *Nírangestán* 119:20, in Bulsara, *Aérpatestán and Nírangestán; Dinkard* 8:20, 23, 26, in Sanjana, *Dinkard; Saddar Bundehesh*, chap. 50, in Dhabhar, *Saddar Nasr and Saddar Bundehesh*.
26. Personal conversation of Jamzadeh with B.M., 1980.
27. Boyce, *Persian Stronghold, passim*. Betteridge comments (personal communication, Oct. 4, 1984), that *sofreh* attendance among Muslims is also a mechanism for repairing and maintaining social bonds. The significant difference in the sense of obligation between Zoroastrians and Muslims seems to be the difference between generalized loyalty to a community and loyalty to members of one's individual network of family and friends. Cf. Fischer, "Zoroastrians," p. 17.
28. Boyce, *Persian Stronghold*, p. 34. Cf. Fischer, "Zoroastrians," p. 162.
29. Boyce, *Persian Stronghold*, p. 36. Although the religious texts make *gæhambar* attendance obligatory for everyone, Boyce notes that Parsi feasts in India were male-only affairs until the nineteenth century. The influence of the surrounding society with regard to the seclusion of women is visible in local Zoroastrian practice.
30. Boyce, *Persian Stronghold*, pp. 38–39.
31. Cf. Fischer, "Zoroastrians," p. 184.
32. Anne Betteridge (personal communication, Oct. 4, 1984) reports a solitary instance of a funerary *sofreh* laid out on the grave of a young Muslim man in Shiraz. While food distributions at funerals and death memorials are common, Muslim *sofreh* appear to be very rare in this context. Betteridge's observation suggests a need for further research.
33. Said Æbdul Qassem Ænjævi Shirazi, *Jæshnha o Adab o Mo'tæqædat-e Zemestan* (Winter festivals, customs, and beliefs) (Tehran: Amir Kabir Publishers, 1352 A.H.); Sadeq Hedayat, *Neyrængestan* (Tehran: Amir Kabir Publishers, 1342 A.H.); Sadeq Homayuni, *Færhæng-e Mærdom-e Særvestan* (Culture of the people of Sarvestan) Publication No. 1, Dæftær-e

Mærkæzi-ye Færhæng-e Mærdom (Tehran: Ministry of Information Publishing House, 1348–49 A.H.); Honæri, *A'inha-ye Noruzi* (New Year's customs); Ibrahim Shokurzadeh, *Aeqayed o Rosum-e 'Ameh-ye Mærdom-e Khorassan* (Popular beliefs and customs of the people of Khorassan) (Tehran: Cultural Foundation of Iran, 1346 A.H.); and Massé, *Persian Beliefs;* all describe rural *sofreh* dedicated to different named personages.

34. Anne Betteridge, "The Controversial Vows of Urban Muslim Women in Iran," in *Unspoken Worlds: Women's Religious Lives in Non-Western Cultures,* ed. N. A. Falk and R. M. Gross (New York: Harper and Row, 1980), pp. 141–55.

35. Honæri, *A'inha-ye Noruzi,* pp. 60–63; Massé, *Persian Beliefs,* pp. 152ff. Typical items include silver *(sim),* small coins *(sekkeh),* garlic *(sir),* vinegar *(serkeh),* a blooming hyacinth plant *(sombol),* the condiment *sumaq,* the dried fruit *senjed,* edible greens of various kinds *(sæbzi),* and growing plants, often sprouted wheat *(sæbzeh).* Many other *s*-initial items are acceptable. Additional components are familiar from the Zoroastrian *sofreh:* a mirror, candlesticks with lit candles, a Qor'an (God's message to man replacing the human portrait), sometimes a portrait of Hazrat Ali, the Prophet's cousin and son-in-law and the special patron of Shi'a Muslims, bread, a bowl of water with green leaves floating in it, a flagon of fragrant rose water, a variety of sweets and dried fruits (often stipulated to be seven different kinds of fruits and nuts, the combination called *ajil* by Muslims or *lork* by Zoroastrians), a cassollette in which wild rue seeds are burned, dyed eggs, and a fish, either alive in a bowl or cooked. Small gold commemorative coins called *sekkeh* (another *s* initial), which during the Pahlavi period bore the image of a current or past shah, are placed on the *sofreh* and also exchanged as gifts at New Year's and for weddings and other family celebrations.

Another custom holds that a candle should be lit on the *sofreh* for each member of the family and allowed to burn down completely. If any candle is snuffed out before it is completely consumed, that individual's life is shortened. This light symbolism recalls a Zoroastrian belief that there should be light wherever there are souls, to protect them from Evil, which is connected with cold and darkness. Boyce considers that the New Year's ceremony was, in fact, the seventh *gæhambar,* dedicated to the principle of fire and light.

36. Selective, but not necessarily optional: Betteridge (personal communication, Oct. 1984) points out that some visits, such as those made to senior family members, are clearly obligatory and that the order of visits must properly represent the hierarchy of family obligations of the particular visitants.

37. Personal communication to Mills, July 1984.

38. Rostam Kavoussi, personal communication to Jamzadeh, 1982.
39. Also in Shiraz, the kerchief is replaced by a garland of green raw silk thread, which is one of the standard gifts of the groom's family to the bride and which she wears around her neck during the contract ceremony. Additional food items appear on the *sofreh* for blessing and to protect the bride from acquiring a co-wife. Note that interpretations of *sofreh* components vary, but tend to center on the bride. Fischer ("Zoroastrians," pp. 200ff) compares Zoroastrian and Muslim wedding ceremonies and *sofreh*, and includes a diagram of a *sofreh* display from a Muslim context.
40. Massé, *Persian Beliefs*, p. 41, reports the bride's haircutting as part of the betrothal ceremonies, prior to the wedding. Mills witnessed such a ceremony at a Bakhtiari wedding in the Marv Dasht plain in southern Iran in 1968. There are portrayals of the ceremony in folktales Mills recorded in Persian-speaking Afghanistan as well.
41. Boyce, *Persian Stronghold*, pp. 38 ff., 58–59. However, Betteridge ("Controversial Vows," p. 151) described preparations for *sofreh* among Muslim city women as similarly communal and sociable. Solitary preparations and consecrations may be more of a feature of rural votive *sofreh* among Muslims; they are certainly more evident in rural ethnographic descriptions such as Shokurzadeh's (*Khorassan*, pp. 12–59).
42. Betteridge, "Controversial Vows," p. 152.
43. Mills, interview with N.V., Philadelphia, July 14, 1984.
44. Ibid.; Betteridge, "Controversial Vows," *passim*.
45. Michael M.J. Fischer, Review of M. Boyce, *A Persian Stronghold of Zoroastrianism*, in *Iranian Studies* 10:4 (Autumn 1977) offers additional insights on the collection and interpretation of data in ethnography. Authors' different orientations to topics such as orthodoxy/heterodoxy make using diverse ethnographies to compare religious practices, as is done here, particularly challenging.
46. Shokurzadeh, *Khorassan*, pp. 28–35.
47. Boyce, *Persian Stronghold*, p. 53.
48. Betteridge, "Controversial Vows," p. 146. Concerning the public/private dichotomy, of which much has been made in literature describing purdah and the social organization and activities of Muslim women, we note that while women do not use the channels of public announcement used by men (e.g., announcements made at communal prayer meetings at mosques), they nonetheless issue general invitations to functions such as *sofreh* by word of mouth. Rather than asserting a dichotomy whereby men's social activities are construed as public because conducted outside the home or in a section of the house designated for the reception of male nonfamily members, and women's social activities as private because they frequently occur in a domestic space, it would be more useful to develop

different maps for the communicative systems or channels of Muslim men and women, whereby both sexes have "public" and "private" alternatives or modes.

49. Honæri, however, in *A'inha-ye Noruzi*, p. 63, describes occasional inclusion of a portrait of Hazrat'Ali, the Prophet's cousin and husband of his daughter Fatimeh, together with the Qor'an on the New Year's *sofreh*.

50. Shi'a Muslims recognize as supreme spiritual authorities twelve *imams*—'Ali and eleven lineal descendants of his. The last *imam* disappeared and is expected to return to lead the community in the last days.

51. Shokurzadeh, *Khorassan*, p. 35.

52. Cf., e.g., Margaret Mills, "A *Cinderella* Variant in the Context of Muslim Women's Ritual," in *A Cinderella Casebook,* ed. Alan Dundes (New York and London: Garland Press, 1984), pp. 180–92; Hedayat, *Neyrængestan,* pp. 58–63; and Shokurzadeh, *"Nokhod-e Moshgel Gosha,"* in *Khorassan,* pp. 51–58. Several *sofreh* descriptions also include an opportunity for the sponsor to tell her own story and so bear witness to the guests concerning the facts of her personal difficulty and its resolution. These personal narratives form a sequel to the formal narratives, whether *rowzeh* proper or origin legends of the rite per se. Cf. Betteridge, "Controversial Vows," p. 151, and Boyce, *Persian Stronghold,* pp. 64, 66.

53. Boyce (*Persian Stronghold,* p. 61) states that men would more commonly visit a fire temple to offer incense or candles and pray on the occasion of some minor difficulty or its resolution, but she also cited examples of male-sponsored charity meals in gratitude for the resolution of difficulties (p. 57). Belivani speculated that Zoroastrian women's votive *sofreh,* especially the one dedicated to "Shah Pæri," are Islamic in origin, in a personal communication to Jamzadeh, summer 1978. Fischer ("Zoroastrians," p. 228) reports fasting as an element in Zoroastrian women's votive *sofreh,* one example of the several departures from Zoroastrian ideas about appropriate forms of worship which would tend to support Belivani's view that this practice has more in common with popular Islam than with orthodox Zoroastrianism.

54. Boyce, *Persian Stronghold,* p. 62; Sadiq Hedayat, *Neyrængestan,* pp. 58–59.

55. Boyce, *Persian Stronghold,* p. 57.

56. Ibid., p. 25.

57. This is the ordinary formula for fictional folktales told in entertainment contexts; it establishes the fictional nature of the narrative. Sacred legends do not have such formulas attached to them; Mills's experience with Persian-language narrative performance in the Herat area, immediately adjacent to Iranian Khorassan, suggests that the formulas might here be an editorial inclusion by Shokurzadeh, since the ritual context of the

narrative would imply an assertion of its truthfulness, not its fictionality.
58. A threat of a traditional mother's curse—she might declare the milk
that nourished her son in infancy *hæræm,* or religiously forbidden to him,
essentially disowning him as her son.

Three

Ambiguous Gender: Male Initiation in a Northern Thai Buddhist Society
Charles F. Keyes

Introduction

Gender identities are problematic for all human beings in the basic sense that biological differences between the sexes do not in and of themselves predetermine how humans will understand maleness and femaleness. Persons acquire such understandings through appropriation of meanings from cultural processes that are articulated with the maturation of a child into an adult. While in modern societies both boys and girls may acquire their gender identities through a common process, in most, if not all, traditional societies, boys and girls pass through distinctive processes. While separate, male and female identities are construed in these processes such that each is predicated on assumed characteristics of the other. Moreover, both are situated with reference to common assumptions about the world; these assumptions in traditional societies are invariably religious in that they are taken as ultimate truths.

In many societies, what have been called "initiatory processes" serve as the primary means for instilling in boys or girls or both a sense of gender identity.[1] The beginning of this process calls into question the world as the child has previously understood it, often by actions that are at once emotionally (and, in many cases, physi-

I have benefited, even when I have not necessarily agreed with them, from the criticisms made on earlier drafts of this paper by Stevan Harrell, Paula Richman, Caroline Walker Bynum, and Jane Keyes.

cally) disturbing and intellectually confusing. Following this experience of disorientation, a new world is opened up for the initiate
through a sequence of ritualized activities. As a consequence of the
initiatory process, a male or female acquires a way, a perspective,
for seeing himself or herself as a man or as a woman in a particular
society.

Most anthropologists who have concerned themselves with
initiatory processes have followed van Gennep in seeing such
processes as constituting rites of passage whereby a child is transformed from an asexual into a sexual person. In van Gennep's
terms: "These are rites of separation from the asexual world, and
they are followed in the same initiatory process by rites of incorporation into the world of sexuality."[2] The child acquires from both
the symbolic and the experiential aspects of the initiatory process a
sense of self as a sexual being in the society he or she will reenter at
the end of the process.

Gender identities are not reducible solely to an awareness of self
as a sexual being; they also entail a social sense of self. As Ortner
and Whitehead have written in their introduction to a recent com-
pendium of anthropological reflections on gender, gender notions
are predicated on the assumption that social differentiation derives
from evaluations of relative "prestige." Each society has a
"prestige structure," that is, "sets of prestige positions or levels
that result from a particular line of social evaluation—the mechanism by which individuals and groups arrive at given levels or positions—and the overall conditions of reproduction of the system of
statuses."[3] In traditional societies, initiatory processes often contribute fundamentally to the reproduction of a system of prestige.
Inherent in any system of prestige is the relative social value that
attaches to male and female gender; such a value is perhaps always
fundamental to the whole system.

But this interpretation of initiation rites, as functioning exclusively to transform an asexual and asocial child into a sexual adult
with a gender-linked potential to assume particular social roles,
permits only partial understanding of the formation of gender
identities acquired during an initiatory process. This process also
produces, as Eliade argues, "a decisive alteration in the religious"
as well as in the "social status of the person to be initiated."[4]
Indeed, I would agree with Eliade that the religious transformation is fundamental: "the function of initiation may be reduced to

67

this: to each new generation it reveals a world open to the transhuman, a world that, in our philosophical terminology, we should call transcendental."[5] In passing through an initiatory process, a person gains a perspective on himself or herself as sharing some quality of maleness or femaleness that transcends the individual self. This quality assumes a givenness, a primordiality, because it is accepted as fundamentally true. One's identity as a sexual being and as a social actor is conditioned by one's sense of being male or female with reference to primordial or ultimate truths.

An initiatory process might be expected to produce in a child an unambiguous gender identity, a sacralized idea of the male or female self that clearly establishes the parameters for the social roles he or she can play. This may well be true in those primitive and tribal societies for which most models of initiation have been developed. I will here, however, consider a different case, that of a Theravada Buddhist society in Southeast Asia in which a man emerges from an initiatory process with a sexual-social identity that is in tension with an ideal male religious identity.

The Monkly Ideal

The Buddha taught that those who would gain permanent release from the suffering inherent in experience motivated by desire must renounce the world. One who follows the Buddhist ideal of renunciation must reject sexuality, leave family behind, and abandon any quest for social prestige or power. From the beginning this ideal was upheld primarily for males. The Buddha reluctantly allowed women to be ordained, but the female order never prospered and it disappeared not only from India but also from Sri Lanka, the only Theravadin society in which it was ever established.[6] The ideal woman in Buddhist societies was one who remained in the world, providing sons and support for the sangha. For males who would be true followers of the Buddha, however, the path that they should follow was unequivocally that of world renunciation.

The salvation ideal that requires a man to turn his back on sexuality, on fatherhood, and on worldly status would seem to leave the role of male householder without positive religious value. If this logic had, in fact, been adopted by Buddhists, there would never have been a Buddhist society, only an esoteric cult of monkly practitioners. As a popular religion, Buddhism had to provide for a role of male Buddhist householder, but in so doing, popular Buddhism developed a paradoxical view of maleness. This view is comparable to that, as shown by Wendy O'Flaherty, found in the Hinduism of the *Puranas*. The mythology of Siva, O'Flaherty writes, shows the Hindu man that "his society demands of him two roles which he cannot possibly satisfy fully—that he become a householder and beget sons, and that he renounce life and seek union with god."[7] In popular Buddhism, a man is expected to leave the world to become a "son of the Buddha" in the quest for Nibbana *and* to assume a place in the world as a householder.

In the Theravadin traditions of Southeast Asia, the contradiction between ideals of maleness was seemingly resolved by the emergence of a practice, dating from at least the fifteenth century, whereby all males were expected to enter the sangha for at least a temporary time. This cultural ideal assumed somewhat different forms in the several Theravadin traditions of the societies today found in the modern states of Burma, Thailand, Laos, and Cambodia (Kampuchea), but most men in these societies, at least until quite recently, would have entered the order as adolescents or young adults, spent from a few weeks to a year or two as members of the sangha, and then returned to lay society to marry and assume adult roles. The man who passed through this Buddhist initiatory process was transformed, as in initiations in other societies, into a mature sexual adult. He was, in the Thai idiom, "ripe" *(suk)* for marriage, not "raw" *(dip)*. Moreover, he acquired prestige, indicated by titles, and knowledge of writing that could be used to enhance his social position within lay society. A very few men remained to devote their lives to the religion, but most men did not become permanent monks. Buddhist initiation was only for males; there was nothing comparable for women in these societies. Females gained a sense of themselves as Buddhist women primarily within the domestic groups in which they grew up.[8]

Even today, when many males in Southeast Asian societies do not follow the traditional ideal and enter the sangha, the rites and texts associated with ordination and sangha membership still provide the most coherent and authoritative perspective on maleness found in these societies. The Buddhist initiatory process functions as a "total social phenomenon" in that it unifies diverse spheres of social action.[9] Buddhist initiation provides simultaneous expression of the religious and moral character of males, whether they remain members of the religious community or return to assume adult roles in lay society. The performance of an ordination rite and the subsequent practice of the "discipline" by those who become members of the sangha constitute in each instance a process of "text-building," as Becker has termed it.[10] That is, a past long fixed by tradition is re-created in the present by actors who are members of a particular social order. From their participation, these actors acquire a perspective on their maleness that is at once shaped by the Buddhist texts of the past and at the same time by the constraints of the present social world in which the initiatory process occurs. The initiatory process begins with a fundamental contradiction and moves toward its mediation. Here the contradiction is how a male can be both a world renouncer, seeking after salvation as the Buddha taught, and also a householder in a society that is essential to the perpetuation of Buddhism. The *practical* resolution to this contradiction, evident in the enhanced sexual attractiveness and social prestige of a man who has abandoned the role of renunciant, still leaves the Buddhist male householder with a logically ambiguous gender identity.

The Male Child in Buddhist Northern Thailand

I will here undertake a (partial) interpretation of the Buddhist initiatory process for men as I have observed it in northern Thailand.[11] While there are some distinctive features associated with the Northern Thai (or Yuan or Khonmµang) Buddhist tradition, a comparable interpretation could also be constructed for any of the other Theravadin traditions of Southeast Asia. In the Northern Thai tradition it has long been the ideal that every boy should be ordained as a novice for at least a lenten period. While among the Lao of lowland Laos or northeastern Thailand and among the Siamese (Central Thai) of the heartland of Thailand it is the pattern to spend a period as a monk after the age of twenty as well as or instead of serving as a novice, such a pattern is not observed among the Northern Thai, although some Northern Thai men have in recent years followed the Siamese pattern and been ordained for a period as a monk. Few Northern Thai men today still observe the pattern of temporary service in the monkhood, but only in the secularized context of the cities has the Buddhist initiatory process lost its totalizing significance.[12] Most Northern Thai men (and women) continue to participate in the process at least as relatives and friends of the large number of boys and young men who enter the sangha each year.

Before considering the characteristics of the process, it is necessary to say something about the experience of Northern Thai boys before they become eligible for ordination. The last child born, whether male or female, will sleep next to the mother, but unlike some other societies, the mother will not focus her attention on the child to the exclusion of the husband. When a mother has an infant child, the husband may sleep separately, often with the males of the family, but he is not denied access to his wife if he chooses to sleep with her. The presence of an infant on the other side of the woman at night does not deter a couple from having sexual relations. A mother typically weans her child when the next child is born; the last child born usually enjoys a longer period of suckling than do his or her older siblings. In large families, older siblings assist both parents in looking after younger children. Fathers, as well as mothers, show physical affection toward their children. In northern Thailand (as in the rest of Theravadin Buddhist Southeast Asia) there does not appear to be an accentuation of sexual rivalry between fathers and sons or a marked degree of identification of sons with mothers, two factors that have been taken in other societies as predisposing to elaborate male initiation rites.

From earliest childhood, Northern Thai males are treated differently from females in some ways, in anticipation of the fact that males will have to make a significant break with the world of their childhood, a break not required of their sisters. Both male and female children in northern Thailand orient themselves first toward a world defined by the boundaries of the household (NT *bān*) into which they are born. The Northern Thai household is organized spatially and ritually to establish linkages between the mother and her matrilineal ancestors and to reinforce ties between mothers and daughters. As they reach sexual maturity, girls will entertain suitors in a place set aside in their natal households; after marriage young women and their husbands reside initially in the same household as the woman's parents. Even when a woman and her husband (and by then probably a child as well) move into a separate household, as all but the youngest daughter will do, the new household will usually share a compound with that of the

71

woman's parents.[13] A typical Northern Thai woman thus passes from childhood to maidenhood to marriage to motherhood and eventually to death within the confines of the same world into which she was born. The pattern is very different for a male.

In farming households, the vast majority of the Northern Thai children, both male and female, participate in the agricultural pursuits of their parental family. While there is some sexual division of labor in agriculture, it is far less marked than in the activities that take place during the nonagricultural season. During that period, young girls usually remain at home where they are taught domestic skills, the most distinctive of which traditionally (and still today in many villages) is weaving. Boys, on the other hand, are likely to go with their fathers to fish and hunt in the surrounding areas. As girls grow older, weaving becomes a significant aspect of female identity.[14] Hunting and fishing are not, however, accorded comparable positive cultural value in the development of male identity. Male identity is formulated, rather, for Northern Thai in terms that have been drawn primarily from the Theravada Buddhist tradition as expressed in the initiatory process.

Gender Ambiguity during Candidacy for Ordination

The Buddhist ordination rite in northern Thailand, as in other Theravadin communities in Southeast Asia, has long been the first means whereby a male separates himself from the world of his family and reorients himself toward another world.[15] The rite of ordination as a novice (P *Sāmaṇra;* NT *pha;* ST *nēn*)[16]—a rite through which even those who are to become monks (P *bhikkhu;* NT *tu cao;* ST *phra*) must pass—is called in Pali *pabbajjā,* "going forth." This name indicates movement away from the life of the householder, a movement clearly symbolized in ritual actions that precede the ordination rite proper.

In northern Thailand a boy or a young man who becomes a candidate for ordination is known as *lūk kāēo,* a term with several meanings. *Lūk,* "child," denotes an actual kin relationship to one's parents, those who are most likely to be the sponsors of the ordination. They, in turn, become known as *phǫ ǫk* and *māē ǫk,* literally "father-leaving" and "mother-leaving," thereby marking their status as parents of one who is "going forth." The *lūk kāēo* is a "precious child," to employ one sense of *kāēo,* both because he is being lost to the family and because his ordination will yield merit (P *puñña;* NT and ST *bun*) for his parents—a reward for their parenting that is precious beyond material measure.[17] *Lūk kāēo* means not only that he is the "precious child" of his parents but that he is also a "child of the religion." *Kāēo,* which also means gem, is a shorthand way of referring to the Buddhist religion, which is based upon the Triple Gems of the Buddha, the *dhamma* (the teachings of the Buddha), and the sangha.[18]

On the day before the ordination proper, a boy or young man becomes a candidate for ordination—a *lūk kāēo*—by first having all the hair on his head shaved off. In doing so, he is prepared to take his place in a sangha whose members all have their heads shaved at least once a month. I agree with Tambiah[19] that the head shaving represents "symbolic renunciation of [male] sexuality."[20] The head shaving marks the beginning of the ordination ritual in the same way that circumcision marks the beginning of male initiation rites in many African societies. Both acts serve to signal (primarily to the initiates themselves) a break with the unconscious maleness of childhood and the beginning of a self-consciousness about male sexuality. While circumcision is a permanent physical alteration that bespeaks a permanent social transformation of the African initiate, head shaving is but a transitory alteration. The act of shaving the head once a month symbolizes a renewal of one's commitment to the discipline of the sangha. Just as one's hair can regrow, so can one's sexual desire reemerge.

The candidate for ordination not only is transformed through a shaving of the head, but also through the costume that he dons for the day (sometimes only part of a day, sometimes extending over two days) before the ordination proper. Throughout Buddhist Southeast Asia, the costume of the candidate is distinguished both from normal clothing and from the robes worn by monks. In northern Thailand the *lūk kāēo* dresses in distinctive clothing said to recall the dress of Prince Siddhatha before he entered on his quest for enlightenment. In Mae Sariang, the *lūk kāēo* dressed in silk lower garments (sarongs), light-colored fancy blouses, and turbans and were bedecked in jewels, usually provided by their mothers. Compared to normal male clothing—dark shirts and dark trousers or check waistcloths—the clothing of the candidates has a distinctly feminine quality. This quality is accentuated by the wearing of female jewelry. Perhaps one might interpret this costume as transforming the candidate into an androgyne prior to his transformation into an asexual member of the sangha. Eliade has proposed that the "ritual transformation of novices into women—whether by assuming women's dress or by subincision" in other societies reflects an (unconscious) effort "to recover a primordial situation of totality and perfection" manifest in the androgynous state.[21] Even if this interpretation cannot be sustained, it remains true that the costume worn by the candidates for ordination, associated as it is with the shaved head, creates an image of ambiguous sexuality.

On "preparation day" *(wan hūam)*, the day on which a boy or young man becomes a *lūk kāēo*, the candidate separates himself from lay society in anticipation of entry into the sangha.[22] The rites of preparation day in northern Thailand—and similar rites observed in every Southeast Asian Buddhist society—re-create a myth that recalls the Buddha's own Great Renunciation of the world in order to seek enlightenment. Prince Siddhatha, the man who would become the Buddha, had been raised in the great palace of his father. While he could have chosen to be a World Emperor *(cakkavatin)*, he had become aware through seeing an old man, an infirm man, and a corpse that *dukkha*, suffering, shapes all human experience. Having also seen a mendicant, he determined to leave the world to seek a way to escape altogether from suffering. The myth of the Great Renunciation tells how Prince Siddhatha left the palace one night at the conclusion of a magnificent party. Turning his back not only on his sleeping wife and infant son but also on the ladies-in-waiting who had fallen asleep in wanton abandon (this scene is a favorite one of artists who paint temple murals), he quietly stole away to where his horse, Kanthaka, was waiting. Flying across the river on Kanthaka, he stopped at a spot where he cut his hair and exchanged his regal costume for the plain robes of a mendicant. Then, with begging bowl in hand, he set off to find the way to achieve ultimate transcendence of worldly desire. Like Prince Siddhatha, every man (the tradition is more ambiguous regarding women) has the potential to exercise the same act of will, thereby renouncing the world and setting out on a course that will eventually lead to the attainment of Nibbana.

Having dressed in finery, the *lūk kāēo* becomes Prince Siddhatha. As a prince he is not allowed to touch the ground with his feet. When he moves any distance during the day, he is expected to ride on a horse—the equivalent of Kanthaka—although when an actual horse is not available a bicycle, the back of a man, an open car, or even, as I observed on one occasion in Mae Sariang, a wheelchair borrowed from a local medical center might be substituted. On the night before the ordination proper, a grand party with all the entertainment, food, and drink that the candidate's parents or other sponsors can afford to provide, is held. This celebration recalls the events at the palace of Prince Siddhatha the night he left home.

During the preparation day the candidate is taken around his home community in procession, with attendants holding elaborate umbrellas over his head to signify his royal status for the day. The procession moves from place to place, where the candidate begs forgiveness for any acts committed intentionally or unintentionally that were offensive to his moral superiors. Once he has entered the sangha, he can no longer act in lay ways, even if he desires to do so, in order to rectify previous offenses to others. In the case of the most elaborate ordination that I observed in Mae Sariang, the three candidates paid visits to the abbot of the local temple-monastery where they had previously acted as lay persons, to older kinsmen, to respected elders, and to the shrine of the village guardian spirits. In acts that symbolically constitute taking leave of the world, the candidate relates himself to significant persons who will constitute the actual social world in which he will live when (and if) he leaves the sangha. This world is fundamentally a male world: the abbot of the *wat* is male, the elders are male, and most of the older kinsmen the candidate visits are also male. The village guardian spirits may or may not be male, but the intermediary through whom the candidate approaches the spirits is male. The events of the preparation day thus serve to move the *lūk kāēo* away from the domestic world of his childhood and toward not only a religious world but also a male-dominated social world in which he will assume a place as an adult.

In leaving behind once and for all the domestic sphere in which he passed his childhood, the candidate perforce ceases to have a child's relationship to his mother. He does not, however, sever his relationship with his mother in the way that initiates in many African or New Guinean societies do. Rather, the ordination rite provides a means whereby the relationship between son and mother is reformulated with reference to sacred Buddhist values while at the

75

same time permitting the son to act independently of his mother in whatever adult role he assumes.

This reformulation begins first with a rite usually held in the home the night before the ordination proper. At this rite, a lay ritual specialist (called in Northern Thai an *ācān*, from Pali/ Sanskrit *ācārya*, "teacher") calls and secures the *khwan*, the "vital essence" of the candidate. The *khwan* is called and secured on every occasion—a wedding, entering a new house, moving to a new community, and so on—when the psyche might undergo a radical shock, stimulating its departure and causing the person to become vulnerable to illness and ultimately to death.

In one calling of the *khwan* of a candidate for ordination that I recorded, the *ācān* told in formal Northern Thai chanting style how the child was conceived and born. He then related how the parents, and especially the mother, cared for the child in its infancy.

> When it was time to sleep, [your] mother lulled you to sleep by singing. [Your mother] feared that her child would be cold. She feared that the evil spirits would come to haunt you, and so [she] made a special banana stalk container in which betel and areca nut had been placed and had the father say: "All spirits which come to deceive [this] child, making him cry, go away from here, don't stay here. May it be so!" When your father had said this, your mother picked you up in her arms and took her precious one [*lūk kāēo*] to bed.[23]

The *ācān* continues to describe how the candidate's merit and virtues have led him to decide to depart from mundane existence which had been, to this point, one of warm dependence on the mother and, to a lesser extent, on the father. In subsequent passages, the ritual specialist warns the candidate of the temptations of the world that he will become aware of once he joins the sangha: young maidens (whose friendships are to be spurned), women of the highest station (presumably supporters of the sangha), and wise men. Although inappropriate as companions of a monk, these persons are ones that a lay male adult would hope to consort with in the world. Finally, the *ācān* concludes with a description of the procession that will accompany the candidates to the *wat* where they will be ordained, a procession consisting primarily of joyous young men and especially young women who will have "lotus blossoms in their hair" and who will "stretch themselves [above the crowd] to stare at groups of boys." In these images the ritual specialist alludes to the interest that maidens will have in a man who has been ordained and thus "ripened." The rite of calling the *khwan* might be likened to an overture to the ordination rite, for it brings together all of the important themes found in more elaborated form in other parts of the process: the obligations that the candidate has to his parents, and especially his mother, for having raised him so that he can "go forth"; the temptations, especially sexual, that a member of the sangha must resist if he is to adhere to the discipline prescribed by the Buddha for his followers; and the attribute of "ripened" maleness that one who has been a temporary member of the sangha acquires.

Maleness Transformed through Ordination

On the day of ordination, the candidate mounts his symbolic Kanthaka and processes from his "palace" to the place of ordination. Ordinations for novices are usually held in the image hall or ordination hall of a *wat*. Ordinations of monks must take place within a consecrated space, a building (called *bōt* in NT and ST, from Pali *posatha* or *uposatha*) set apart from other buildings in a *wat* by stone markers (P *sīmā;* NT and ST *sēmā*).[24] It is normally taboo in northern Thailand for women to enter an ordination hall, although in Mae Sariang the district abbot, who was also often the officiant at ordinations, permitted mothers and older female relatives of candidates to sit just inside the entrance to the ordination hall at his *wat*. While the taboo against women entering an ordination hall has no Buddhist charter and is not observed in central Thailand, it is in keeping with other Buddhist ideas about women representing a threat to the disciplinary purity of the sangha. The ordination hall is fundamentally a place where the sangha convenes for its communal acts, including that of receiving new members into the order. In this place the laity in general and women in particular have no significant religious role.

On entering the place of ordination, the candidate literally turns his back on his family and other laity who have accompanied him in the procession and faces the clergy who will receive him into the sangha. If a person is to be ordained as a monk, a full chapter of not less than five monks must be present; in northern Thailand such ordinations typically involve at least ten monks. If he is to be

77

ordained as a novice, only one monk, a qualified *thera* or "elder" who has spent ten years in the sangha, is required; but other monks may also be present.

The first thing a candidate does on entering the place of ordination is to change out of his princely costume. He dons instead plain white robes. White robes are indicative for Northern Thai, as well as for those in all other Theravadin societies, of purity which, in Buddhist terms, implies abstinence from indulging one's sensual, especially sexual, appetites. While aspirants for entrance into the sangha wear white robes for only a very brief time, some lay persons—especially those women who become Buddhist nuns (NT *māē cī;* ST *māē chī*)—are "ordained in white" (NT and ST *būat khāo*) for prolonged, even lifelong, periods, thereby signifying that they are observing the norms of abstinence. The white dress of candidates can be compared to the nudity (sometimes accentuated by the application of white color to the skin) of African boys after they cross the threshold of an initiation school. In both cases, outward signs of previous social identities are eliminated. Having become socially naked in his white robes, the candidate then presents himself to the monks who will ordain him.

In Mae Sariang I observed that when a candidate presented himself, he offered the officiating monk a fresh coconut with a hole drilled in it and an unlit candle placed in the hole. Several similar offerings were made in subsequent parts of the ritual. My first thought in attempting to interpret the candle-in-coconut was to see it as signifying sexual union that was foresworn (at least temporarily) when a man entered the sangha. I was, however, unable to elicit any native exegesis or to link the symbol with other symbols in any way that would support such an interpretation. Northern Thai and other Southeast Asian Buddhists see the coconut as signifying purity because the liquid inside is never exposed to outside impurities before the nut is cracked. At funerary rites, the liquid from a coconut is poured on the face of the deceased in order, I was told by informants, that the person might be reborn as "pure" as the liquid. The candle figures prominently in well-known Buddhist texts as a metaphor for the linkage of one life to the next. Given these meanings, I now interpret the candle-in-coconut as a symbol of death and rebirth. One who enters the sangha "dies" as a sexual being and is reborn as one who is sexless; one who enters the sangha also accrues great merit that will redound to his benefit when he truly dies and is reborn.

After making the offering of the candle-in-coconut, the candidate requests, in formalized Pali, to enter the order.[25] He then gives the robes he will wear as a member of the order to the preceptor. The preceptor in the Mae Sariang ordinations I observed then instructed the candidate in the vernacular regarding the role of the sangha. After this instruction, the preceptor hands back the robes to the candidate, placing the shoulder cloth on the candidate's person and giving him the remaining pieces. The candidate withdraws, moving backward on his knees, until he is out of the semicircle of monks. Then he stands and walks to a corner of the ordination hall where he once again changes clothes, this time exchanging his white robes for the yellow ones allowed members of the sangha. Having changed, he again returns to kneel in front of the preceptor or one of the other monks who acts as an "instructor." The candidate then requests, in Pali, to take refuge in the Triple Gems and to receive the Ten Precepts that he must follow as a novice. He repeats the precepts after the monk who gives them to him. While the precepts are recited in Pali, their meaning is generally understood:

To refrain from killing living creatures.
To refrain from taking what is not given.
To refrain from sexual relations.
To refrain from speaking falsely.
To refrain from intoxicants which are the occasion for heedlessness.
To refrain from eating at improper times (i.e., after the midday meal).
To refrain from dancing, singing, music, and going to see entertainments.
To refrain from adorning the body with flowers, scents, and ointments.
To refrain from sleeping on a high or wide bed.
To refrain from accepting gold or silver.

These ten rules of training constitute the base of the discipline of the sangha and are derived from doctrinal premises regarding the "hindrances" that one must overcome if one is to transcend suffering (the first four) and incorporate means by which detachment

79

from the world can be achieved (the last six). The 227 rules that monks, as distinct from novices, must obey are elaborations of these ten (especially the first four), to which have been added regulations that order relationships between members of the sangha.

Up to the point where the ten precepts are given and received, the ordination ritual is the same for both novices and monks. At this point the ordination of the novice is complete. If the candidate is to be ordained as a monk, he withdraws from the monks once again and goes to where he is given his alms bowl. In Mae Sariang, the monk-to-be always received the bowl from his mother. As a woman the candidate's mother cannot give the alms bowl directly to her son since he is now a novice and as a member of the sangha he is forbidden physical contact with any woman. The mother places the bowl on a white cloth that has been laid in front of her novice-son. By this act a mother signifies that she no longer has particular responsibility for nurturing her son. He will now be nurtured by all (albeit usually women), who will place food in his alms bowl.

Having received his bowl, the candidate then moves back, on his knees once again, to a place in front of his preceptor. During the ritual in Pali that follows, the aspirant requests "dependence" and the clergy then rehearse his qualifications and ask for any objections to his being admitted to the order. When the monks remain silent, assent is assumed, and the new monk is incorporated into the sangha.

After completion of the ordination rite proper, the laity are the first to leave the place where the ritual has taken place. When the new novice or monk comes out, some of his relatives—mainly women, including his mother—place coins in the novice's shoulder bag or the monk's alms bowl. The alms are offered because the new novice or monk, like any member of the sangha, is a "field of merit." Whereas prior to ordination the boy or young man had needed the support of his kinsmen to ensure his physical well-being, his kinsmen now offer him support in order to ensure their religious well-being.

A new monk is expected to deliver a sermon following his ordination. He will not give an extemporaneous speech, but will read a traditional text. The most popular Northern Thai text to be selected for delivery by a new monk is one entitled *ānisong būat*

(P *pabbajānisaṁsa*), "Blessings of Ordination." The text consists of a myth that tells of the great merit gained by a mother who allows her son to become a novice.[26] While the myth also tells of how subsequent ordination as a monk permitted the central actor to transfer merit to his father, the key relationship is clearly that of mother and son. The myth underscores what has in fact happened in the ritual: a son has "gone forth," leaving his mother-centered home, and has entered a religious brotherhood. In so doing, the son fulfills his filial obligations by transferring merit to his parents, especially his mother.

With the reading of the sermon, the ordination rite is complete. The laity disperse, returning to their homes. The new monk or novice, however, remains at the *wat* to begin a new life as a member of the sangha. He is now bound by the discipline of those who have renounced the world. Traditionally in Mae Sariang and elsewhere in northern Thailand, a new novice or monk secluded himself in the grounds of the temple-monastery for three days following the ordination. During this period, called in Northern Thai "living in karma" *(yū kam),*[27] he should meditate and take only one meal instead of the usual two allowed members of the sangha. This period of strict asceticism was believed to prepare the new member of the sangha for life shaped by a strict discipline. Even today, when this transitional rite is rarely, if ever, observed, the new novice or monk must act in accordance with the ancient code derived from the *Vinaya-piṭaka,* the "basket of discipline," for those who renounce the world.

World Renounced, World Restored

The "discipline" to which a member of the sangha must subject himself consists, as Holt has argued, of "more than adherence to a general moral norm."

> Rather, it consists of being completely aware of the nature of one's actions. That is to say, mindfulness and concentration are intricately involved in the process of discipline. A disciplined action is more than just the avoidance of killing, lying, stealing and sexual misconduct. It is the effective expression of one who has been converted to a way of looking at the world, one who has embraced the perspective and world view realized by the Buddha and expounded in his central teachings.[28]

81

Disciplined action serves to generate the new perspective a man gains on himself through making him aware of the *tanhā* (desires) that bind him to the world and conduce to continual *dukkha* (suffering) in that world.

Dukkha results not only from actions that produce physical or mental pain but also from the cessation of experiences that are pleasant and from separation from persons and things to which one has formed a strong attachment. Desire for things that are (temporarily) pleasurable, desire for things that are impermanent, as well as desire for things that have immediate painful consequences all lead to *dukkha*. To escape the world of sentient existence *(saṁsāra)* characterized by *dukkha*, the follower of the Buddha knows that he must root out desire. Desire is conceived of as arising from the predispositions to yield to the temptation of the cardinal vices *(kilesa)* of *rāga* (lust), *lobha* (greed), *dosa* (anger), and *moha* (delusion). Ordination into the Buddhist sangha gives a man the most effective means available to destroy these predispositions in himself.

This means is the *vinaya* (discipline), formulated as the ten precepts for novices and the 227 training rules (P *sikkhapada;* NT and ST *sikkhābot*) for monks.[29] Those who break the precepts or the rules are deemed guilty of offences (P *āpatti;* NT and ST *ābat*) for which various penalties are meted out by the sangha. These penalties fall into three categories:

> The heavy offence . . . which causes one committing it to fall from the state of bhikkhuhood [i.e., to be expelled from the order]; the middle . . . causing the offender to live on probation, that is to practice in a certain way making it difficult for oneself [to commit the offence again]; and the light offence . . . which causes the offender to confess in front of a bhikkhu (or bhikkhus) so that having carried out the prescribed discipline, he will be free from the offence.[30]

There are four offences that bring *pārājika,* "defeat," thus forcing a monk to leave the sangha. One is defeated if, while a member of the order, one engages in "sexual intercourse even with a female animal,"[31] if one steals something of such value that if caught one would deserve capital punishment, if one murders another human being, or if one falsely claims to have the powers of an arahat, a Buddhist saint. Each of these *pārājika* offences is an extreme version of the cardinal vices of lust, greed, anger, and delusion.[32] Of these four, the first—prohibiting sexual intercourse—has been most stressed. Sexual offences also constitute the first five of the next category of most serious offences, those that cause the sangha to both judge the offence and supervise the punishment (thus the name, *sanghādisesa*, the fault that has "*Sangha* at the beginning [*ādi*] and at the end *sesa*").[33] Prince Vajirañānavarorasa, the highly influential Prince Patriarch of the Thai sangha, who died in 1921, wrote in his commentary on the training regulations that 'woman' is the "base of *sanghādisesa*,"[34] the second most serious class of offences.

Most lay persons consider the sexual purity of monks as the most distinctive attribute of those who join the sangha. While few are ever expelled for a serious sexual offence, the inability of most men to commit themselves to a life of sexual abstinence is the reason most often mentioned for why men do not remain as members of the sangha. To leave the sangha because one cannot forever forego sexual relations is not, however, the same as being "defeated." Quite the contrary; the man who has spent a period of time—ideally at least one rains-retreat (lenten) period of three months—as a novice or as a monk and who has during that period adhered strictly to the discipline gains esteem in the eyes of those in the world to which he returns.

The man who has emerged from a period in the sangha is considered to be much more desirable as a marriage partner than are men who have never been a novice or a monk. Esteem is not limited, however, to maidens seeking husbands. Throughout Thailand, the man who has been a member of the sangha is socially recognized by a title that indicates his previous status in the order. In northern Thailand, a man who has been a novice, but never a monk, is known by the title *nǫi* (equivalent to the Central Thai *chīang*), while the man who has been a monk, whether or not he had ever been a novice, is called *nān* (equivalent to the Central Thai *thit*). Writing of a village in the northern Thai province of Chiang Rai, Moerman reports: "Actually these titles have become more than honorific for almost without exception the political leaders and moral counselors of the village have served in the temple."[35] Moerman's observation echoes that of Kingshill, who found in a village near Chiang Mai that "seventy percent of the village 'leaders' have at one time or another been a priest or novice, a percentage more than twice as high as that for village men as a group."[36]

Prior to the 1930s the only access to literacy was through instruction provided in *wats*. Monastic education served to provide the student who was either a novice or a novice-to-be and who might also become a monk with access to the *dhamma*. More precisely, the monastic student learned to read so that he could recite the Pali liturgy used in Northern Thai rituals. If he later became a monk, he would also use his knowledge of reading in reciting the Pali texts containing the essential "acts of the Sangha" and the traditional vernacular texts that made the *dhamma* accessible to the laity. While the literacy acquired at the *wat* was meant to be used for religious purposes, it could also be used to read other texts that dealt with astrology, herbal medicine, love magic, customary law, and various folk arts. Those who needed literacy for clerical and other work in the premodern (prior to the 1890s) administrative structure of northern Thailand would also have obtained literacy through monastic education. Such literacy was, in short, a prerequisite for an array of traditional roles in Northern Thai society. What Phya Anuman Rajadhon wrote of traditional central Thailand was also true of the north: "Whatever knowledge a monk has gained during his monkhood will be turned into useful occupation."[37]

Until the introduction of compulsory mass education, literacy was an exclusive prerogative of males.[38] The illiterate male was distinctly disadvantaged relative to those who had acquired literacy at the *wat* in the competition for status in the public sphere of Northern Thai society. The implementation of compulsory education laws has radically undermined the significance of literacy for males. While access to literacy in Yuan (the traditional Northern Thai script) can still be obtained only through monastic education, such literacy today has a very limited function in Northern Thai society, where most occupations require literacy in standard Thai, the medium of instruction in public schools.

Compulsory education has created a direct conflict with temporary service in the novitiate. The school schedule does not permit a three-month absence during the lenten period. Thus, while boys are attending school between the ages of about seven and thirteen or fourteen, they cannot be ordained for the traditional period. If they are ordained, it must be for a short period during school holidays or else following completion of the required six grades.[39]

The introduction of government-sponsored mass education can be seen as the primary cause of the decline in certain sectors of Thai society of ordination and temporary subservience to the discipline. This decline is evident in statistics that show a reduction in monks as a percentage of the total adult Buddhist male population from 6.0 percent in 1927 to 2.3 percent in 1970 and in novices as a percentage of the total adult Buddhist male population from 3.9 percent in 1927 to 1.7 percent in 1970.[40] The decline in monastic experience has not been equally significant in all parts of Thai society. In rural central and northeastern Thailand, most men still continue to realize the ideal of entering the sangha for a temporary period as a monk.[41] The most marked reduction in percentage of men who have been ordained is to be found in urban areas throughout the country. There has also been a decline in rural northern Thailand that is a direct consequence of the conflict between the traditional ideal of ordination as a novice and the modern requirement for boys to attend government-sponsored schools.

The recent decline in monastic experience among males in Thailand reflects a process of secularization that may well lead to the emergence of a new conception of maleness. For the present, however, most men, and especially men in rural areas, still obtain an understanding of maleness from the totalizing pattern that is entailed by the ordination of men into the sangha, the submission of men to the discipline of the religious order, and, in most cases, the reentrance of most men after temporary monastic experience back into the world. Monastic experience serves as the source for a perspective on maleness that is, paradoxically, both world rejecting and world affirming.

The Buddhist Problem of Male Gender

Once a boy or man has been ordained, he assumes a new gender identity, one that is neither male or female. The term used for gender in Northern Thai (as also in standard Thai)—*phēt* (P *vesa;* Skt. *vesa,* "apparel, appearance")—is also used to refer to the fundamental character of one who has been ordained. The gender of the renunciant does not spring, as does that of "natural" males and females, from a biological sexual attribute. Nor is it a consequence of a physical mutilation. Rather one acquires sangha-gender (NT and ST *phēt yāng song*) through a uniquely human endeavor whereby one subjects oneself to a "discipline" that makes it possible to transcend "natural" sexuality. That this discipline is applicable only to males in the Theravadin tradition reflects a religious perspective that views maleness and femaleness very differently.

Both men and women in Theravadin societies acquire, primarily through participation in the ritual life of the communities in which they live, the same Buddhist understanding of suffering *(dukkha)*, and of the idea that suffering is rooted in desire *(tanhā)*. In the psychology of popular Buddhism, however, males and females are seen as motivated differently by desire. This difference bespeaks a basic unreflected assumption characteristic not only of Buddhist societies but most, if not all, traditional societies:[42] roles that define women in terms of their relations as wives or sex partners of men and as mothers of children while men's roles are defined in terms of public activities to which prestige attaches.

In northern Thailand, as in other Southeast Asian Theravadin societies, a girl grows into adulthood within a domestic sphere that is focused on her mother. After marriage, she initially remains with her parents, and when she does move into a separate household it will typically be one that is in the same compound as her parents' domicile. Separation from her mother rarely occurs until her mother dies, by which time she will usually have children of her own. A Northern Thai woman thus acquires an identity within a domestic sphere, an identity predicated primarily on the mother-child relationship. As I have argued elsewhere, Buddhist texts and rites posit a direct correspondence between the worldly identity of a woman as a mother of children and the primary religious identity of a woman as the nurturer of the religion.[43] Whatever significance female renunciation may have had at the time when an order of *bhikkhuni* existed in India or Sri Lanka (but never in Southeast Asia), no Northern Thai woman nor any other woman in the Theravadin societies of Southeast Asia can alter her gender identity by ordination.

As a late adolescent or a young woman, the desire that is most likely to beset a female is that of lust *(rāga),* that is, sexual attraction to a man. Such attraction is to be conquered not by withdrawal from the world, but through the forging of a marriage relationship so that it can be channeled toward the producing of a child, an act that is essential to the attainment of full adult female identity. As a mother, a woman faces another type of desire, that of attachment (P *upādāna;* NT and ST *tit*) to her children. This attachment is most pronounced for a woman in relationship to her male children, who will, unlike her female offspring, leave home not only to marry but also to assume roles in the public sphere. The separation of a woman from her son is least painful if his detachment occurs first through ordination into the sangha, an act by which he generates "merit" for his mother. Such merit, Northern Thai say, is partial compensation for her nurturance of him as a child. As a woman grows older and her daughters assume many of the domestic functions she previously performed, she still does not leave the domestic sphere in quest of salvation. Rather, she will intensify her offerings of food, prepared at home and carried to the temple-monastery to present to those who are her surrogate sons in the faith.

The characteristic desires that a male must contend with are perhaps best summarized with reference to a macho ideal that contrasts strongly with that of the monk. This ideal is that of the *nakleng,* a type of male whom Thak Chaloemtiarana has characterized as "a person who is not afraid to take risks, a person who 'lives dangerously,' kind to his friends but cruel to his enemies, a compassionate person, a gambler, a heavy drinker, and a lady-killer."[44] The *nakleng* epitomizes the man who accentuates desire for power, wealth, pleasure, and sexual domination. Although the *nakleng* would seem to make a mockery of Buddhist values, the man who is able to pursue his desires to the fullest without bringing suffering as an immediate consequence gains the respect and often the support of many of his fellow men living in Buddhist societies.

The time-lapse morality inherent in practical Buddhist thought provides Northern Thai and other Buddhists with a means to explain why sometimes the wicked flourish like the leaves of the Bodhi tree. The *nakleng,* or any man who is very effective in acquiring and wielding power and wealth, is deemed to possess a great store of positive kamma, to have merit *(mī bun),* from previous existences. Even though it may be assumed, even by a *nakleng* himself, that present actions motivated by sexual, aggressive, avaricious, and deceitful desires will sooner or later result in suffering, the high worldly status gained through these actions holds great appeal for some men.

The this-worldly ideal of the *nakleng* juxtaposed with the other-worldly ideal of the monk would seem likely to divide sharply the male populations of Buddhist societies. Perhaps urban Thailand may become a society in which a very small number of men withdraw totally from the world while the vast number who remain in the world engage in a perpetual Hobbesian war with each other. One can also see in Cambodia today a society struggling to regain some sort of moral balance after the *kāliyuga* (dark age) rule of the Khmer Rouge, during which the sangha was all but totally destroyed. Whatever is to be made of these contemporary cases, in traditional Buddhist societies, such as existed and still exist at least in rural areas in northern Thailand, the Buddhist initiatory process functioned to produce a dominant type of male who was neither supermoral monk nor amoral egotist. The ideal male is a man who has morally tempered his desires through temporary submission to the discipline of the sangha and has then returned to play an active role in society.

As the Northern Thai boy approaches adulthood, he has a choice to enter or not to enter the Buddhist order. Buddhist initiation is not compulsory for males in northern Thailand, or in other Theravadin societies of Southeast Asia, as initiation is in many small-scale horticultural societies in Africa and New Guinea. The noncompulsory nature of Buddhist initiation reflects an assumption fundamental to Buddhist teachings—that the decision to traverse the Path should be impelled by awareness that desire in oneself leads to suffering and must, therefore, be rooted out. The boy who stands on the threshold of manhood, however, is not likely to find desire-driven suffering to be especially characteristic of his experience. If he chooses to enter the order, it will most likely be for social rather than religious reasons. Perhaps most compelling would be his mother's wish that he be ordained in gratitude for her nurturing him through infancy and childhood. In addition, his father and other adult men may have impressed on him the status enhancement that will be gained by a temporary stay in the sangha. Further, and perhaps especially salient for older boys, will be the attractiveness that a former member of the sangha has for unmarried girls.

While a boy or young man may enter the sangha for social reasons, the disciplined life that he leads as a member of the order
often breeds some religious understanding of self. The self-
reflection that the disciplined life stimulates may serve to dispel
"delusion" and lead one to recognize the truths about suffering
and the cause of suffering which is desire. As an "aware" person,
he will more likely seek to control his natural passions.

This awareness can lead the young member of the sangha in two
different directions, each of which leads to gender identities that
are quite distinctive not only from each other but also from that of
the *nakleng*. He may choose to remain a member of the order,
pursuing the elimination of desire in a quest for ultimate salvation.
In this case, he will abandon forever a maleness that is expressed
through sexual and (lay) social activity.[45] On the other hand, he
may and in most cases will return to the world and assume an adult
male role. If he remains "aware," then he can be expected to exercise some control over his natural passions. The man who has led a
"disciplined" life as a temporary member of the sangha should
emerge from this experience able to temper his sexual passions and
enter into a stable marriage. He should also be able to rein in
aggressive desire and play an active role in community affairs without arrogating power to himself. He should be able to engage in
productive and other economic activities without greed.[46] And he
should be a man who can speak truly and wisely, drawing upon the
knowledge he has gained as a member of the sangha.

The morally tempered male householder would appear to be a
satisfactory compromise between two quite contradictory ideals of
maleness found in Northern Thai culture. For many it is indeed a
satisfactory *practical* compromise, especially as the man who
passes through the Buddhist initiatory process emerges with an
identity that is unequivocally distinguished from female identity.
Nonetheless, the initiatory process in northern Thailand, as in
other Theravadin societies in Southeast Asia, does not eliminate
an inherent *theological* ambiguity in male identity. Despite the
enhanced social prestige a man who has been ordained attains on
leaving the order, he still has not been successful in assuming the
religiously valued identity of one who totally transcends his "natural," *tanhā*-rooted maleness. On the other hand, the man who
tempers his desires while acting in the world may find himself at a
distinct disadvantage relative to those who accentuate their "natu-

ral" maleness. Yet, while the ambiguity contained in the Buddhist perspective on maleness may stimulate in some a feeling of tension regarding their gender identity,[47] elimination of this ambiguity would undermine the fundamental basis on which Buddhist societies in Southeast Asia rest. The ideal male in a Buddhist *social* order is one who acts in the world while having acquired detachment from worldly passions.

Notes

1. Van Gennep first proposed viewing initiation rites as "initiatory processes" entailing the meaningful shaping of a child into an adult. See Arnold van Gennep, *The Rites of Passage,* trans. Monika B. Vizedom and Gabrielle L. Caffee (1908; reprint, Chicago: University of Chicago Press, 1960). Van Gennep's ideas have been elaborated in Turner's work in what he calls the "ritual process." See especially, Victor Turner, *The Forest of Symbols* (Ithaca: Cornell University Press, 1967), and Victor Turner and Edith Turner, *Image and Pilgrimage in Christian Culture* (New York: Columbia University Press, 1978).
2. Van Gennep, *Rites of Passage,* p. 66.
3. Sherry B. Ortner and Harriet Whitehead, "Introduction: Accounting for Sexual Meanings," in *Sexual Meanings: The Cultural Construction of Gender and Sexuality,* ed. Ortner and Whitehead (Cambridge: Cambridge University Press, 1981), p. 13.
4. Mircea Eliade, *Rites and Symbols of Initiation: The Mysteries of Birth and Rebirth,* trans. Willard R. Trask (New York: Harper Colophon, 1975), p. x. This volume was originally published as *Birth and Rebirth* in 1958.
5. Ibid., p. 132.
6. Paula Richman's chapter in this volume considers female renunciation as portrayed in an early Tamil Buddhist text. Even in this text, the female renunciant, Maṇimēkalai, does not break with what I take to be the defining characteristic of female gender in Buddhist societies, namely that of nurturing mother. After succeeding in withdrawing from the temptations of the world, Maṇimēkalai acquires a magical alms bowl. In contrast to the alms bowl of the monk, which is used to receive food offered by the laity, Maṇimēkalai's alms bowl produces food that she then uses to feed the world. In contemporary Thailand as in contemporary Sri Lanka, there is growing criticism of the exclusion of women from the sangha. Some efforts have been made in both countries to reestablish an order of *bhikkhuni,* a female sangha, but these efforts have as yet met with little success among women as well as with little acceptance by men. If a radical

change is ever effected in the culture of gender short of a total break with Buddhism, it will probably come about as a consequence of a decline in the significance of the sangha/laity distinction. In this connection I would point to the fact that meditation masters in Thailand today are not necessarily members of the sangha; at least one highly respected teacher of meditation is a woman.

7. Wendy Doniger O'Flaherty, *Siva: The Erotic Ascetic* (Oxford: Oxford University Press, 1981), p. 38. This volume was first published in 1973 as *Asceticism and Eroticism in the Mythology of Siva*.

8. I have discussed the Buddhist perspective acquired by women in rural Thai society in another paper. See Charles F. Keyes, "Mother or Mistress but Never a Monk: Buddhist Notions of Female Gender in Rural Thailand," *American Ethnologist* 11.2 (1984):223–41. In Burma, the ear-boring ceremony *(natwin)* carried out for girls has some characteristics of a female initiation, but it is distinctly subordinate to the male ordination rite *(shinbyu)* with which it is invariably associated. See Melford E. Spiro, *Buddhism and Society* (Berkeley: University of California Press, 1970), pp. 234–47.

9. Marcel Mauss, *The Gift: Forms and Functions of Exchange in Archaic Societies,* trans. Ian Cunnison (1925; reprint, New York: W. W. Norton, 1967), pp. 1, 76–79.

10. A. L. Becker, "Text-Building, Epistemology, and Aesthetics in Javanese Shadow Theatre," in *The Imagination of Reality,* ed. A. L. Becker and Aram Yengoyan (Norwood, N.J.: Ablex Publishing, 1979), pp. 211–43.

11. My interpretation is based primarily on ethnographic research carried out in 1967–1968 in Mae Sariang, a district center located near the Burmese border in northwestern Thailand. Additional research was carried out in 1973–1974 when I served as Fulbright lecturer at Chiang Mai University in Chiang Mai, the major city of northern Thailand. I also draw on studies I have made over a number of years of Northern Thai ritual texts. Because of space limitations, I cannot here discuss many of the implications that the rites had for the Northern Thai communities in which they were performed.

12. See Charles F. Keyes, "Buddhism in a Secular City: A View from Chiang Mai," in *Visakha Puja B.E. 2518* (Bangkok: Annual Publication of the Buddhist Association of Thailand, 1975), pp. 62–72.

13. See Richard Davis, "Muang Matrifocality," *Journal of the Siam Society* 61 (1972):53–62; Ann Hale, "Reassessment of Northern Thai Matrilineages," *Mankind* 12 (1979):138–50; Marjorie Muecke, "Thai Conjugal Family Relationships and the Hsu Hypothesis," *Journal of the Siam Society,* forthcoming; Andrew Turton, "Matrilineal Descent Groups and Spirit Cults of the Thai Yuan in Northern Thailand," *Journal of the*

Siam Society 60.2 (1972):217–56; Turton, "Architectural and Political Space in Thailand," in *Natural Symbols in South East Asia,* ed. G. B. Milner (London: School of Oriental and African Studies, 1978), pp. 113–32; Gehan Wijeyewardene, "Matriclans or Female Cults: A Problem in Northern Thai Ethnography," *Mankind* 11 (1977):19–25; idem, "Scrubbing Scurf: Medium and Deity in Chiang Mai," *Mankind* 13 (1981):1–14. An about to be completed dissertation by Chayan Vaddhanaputhi contains perhaps the best discussion to date of the matrilineal influences associated with the Northern Thai household.

14. For a similar linkage between weaving and female identity, see Kathryn ƹ. March, "Weaving, Writing, and Gender," Paper prepared for a symposium entitled "Cloth and the Organization of Human Experience," sponsored by the Wenner-Gren Foundation for Anthropological Research, and held at Troutbeck, Amenia, New York, 1983. Also see H. Leedom Lefferts, Jr., "Textiles, Buddhism, and Society in Northeast Thailand," Paper prepared for the same symposium, for a case related to that of northern Thailand.

15. Ordination is undertaken not only as a rite of passage for those who will spend a temporary period in the sangha or as a prelude to lifelong mendicancy. Some boys (and occasionally men) are ordained at funerals "in front of the corpse" (*būat nā sop*) in order to make merit for the deceased. It would complicate discussion to consider here this form of ordination as well, but an analysis would show, I believe, that it also entails the same Buddhist perspective on maleness.

16. Pali terms (indicated by P) used in this paper are given in the romanization used by the Pali Text Society. In transliterating Northern Thai (NT) terms, I indicate vowel length but not tone; I do the same for the Standard Thai (ST) equivalents I provide for some Northern Thai words. In transliterating Northern and Standard Thai, as in transliterating other Southeast Asian languages written in Indian-derived scripts, one must choose whether to indicate the orthographic or spoken versions of words. Both languages have borrowed many words from Pali and Sanskrit and in so doing have preserved the original spelling even though they are pronounced quite differently. Here I transliterate according to the spoken language, giving Pali equivalents when relevant. For both Northern Thai and Standard Thai terms, I employ the signs ǫ and ụ for the phonetic values /ɔ/ and /ɨ/.

17. On the implications of merit transference of a son to his parents during ordination, see Charles F. Keyes, "Merit-Transference in the Kammie Theory of Popular Theravāda Buddhism," in *Karma: An Anthropological Inquiry,* ed. Charles F. Keyes and E. Valentine Daniel (Berkeley and Los Angeles: University of California Press, 1983), pp. 261–86.

18. Cf. Sangūan Chōtosukkharat, *Praphēni Thai phāk nụa* (Northern

Thai customs) (Bangkok: Odean Store, 1969), pp. 295–96. In other parts of Thailand and in Laos a candidate for ordination is called *nāk,* naga, a term that designates a serpent god that is associated with water and (male) fertility. The term is also sometimes used in northern Thailand as an alternative to *lūk kāēo.* This designation for candidates for ordination is chartered in a myth found in the canon itself (*Mahāvagga,* 1:63, 1–4). Tambiah has suggested that the point of the myth "is that a human being in entering the status of ascetic monk leaves behind and renounces the attributes of *nag*—virility or sexuality and similar attributes of secular life; or, to put it differently, *nag* and monk . . . are opposed states and through ordination of man makes the passage from one status to the other"; see Stanley J. Tambiah, *Buddhism and the Spirit Cults in North-East Thailand* (Cambridge: Cambridge University Press, 1970), p. 107. It seems to me that identification of a candidate with the naga accentuates his "natural" maleness, a maleness that will be fundamentally transformed through ordination whether or not a man remains an ascetic monk for life.

19. Tambiah, *Buddhism and Spirit Cults,* p. 104.

20. E. R. Leach in his paper "Magical Hair," *Journal of the Royal Anthropological Institute,* 88 (1958):147–64, argues that this head shaving should be interpreted as "symbolic castration." Such an interpretation is at odds with the stance taken in the Buddhist tradition regarding the sexuality of members of the sangha. There is explicit prohibition against eunuchs entering the sangha. See Prince Vajirañānavarorasa, *The Entrance to the Vinaya: Vinayamukha, Volume One* (Bangkok: Mahāmakutarājavidyālaya, 1969). Moreover, it is deemed essential that one who demonstrates his adherence to the discipline (P *vinaya*) be biologically capable of performing sexually while controlling completely the desire to do so.

21. Eliade, *Rites and Symbols,* p. 26.

22. The activities of the preparation day might be said to constitute a "separation phase" according to the analytical scheme of van Gennep, who divided the ritual process into the three phases of separation, limen (or transition), and incorporation or aggregation. It should be noted, however, that the candidate is more of a "liminal person"—in Turner's (*Forest of Symbols)* sense—during the activities of the preparation day than he is during the ordination proper. While I follow Turner and van Gennep in analyzing rituals "processually," I do not believe that an analysis of a particular ritual process should employ the van Gennep/Turner scheme in a mechanical fashion.

23. Excerpt from an oral text recorded on July 5, 1968, in Mae Sariang. The translation was made by Professor Sommai Premchit of Chiang Mai University and myself.

24. It is also possible, but rarely done at least in Thailand, to hold ordinations over water in an area that has not been previously consecrated.

25. From this point on, the ritual is conducted primarily in Pali liturgical forms that bring the ancient past of earliest Buddhism into the present and make ordinations performed in northern Thailand the same as ordinations performed in other Theravadin societies past and present. The language of this liturgy can be traced to canonical sources in the *Vinaya-piṭaka*, that basket (*piṭaka*) of the scriptures that relates the story of the evolution of the discipline (*vinaya*) incumbent upon those who commit themselves to being "sons of the Buddha."

For English translations of the ordination rite as performed in Thailand see Prince Patriarch Vajirañāṇavarorasa, *Ordination Procedure: Upasampadāvidhī* (Bangkok: Mahāmakutarājavidyālaya, 1973), and Kenneth E. Wells, *Thai Buddhism: Its Rites and Activities* (Bangkok: Suriyabun Publishers, 1975), pp. 136–52.

26. For extended discussions of this myth, see Keyes, "Merit-Transference," and "Mother or Mistress."

27. The term *living in kamma* is also applied to a traditional rite held in the cool season during which members of the sangha withdraw to a cremation grounds to meditate on the dissolution of the physical body. More interesting for a consideration of gender, the term is also sometimes used to refer to the postpartum customs observed by a woman. In all cases where the term is used, there is a sense that one is at a threshold that may mark a significant change in one's kammic destiny.

28. John C. Holt, *Discipline: The Canonical Buddhism of the Vinaya-pitaka* (Delhi: Motilal Banarsidass, 1981), p. 65.

29. Prince Vajirañāṇavarorasa's *Entrance to the Vinaya* provides an interpretation of the training regulations that have become standard for the Thai sangha.

30. Ibid., p. 12.

31. Ibid., p. 27.

32. While this is the case for the first 4 training regulations, the remaining 223 cannot all be derived from prohibitions against the four vices. Many have to do with conduct appropriate to a member of the sangha.

33. Ibid., p. 55.

34. Ibid., p. 57.

35. Michael Moerman, "Ban Ping's Temple: The Center of a 'Loosely Structured' Society," in *Anthropological Studies in Theravada Buddhism*, ed. Manning Nash et al., Cultural Report Series, 13 (New Haven: Yale University Southeast Asia Studies, 1966), p. 156.

36. Konrad Kingshill, *Ku Daeng—The Red Tomb* (Bangkok: Bangkok Christian College, 1965), p. 124.

37. Phya Anuman Rajadhon, *Life and Ritual in Old Siam*, trans. and ed. William J. Gedney (New Haven: HRAF Press, 1961), p. 83. Also see Stanley J. Tambiah, "Literacy in a Buddhist Village in North-East Thai-

land," in *Literacy in Traditional Societies,* ed. Jack Goody (Cambridge: Cambridge University Press, 1968), pp. 86–131.

38. March, in "Weaving, Writing, and Gender," reports a similar relationship between maleness and literacy among the Mahayanist Tamang of Nepal. While most Northern Thai men, like the Tamang men March studied, used their literacy primarily for reciting fixed texts rather than reading for understanding, a few Northern Thai monks, even in rural monasteries, would study texts, thereby reading them to gain a deeper insight into the world than most who entered the order would have. Even today such men are called *khūbā ācān,* "learned teachers."

39. Until the late 1970s, only four grades of primary school were required and boys would, thus, have been free to enter the novitiate for a three-month or longer period after the age of eleven or so.

40. Statistics calculated on the basis of data presented by J. A. Niels Mulder in *Monks, Merit, and Motivation: Buddhism and National Development in Thailand,* 2d rev. ed., Center for Southeast Asian Studies, Special Report 1 (DeKalb: Northern Illinois University, 1973), p. 10.

41. Terwiel found that in a village in Ratburi Province in the Central Plains, where he carried out a study in 1968, 76.8 percent of adult men had been or were serving as monks. See B. J. Terwiel, *Monks and Magic: An Analysis of Religious Ceremonies in Central Thailand,* Scandinavian Institute of Asian Studies Monograph Series 24 (London: Curzon Press; Lund: Studentlitteratur, 1975), p. 99. In the village of Ban Nǫng Tʉn in northeastern Thailand where I have carried out research over a period of twenty years, I found that in 1963 69.9 percent of adult men had been or were monks and 38.6 percent of the same population had been novices. In a new survey made in 1980, I found that 70.3 percent of adult men had been monks and that 24.5 percent of the same population had been novices.

42. See Ortner and Whitehead, *Sexual Meanings,* esp. p. 19.

43. See Keyes, "Mother or Mistress."

44. Thak Chaloemtiarana, *Thailand: The Politics of Despotic Paternalism* (Bangkok: Social Science Association of Thailand and Thai Khadi Institute, Thammasat University, 1979), p. 339.

45. I do not wish to leave the impression that monks have no social role; they certainly do and have had since at least the time when King Aśoka in the third century B.C. assumed royal patronage for the sangha. Still, the social role of the sangha is constrained by its fundamental religious character.

46. In another paper I have argued that the experience of temporary monkhood (as distinguished from temporary novicehood) still undertaken by most male villagers in northeast Thailand lies at the root of an economic ethic that is in some ways comparable to the Puritan ethic as dis-

cussed by Max Weber. The tempering of greed learned by northeastern Thai as monks can be linked to their ability to forego immediate gratification and accumulating capital. See Charles F. Keyes, "Economic Action and Buddhist Morality in a Thai Village," *Journal of Asian Studies* 62.4 (1983):851–68.

47. While I cannot pursue the point here, I suggest that such a tension may be related to the quite high incidence of and tolerance for male homosexuality found in Thai society.

Four

Men, Women, and Ghosts in Taiwanese Folk Religion
Stevan Harrell

Encounters with ghosts are an important part of Taiwanese folk religion. Ghosts, the unhappy or unsettled spirits of deceased persons, represent social anomalies, otherwise inexplicable misfortunes, and fear. The occurrence of ghosts and encounters with them are gender-specific in a variety of ways. Both the gender of ghosts and the way men and women interact with ghosts tell us something about the nature of gender relations in Taiwanese society. In addition, variation between the theory of what ghosts represent and the practice of interacting with them when they appear can provide insights about the relationship between theory and practice as related to the general issue of gender and religion.

Taiwanese Folk Religion

Before examining the issues of gender and ghosts, I need to describe the most important beliefs of Taiwanese folk religion and the place of ghosts in this belief system. The folk religion of the Taiwanese, Hokkien-speaking Chinese whose ancestors immi-

This chapter is based partly on field research near Sanxia, Taiwan, in 1972–1973 and 1978. The author is grateful for the financial assistance of the National Institute of Mental Health and the Joint Committee on Contemporary China of the American Council of Learned Societies and the Social Science Research Council. Also the author wishes to thank the Institute of Ethnology, Academia Sinica, Taiwan, for sponsoring the research.

grated from Fujian Province in the seventeenth through nineteenth centuries, is a variant of a similar set of beliefs and practices found outside the educated elite in all parts of China.[1] These beliefs and practices are directed toward achieving harmony in the cosmos, in society, and within the individual. Harmony will bring wealth, prosperity, and happiness, while disharmony will bring poverty and disaster. In the pursuit of harmony, an entity, such as the cosmos or the society, is conceived of and treated as a system of interrelating parts. Harmony is the smooth and proper working of parts in the system, while disharmony is the conflict between parts. If divination or just plain common sense indicates that a system is in disharmony, then people can take measures to put it aright again. For example, rites of passage must be performed at times that fit harmoniously into the cycle of hours, days, months, and years. If people are, for example, married or buried at the wrong time, misfortune will befall them or their relatives. But divination makes it possible to know in advance the proper time to perform such a rite, so simple recourse to a diviner, plus a bit of planning, can assure that the rite will fit properly into the cosmic temporal scheme. Similarly, everyone has a proper status in society, with a concomitant role to perform. When people perform these roles correctly, when son is filial to father and wife dutiful to husband, for example, the whole society will work harmoniously, and all members will share in its prosperity.

We can understand interaction with supernatural beings in Taiwan only if we look at the supernatural beings themselves as part of these cosmic and social systems. In folk theory, most supernatural beings are the souls of deceased persons—while people live, their souls ordinarily remain with them, but after they die, the souls assume an independent existence.[2] As a matter of fact, most souls simply turn into ancestors—spirits to be revered, honored with places on the wooden altar in the parlor of every house, propitiated with incense offerings morning and night and with food on special occasions.[3] But the ancestors rarely intervene actively for good or evil in the affairs of their descendants, unless the descendants worship them improperly or otherwise neglect them. If the world worked with ideal smoothness and harmony, ancestors might well be the only kind of spirits inhabiting this cosmos. But in fact, crises, disasters, and conflicts occur all the time, and they bring forth both heroes and victims. The heroes, those who have led unusually meritorious lives on earth, are exalted after death. They have power to help people and become deified by the parallel processes of popular devotion and "bureaucratic" appointment from the supernatural ruler, the Jade Emperor. They are the local gods, worshipped and supplicated in temples, in processions at festival time, and on home altars all over the island. While inter-action with the ancestors is indicative of harmony, or at best serves to preserve it, interaction with the gods can not only preserve but also restore harmony. People go to the gods for help when some-thing is wrong, promising offerings and devotion in return for advice and assistance.

The spirits that concern me most directly here are the victims of disharmony—the ghosts. While in theory everyone's soul becomes a ghost of a sort upon death, almost all such "ghosts" are peace-fully enshrined as family ancestors and cause little trouble to any-one. But some slip through the net. For example, despite every-one's best efforts, forgetfulness, anonymous death in a large disaster, and petty quarrels can all cause someone who ought to be an ancestor to remain unworshipped. Such a person is both a vic-tim of social disharmony and a cause of cosmic disharmony and, like all aspects of disharmony, becomes dangerous to members of the cosmic and social system. Such a "hungry ghost" preys on inno-cent living people (particularly small children and those who are at a vulnerable point in the temporal cycle) in order to gain the other-worldly sustenance denied it by not becoming an ancestor. Or someone dies an unnatural death—by suicide, drowning, war, or, in modern times, by motorcycle or coal mine accident. Such a person's spirit, despite efforts to mollify it, remains angry and will prey on the innocent living, not so much in desperation as out of resentment and desire for revenge.[4] Often the spirit lurks around the place of death—frequently a river, a bridge, or a dark and hid-den spot—waiting to accost unsuspecting victims and cause them to take fright, causing sickness, psychosis, or even death. In an-other example, a teenage girl, who ought to look forward to mar-riage and motherhood, dies unmarried. Her spirit may become dissatisfied and cause trouble to her family until she is married, usually to a living man, giving her a proper place as a wife and mother on her husband's ancestral altar.[5]

In all these examples, ghosts are personifications of anomalies, of disharmonies, of what ought not to have happened and would not have happened had the cosmic and social orders been running properly. But ghosts are more besides. Ghosts are also explanations for random disasters. In the same way that Azande, for example, ascribe "unfortunate events" to the actions of witchcraft,[6] Chinese use ghosts as a common explanation for misfortunes that cannot be explained otherwise. Ghosts are far from the only way of explaining unfortunate events: if, for example, one has neglected to follow the easy procedure of divining the proper day and time for a wedding, or the more difficult and expensive process of choosing a fitting burial spot for a parent, one has risked causing a disharmonious relationship, and many misfortunes are attributed to just such negligence. Other misfortunes, particularly illness, can be caused by neglecting to take the proper medications that keep the bodily system running smoothly. Sorcery—deliberate and malicious use of charms and other magical means to harm a rival—is another cause. And of course there is just plain stupidity—some misfortunes need no supernatural explanation at all. But other things are harder to pin down. Some people who do the proper rituals, always consult diviners, have no known enemies, and are in fact very intelligent, nevertheless suffer misfortunes of one kind or another. In cases like this, anonymous ghosts tend to be invoked as explanations. Because ghosts are alien to order and to the ordering morality that creates harmony, they attack at random. People are rarely completely safe from them. In this sense, ghosts are personifications of the randomness of suffering.

Ghosts, however, personify more than just anomaly and the randomness of suffering. They also personify what frightens. The places they inhabit—streams and bridges in a country of nonswimmers, dark corners where people cannot see clearly, the outer edges of villages where the social order does not rule uncontested, coal mines that tend to collapse and kill workers—would be fearsome enough to people who had no notion whatsoever of ghosts or ghostly powers. Individuals who encounter ghosts typically either take fright—an actual sickness—or at least come away very shaken. In fact, when ghosts are thought to be lurking in the vicinity—during the seventh month of the lunar calendar, or at any time when there is evidence of their causing misfortunes—people speak of ghosts in hushed tones, if at all, and usually call them by some sort of polite euphemism. For example, a teenage girl in the village where I lived once developed an acute psychosis. After several days and no improvement in her condition, her relatives called in a spirit medium so they could ask a god's diagnosis and prescription. One of the possible causes the god mentioned was that an *ong-si kui*[7]—a ghost who had died a violent death—had attacked the girl at a dark intersection on her way home from work. When a neighbor woman, herself not related to the victim or otherwise involved, reported this to a friend of hers, she said the god had mentioned an *ong-si Hit-o-e*—one of those who died a violent death. When I told my landlady's teenage daughter about this, she shuddered at my direct mention of the angry ghost.

The Relative Importance of Various Aspects of Ghosts

These three aspects of ghosts, as personifications of anomaly, of the randomness of suffering, and of the frightening, are probably all present to some degree in any Taiwanese person's ideas about ghosts and in every encounter that a Taiwanese has with ghosts. But the importance of each aspect will vary in different contexts. First, ghosts as conceived of in the abstract will be different from ghosts as interacted with in a variety of situations. Second, ghosts as interacted with in one kind of situation will differ from ghosts as interacted with in a different kind of situation. Finally, ghosts encountered in the same kind of situation will look different to different people. In all three of these variations, the gender of the ghost is one characteristic that changes. In addition, the gender of the person interacting with the ghosts is important in understanding the last two of these three kinds of variation. Because men and women tend to interact with ghosts in different kinds of situations, men perceive ghosts differently than do women. And because men and women are subject to different kinds of misfortunes and are frightened by different kinds of things, insofar as ghosts represent misfortunes or frightening things, men and women perceive ghosts differently in the same kinds of situations. Gender is thus an important facet both of ghosts and of the way people interact with those ghosts. To understand the connection between men, women, and ghosts more clearly, let us examine the three kinds of variation in more detail.

People who are actively involved in living a certain religious tradition every day are also likely to be actively involved in thinking about it, analyzing it, considering what its different parts mean.

And although there is certainly a close connection between belief and behavior, between analysis and action, there is not necessarily an identity. What people tell us when we ask analytical questions about, for example, what ghosts are, how they arise, and how they can be expected to interact with people may not be the same as what people actually do when faced with ghosts either as hallucinations or as presumed agents of misfortune. In particular, when people see ghosts, what they actually see may be at odds with what they think about when they try to theorize about the nature of ghosts either in response to an anthropologist's question or in a casual discussion with other interested natives. Any analysis of the gender of ghosts must take into account possible differences between the ghosts as part of a "theology" and ghosts as part of religious practice. This point has been missed by previous, otherwise good, analyses of the place of ghosts in Taiwanese folk religion. Arthur Wolf, for example, has based his discussion entirely on the folk theory of religious beliefs and has thus seen ghosts as a supernatural reflection of outcasts of the social order, predominantly male beggars, bandits, and other wanderers.[8] David Jordan, on the other hand, has explicitly recognized that there is a difference between folk theory and behavior, between what he calls a "theological model" and an "action model," and has gone so far as to show that the differences between the two models derive partly from the difference between supernatural beings as explanatory devices and as sources of help in times of crisis.[9] But he has missed the issue of the gender of ghosts, even though his own data indicate that ghosts as personifications of particular kinds of structural anomalies are in fact always female. I will return to Jordan's data later in this chapter.

If different aspects of ghosts are important in theory and in practice, their importance also varies among different kinds of practice—among different kinds of situations in which people encounter ghosts. Whether the occasion is calendrical or critical; whether the ghosts are propitiated publicly or privately, en masse or individually; whether their presence is merely assumed, derived from indirect evidence such as people's illness or misfortune, or from the direct evidence of seeing them as nighttime apparitions, all affect which aspects of ghosts are predominant. In general terms, ghosts propitiated as part of mass celebrations represent anomalies in the larger social order; ghosts propitiated as a result of childhood illnesses represent the randomness of misfortune; ghosts propitiated as a result of familial crises represent anomalies in the domestic order; and ghosts seen as apparitions represent repressed fears. The importance of these various kinds of representations is, again, closely tied to the gender of the perceiver and plays a large part in determining the gender of the ghosts. Large-scale social anomalies, the beggars and bandits of Wolf's formulation, tend to be male in Chinese society, and the people who interact with them may be either men or women. The agents of random misfortune are vague and anonymous, and we cannot really determine their gender. Those who make offerings to them, however, are almost always women. Domestic anomalies, persons who have been left out by the ordinary workings of the family system, tend to be female, as do those who propitiate them. Finally, apparitions, expressions of otherwise repressed fears, tend to be of a nature strange and threatening to the person seeing them. In most cases, then, they tend to be of the opposite gender to the observer. Since the observers are usually male, the ghosts, barring special circumstances, are usually female.

This leads us to the third factor in the relative importance of different aspects of ghosts and in determining the ghosts' gender. This factor is the perspective of the individual perceiver. As is illustrated abundantly elsewhere in this volume, in all religious traditions, people in different social roles have different perspectives on their religions; this is especially evident if we look at the differing perspectives of men and women. But such differences in perspective are probably particularly apparent in traditions such as the Chinese folk religion, where little if any doctrinal authority exists to check or restrain innovation. In Chinese folk religion, people are free to reinterpret doctrine and practice, subject only to the vague and informal pressures of social and cultural conformity.[10] This relative freedom of interpretation, coupled with the differences in perspective we would expect according to different places in the social organization—gender, age, education—and differences in individual religiosity, suggestibility, and other aspects of personality, means that there will be almost as many perspectives as there are actors in the system. Nevertheless, because there is a certain uniformity to all men's and to all women's experience, we find interesting differences in religious perspective that are attributable to gender differences.

In the interaction of these three factors—the difference between analysis and action, the difference between ghosts in their various situational contexts, and the difference among the perspectives of different actors—the relationship between ghosts and gender becomes clear. This will be evident if we examine in turn the various kinds of situations in which ghosts figure, keeping in mind that the theoretical nature of ghosts is much more important in some situations than in others and, at the same time, that certain kinds of actors are much more likely to encounter ghosts in one kind of situation than in another.

Ghosts in Different Kinds of Situations
The Communal Festival Called Pudu

According to the folk religious interpretation of the Chinese lunar calendar, the seventh month, which usually starts sometime during the first half of August in the Gregorian calendar, is the time for ghosts. People well versed in spirit lore say that during this time, the gates to the world of the spirits (the [M] *yin* realm) are opened and ghosts thus in some sense are "allowed out" during that time. In fact, many temples have a small door near the back wall, at one side, called the ghost door. On the first day of the seventh month, this door is ceremonally opened, and it is closed again on the last day of the month. Some people say that ordinary visits to temples to worship the gods will be inefficacious when the ghosts are out (although people still go), and no sane person would think of having a wedding during the seventh month: a common proverb says *chit-ge chua kui-po,* "In the seventh month, take a ghost wife," that is, a woman married in the seventh month is not long for this world. During the seventh month also, ceremonies are held to honor the anonymous and presumably dangerous dead whose bones have been dug up during construction projects and are gathered in communal roadside shrines. If some of these dead eventually become powerful gods through a process of popular consensus, everyone still recognizes that they were once ghosts.

The most important and largest-scale homage to the ghosts comes in most Taiwanese communities on the fifteenth day of the seventh month, in the great communal festival of [M] *Pudu.* About the middle of the afternoon, after most households have already worshipped Tho-te Kong, the local tutelary deity, and their own ancestors, they begin to put out offerings for the anonymous ghosts. As befits ghost offerings, these are placed outside the house (nobody wants to invite the ghosts in) and facing away from the house, in the direction from which the ghosts will be coming. These offerings are many and various—the ghosts are legion, and people, not knowing them individually, have no idea exactly what they want. So there are fruits and vegetables of all sorts (raw and uncut, since they are not inviting the ghost to eat), flesh, fish, and fowl, eggs and raw rice, cigarettes, beer and wine, and a basin of water with a washcloth in it for the ghosts to tidy up before taking the food. People burn silver spirit money of a lower denomination than that given to the ancestors and contrasting even more with the gold given to the gods. Those who live amid rice fields make a trail of incense sticks from the nearest path to the courtyard of the house—some say it is so the ghosts will be sure to find the way there and thus go away satisfied; others, so the ghosts will be sure to find a way out again and thus go away. There is banter and levity of this sort all around, and although people are careful to refer to the ghosts by some euphemism so as not to offend them, they do not seem very concerned; indeed they seem more concerned with the good show and with the good meal afterward than with any immediate danger from the ghosts.

If one asks the villagers to whom they are offering, the euphemism they will use is *hou hia:-ti-a*, the good brothers. That is about all anyone will want to say at the time, but on other occasions they will explain that *good brothers* is really a polite way of referring to the anonymous mass of ghosts who are hungry and wandering because they are homeless, because they have no descendants to care for them. The great masses of *hou hia:-ti-a* are not, as far as I know, worshipped collectively on any other occasion.

The *Pudu* festival thus makes only a vague reference to the gender of ghosts—one assumes that *hia:-ti-a*, or brothers, are male, but their gender is not a very salient feature of the ghosts themselves or of the festival held to propitiate them. This unimportance of gender can be explained by two facts—that the *hou hiu:-ti-a* are anonymous and never identified as individuals, and that the *Pudu* is, above all, a collective ceremony. As mentioned, people do not display much emotional involvement in the *Pudu* festival. Aside from being a good time and an excuse to eat and drink, it is basically a prophylactic ritual. People do not worship the *hou hia:-ti-a* at *Pudu* time because they have seen a ghost or because they have determined that a ghost is causing them misfortune; they worship because it is part of the ritual calendar. Thus they never identify any characteristics of the individual ghosts worshipped at that time. They are simply the anonymous good brothers, out there, but nameless and faceless. Moreover, everyone, men, women, and children, worships together at *Pudu* and does it publicly. Thus a consensus develops about what people are doing and why they are doing it. In this kind of a situation, it would be hard to conceive of a behavioral interaction with ghosts that deviated far, if at all, from the agreed-on folk theory. And as we have seen, the folk theory tends to assume that ghosts are male, but does not dwell on the point. From the perspective of the *Pudu* festival, ghosts are personifications of anomalies, and that is all, and they are very vague personifications of very generalized anomalies at that.

Placating Ghosts to Cure Random Misfortunes

If the *Pudu* rite is a collective as well as a prophylactic one in which the community as a whole propitiates anonymous ghosts to ward off undefined misfortunes, there are other rites, curative rather than prophylactic in nature, in which individuals attempt to chase away the already present influence of equally anonymous ghosts. This happens, more often than not, when a child is ill—not ill with an ordinary illness that can be cured with herbs or with a shot from a Western-style doctor, but down with a vaguer, more lingering illness, whose symptoms are poorly defined and which seems intractable to either herbal or biochemical medicines. Often in a case such as this, a relative, usually a mother or a father's mother, but occasionally a father or father's father, will ask a diviner what is wrong with the child. This can be done at a temple by means of mechanical divination devices, but a professional spirit medium is more reliable for this kind of advice. Most spirit mediums hold regular consultations in temples or in shrines in their own homes, becoming possessed at definite times each day by a god with a reputation for the healing arts. Such a god, speaking through a medium, may give a number of different answers, including simply that the child has a physical illness that ought to be treated by a physician;

one of the most common answers is that the child has "run into conflict" (*chiong-tiou*) in a particular direction. This is a euphemism for an attack by ghosts coming at the child's house from that direction. If this is the diagnosis, the prescription is simple—someone in the family, most often again a mother or grandmother—must place an offering in a secluded spot outside the house, usually beside a path, in the specified direction. Walking about a village in the morning, one can sometimes see a bowlful of rice dumped upside down, a couple of strips of fat meat, perhaps a vegetable or two, and two sticks of incense sticking in the ground, remains of offerings made the night before. The supplicant usually talks to the ghosts, asking them to withdraw their influence and promising another, similar offering in the same place three days hence if the child recovers. (The child, of course, usually does—such measures are not appropriate for major illnesses anyway.)

This kind of interaction with ghosts differs in several respects from the interaction of *Pudu*. As mentioned, the action is curative rather than preventative. Individuals put out the offerings not as part of a public festival but as a private act of supplication, and they do it not out of a sense of social obligation but out of a desire to cure the child. The ghosts in this case are less theoretical, more real; less collective, more individual. Nevertheless, the ghosts are still anonymous—the god who made the diagnosis never said whose ghosts they were, and the women who put out the offerings never, to my knowledge, see the ghosts come to take them. (In fact, everyone knows that dogs usually eat them.) As personifications of random misfortune, these are still in a sense random ghosts, even more anonymous than those worshipped at *Pudu*. There people at least talk about worshipping a particular kind of spirit (the good brothers). But when offerings go out beside the path at night, it is just because the child has a "conflict"—a very impersonal threat—in that direction. Once again, as in *Pudu*, interaction with ghosts in this context does not require that people know anything about the ghosts. For a nighttime offering, the only necessary knowledge is which direction the ghosts are attacking from. Ghosts who attack at random are, from the theoretical perspective, souls so lost that they are completely forgotten. And the kind of formulaic interaction with them—put out the rice and other offerings, say a little invocation, burn some spirit money, and then come back in three days and do it again—demands no deviation from the theoretical perspective. The ghosts' gender is thus irrelevant here. The gender of the persons interacting with the ghost is not, however. This kind of ghostly attack almost always comes to children, and it is mothers and grandmothers who do most of the child care and who are likely to consult with doctors or spirit mediums about childhood illnesses. Ghosts who attack at random are thus primarily the concern of women.

Placating Specific Ghosts Who Have Been Wronged and Have Thus Caused Misfortunes

If *Pudu* and "conflict offerings" both deal with anonymous ghosts, the one primarily as personifications of anomalies and the other primarily as personifications of random misfortune, there are two other contexts in which people interact with individual, identified ghosts. The first of these concerns what David Jordan has called "family ghosts."[11] The second concerns actually seeing ghosts, usually as nighttime apparitions. In both of these contexts, the ghosts are predominantly female. Let me explore some of the reasons why.

Family ghosts, spirits that cause trouble in families and have to be either exorcised or placated, are a common occurrence in all parts of Taiwan, and indeed all over China. They come in a variety of forms, but all have at least one thing in common: they are girls or women who have been deprived of their proper place in family and society as wives and particularly as mothers. As Jordan clearly explains, a girl who dies unmarried cannot have a place as an ancestor on her father's altar. Her family can worship her in a back room somewhere, or donate her spirit table to a Buddhist "vegetarian hall," but in some cases they choose to find a husband for her, marrying her to a living man in a posthumous wedding (usually with a considerable dowry to sweeten the proposition for the husband's family) and having her spirit tablet enshrined on her husband's family's ancestral altar.[12] In this way, a dangerous ghost, an anomaly in the family system, has been domesticated by placing her posthumously in the normal structural position of a wife and, at least for purposes of ancestor worship, a mother. Jordan also mentions cases of older women who have been deprived of their rightful places as mothers *after* they die because their daughters-in-law remarried out of their families or had adulterous relations, disrupting the proper order of the family system.[13]

Jordan is not the only observer who mentions this kind of anomalous female ghost. R. F. Johnston, a British colonial official at Weihaiwei in Shandong in the early twentieth century, related several stories of the trouble caused by the ghosts of suicides in the villages of that area. Usually, he said, the suicides were young women escaping from an impossible husband or mother-in-law.[14] And Jack Potter, in an analysis of female spirit mediums in still another part of China, comments: "That most malevolent ghosts are female is surely no accident. Ground down by the lineage and family system . . . they are the most downtrodden group in village society. . . . The frustrations of Cantonese women from one village could supply enough discontented, angry, revengeful, ghosts to populate ten village hells."[15] Potter, of course, is speaking only about one context in which people encounter ghosts—the context of family crises. But in this restricted context, his analysis is correct. Cantonese spirit mediums, themselves usually women frustrated in their attempts to assume the ordinary female status of mother, control familiar spirits, who in turn battle against these malevolent ghosts who, like their sisters in Taiwan and Shandong, are mostly women. The reason is clear—they are personifications of social anomalies, and the particular anomalies they represent, those of the kinship and family systems, bear more heavily on the women. Men who fail to reproduce or to lead a normal family life leave the village context altogether—they become the anonymous ghosts of the good brother type. A childless man who remains in village society will usually have a descendant adopted for him and thus, even if artificially, take his place in the kinship system. But an unmarried woman or a wronged mother-in-law has no such easy recourse and at the same time does not ordinarily leave the system altogether. She thus becomes an identifiable ghost who somehow has to be reabsorbed into the family system.

One might legitimately ask why it is so easy to take care of the anomalous male, who can obtain an adopted status, while the unmarried or otherwise anomalous female has no such options open to her. The answer is simply that in the Chinese patrilineal system, a woman's only correct place is as a mother, and as a mother in a different household from the one she was born in. If anything—failure to marry or the unfilial conduct of a son or daughter-in-law are two examples—threatens that status, there is no easy way for a woman to get it back. She must become a ghost and assert herself by causing misfortunes.

If female ghosts arise from women in anomalous family statuses, so do female gods. Neither of the two most prominent female deities in southern Chinese folk religions is thought of as a wife and mother. [M] Guanyin (Kuanyin), the Buddhist-derived female deity often referred to in the Western literature as the Goddess of Mercy, appears to be a feminization of an originally male bodhisattva of the Pure Land tradition, Avalokitesvara.[16] And the deity known as Ma Co in Taiwan and as (M) Tian Hou in Guangdong is thought to have been a young girl who died a virgin. In the supernatural world, as in earthly society, the women who stand out, who have other than ordinary status, are those who do not go through the normal progression ending in mother and ancestor. Though a few become gods, the majority, of course, become the family ghosts of the sort discussed by Jordan and Potter.

Interaction with ghosts in this context differs from that in the previously discussed contexts of *Pudu* and conflict offerings because the ghosts in this case are identified. Since individual females are much more likely to be identifiable as the victims of structural anomalies in the family, it is they who become the family ghosts. But interaction with ghosts in this context still resembles that in the *Pudu* and conflict contexts in one way: ghosts in this case are both manifestations of anomaly and representations of misfortune (though in this case hardly random misfortune) and as such do not look very different from the perspectives of different actors. In the cases described by Potter, the female spirit mediums are the diagnosticians and thus play the active role in seeing their deceased counterparts, the anomalous females who have become ghosts. If men become involved in such interactions at all, they tend to go along with the diagnosis. Everyone agrees that family ghosts are mostly female.

Seeing Ghosts

The situation looks somewhat different when we consider actually seeing ghosts. Seeing ghosts (unless one has a close and sudden encounter with one and thus becomes ill) usually accompanies no particular misfortune, so the apparitions do not represent either social structural anomaly, which by deduction from the general theory of harmony must always cause misfortune, or any kind of explanation of misfortune, random or otherwise. The apparitions that people see can only represent fears, often fears that arise out of projected hostility. If this is true (I have no proof, but this explanation seems most reasonable), then individuals seeing ghosts from the perspective of different positions in the social structure will have different kinds of people to fear, and thus will see different kinds of ghosts. We need to look at who sees ghosts, what kinds of ghosts they see, and whether these ghosts are the sorts of people they would have reason to fear or hate and thus project the threatening qualities of ghostliness onto.

First, who sees ghosts? In a survey of individual differences in belief in folk religious doctrine, I asked approximately sixty adult residents of the Taiwanese village where I lived whether they had ever seen ghosts.[17] In response to this question, some people reported others' experiences instead of, or in addition to, their own. Most had not seen ghosts and did not spontaneously tell stories about others' having seen them. Many gave a folk theoretical answer for why they had not seen them—only people, they said, whose "luck" is very low *(un khat kei e lang)* could see ghosts. This explanation, like all folk analytic explanations, sees ghosts in terms of anomalies. Individuals' "luck" *(un)*, which is their likelihood of sickness or other misfortune during a particular period, usually one to three years, is the outcome of a complex series of relationships between the cosmic affinities of the time they were born and those of the period in question. Most individuals have rather ordinary luck during any given period, and for one's luck to be really low seems to require an unusual, and thus anomalous, malconjunction of cosmic affinities. But in fact, who saw ghosts and who did not seemed to have more to do with gender than with birth dates. Of seventeen reported sightings of ghosts, only two were made by females, and one of these was a hearsay report. Most of the older women asked reported that only men ordinarily went out of the house, or at least out of the village, in the middle of the night. The one woman who had herself seen a ghost, however, had seen a male. It was when she was a child, she said, and the ghost had been very big and tall. She did not see his face or clothes distinctly, however, and he quickly disappeared. The other report of a woman seeing a ghost was hearsay and concerned a woman having seen the ghost of a drowned man lurking in a river waiting to capture travelers attempting to ford. This sounds more like a piece of folklore than a personal account, but nevertheless the ghost the woman saw was male.

The great majority of the sightings my informants reported, however, were by men. And they formed an interesting pattern. Of the fifteen ghosts the informants themselves had seen, or reported that their friends and neighbors had seen, six were of unidentified sex. Of the remaining nine, four were female and five male. The male ghosts, however, were not the spirits of ordinary Taiwanese men. Of the five male ghosts seen by males, four were foreigners—two Japanese and two Americans. And in every case, they were huge and fearsome. For example, an old man told me a story that happened during the Japanese colonial period. He had been walking near the hills in back of the village, he said, when he saw someone extremely tall—so tall that he himself would only come up to the man's breastbone—and wearing Japanese clothes. My informant said that the ghost vanished quickly, but he thinks it was the ghost of a Japanese who had been killed in the area. Another story told of a planeload of Americans who had crashed in the mountains to the south of the village. People who looted the wreck got sick, and some of them could hear the American ghosts in the wreckage, babbling, my informant told me, in their strange, incomprehensible language.

One thing these stories of Japanese and American male ghosts all share is that the ghosts had been wronged (crashed in a plane and the wreckage looted, for example, or killed by someone) and would probably want to avenge themselves. And, as Japanese or Americans, both somewhat strange and mysterious, they appeared as ghosts. Since in this area many more Taiwanese men than foreigners had been killed in mining accidents, in resisting the Japanese occupation, and in other ways, it is striking that Taiwanese men almost never saw Taiwanese male ghosts.

Thus it becomes much clearer why almost all ghosts seen by men but of unspecified ethnicity (and thus presumably Taiwanese) were women. For example, one man reported that when he had been a pushcart-railway worker, he had gotten up in the middle of the night to go to work and had seen a ghostly woman sitting by the side of the road, sewing. He could not see her face clearly. The same man who reported the Japanese soldier ghost reported that a friend of his once saw a woman by an irrigation ditch, washing her hair at night. He thought she was a ghost and asked a Japanese policeman to come. The policeman did not believe him, but took his sword with him anyway, and sure enough, there she was. He struck with his sword and she vanished, but there was a little blood on the sword. The other stories of female ghosts were similar—men did not see their faces, but they were sitting by a road or stream, doing an ordinary female activity such as sewing or washing their hair.

Other investigators report the same thing—that when men see ghosts, the ghosts are usually female.[18] Wolf introduces another theme, without much comment, into stories of encounters between living males and female ghosts—the theme of sexual threat. Wolf not only reports the story of a vengeful female ghost who squeezed a man's testicles until he screamed with pain in his sleep, he also reports the common belief that when a living man takes a spirit bride, her ghost actually comes to him the first night of the union and that her insatiable sexual demands leave the groom absolutely exhausted the next day.[19] And a large body of lore, reported by Johnston and other observers, mostly from north China, tells of the evil fox-spirits that manifest themselves as beautiful women and seduce men to their ruin.[20]

A pattern seems to emerge in all this. People see the kind of ghosts who would be likely to frighten them in life. Armed Japanese, huge Japanese or American men, and insatiably seductive females all can be very threatening to the average Chinese male. But the girl sitting by the roadside sewing or washing her hair seems to pose no such direct threat, until we realize that, from the Chinese male's perspective, all women present a threat. It is they who are introduced into the patrilocal, patrilineal family as strangers and thus lead to its breakup and demise. It is they who, from the male's perspective, are the amoral creatures who act only from selfish motives, not from moral reasoning. I was once told by a village man that all the world's troubles could ultimately be traced to women, and most of his male compatriots would probably agree at least to some extent. Also, as pointed out by Potter, women are downtrodden and thus, like the vengeful ghosts who lurk near the place of death, out for revenge. But the vengeful ghosts are never or almost never seen, while the ordinary female ghosts are seen quite frequently. This is precisely because the

Chinese male feels somewhat guilty for the oppression of women in his society and at the same time very afraid of the destructive power of females in the kinship system. Whereas the vengeful ghosts are anomalous, like the women who die unmarried, the ordinary women ghosts are not anomalous at all. They are simply fearsome and at the same time have cause for wanting to get back at the system that oppressed them. No wonder they enter into the projective imaginations of so many men.

Summary

We can now review the relationship of the gender of ghosts to the different perspectives of those who interact with them. In the first two contexts, *Pudu* and conflict offerings, ghosts are both anonymous and invisible, so their gender conforms to the folk analytic perspective—they can be either gender, though perhaps in the case of *Pudu,* since they seem to be thought of as wandering gangs, they may be predominantly male. Because of the nature of gender roles in the society, however, in the first context both women and men interact with the ghost, while in the second primarily the women interact with it. In the third context, that of identifying and placating family ghosts, the ghosts are identified with those who have suffered because of specific anomalies in the family system. Since it is usually women who suffer in these anomalous positions, the family ghosts are usually women, as are those who interact with them. In the final context, that of seeing ghosts, the ghosts are anonymous and thus are not associated with any particular anomaly, but they are seen and therefore are likely to have a gender. In general, such ghosts represent categories of fearsome persons. From the perspective of any Taiwanese, Japanese and Americans probably fit this category, but from the perspective of either gender, Taiwanese of the other gender are fearsome. The difference is that women's fear of men is in a sense open and legitimate. Men's power to oppress women is a recognized part of the social system. Men's fear of women, on the other hand, must remain covert. Women's power is not part of the system; rather women have the power to subvert the system. So powerful goddesses, though they exist, are not reflections of female power. That power is manifested supernaturally by the ghosts who, like the disruptive female in the patrilocal family, can never be fully controlled.

114

Thus, to answer the simple question of the nature of ghosts in Taiwanese folk religion, we need to take gender issues into account. We find that a number of previously puzzling aspects of ghosts become clear once we consider them in light of the different roles and perspectives of men and women in the religious system.

Notes

1. The best accounts of Hokkien folk religion in Taiwan are Arthur P. Wolf, "Gods, Ghosts, and Ancestors," in *Religion and Ritual in Chinese Society,* ed. Arthur P. Wolf (Stanford: Stanford University Press, 1974), and David K. Jordan, *Gods, Ghosts, and Ancestors* (Berkeley and Los Angeles: University of California Press, 1972).
2. Stevan Harrell, "The Nature of the 'Soul' in Chinese Folk Religion," *Journal of Asian Studies* 38 (1979):519–28.
3. Wolf, "Gods, Ghosts, and Ancestors," p. 177.
4. Wolf, "Gods, Ghosts, and Ancestors," p. 170.
5. Ibid., pp. 150–53; Jordan, *Gods, Ghosts, and Ancestors,* pp. 146–50.
6. E. E. Evans-Pritchard, *Witchcraft, Oracles, and Magic among the Azande* (Oxford: Oxford University Press, 1937), pp. 63–82.
7. Most native terms are romanized in the Quanzhou dialect of Hokkien, as spoken in the Sanxia area in northern Taiwan. A few terms are romanized in Mandarin Chinese according to the pinyin system. These terms are indicated by an *M* preceding the romanization on their first occurrence.
8. Wolf, "Gods, Ghosts, and Ancestors," pp. 170–72.
9. Jordan, *Gods, Ghosts, and Ancestors,* pp. 169–71.
10. Stevan Harrell, "When a Ghost Becomes a God," in *Religion and Ritual in Chinese Society,* ed. Wolf.
11. Jordan, *Gods, Ghosts, and Ancestors,* pp. 138–71.
12. Ibid.
13. Ibid., pp. 155–64.
14. R. F. Johnston, *Lion and Dragon in Northern China* (New York: E. P. Dutton, 1910), pp. 219–27.
15. Jack M. Potter, "Cantonese Shamanism," in *Religion and Ritual in Chinese Society,* ed. Wolf, p. 229.
16. Kenneth K. S. Chen, *Buddhism in China* (Princeton: Princeton University Press, 1964), pp. 341–42.
17. The sample included married adults only. Because of time pressure, I interviewed only people under forty and over sixty. Half the respondents belonged to the older group and half to the younger; half were men and half women in each group.

18. Wolf, "Gods, Ghosts, and Ancestors," p. 146; Robert Weller, personal communication.

19. Wolf, "Gods, Ghosts, and Ancestors," p. 151.

20. Johnston, *Lion and Dragon in Northern China,* p. 289. It is not entirely clear whether fox-spirits have the same origin as other ghosts; it is clear enough, however, that they represent something similar to the family ghosts, the ghost brides, and most apparitions—they represent the seductive female who threatens the patrilineal order.

Five

The Priesthood and Motherhood in The Church of Jesus Christ of Latter-day Saints
Carolyn M. Wallace

This chapter examines various points of view—male and female, official and informal—among members of The Church of Jesus Christ of Latter-day Saints concerning the LDS priesthood and motherhood. When church members discuss doctrine, they use the concepts of priesthood and motherhood to clearly delineate responsibilities based on sex. They say, "Men have the priesthood; women have motherhood." LDS church leaders emphasize men and women's equality and the importance of the plan of salvation, but at the same time they stress differences: "We recognize men and women as equally important before the Lord, but with differences biologically, emotionally, and in other ways."[1]

The LDS priesthood and motherhood may be complementary, but, as the following analysis demonstrates, they are not symmetrical. While both LDS men and women appear to accept the spiritual significance of the priesthood, which stresses men's obligation to

The formal name, The Church of Jesus Christ of Latter-day Saints, is abbreviated to LDS church in this chapter; non–LDS church members often call its members Mormons.

This chapter is based on research conducted in 1978 and 1979 in Seattle, Washington, and Salt Lake City, Utah. Many of these ideas are discussed in somewhat different ways in the author's Ph.D. dissertation (C. M. Wallace, "Daughters of God: Meanings of Womanhood in The Church of Jesus Christ of Latter-day Saints," Ph.D. diss., University of Washington, 1982). The author wishes to thank Constance Faulkner, Irene Peters, Susan Starbuck, and Carolyn Woodward for their comments on previous drafts of this paper.

carry out its responsibilities and women's obligation to support it, motherhood remains problematic. Men accept their roles as spiritual leaders and fathers just as women accept their roles as supporters of the priesthood and childbearers. Men, however, address women's role as mother without making a clear distinction between a mother's responsibility in giving birth to children (maternity/biological motherhood) and her responsibilities in rearing children (nurturing/social motherhood). LDS women, on the other hand, do make this distinction, particularly when talking in informal settings. Their biological maternity provides them an accepted role in the plan of salvation; what LDS women find problematic are the stresses of nurturing motherhood.

This chapter explores the asymmetry between the priesthood and motherhood by investigating male and female perspectives on the two concepts. Priesthood and motherhood are best understood in the context of LDS beliefs about salvation, the focus of the next section of this chapter. Following that, a section discusses male and female perceptions of the priesthood, whose public and private components structure LDS men's experiences in particular ways. The section on motherhood examines the official notion of motherhood promulgated by church leaders, contrasting it with women's attempts to interpret the experience of motherhood. The final section addresses relationships among LDS doctrine, the priesthood, motherhood, and women's experiences.[2]

Gender and the Plan of Salvation

The spiritual and social significance of the priesthood and motherhood grow out of LDS doctrine about the family, which the church considers the basic unit of both this society and the future life. Human spiritual development depends upon the family as the vehicle of salvation. The obligations associated with the priesthood and motherhood require men and women to take distinct actions as family members during earthly life, thereby assuring not only their personal salvation but also the continuation of the larger eternal process entailed in the divine plan of salvation. Although the priesthood and motherhood both contribute to the attainment of salvation and spiritual maturity, differences between the two roles make them asymmetrical.

LDS doctrine posits continuity between the past, the present, and the future.[3] It holds that humans begin as spirits created during a premortal life called the preexistence. Created by a Heavenly Father and a Heavenly Mother, all spirits begin the process of attaining perfection as members of a heavenly family. This process, called eternal progression, continues when spirits assume mortal bodies on earth, where they live in human families. Spiritual maturity, defined as becoming a perfected being, occurs in the future life in eternal family groups.

God's plan of salvation encompasses space and time by delineating the responsibilities of individuals in each of the three phases of existence and defining their spiritual importance. God's laws and commandments provide order and purpose for the universe and all within it and give meaning to life, death, and eternity. The plan of salvation offers all spirits the possibility of salvation and spiritual maturity. Premortal existence, earthly life, and the future life are essential components of eternal progression.

Mortal existence is crucial to eternal progression because spirits obtain a physical body and gain the opportunity to live by faith, prepare for eternal life, and experience death. The physical body, which is considered the temple for the spirit, is necessary for the perfectability that LDS church members strive to attain. Women's place in LDS doctrine rests on their ability to create and give birth to new life, thus providing mortal bodies to spirits. Since spirits cannot attain spiritual maturity unless they live in the embodied state, maternity is an indispensable function.

The family is particularly important to eternal progression. As the basic unit of society, the family provides the context for spirits' mortal development into perfected beings and members of the highest of the three heavenly kingdoms, the celestial kingdom. Parents have the responsibility to teach their children about the plan of salvation. LDS church members hold that men and women have different roles in divinely given family organization: women create bodies for spirits and nurture them, while men, through the priesthood, link mortal existence and the future life.

Spiritual maturity depends on rituals whose efficacy rests on the spiritual significance attached to the priesthood. Only those who are baptized into the LDS church, receive the Holy Spirit, and participate in temple rituals become eligible for the celestial kingdom. Marriage in the temple (celestial marriage) is particularly important because it creates eternal family units that endure in the celestial kingdom, providing family members adhere to God's commandments. Only those who fulfill these requirements will become perfected beings who, living as members of multigenerational families, will have the power to create new worlds and spirits.

From this brief outline of beliefs, we can see that the role women play in the divine plan of salvation centers on maternity, a biological function, while the role men play centers on exercising the spiritual authority of the priesthood, a social act with profound implications for the process of eternal progression. Thus official LDS doctrine defines gender roles as asymmetrical. In Sherry Ortner's terms, the female role is defined as "nature," based in biology, while the male role is defined as "culture," based in an authority to perform certain social and religious acts.[4] But LDS doctrine also explicitly posits the two asymmetrical roles as equal. Given these doctrinal formulations, do the two sexes, posited as equal and asymmetrical, perceive themselves to be so in all contexts? I shall investigate how men and women see priesthood and motherhood in the following contexts: the general church conferences, worship services, and meetings held especially for LDS women.

Perspectives on the Priesthood
LDS Men and the Priesthood

LDS doctrine defines the priesthood as the "power to act in the name of God,"[5] a definition stressing a culturally defined capacity rather than any particular biological endowment as the basis for membership in the LDS priesthood. This definition contrasts clearly with definitions of motherhood, which are explicitly based on the biological capacity to bear children. The following statement, made by a man during a local (ward) worship service, summarizes the responsibilities of males:

> The purposes of existence are the following: to be proved by God; to receive a body of flesh and bones; to prove we can keep our second estate; to develop our gifts and talents; to account to God for our stewardship; to meet the requirements for celestial glory—for men, to

be a High Priest in the Melchizedek priesthood; to be sealed to a companion for time and eternity [celestial marriage]; and to have children, who are a heritage of the Lord.

Through the performance of rituals and through continuation of what are called "patriarchal chains,"[6] lineages traced through males with membership in the priesthood, the priesthood plays essential roles in the plan of salvation.

The male members of the LDS church who are twelve years of age or older and who meet the church's standards become members of the LDS priesthood, which has two orders, the Aaronic (lower) priesthood and the Melchizedek (higher) priesthood. Each priesthood order is comprised of three grades, with particular responsibilities for conducting rituals and managing church programs. The grades of the Aaronic priesthood move in progression from teacher to deacon and then to priest, with an associated increase in what are considered the spiritual authority and responsibilities of the priesthood. Elder, the first grade of the Melchizedek priesthood, possesses all the spiritual authority available to the priesthood. The other grades, called seventy and high priest, are distinguished primarily by their specific duties for maintaining the church and its programs. Membership in each grade requires a brief ritual, which can only be performed by a member of the priesthood who holds a higher grade. When LDS church members refer to the priesthood, they include both those males who are its members in all grades and its assumed spiritual authority.

The priesthood is so important to salvation and spiritual maturity, only its members can perform those rituals that are required for the attainment of the celestial kingdom. Women can perform none of these crucial rituals, and thus they must depend on the priesthood.

Baptism is necessary for membership in the LDS church and a prerequisite for membership in the celestial kingdom. Only the priesthood has the authority to conduct the ritual that publicly affirms church membership and confers the Holy Ghost as inner spiritual guide. While these rituals establish church membership, the temple rituals extend the spiritual authority of the priesthood through time and space by instructing faithful church members about their obligations to themselves and the church. Access to an LDS temple has certain restrictions: only those church members who receive permission from designated priesthood leaders may enter a temple and participate in temple rituals. Participation in these rituals, including what are called the endowment ceremonies, requires church members to demonstrate through their actions their worthiness to enter a temple and their intention to remain faithful adherents to church doctrine and standards of conduct. Couples desiring celestial marriage must have participated in the endowment ceremonies. The celestial marriage ceremony binds a man, a woman, and their children into a mortal and an eternal family. So long as church members remain faithful to the church and live according to its standards, the bonds established by celestial marriage are considered eternal as well as temporal ones. Members of the priesthood officiate at all of these rituals, demonstrating its spiritual authority.

The priesthood also establishes the patriarchal chains that link families through the generations. Thus women are dependent on the priesthood in another way as well: only the priesthood establishes the possibility of multigenerational family units. Spiritual maturity occurs in eternal families, which are joined by ties traced through members of the priesthood. These patriarchal chains eventually establish genealogical links to the Old Testament figure Adam, considered the first spirit to experience the mortal state. The patriarchal chain thus establishes an order on earth as well as in heaven, an order that both expresses and depends on priesthood authority.

Male church leaders emphasize the spiritual significance of the priesthood in their lectures at general church conferences. The church holds these conferences twice each year in Salt Lake City, Utah. The speakers at these meetings are all priesthood leaders, with the exception of the general president of the Relief Society (the auxiliary organization for women), who speaks at one conference session. One session of each general conference is devoted solely to the priesthood. Although only males attend this session in Salt Lake City or participate via the church's communications network, the proceedings are published in the church's general magazine and conference reports and are available to both men and women.[7] This session emphasizes the spiritual obligations of members of the Aaronic and Melchizedek priesthoods.

The speakers at these sessions stress that the priesthood is the cornerstone of the church. One speaker, for example, cautions his listeners: "Each priesthood bearer must take advantage of every opportunity to testify of the Savior and teach and exemplify gospel truth, letting his light so shine before friends and strangers alike to perpetuate the truth concerning our Savior, Jesus Christ."[8] Although men's obligations to the church are often posed in general terms, called "honoring the priesthood," two elements stand out: the need for obedience to the church president, who is considered a prophet, and the importance of carrying out the duties associated with the priesthood and other church assignments. Because all church programs depend on the priesthood, "the full weight of governing the Church rests squarely on the priesthood."[9] Another leader's words indicate that the importance of the priesthood to the church cannot be overestimated: "We belong to the Church of Jesus Christ. . . . We hold the priesthood of God, and the progress of the Church depends on us and how fully we magnify our callings and follow the instructions of our present-day prophet."[10] Thus, the success or failure of the church rests with its priesthood members.

In addition to gradually undertaking greater and greater responsibilities in the priesthood, men fulfill their soteriological duties through missionary service. As missionaries they present the plan of salvation to the world. At the general church conferences young men regularly hear of their obligation to serve as missionaries: "There is a growing need for more missionaries. . . . Young men, with the encouragement of their parents, should begin early in life to prepare."[11] Missionaries convey the plan of salvation throughout the world, enabling others to join the LDS church and thereby have the possibility of the celestial kingdom. Besides proselytizing, missionary service further socializes church members into active support of its programs. For example, church leaders stress that serving as a missionary prepares young men for a lifetime of church activity. One church leader called missionaries "a royal army,"[12] which develops personal attributes that also benefit the church. The missionary experience, like all church service, requires "a desire to serve, the patience to prepare, and a willingness to labor."[13]

Even fatherhood is secondary to the priesthood for males. Church members' discussions of fatherhood show this clearly: priest-as-father contains both spiritual and social significance, while father in itself has limited spiritual significance. The function of the priesthood is crucial: men must learn God's will for their families and then carry it out. One man's remarks in a talk given at a ward worship service illustrate how men use the priesthood to provide its spiritual benefits in family life: "The priesthood is a father's best tool. It can be used to give a blessing and a name, for baptism and confirmation, and for healing. Our prayers should be sincere. We should pray for our children—a different prayer for each child because each is different and has different needs." Thus a father can only fulfill his role properly if he performs the ritual duties (such as blessing, baptism, or confirmation) of the priesthood properly.

In sum, male perceptions of the priesthood are defined in terms of its spiritual power and the capacity to act in ways conducive to LDS soteriological goals. As can be seen from doctrinal summaries and the statements of members of the priesthood, both prominent church leaders and participants in ward churches, the priesthood entails the acquisition of its various grades, the performance of rituals essential to the process of eternal progression, and service to the church. Even fatherhood is subsumed under the priesthood.

As we shall see in the second part of this chapter, the basis of the priesthood differs markedly from the basis of motherhood. Priesthood is a public and cultural role, which subsumes biological fatherhood. In contrast, motherhood is based primarily on women's biological capacity to bear children. In the official definition of the female role, the more public and cultural aspects of "mothering" (i.e., rearing and educating the child) are subsumed into the biological aspect.

LDS Women and the Priesthood

Neither LDS men nor women seem to have difficulty defining, accepting, or understanding their individual relationship to the priesthood. Women acknowledge and depend upon the priesthood for access to salvation and the celestial kingdom as well as for the existence of the church and the organizations for women and young women. Women clearly feel a commitment to support the priesthood.

Discussion of the relationship of women to the priesthood and its functions takes place when all the female members of the church twelve years and older gather approximately once a year for a meeting that emphasizes women's place in the church and their obligations as faithful LDS women.[14] This meeting, like sessions of the church general conferences, takes place in Salt Lake City; it is broadcast to local LDS churches via the church's communications network. The women who serve as the presidents of the auxiliary organizations for women (the Relief Society), young women (the Young Women), and children (the Primary) speak at these meetings,[15] as does a highly placed priesthood leader. The female leaders in particular emphasize the importance of the special women's meeting. Not required by the scriptures nor part of the auxiliary organizations, the women's meeting only occurs at the pleasure of the priesthood and under its aegis.

One topic remains constant from year to year: the significance of the priesthood for the auxiliary organizations and for women generally. A former Young Women president emphasized the privilege that LDS women enjoy to meet together under priesthood authority in her remarks at one of these meetings: "We see it [the special women's meeting] as a significant enveloping of all of us under the mantle of the mouthpiece of the Lord, President Spencer W. Kimball."[16] Another woman (the Primary president) thanked priesthood leaders for the authority that makes these meetings possible: "May I add my appreciation for this blessed opportunity to be together again as women throughout the world, gathered together to hear words of encouragement and direction."[17]

These remarks express gratitude and indicate the recognition that the women's meeting (like the Relief Society, the Young Women, and the Primary) depends upon the priesthood. LDS doctrine establishes the authority and necessity for members of the priesthood to provide spiritual guidance to church members. The special women's meeting is not structurally or organizationally required; only priesthood leaders possess the authority to give permission for the meeting.[18] Priesthood leaders' attendance reinforces their spiritual and organizational authority and makes clear the contrast between priest and nonpriest.

An analysis of comments made during several of these women's meetings indicates that faithful LDS women feel the need and responsibility to recognize, respect, and support the priesthood, thereby helping to advance those general purposes to benefit all church members. A former president of the Young Women clearly stated women's obligations to assist the priesthood:

> Through this is the day of women, I pay tribute to the men who lead us, who bless us, who pray over us and with us, and who would gladly raise their voices more frequently in our defense, if only we would let them raise their voices! It is exciting to be an active participant as a woman in all that is being done for us by the brethren. . . . Brethren, thank you. . . . We honor the priesthood of God which you bear and appreciate the errand you are on. We women want to help, and not hinder.[19]

She implies that women do not need to do more for themselves: those women who truly understand the significance of the priesthood find such actions unnecessary.

Women in these meetings express their belief that cooperation between women and the priesthood creates a strong church. For example, the Young Women president called on LDS women to express by their actions the supportive relationship between the priesthood and women's participation in the church. She found the cooperation between those members who hold the priesthood and women the source of the strength of the church and the significance of women's roles. By exhorting women to appreciate the priesthood and allow it to be used to their benefit, women enhance the church's primary purpose—to advance the plan of salvation.

In local (ward) churches as well, women indicate great respect for the priesthood. Members stress the benefits that accrue to all when men fulfill their priesthood responsibilities. For example, one woman church member discussed men's personal qualities and their priesthood obligations at a ward worship service:

> Priesthood holders should attend all church meetings, especially priesthood meetings, and be a good example in all things. They are important to women as home teachers [who visit members' homes monthly], as a good friend and companion, and because they can perform ordinances. I need example, kindness and leadership from the priesthood. If they do what they ought to do, they'll be good examples to all of us.

By locating the primary expression of maleness in the priesthood, she stresses the appropriate actions that members of the priesthood undertake: attending church meetings; exemplifying correct behavior; visiting church members and making available the priesthood's guidance and spiritual authority; and conducting those rituals necessary for eternal progression.

The remarks of these women, one a well-known leader in the church and the other a participant in ward activities, focus on the same issue: how the priesthood benefits women. There are two sides to this question: the actions that members of the priesthood take and the women's responses to those actions. Their responses reveal a set of obligations that extend beyond mere acceptance of the ways in which the priesthood benefits women.

One obligation requires LDS women to assist members of the priesthood, enabling men to fulfill their prescribed responsibilities. "Supporting the priesthood" encompasses a variety of actions, including church members' voluntary acceptance of church jobs and positive responses to the priesthood's requests for time, effort, or money for church programs. "Supporting the priesthood" also involves women making personal sacrifices. One woman, wife of a man with many priesthood obligations, analyzed her duties this way in a talk given at a ward worship service:

> An example from my own life is supporting my husband in his priesthood callings [assignments]. It's important for me to do these things: be cheerful when he goes to meetings; not complain when he comes home; free myself of resentments, so then our family will be cooperative; and have a positive attitude and good will.
>
> Our attitude is very important. Women's responsibility is to support men who want to magnify their priesthood calling. Here are some suggestions on how we can do this. We need to feel good about ourselves in order to be self-reliant. We must assess our strong points and our weaknesses and then resolve to make changes that will help us to achieve our goals. We can learn to exercise will-power, self-control and discipline. Finally, we should set aside a block of time one to three times a week to do something for ourselves.

Clearly, women recognize both the authority of the priesthood and its members and women's obligation to facilitate male performance of those duties required by the priesthood.

In order to adequately uphold the work of priesthood members this speaker, like the leaders of the auxiliary organizations, encourages women to develop attitudes and actions that demonstrate their recognition of the relationship between women and the priesthood. She understands women's responsibilities to act in ways that allow men to carry out those activities appropriate to the priesthood. She does not question the necessity for women to adjust to the demands the priesthood places on men. The problem is not conceived in structural terms; instead it is perceived as requiring personal adjustments on the part of women. In this formulation, the crucial issue is clear: the ways women must examine their attitudes and actions and direct them toward supporting the priesthood. Important topics include women's images of themselves and their ability to demonstrate their support of the priesthood. This speaker links these issues to a theme discussed later in this chapter, the notion that correct actions are insufficient in themselves unless they arise as part of personal spiritual development.

The conceptions LDS women and men hold of the priesthood reveal similarities: both women and men accept the primacy of the priesthood in the church and the family. LDS doctrine provides a more encompassing set of spiritual and social roles for men via the priesthood than it provides for women via motherhood. Although LDS doctrine posits complementarity between LDS males and females in the plan of salvation, only members of the priesthood have fundamental organizational roles in the church. For example, only members of the priesthood can hold the positions of church president, member of the Quorum of the Twelve Apostles (second in authority to the church president), stake (unit composed of wards, commonly ten) president or high councilman, ward bishop (highest leader in a local church), ward clerk, or president of the ward Teachers Quorum of the Aaronic priesthood.

LDS church organization is based on the priesthood, which bears responsibility for all church programs. These diverse programs, including, for example, the auxiliary organizations, the missionary program, and building construction and maintenance, are intended to carry out God's command to spread the gospel. Their goals are spiritual. As LDS doctrine establishes the spiritual primacy of the priesthood as the organizational principle of the church, it also establishes asymmetry between males and females. So while women play important roles in many church programs, their participation is fundamentally different from that of men: women participate in programs that do not have the structural significance attached to the priesthood. For example, although women speak in ward worship services, participate in conferences, and constitute the overwhelming majority of workers in the auxiliary organizations (which also include the Sunday School), they perform these activities and fill church jobs at the request of the priesthood. While more LDS women now serve as missionaries, having similar training and obligations to preach the gospel and be positive examples for the church, they cannot baptize those whom they proselytize and bring to church membership. However important to the church and to women's (and men's) spiritual development, women's participation in these programs remains secondary because the priesthood bears primary responsibility for the church. A widely quoted LDS aphorism expresses the matter succinctly: "If the priesthood were functioning correctly, the auxiliary organizations [which include the Relief Society, the Young Women, and the Primary] would not be necessary."

These structural differences do not lead to men's and women's having basically different views of the priesthood. The differences lie instead in the ways in which men and women understand "supporting the priesthood." Simply put, both men and women need to direct their actions toward enabling the priesthood to fulfill its responsibilities. For men, the doctrine of the priesthood provides clear direction for their actions. For women, the situation is somewhat different: their acceptance of the necessity to act in support of the priesthood requires them to respond to the priesthood. The combination of the requirement that women support the priesthood and fulfill their roles as mothers creates tension between women's roles as based in LDS doctrine and women's experiences.

Perspectives on Motherhood
LDS Church Leaders' Views on Motherhood

Motherhood is the female complement of the male priesthood. As established in LDS doctrine and understood by church members, motherhood constitutes the earthly expression of divinely given creative power to give birth to embodied spirits and thus provide them with the opportunity for salvation and spiritual maturation. Male church leaders tend to depict motherhood primarily in terms of maternity. When they recognize nurturing motherhood, it is usually subsumed under maternity. In contrast, LDS women separate these two functions. Church leaders stress the significance of maternity to the plan of salvation. Remarks by a former church president at one of the women's meetings locate maternity in the divinely established order of the universe: "This [maternity] is the great, irreplaceable work of women. Life cannot go on if women cease to bear children. Mortal life is a privilege and a necessary step in eternal progression. Mother Eve understood that. You must also understand it."[20] Because of women's biological capacity to provide spirits with a mortal body, these remarks stress that maternity constitutes women's fundamental contribution to God's plan for the universe. Male church leaders underscore the equality between men's roles and women's roles. For example, when the former church president addressed the special women's meeting, he urged LDS women to consider their social roles in a spiritual context of equality:

> The scripture and the prophets have taught us clearly that God, who is perfect in his attribute of justice, "is no respecter of persons" (Acts 10:34). . . . We had full equality as his spirit children. We have equality as recipients of God's perfected love for each of us. The late Elder John A. Widtsoe wrote: "The place of woman in the Church is to walk beside the man, not in front of him nor behind him. In the Church there is full equality between man and woman. The gospel, which is the only concern of the Church, was devised by the Lord for men and women alike" (*Improvement Era,* March 1942, p. 161).

This spiritual context, with its assumed equality between the sexes, provides the basis from which to postulate complementarity between men and women:

> Within these great assurances, however, our roles and assignments differ. These are eternal differences—with women being given many tremendous responsibilities of motherhood and sisterhood and men being given the tremendous responsibilities of fatherhood and the priesthood—but the man is not without the woman nor the woman without the man in the Lord.[21]

Both the differences and the complementarity between men and women are seen as part of the divine plan.

The ideas expressed in this last quotation are worth pondering because these remarks illustrate the asymmetry of motherhood and priesthood. Motherhood does not have spiritual significance similar to that of the priesthood. Nor do male church members usually distinguish maternity and nurturing motherhood, although they do recognize differences between the priesthood and fatherhood. Finally, the term *sister* reminds members of women's status as daughters of heavenly parents and members of Christ's church, but no further comparison is possible because sisterhood complements neither fatherhood nor the priesthood; it is not parallel to them.

When male church leaders' discussion of motherhood includes both maternity and nurturing motherhood, they treat the two as if they were both part of the same role, allowing women to act according to a divine plan. According to a former church president, sacred maternity is immediately followed by sacred nurturing: "Mothers have a sacred role. They are partners with God, as well as with their own husbands, first in giving birth to the Lord's spirit children and then in rearing these children so they will serve the Lord and keep his commandments."[22] Although his comments suggest the profound importance of motherhood, the fusion of childbearing (maternity) with child rearing (nurturing) obscures their spiritual and social differences. Women's contribution to the plan of salvation is maternity; their contribution to social life is nurturing motherhood.

When male speakers discuss nurturing motherhood, they discuss it as a component of eternal progression. For example, one speaker in a ward worship service assessed his mother's example: "Home is where we learn what is right and to be good and kind. I also learned about obedience, freedom, making decisions, the joys of uniqueness and humor, support and gospel principles, which freed me from the constraints of the world. As a wife and mother, she shares in the priesthood and is the supporter of the home." This speaker sees nurturing motherhood entirely in soteriological terms. Mothers teach children proper values and therefore assist in eternal progression. Mothers' spiritual role rests on helping their children develop the faith and commitment to God's commands that prove worthiness for the celestial kingdom.

While the church president and the presidents of the Relief Society and the Young Women exhort women to understand and appreciate maternity because it is integral to the plan of salvation, they also urge women to remember that they are partners with the priesthood in carrying out the church's main purpose. A former

Relief Society general president framed women's work in relation to that of the priesthood: "We are the people raised up to do this work; we, the women of the church, hand-in-hand with the men— our husbands, our sons, our brothers in the priesthood. May the Lord bless us as women with that eternal perspective."[23] Elaborating on church doctrine, she urges women to become partners in the work of the church by influencing others to follow God's commandments and thereby reap eternal rewards. A former president of the Young Women similarly presented traditional church doctrine when discussing women's obligation to the priesthood:

> Sisters, this church is the saving remnant of the world. And what is our part as women in all of this? The girl is the future mother of the man. The woman is companion to the priesthood. She is molder of the next generation. As women ours is the gift to love, to influence for good, to marry, and to mother—but according to the timetable of the Lord for us.[24]

For her, women must concentrate on their roles in the family and the church, especially in relation to the men who hold the priesthood.

In sum, when male church leaders or females who hold leadership positions in the auxiliary organizations speak to church members, they present a strictly doctrinal view of motherhood. The discussion of maternity in church conferences and the special women's meeting occurs in contexts where spreading the message of God's plan of salvation is paramount. Insofar as maternity is crucial to fulfilling what are considered divine commandments, speakers accentuate maternity and pay less attention to nurturing motherhood, or they see the latter only as an extension of the former.

LDS Women's Experience of Motherhood

While church leaders present glowing descriptions of motherhood, women in LDS wards express their concerns about the experience of motherhood. Presupposing maternity, they emphasize nurturing motherhood. These concerns appeared more clearly in a special training session for ward Relief Society leaders and teachers that was held prior to the beginning of the church educational year.

An informal workshop for ward teachers of Mother Education lessons highlighted the contrasts between doctrinal formulations of motherhood and the experience of motherhood that participants had undergone.[25]

Women's discussion of motherhood at this meeting directly addressed the problems mothers face. The topic of raising children dominated the seminar. The seminar leader, introduced as a college graduate and a mother with training and experience in teaching, began by examining "some of the overwhelming feelings of being a mother." She cited examples—caring for several small children, dealing with children born in close succession, and balancing the physical demands of caring for a home and children—and concluded, "It's not easy to be a mother. It's a physical and emotional drain." Then, like the church president and the presidents of the Relief Society and Young Women, she called attention to women's experiences. In contrast to those leaders, however, she did not idealize maternity and nurturing motherhood. Instead, she acknowledged that difficult circumstances and discouragement comprise part of women's experience of motherhood.

Although the training session leader appreciated women's emotional reactions to the experience of motherhood, she encouraged practical solutions to problems: "Help women know when they feel overwhelmed and then have them think of ways to overcome pressures." In addition to problem solving, she urged women to accept themselves. Her comments are important both as advice to women and as indirect references to problems with women's images of themselves: "The point is that you can't be someone you're not. It's not necessary to judge yourself by others. It's not necessary to criticize or to complain about what you're doing or what others are doing. You may not be able to do what everyone else does, but you can appreciate what others can do."

In a church with high standards for its members, women sometimes feel inadequate in comparison to their own and others' (or what they think are others') standards of achievement. Women may compare themselves negatively with others, deciding that their attainments are minor. The seminar leader emphasized the futility of such actions and urged LDS women to appreciate themselves.

Discussion of these questions also occurs in ward Relief Society meetings. During one such meeting, the Mother Education lesson

133

teacher presented a theory for using female skills, linking actions and emotions to spiritual principles:

> Acting is usually appropriate and controlled behavior. There are different actions, depending on the situation. . . . When acting, you feel proud, self-confident, and powerful. Christ's example also included an emphasis on calm and loving behavior.

Then she specified some of the consequences of appropriate actions:

> The main benefit of acting is that it teaches children ways of behaving. This is how we all learn to parent. Acting also improves communication between people. There are pitfalls to reacting. Communication barriers are set up and physical and emotional tension are created. There is loss of mutual respect between spouses and loss of self-esteem. It also sets you up to be defensive and to retaliate. Defensiveness leads to rationalizing our behavior. Reacting also causes negative responses in our children, including lying, cheating, and sexual offenses.

She constructed a simple model of behavior: acting produces positive responses from others, while reacting produces negative responses. If women act correctly, they will enjoy self-esteem and others' respect. Otherwise, they risk the loss of both self-esteem and others' respect. Her advice was specific: "You LDS mothers can plan to act instead of reacting. There are two steps in this process: (1) predict your child's behavior and plan your actions ahead of time; and (2) work on yourself." This teacher expected mothers to use their knowledge about themselves and their children both to anticipate situations and to figure out appropriate responses.

Several mothers had trouble accepting this formulation, however reasonable it might sound. One mother felt that her family challenged her efforts: "Sometimes I feel as if there's a conspiracy against me at home. Rules are disobeyed and chores aren't done in spite of my efforts at cooperation." Another clearly saw the limits of her responsibilities: "I try to maintain a clean and orderly home, but it seems as if the children only mess it up. Then they won't help around the house." Another mother was simply frustrated: "It's hard for me to get my family's cooperation at home." The overall informal message of these comments seems to be that although the ideal for a perfecting mother is attractive to these women, they are not sure how to live up to that ideal.

Each of these mothers accepted responsibility for the home, attempted to fulfill her responsibility to be a good mother, and evaluated her attempts to create positive and cooperative family life. However, these mothers often saw their efforts undermined by their children's uncooperative behavior. These women agreed they had problems to solve. But no one at the meeting proposed any specific solutions: instead, the women turned inward and discussed ways to control their emotions and conduct as a means of solving their problems.

These women emphasized personal responsibility as a crucial component in motherhood. Their comments show how personal issues can be construed in spiritual terms, shifting the attention from ordinary experience to abstract spiritual principles. One woman stressed individual responsibility: "People are sometimes reluctant to admit that they do have some choices. It's very hard to achieve our own ideals, so the best choices are our own." Other women stressed learning to control feelings. One said, "People have a variety of feelings—so we're not always on an even keel. Without this, it would be boring and we'd never progress." Their comments suggest that because emotions are essential to earthly experience, everyone must learn to choose appropriate ways of handling emotions. These women concluded that they need to be prepared for the consequences of their actions: "You can always pray for help in being good mothers. But remember that prayers are often answered with opportunities and challenges."

By accepting an obligation to adhere to spiritual standards and to set good examples for their children, these women also appeared to hold themselves responsible for both their own and their children's conduct, or at least for the implications of their children's conduct. To this standard, they added their expectation to pay even closer attention to their own actions, judging them according to their ultimate spiritual context and significance.

LDS women, who presuppose maternity's spiritual significance, place greater stress on nurturing motherhood than on biological maternity in discussions at ward Relief Society meetings. Although maternity possesses doctrinal importance, women give maternity far less attention than understanding nurturing motherhood and its emotional strains. These differences in perceptions of motherhood merit some attention. First, beyond recognizing maternity's profound spiritual meaning, not much remains for discussion. Women are either mothers or they are not.[26] Church leaders' remarks about motherhood, whether made by men or women, reinforce the spiritual primacy of maternity. Second, nurturing motherhood provides a context for women to evaluate themselves and their contributions to the plan of salvation. The social context of nurturing motherhood allows them to act on spiritual principles. But since raising children is anything but abstract, women emphasize the day-to-day experience of motherhood more than its spiritual significance.

Conclusion

This chapter has examined several perspectives on the priesthood and motherhood in the LDS church. First, men's perspectives on the priesthood were outlined. Second, women's perspectives on the same topic were examined. Both men and women understand the nature of the LDS priesthood, recognize its significance to the church, and act accordingly.

The analysis of motherhood reveals that although it is held to be equal to the priesthood, they are asymmetrical in many ways. While the priesthood comprises the inseparable components of spiritual duties and fatherhood, motherhood remains simply motherhood. The priesthood exists because of LDS doctrinal formulations, whereas motherhood exists with or without that doctrine. Further, the priesthood's significance rests on nonbiological criteria while motherhood rests on female reproductive activity. The doctrine concerning the priesthood continues to be elaborated upon, in contrast to motherhood, which appears complete and requires only reinforcement.

One aspect of the asymmetry between the priesthood and motherhood is clearly revealed through an examination of men's and women's perspectives, as church leaders or participants in ward activities: while LDS church members divide the priesthood into carefully distinguished grades and ranks, the nature and facets of motherhood are telescoped in doctrine and discussion of LDS tenets. LDS males tend to see nurturing merely as a corollary to maternity. In contrast, LDS women themselves focus on nurturing motherhood rather than on maternity as having the primary meaning of motherhood.

Church leaders' discussion of motherhood is directed toward its spiritual significance not only because maternity constitutes the core of motherhood and complements the priesthood, but also because of the context provided by church conferences and other large meetings. In these settings, the significance of the priesthood and motherhood to eternal progression dominates discussion. Both men and women in church leadership positions put forth a doctrinally based viewpoint on motherhood. These "official" perspectives on motherhood stand in sharp contrast to women's discussion of motherhood in those church meetings not requiring the presence of members of the priesthood. In more informal settings, such as Relief Society seminars or meetings, women seek to reconcile their experiences of motherhood with its spiritual importance. They seek to resolve the discontinuities between maternity and nurturing motherhood by formulating personal questions. The informal perspective on motherhood, based on private rather than public experience, remains particular to LDS women. It appears to be the one place where women take on a gender role more complex than that assigned to them by official doctrine.

Further clarification of these perspectives is complicated by the structure of the LDS church: for example, attendance at some meetings is restricted to priesthood members only. Other questions seem unlikely topics of discussion in meetings or are inappropriate because too personal or because of the presence of a non-LDS church member. Finally, the LDS church's concern for enhancing its members' faith and fulfilling its spiritual purposes has resulted in its leaders' emphasis on certainty rather than on ambiguity or contradictions in its members' experiences.

Notes

1. The Church of Jesus Christ of Latter-day Saints, "First Presidency Statement on the ERA," 1976.
2. Most studies of LDS doctrine and church organization address its historical, economic, and religious development. See, for example, James B.

Allen and Glenn M. Leonard, *The Story of the Latter-day Saints* (Salt Lake City: Deseret Book Company, 1976); Leonard J. Arrington and Davis Bitton, *The Mormon Experience* (New York: Alfred A. Knopf, 1979); Mark P. Leone, *The Roots of Modern Mormonism* (Cambridge: Harvard University Press, 1979); and Thomas F. O'Dea, *The Mormons* (Chicago: University of Chicago Press, 1957).

Other studies examine women's roles in the church's development. Among these studies are Leonard J. Arrington, "Blessed Damozels: Women in Mormon History," *Dialogue: A Journal of Mormon Thought* 2 (1971):22–31; Vicky Burgess-Olson, ed., *Sister Saints* (Provo, Utah: Brigham Young University Press, 1978); Claudia Bushman, ed., *Mormon Sisters* (Salt Lake City, Utah: Olympus Publishing Company, 1976); Lawrence Foster, "From Frontier Activism to Neo-Victorian Domesticity: Mormon Women in the Nineteenth and Twentieth Centuries," *Journal of Mormon History* 6 (1979):3–21; Kenneth W. Godfrey, Audrey M. Godfrey, and Jill Mulvay Derr, *Women's Voices: An Untold Story of the Latter-day Saints, 1830–1900* (Salt Lake City, Utah: Deseret Book Company, 1982); Marilyn Warenski, *Patriarchs and Politics: The Plight of the Mormon Woman* (New York: McGraw-Hill, 1978).

Two scholarly studies of the relationship between ideas about sexuality and gender roles in nineteenth-century utopian communities in the United States discuss the Mormons. They are Lawrence Foster, *Religion and Sexuality: Three American Communal Experiments of the Nineteenth Century* (New York: Oxford University Press, 1981), and Louis Kern, *An Ordered Love: Sex Roles and Sexuality in Victorian Utopias—The Shakers, the Mormons, and the Oneida Community* (Chapel Hill: University of North Carolina Press, 1981).

3. The LDS church recognizes the *Book of Mormon,* the *Doctrine and Covenants,* and the *Pearl of Great Price* as scriptures that supplement the King James Version of the Bible.

4. Sherry B. Ortner, "Is Female to Male as Nature is to Culture?" in *Woman, Culture, and Society,* Michelle Z. Rosaldo and Louise Lamphere, eds. (Stanford, California: Stanford University Press, 1974), pp. 67–88.

5. Bruce R. McConkie, *Mormon Doctrine,* 2d ed. (Salt Lake City, Utah: Bookcraft, 1979), pp. 594–95.

6. Ibid., pp. 558–59.

7. Both women and men may attend conference sessions other than the priesthood session. The texts of all talks given in sessions of the conferences are published in conference reports and the church magazine, *Ensign.* Most of the discussion of the priesthood in this paper draws upon the published proceedings of the priesthood sessions.

8. Joseph B. Wirthlin, "Let Your Light So Shine," *Ensign* 8 (Nov. 1978):36–37, esp. 37.

9. William R. Bradford, "The Governing Ones," *Ensign* 9 (May 1979):37–39, esp. 39.

10. N. Eldon Tanner, "Put On the Whole Armor of God," *Ensign* 9 (May 1979):43–46, esp. 46.

11. Spencer W. Kimball, "The Lord Expects Righteousness," *Ensign* 12 (Nov. 1982):4–6, esp. 6.

12. Thomas S. Monson, "The Army of the Lord," *Ensign* 9 (May 1979):35–37, esp. 35.

13. Ibid., pp. 35–37, esp. 37.

14. The Relief Society met yearly in a general conference until 1974. A special meeting for church women was not held again until 1978. Since then, women have had a special meeting approximately once a year.

15. These women, who have long histories of service in the church, are appointed by the First Presidency (the highest level of authority) for an indefinite period. The Relief Society and Young Women general officers quoted in this paper served until April 1974, when the First Presidency appointed new officers.

16. Elaine Cannon, "If We Want to Go Up, We Have to Get On," *Ensign* 8 (Nov. 1978):107–108, esp. 107.

17. Naomi M. Shumway, "Teaching Our Little Women," *Ensign* 9 (Nov. 1979):104–105, esp. 104.

18. The talks at these meetings are published in the church magazine, *Ensign.* Although I attended several of these meetings in local LDS churches, I quote from the published talks.

19. Elaine Cannon, "Our Mighty Errand," *Ensign* 9 (Nov. 1979):106–107, esp. 107.

20. Spencer W. Kimball, "Privileges and Responsibilities of Sisters," *Ensign* 8 (Nov. 1978):102–106, esp. 105. President Kimball died in November, 1985; his successor is Ezra Taft Benson.

21. Spencer W. Kimball, "The Role of Righteous Women," *Ensign* 9 (Nov. 1979):102–104, esp. 102.

22. Kimball, "Privileges and Responsibilities of Sisters," pp. 102–106, esp. 106.

23. Barbara B. Smith, "Women's Greatest Challenge," *Ensign* 8 (Nov. 1978):108–109, esp. 109.

24. Cannon, "If We Want to Go Up, We Have to Get On," pp. 107–108, esp. 108.

25. Mother Education is one of several lesson series prepared by the Relief Society General Board and approved by the appropriate educational department of the church. Each monthly lesson, addressing a

particular topic, is published in a lesson manual containing all Relief Society lessons.

26. Because motherhood carries fundamental spiritual significance, it is an essential component of the female experience. One result is the awkward position of single women and, to a lesser extent, childless married women in the LDS church. As long as these women adhere to the church's standards, they expect to be rewarded with marriage (in the case of single women) and motherhood in the next life.

Part 2

Gender as Polysemic Symbol

Six

The Portrayal of a Female Renouncer in a Tamil Buddhist Text

Paula Richman

In the Tamil Buddhist epic, *Maṇimēkalai*,[1] the author, Cāttaṉār, tells the story of a courtesan's daughter who renounces her hereditary occupation and becomes a Buddhist nun. How should one interpret this portrayal? In this chapter I provide two ways of analyzing Cāttaṉār's description of Maṇimēkalai's progress upon the path of religious renunciation. First, I consider the role of Tamil literary conventions in the unfolding story of Maṇimēkalai's religious quest, discussing the way these conventions help advocate female renunciation to a group of people among whom women have never become ascetics. From this perspective, Cāttaṉār's portrayal is gender-specific—it directly concerns the ways in which women can renounce sexual love and become Buddhist nuns. Second, I discuss the role of craving in Buddhist doctrine and the way Maṇimēkalai's status as a courtesan makes her a model of renunciation for all human beings. From this perspective, Cāttaṉār's portrayal is unmarked for gender—all those seeking enlightenment must overcome craving as Maṇimēkalai does. These two complementary interpretations demonstrate how Cāttaṉār's por-

A Fulbright-Hays Doctoral Dissertation Abroad Fellowship, granted for the study of *Maṇimēkalai* in India from December 1979 to February 1981, enabled the author to conduct the research upon which this article is based. The author is also grateful to Caroline Walker Bynum, Norman Cutler, Michael Fisher, Stevan Harrell, Jane Hunter, and Charles Keyes for their helpful comments on drafts of this article.

143

trait of a female renouncer can be seen as a model specifically for women as well as for all (male and female) human beings.

Introduction

Maṇimēkalai is a sixth-century Buddhist epic composed by Cīttalai Cāttanār in Tamil.[2] The second Tamil epic ever written,[3] *Maṇimē-kalai*'s main story is introduced as a sequel to Tamil's first epic, *Cilappatikāram*.[4] Despite the rather tenuous plot connections between the two epics, *Maṇimēkalai* is unique in being the only extant Tamil Buddhist epic.[5] Although Cāttanār's text is Buddhist in ideology, vocabulary, and character, he has carefully presented Buddhist ideas in a manner that will allow an audience relatively unfamiliar with Buddhism to understand and accept them. Because it is an epic, the text's didacticism manifests itself in story form.

Maṇimēkalai contains thirty chapters and is composed of a main story and sixteen minor stories.[6] Its main story, with which this chapter is concerned, depicts the spiritual growth of the heroine. Maṇimēkalai, a courtesan's daughter, decides to renounce her hereditary occupation and become a Buddhist nun, even though she feels attracted to a prince and he longs to have her as his mistress. The main story thus focuses largely on Maṇimēkalai's conflict between love and her attraction toward the Buddhist path.

First and foremost, *Maṇimēkalai* concerns female renunciation—its obstacles and successes. *Maṇi-mēkalai* means "jeweled girdle," the sort of ornament that Maṇimēkalai, daughter of a popular dancing girl in Pukār, would normally wear.[7] It would also be normal for the impetuous Prince Utayakumaraṉ to become attracted to her. Indeed, he does. What is abnormal, however, is Maṇimēkalai's unalterable decision to reject both the glamour of being a public woman and the prince's attention in order to embrace Buddhism. Because this decision would seem so unusual to the text's intended audience, it affords Cāttanār the opportunity to explain the motivation behind the young girl's resolution to become a renouncer.

In *Maṇimēkalai* Cāttanār explains many of the key concepts of Buddhism and advocates the practice of several of its virtues, including female renunciation, as part of his overall effort to persuade his audience to accept the validity and viability of the

144

Buddhist worldview. Around the time *Maṇimēkalai* was written, significant developments in Buddhist philosophy and monastic life occurred at places such as Kāñcīpuram and Kāvirippaṭṭinam in Tamilnadu.[8] It is against this background of growing interest in Buddhism throughout Tamil country that we must see Cāttaṉār's endeavor to convince his audience, whose members would be largely unfamiliar with Buddhism, that renunciation was an admirable religious undertaking for women.

Cāttaṉār depicts Maṇimēkalai as a woman pulled in two directions—she feels attracted to both Prince Utayakumaraṉ and the Buddhist path. Maṇimēkalai can devote herself fully to her quest for religious liberation only after she has understood and rejected her attachment to the prince. The conflict Maṇimēkalai feels between love and renunciation gives the epic its dynamic quality and provides the impetus for its events. Depicting both her increasing detachment from her desire for the prince and also her growing commitment to Buddhism, the four sections of the text alternately focus upon Maṇimēkalai's relationship with the prince and with the Buddhist path.

In the first section of the epic (chaps. 1–5), Cāttaṉār describes how Prince Utayakumaraṉ first becomes fascinated with Maṇimēkalai. As the epic opens Maṇimēkalai's mother, Mātavi, announces that she will not dance at the annual city festival this year. After seeing the terrible suffering of her lover, Maṇimēkalai's father, Mātavi has decided to give up the life of a dancing girl to become an ascetic and desires that her daughter do the same. Soon afterward, while Maṇimēkalai is making a flower garland, she thinks of her father's execution (resulting from a false accusation that he had stolen the queen's jeweled anklet) and begins to weep. Since her tears have ruined the flowers, she sets off with her companion Cutamati to pick some fresh blossoms in a garden on the other side of town. It is to this garden that Prince Utayakumaraṉ will eventually come in hopes of meeting with her.

After the prince subdues a rampaging, sexually maddened elephant that had run loose through the city and terrified its inhabitants, he hears from one of the townspeople that the extraordinary Maṇimēkalai has just passed. He immediately sets off to find her. When he reaches the garden he meets Cutamati, who tells the prince of her own conversion to Buddhism and concludes her tale with a lecture on the impermanence of the human body.

At this point, the prince catches sight of Maṇimēkalai, who has locked herself in a glass pavilion in the grove to escape from him. Seeing that his pursuit is hopeless, Utayakumaraṉ finally departs in frustration. As he leaves, he vows that Maṇimēkalai's grandmother, the matriarch of the courtesan community, will arrange for him to enjoy union with the girl. As soon as he departs, Maṇimēkalai confesses to Cutamati that, despite all her resolve, her heart has followed after the prince. She then expresses the hope that she will overcome her love for him.

In this first section, Cāttaṉār sets up the dimensions of Maṇimēkalai's conflict. Although she has decided to renounce her hereditary role as a courtesan, the world does not recognize her decision. Prince Utayakumaraṉ and the townspeople find it difficult to accept that this lovely young girl would give up the life of a dancer to become an ascetic. To complicate matters even further, Maṇimēkalai herself feels ambivalent about her decision because she is attracted to the prince.

In the second section of the narrative (chaps. 7–16), Cāttaṉār shifts his focus away from the love story to chart the path of Maṇimēkalai's spiritual progress. After the prince's departure, the goddess Maṇimēkalā, after whom the girl was named, arrives at the garden and takes the girl to Maṇipallavam Island, where a dharma seat discloses many events that transpired in her past lives.[9] The goddess reveals that because Utayakumaraṉ was her husband in a former birth, the girl feels drawn to him. The goddess discourages her from any further relations with the prince and tells her what she must do to fully practice virtue. To help Maṇimēkalai, the goddess teaches her special mantras (sacred syllables) that will enable her to change her bodily form, fly, and rid herself of hunger.

After the goddess departs, the guardian of the dharma seat leads Maṇimēkalai to a pond where, on the anniversary of the Buddha's birth each year, a bowl appears that is destined always to be filled with food. The bowl awaits a person who is intent on performing compassionate deeds. Accordingly, it enters Maṇimēkalai's hands and she vows to nourish hungry people from it.

This second section of the epic portrays Maṇimēkalai's initiation into Buddhism. Her trip to Maṇipallavam Island removes her from the clutches of the prince and brings her to a holy place. This island gains its significance from the presence of the dharma seat, where the Buddha once sat, and the pond from which the inexhaustible begging bowl emerges. Through the gift of the bowl, she receives the ability to nourish countless suffering people, thus practicing the Buddhist ideals of compassion *(karuṇa)* and giving *(dāna)*. She also learns that her present experiences are direct correlates of the deeds that occurred in her past life. In addition, she receives miraculous powers that will enable her to discharge the tasks she has undertaken, in spite of any obstacles she might encounter. In sum, in the second section of the epic, Maṇimēkalai is unencumbered by Utayakumaraṉ's advances and free to deepen her ties to Buddhism.

In the third section of the narrative (chaps. 17–24), Cāttaṉār again focuses upon the attraction between Maṇimēkalai and Utayakumaraṉ. He begins the section by describing the wonders of Maṇimēkalai's miraculous begging bowl. After Ātirai, who is known throughout the city as a chaste and virtuous housewife, places alms in the bowl, it never again becomes empty. Wandering through the streets of the city, Maṇimēkalai distributes food to the needy. Cāttaṉār compares her generous acts to rains nourishing the land and to a cow nurturing its calf. Because she is so virtuous, Maṇimēkalai convinces the king to transform the city prison into a house where suffering people can receive aid.

In contrast to Maṇimēkalai's desire to end the hunger of many starving people, Utayakumaraṉ becomes increasingly possessed by his obsession to unite sexually with Maṇimēkalai. Maṇimēkalai's grandmother Cittirāpati schemes with him to thwart the girl's vow of asceticism. Furious at the way Maṇimēkalai's renunciation has brought criticism upon the courtesan community, she vows before an assembly of dancing girls to arrange for Utayakumaraṉ to obtain his desire.

Maṇimēkalai then uses one of her mantras to take on another form—that of a woman named Kāyacaṇṭikai—so that she can avoid the prince's attentions. Unfortunately the prince eventually recognizes her despite her transformation and follows her about relentlessly, talking of her beauty. At the moment Maṇimēkalai begins to lecture the prince on the transience of the beauty of the human body, Kāyacaṇṭikai's husband appears. Seeing a woman whom he assumes to be his wife conversing intimately with another man, he is overcome with anger. When the prince returns to the temple late that night, determined to have his way with Maṇimēkalai, Kāyacaṇṭikai's husband lies in wait. Thinking that the prince

147

seeks his wife, the jealous husband slices him to pieces with his sword.

Reactions to the murder of Utayakumaraṉ form the core of the last part of this section. His death serves as the occasion for a series of religious discourses. As the discourse evolves, the focus shifts from the specific circumstances of the prince's death to an explanation of the underlying cause of the situation, according to Buddhist philosophy.

Thus, in the third section of the epic Cāttaṉār depicts the beneficial results of Maṇimēkalai's giving, the violent end of Utayakumaraṉ's lust, and the intellectual aftermath of the prince's murder. The "anti–love story" builds to a tragic climax, heightened by the forces arising from the schemes of Cittirāpati and a jealous husband's mistaken identification. The violent death abruptly ends the relationship between Maṇimēkalai and Utayakumaraṉ. This section culminates with a series of discourses arising from Utayakumaraṉ's death. As Buddhist authors in several cultures have long realized, the grief and separation that death invokes provide an appropriate starting point for an exposition of life's impermanence. Cāttaṉār has used Utayakumaraṉ's death as a suitable occasion for Buddhist preaching.

In the very last section (chaps. 25–30), Cāttaṉār shifts his focus entirely away from the love theme and toward Maṇimēkalai's attainment of ever higher levels of religious understanding. To this end, Cāttaṉār portrays the stages through which Maṇimēkalai passes as part of her ongoing training in Buddhist philosophy. These stages involve visits to learned men who specialize in each of the major non-Buddhist religious viewpoints.[10] Each of the learned men in Vañci presents an extremely terse summary of his particular religious system. Maṇimēkalai hears discourse after discourse, but finds none satisfactory. No Buddhist spokesman presents his views, but Maṇimēkalai's interspersed comments and criticisms indicate the Buddhist perspective from which all other discourses are evaluated.

Afterward, Maṇimēkalai goes to Kāñcī both to relieve the famine there with her miraculous bowl and to study with the great Buddhist sage Aṟavaṇa Aṭikaḷ. Now that she has learned and rejected other philosophical viewpoints, Aṟavaṇar deems her ready for comprehensive and detailed instruction concerning valid and invalid forms of argument. Cāttaṉār devotes an entire, lengthy chapter to Aravaṇar's exposition, outlining the component parts of syllogisms and the circumstances under which individual components of an argument may be judged fallacious or true. In this session of instruction, which is directed solely to Maṇimēkalai, one sees a progression in the type of teaching Maṇimēkalai receives: first Aravaṇa Aṭikaḷ sets out the terms of argumentation, and only afterward does he reveal the major arguments that comprise the Buddhist worldview.

As the final stage of Maṇimēkalai's higher education, Cāttanār then provides what might be termed a "Buddhist manual," a chapter densely packed with explanations of key Buddhist tenets. At the end of this chapter Cāttanār describes Aravaṇa Aṭikaḷ's preaching as "free of any inconsistency," implicitly contrasting it with the words of the Vañci philosophers whose speech contained flaws. Having heard this discourse composed of *dhamma* (Buddhist teaching, truth, or law), Maṇimēkalai dedicates herself to avoiding rebirth. In this way, Cāttanār's epic culminates with the ripening of Maṇimēkalai's renunciation and her commitment to the Buddhist path.

Having briefly reviewed the epic's plot and the salient characteristics of Maṇimēkalai's progress toward total renunciation, we must now ask why Cāttanār portrays her renunciation in the way that he does. More specifically, why does he portray Maṇimēkalai's religious progress as the avoidance of lovers' union? And why does Cāttanār choose a courtesan as the heroine of his epic? The first interpretation below proposes an answer to the former question while the second interpretation addresses the latter.

The Portrayal of Renunciation for Women

Cāttanār's portrayal of Maṇimēkalai's renunciation is structured so as to explain female renunciation as the noncompletion or nonfulfillment of a woman's role as lover. Cāttanār describes a new idea, female renunciation, by showing how it differs from an old and familiar idea, the union of a woman and her lover. In ancient Tamil literature, poets portrayed this union according to a highly schematized set of literary conventions. Cāttanār, always resourceful in the service of persuasion, uses these conventions and then twists them to define and advocate female renunciation. To see how Cāttanār uses these conventions didactically, one must investigate the status of female renunciation before Cāttaṉār, the conventional portrayal of the heroine in love poetry, and the way Cāttaṉār's portrayal of Maṇimēkalai ultimately departs from those conventions.

None of the existing literary evidence prior to *Maṇimēkalai* suggests that the Tamils were familiar with the idea of female renunciation. Even for males, a life of asceticism is relatively rare, although ancient Tamil literature contains enough scattered descriptions of male ascetics to assume some familiarity with the idea.[11] Since we lack any reference to female renouncers, we may assume that female renunciation was not a popular practice among ancient Tamils.

Whereas the classical texts do not mention renunciation for women, they are rife with descriptions of a woman's role as lover. Tamil love poems, comprising more than half of the 2,389 extant poems dating from the first to the third centuries A.D., were composed according to a shared vision that manifested itself in a body of literary conventions. These conventions, which have as their core the correlation between five natural landscapes and five phases of love, provided poets with an extensive set of shared symbols. In the afterword to his recent translation of a selection of these poems, A. K. Ramanujan describes the consensual nature of their poetic vision and explains the logic behind its name, *Caṅkam* poetry:

> the Tamil poets used a set of five landscapes and formalized the world into symbolism. By a remarkable consensus, they all spoke this common language of symbols for some five or six generations. Each could make his own poem and by doing so allude to every other poem which had been, was being, or would be written in this symbolic language. Thus poem became relevant to poem, as if they were all written by a single hand. The spurious name *Caṅkam* ('Fraternity,' 'Community') for this poetry was justified not by history but by the poetic practice.[12]

This shared vision included a highly stylized representation of female behavior as lover or beloved.

If the poets shared a common language, so did their audience. Both the *Caṅkam* poets and Cāttaṉār were able to take for granted their audience's familiarity with the motifs and conventions they incorporated into their poems. As Kenneth Bryant says, commenting about the nature of poetic convention in South Asian literature: "The first assumption is that a poem is a message, from a given poet to a given audience, whose proper transmission depends upon (among other things) poet and audience sharing a common language, and not only language in the ordinary sense, but also the more specialized language of poetic convention."[13] Cāttaṉār's readers had been schooled in this specialized language of poetic conventions, so he could take for granted his audience's knowledge of them. With them he could arouse certain expectations in his reader's mind, stretch the conventions to their limits, and ultimately go beyond them—all in the service of advocating that women become renouncers.

According to Tamil literary convention, poets most appropriately portray each phase of love against the background of a particular landscape. The portrayal of love displays five phases, encompassing both love in union and love in separation. These five are associated with five landscapes:

kuṟiñci (mountain)	clandestine lovers' union
mullai (forest)	patient waiting, domesticity
marutam (countryside)	man with courtesan and wife sulking
neytal (seashore)	anxious waiting
pālai (wasteland)	separation mixed with danger

Each landscape possesses an extensive set of characteristic features called *karupporuḷ*, "native elements," in categories such as appropriate time of day, flora, fauna, and presiding deity. Because of the way the situations of love are correlated with these elements, the poem's reader can easily identify the phase of love and landscape of a given poem merely by noting the presence of a particular native element. The system of native elements enables the poet to call up an entire landscape simply by mentioning a few: "As a result of this theory of composition, Tamil poets were able to use concise descriptive passages to create poems with complex layers of meaning, since reference to even one element of a landscape evoked the full range of subjects and themes associated with the landscape."[14] If one looks at Cāttaṉār's portrayal of Maṇimēkalai's renunciation with this system of correlations in mind, the way he depicts the young girl's interaction with Utayakumaraṉ reveals an inner logic.[15]

Cāttaṉār's use and modification of Tamil literary conventions

Table 6.1
The Five Landscapes, Their Corresponding Phases of Love, and Selected Native Elements

Landscape (*tiṇai*)	Phase of Love (*uṟi*)	Native Elements (birds, beasts, and deities) (*karupporuḷ*)
Kuṟiñci mountain	Clandestine lover's union	Peacock, elephant, *Murukaṉ*
Mullai forest	Patient waiting, domesticity	Forest hen, deer, *Māyōṉ*
Marutam countryside	Lover with courtesan and wife sulking	Heron, buffalo, *Indra*
Neytal seashore	Anxious waiting	Seagull, shark, *Varuna*
Pālai wasteland	Separation mixed with danger	Dove, wild dog, *Kāli*

Sources: Nārkavirāca Nampi, *Akapporuḷ Vilakkam* (Tinnevelly: SISS, 1979), p. 24A; A. K. Ramanujan, *The Interior Landscape* (Bloomington: Indiana University Press, 1975), p. 107; M. Shanmugan Pillai and David Ludden, *Kuṟunto-kai: An Anthology of Classical Tamil Love Poetry* (Madurai: Koodal Publishers, 1976), p. 30; Kamil Zvelebil, *The Smile of Murugan* (Leiden: E. J. Brill, 1973), p. 100; and my own reading of classical Tamil poetry.

clearly suggest the true nature and importance of female renunciation in the scene (chap. 4 of *Maṇimēkalai*) where Maṇimēkalai,
Cutamati, and Utayakumaraṉ go to the garden. In this scene,
Cāttaṉār prepares his audience for a lovers' tryst, facilitated by a
go-between. Through his use of the appropriate native elements,
Cāttaṉār arouses his audience's expectation that clandestine union
will occur.

The native elements Cāttaṉār incorporates into his narrative
would immediately bring to the mind of the Tamil listener the landscape of *kuṟiñci* (the mountains), the appropriate setting for the
secret meetings of lovers. Although the plot has developed in such
a way that Maṇimēkalai could not possibly run off to the mountains at this particular moment in the story, Cāttaṉār describes the
garden as if it were a mountain setting. The description of the
garden and the grove within it contain the native elements associated with the mountain landscape (see table 6.1): the rutting ele-
phants, scampering monkeys, and dancing peacocks figure prominently in *kuṟiñci* poems. The high trees in the grove to which
Maṇimēkalai retires block out the sun. The resulting dark and mysterious environment suggests night, the appropriate time for lovers
to steal away and meet in the *kuṟiñci* landscape. The deserted and
remote location of the grove, as well as the wild calls of the animals
that inhabit it, create a mood appropriate for a clandestine tryst.
The deity Murukaṉ, mentioned in the description of the grove,
presides over the *kuṟiñci* landscape, according to tradition. Thus,
for those versed in poetic convention, the description of the garden
and the grove within it call up the landscape of secret lovers.

In a similar way, Cāttaṉār creates an expected scenario for
Prince Utayakumaraṉ. The reader first encounters the dynamic
young prince in association with a wild elephant in rut. In accordance with the ancient Tamil technique of suggestion, the image of
the rutting elephant suggests the intensity of Utayakumaraṉ's
desire for Maṇimēkalai. When he reaches the garden, he tells her
friend Cutamati that Maṇimēkalai's eyes are like carp and her
teeth resemble pearls. These phrases formulaically express Utayakumaraṉ's appreciation for the beauty of the heroine and his intention to pursue the girl to obtain her sexual favors. In numerous
classical love poems, the hero begins his courtship with phrases
like these, in which parts of a woman's body are compared to
natural objects.[16] In sum, Cāttaṉār's description of the prince leads

the reader to expect that he will succeed in uniting with Maṇimēkalai.

Cutamati, Maṇimēkalai's companion, is also a stock figure. In
the portrayal of the phases of love, a girlfriend almost always acts
as a confidant to the heroine and as a go-between for the two
lovers. In the garden, Utayakumaraṉ approaches Cutamati and
praises Maṇimēkalai because he, and Cāttaṉār's audience ·at this
point, assumes that she will facilitate a meeting between the two
lovers.

Maṇimēkalai's feelings of lovesickness, after the departure of
the prince, provide yet another example of the presence of conventional elements in this account. The heroine traditionally confesses
to feelings of lovesickness after the lovers' union. Classical poems
whose subject is love in separation are replete with such expressions of longing.

Up to this point, everything in Cāttaṉār's tableau accords with
expectation. The site, the cast of characters, the formulaic language, and the sequence of events all suggest that a tryst will take
place. Cāttaṉār's use of the conventions has aroused the expectations of his audience. In fact, however, nothing even remotely like
a lovers' meeting occurs. There is no meeting, no sexual union, and
no need for a go-between. What, then, is Cāttaṉār's reason for setting up such a scene? Cāttaṉār uses the occasion to demonstrate
that it is possible for a woman to become a renouncer.

First, Cāttaṉār transforms Utayakumaraṉ's phrases about
Maṇimēkalai's beauty into a starting point for a discussion of the
decay of the human body. Whereas Utayakumaraṉ sees only
Maṇimēkalai's present physical form, Cutamati urges him to realize how her body will decay as time passes. She pushes him to see
the body as an object worthy of disgust rather than as an object of
desire. Moving from the particular to the general, Cutamati attempts to persuade the prince that all such desires are inappropriate.

In addition to Cāttaṉār's use of the occasion as a starting point
for preaching, the entire structure of the incident illustrates how
women can become renouncers. The culmination of this scene of
failed union between lovers comes when Utayakumaraṉ sees that
Maṇimēkalai has locked herself inside the glass pavilion in the
garden. Thus, she is enclosed and unattainable. Her beautiful body
is not available to be enjoyed by the prince. Utayakumaraṉ's lust,

as that of the rutting elephant he subdued earlier that day, must be frustrated because their union cannot occur. Finally, at the end of the scene, Maṇimēkalai devoutly wishes that her love for the prince cease.

The image of Maṇimēkalai's enclosure is Cāttaṉār's image of female renunciation. Cāttaṉār uses Tamil literary conventions but then twists them so that his readers' expectations are not fulfilled. He manipulates the conventionalized portrait of love to demonstrate, to an audience unfamiliar with the idea, what is entailed when women become renouncers. The essence of Cāttaṉār's portrayal is unfulfilled union. A nun does not act according to the scenario outlined for a woman as lover. Instead she renounces intimate relationships characterized by desire. She sets herself apart from such relationships, just as Maṇimēkalai sets herself apart in the glass pavilion to free herself from Utayakumaraṉ. Cāttaṉār portrays Maṇimēkalai's nunlike determination to free herself from sexual relationships as exemplary.

Cāttaṉār's masterful assembly of the elements in this scene sets female renunciation in high relief. Whereas the portrayal of love in Tamil poetry dwells upon inner feelings, intimate personal relations, and the sexual realm, Cāttaṉār's portrayal of Maṇimēkalai's renunciation dwells upon the way bonds to this inner, sexual sphere must be cut. Thus, female renunciation can be seen as the absence of passionate relations between men and women. Once he has explained this to an audience unfamiliar with female renunciation, he can go on to describe both Maṇimēkalai's decision to become a Buddhist nun and her feeding of the hungry people of Tamilnadu with her miraculous bowl.[17]

Using the insights gained from a close look at this one example of a scene from *Maṇimēkalai,* the larger pattern of the epic can be discerned. Throughout the epic, other scenes use the same techniques. Further, the structure of the epic itself holds the same message of renunciation. *Maṇimēkalai* unfolds as a series of four sections of narrative explicating and advocating female renunciation. While the first section describes Maṇimēkalai's relationship to Utayakumaraṉ, the second focuses upon her progress on the path of commitment to Buddhist monasticism. The same pattern is then repeated: in the third section Maṇimēkalai's relationship to Utayakumaraṉ occupies center stage, while the fourth section again shifts to Buddhist philosophy. Thus, the narrative defines

Maṇimēkalai's spiritual progress as both a turning away from her love for the prince and a turning toward commitment to Buddhism. Cāttaṉār uses Tamil literary conventions to define precisely how Maṇimēkalai's behavior is not conventional. In sum, Cāttaṉār's portrayal of Maṇimēkalai—both in the scene analyzed above and in the epic as a whole—can be seen as an example of one of the types of renunciation demanded as part of the discipline of a Buddhist nun.

The Courtesan as a Symbol of Human Desire

Cāttaṉār's heroine is not only a model of female renunciation. Because she hails from the courtesan community, her renunciatory act can be viewed as an example for all (female and male) human beings. In both Hindu and Buddhist South Asian literature, authors associate courtesans with the rule of passion. Themselves motivated by craving, they excite craving in others. According to the Four Noble Truths, the primary formulation of early Buddhist doctrine, this craving causes suffering, the primary characteristic of existence.

Because courtesans are particularly associated with craving, one who becomes a Buddhist nun demonstrates in a dramatic fashion the Buddhist directive to eliminate craving. Maṇimēkalai renounces the life of a person enmeshed in craving on the basis of her birth in order to pursue the monastic life, a form of discipline designed to gradually free a person from craving. Thus, Cāttaṉār provides a model of religious transformation for any human being trapped by his or her desires and passions. To demonstrate the significance of Cāttaṉār's decision to make his protagonist a courtesan, I provide an overview of the image of the courtesan in South Asian literature, discuss the doctrinal significance of the concept of craving *(taṇhā),* and indicate the extent to which courtesans entered the Buddhist monastic order.

Conventionally, the courtesan attracts a client by exciting his sexual desires, extracts as much money as possible from him, and abandons him when he becomes penniless. Then she moves on to her next victim. Sānudāsa, originally a "paragon of virtue" portrayed in the *Bṛhatkathāślokasaṃgraha,* exemplifies such a victim. At first he is said to uphold an "excessive and unworldly morality"; he respects his wife and behaves as a dutiful son should. However, after he comes under the influence of the courtesan Gangā, her mercenary mother, and their supply of liquor, he loses the entire savings of his family. His behavior leads to the absolute impoverishment of his kinsmen. When he runs out of money, the courtesan's mother rubs him with a repulsively smelly oil (so that all will scorn him) and unceremoniously boots him out of the brothel.[18]

The depiction of the havoc wrought by Gangā upon innocent Sānudāsa is by no means atypical. The specific theme of a man who bankrupts his family through attachment to a prostitute appears frequently throughout Indian literature. In a branch story from *Maṇimēkalai,* the same fate befalls a man named Cātuvan. Although married to a virtuous woman, he neglects her to spend time with a courtesan. When all sources of his wealth are depleted, his mistress loses interest in him. At this point, we are told, the courtesan "pointed out to him the excellence of other men. Then with a wave of her hand, she dismissed him because he had no money."[19] Also of relevance is the presence of the same pattern in *Cilappatikāram,* the Tamil text closest to *Maṇimēkalai* in date and genre. There Kōvalan (Maṇimēkalai's father) abandons his wife for a dancing girl (Maṇimēkalai's mother), loses all his money, and must leave home in an attempt to regain his fortune. In each of these stories the man loses his fortune because of the courtesan's desire for gifts and money.[20]

In several noteworthy texts, the courtesan's indifference to her clients and thirst for money is presented as her duty. In some stories, authors go so far as to proclaim that a courtesan's hereditary code for conduct necessarily entails this mercenary attitude. Even the unfortunate Sānudāsa realizes that a courtesan differs from a virtuous wife in the same way that an outcaste differs from a Brahmin. He points out that this difference is entirely appropriate: "Let her [Gangā, the courtesan] follow the path of her mother and grandmother. A courtesan who, like a wellborn wife, is faithful to one man for a long time is remiss: the righteous don't approve of an outcaste who studies the Vedas."[21]

Cittirāpati, Maṇimēkalai's grandmother and matriarch of the courtesan community, makes the same point in a more sustained manner in chapter 18 of *Maṇimēkalai.* In her address to an assembly of dancing girls, she clearly contrasts the disparate codes for conduct of a chaste wife and a courtesan. Rather than dying on a pyre like a proper and faithful wife, a courtesan should abandon

157

men, after taking all their money. Cittirāpati uses three similes to explain the way a courtesan should move heartlessly from client to client. First, she compares the courtesan to the *yāl* (lute) that continues to be played though the particular minstrel who has owned it may die. Further, she says that the prostitute resembles a bee who abandons the flower after sucking it dry of its honey. Finally, the courtesan is like Lakṣmī, the goddess of prosperity, who leaves a person once the sum of good karma accrued (from good deeds done in the past) has been exhausted.[22] In both the discourse of Sānudāsa and the speech of Cittirāpati, this craving to "suck out" all the wealth of the client is raised to the level of a normative code for conduct.

If the conduct of the courtesan demonstrates craving in the form of greed, the conduct of her client epitomizes craving in the form of sexual desire. In many literary portraits of a good man brought to ruin by a courtesan, the author portrays the client as at the mercy of his desires. Once netted, Sānudāsa seems incapable of releasing himself from the attractions of brothel life. Similarly, in *Maṇimē-kalai,* Cāttanār portrays Prince Utayakumaraṉ as ruled by and obsessed with his desire for Maṇimēkalai.

This all-consuming nature of sexual desire, as exemplified by both Sānudāsa and Utayakumaraṉ, makes it particularly threatening to anyone seeking to develop control over his or her passions. For this reason, in many tales from early Buddhist texts, courtesans are described or depicted as a menace to the Buddhist monk and nun. I. B. Horner, in summarizing these stories, comments:

> not without reason was it [the courtesan profession] regarded as unpraiseworthy and inestimable by the world, and as contaminating by the almspeople, however much it might be thought at the same time to be due to the working of karma. Some courtesans tried to tempt the almswomen back from the holy life, hence the ruling that they were not to be associated with; some tried to break in upon the meditations of the almsmen, and even if they did not try their presence was a menace to mental calm: while others were the cause of strife among men, obstacles in the path of freedom from lust, and hence obstacles in the path of tranquility.[23]

Precisely because courtesans were perceived as associated with craving, they were feared. They were thought to tempt renouncers to enter once again into the realm of craving, thus ending their spiritual progress. Horner gives examples of such concerns from Buddhist texts such as the *Jātakas,* the commentary on the *Therīgāthā* and the *Theragāthā,* and the *Dhammapada.*[24] The same anxiety about the dangers of sexual desire underlies many of the injunctions regulating interaction with women, which are in the *Vinaya,* the Buddhist rule of discipline that governs monastic life.[25]

To summarize, in the relationship between courtesan and client, craving rules. It characterizes the courtesan's behavior and goals as well as the desires of her client. As a courtesan, then, Cāttanār's protagonist Maṇimēkalai would be strongly associated with such passionate desire insofar as she conforms to the typical image of a courtesan. In fact, however, Maṇimēkalai entirely renounces both the role and image of a courtesan because she seeks to eliminate craving completely.

According to Buddhist doctrine, *taṇhā* (craving) causes suffering. The aim of the Four Noble Truths, the set of central doctrinal formulations in Indian Buddhism, is to explain how suffering arises and how it can be eliminated. The First Noble Truth describes existence as characterized by suffering, *dukkha.* In characterizing existence in this way, the Buddha does not deny that happiness and pleasure exist. Rather he shows that all such pleasures are transitory and ultimately lead to suffering.

The Second Noble Truth proclaims that *taṇhā* creates those kinds of suffering that mark phenomenal existence. *Taṇhā* produces rebirth after rebirth, each one bound up with passionate desires. Buddhist texts divide *taṇhā* into three types: thirst for sense pleasures *(kāma-taṇhā),* thirst for existence and becoming, and thirst for nonexistence. The first type, *kāma-taṇhā,* concerns us here. In its most general sense *kāma* denotes all kinds of desires and pleasures. In a more marked usage, *kāma* refers to sexual pleasures (as in *kāma-sūtra*). As we have seen, courtesans are associated with desires, both monetary and sexual.

The Third and Fourth Noble Truths reveal how craving can be extinguished. According to the third, one eliminates suffering by cutting off craving. The fourth sets out a way to eliminate craving, entitled the Eightfold Path. It entails right understanding, right thought, right speech, right action, right livelihood, right effort, right mindfulness, and right concentration.

Before going on to look at the relationship between Maṇimēka-

lai's renunciation and these Four Noble Truths, a bit more attention to the meaning of *taṇhā* in Buddhist tradition is needed. The
Sanskrit term *tṛṣṇā,* derived from the root *tṛṣ* (to be thirsty), means
"thirst" in its literal sense and "desire" and "greed" in its more
figurative sense. One finds both the literal and the figurative meanings as well for the Pali form of the term *taṇhā.* Literally *taṇhā*
denotes "drought" and "thirst." Figuratively it means "craving,"
"hunger for," "excitement," and the "fever of unsatisfied longing."
Rooting out *taṇhā* is the key to all spiritual progress: "just as
physical thirst arises of itself, and must be assuaged, got rid of, or
the body dies; so the mental 'thirst,' arising from without, becomes
a craving that must be routed out, quite got rid of, or there can be
no Nibbāna [Nirvāna]."[26]

We know that Maṇimēkalai desires to eliminate her own craving
because she expresses the hope that her feelings of longing for the
prince end. More specifically, Maṇimēkalai's act of renunciation
may be seen as a way of ensuring right livelihood, the fifth step on
the Eightfold Path. As Walpola comments: "Right livelihood
means that one should abstain from making one's living through a
profession that brings harm to others, such as trading in arms and
lethal weapons, intoxicating drinks, poisons, killing animals,
cheating, etc., and should live by a profession which is honorable,
blameless and innocent of harm to others."[27] By renouncing her
hereditary occupation as a person whose income depends upon
encouraging craving in others, Maṇimēkalai advances upon the
path to eliminating suffering.

Maṇimēkalai was not the first woman in the Buddhist tradition
to renounce her status as a courtesan in favor of Buddhism, but she
is the first in a Tamil text. According to non-Tamil Buddhist texts,
at least four well-known North Indian courtesans converted to
Buddhism, entered the order, and became *arahats* (those who attain salvation). Certain verses in the *Therīgāthā* are attributed to
two of these women. A third, Ambapālī, attained fame as a great
Buddhist donor through her support of the order. According to
tradition, the Buddha refused an invitation from the princely
Licchavi family in order that he and his followers might dine at
Ambapālī's house. Her support for the order culminated with the
gift of a mango grove where the community might dwell. Eventually she attained arahatship.[28] As these examples show, escape

from the courtesan life by adopting the life of a renouncer was an option for women in Buddhism. As Horner comments,

Prostitution was regarded as a condition to which a person was reborn as a desert for some offence which, as it was thought, had overtaken her in a previous existence. By willing to change, by willing to strive against the stream, and to cultivate the upward mounting way and to live well, a woman could become different, could grow, and escape from the prison of sense-desires.[29]

Thus, according to Buddhist texts outside of Tamilnadu, a pattern of courtesans joining the monastic order had been established. Cāttaṉār is the first to portray such a courtesan in a Tamil text.

Maṇimēkalai's renunciation of the life of a courtesan, then, indicates the triumph of spiritual discipline over craving. This triumph is not gender-specific; it would be a victory for either men or women. The courtesan, as one whose normative social role centers on inciting others to let themselves be ruled by craving, symbolizes a life sunk in passion. When such a person becomes a renouncer, she demonstrates that the Buddhist path is open even to those whose attachments and passions have been the strongest. Such a path, then, is appropriate for all human beings.

Conclusion

In this chapter I have indicated the ways in which gender symbolism can have more than one meaning in the same text. On the one hand, in emphasizing the Tamil cultural assumptions that shape portrayal of gender, I stressed the need to interpret the text in terms of the Tamil literary conventions for describing the heroine in love poems. In this light Cāttaṉār's portrayal of Maṇimēkalai can be seen as a way to use and twist the conventional portrait of love to demonstrate to an audience unfamiliar with the idea of female renunciation what it entails for a woman to renounce. Maṇimēkalai's renunciation is pictured as unfulfilled union. Thus, Cāttaṉār specifically defines a nun as a woman who does not act according to the expected scenario for union between a man and a woman. This perspective on the text explains why Cāttaṉār uses the overall narrative pattern he employs, which alternates between focus on Maṇimēkalai's relationship with the prince and her attraction toward Buddhist renunciation.

On the other hand, in emphasizing the role of the courtesan as a symbol of desire par excellence, I also stressed the need to interpret the text in terms of Buddhist doctrine concerning craving. In this light, Cāttaṉār's choice of a courtesan for his protagonist can be seen as providing a model of renunciation for all human beings, not only women. Courtesans possess codes for conduct that encourage them to exercise greed and incite men to become obsessed by desire. After being sunk in craving, the courtesan who renounces her occupation begins to eliminate craving systematically and also prevents herself from becoming the object of men's craving. From this second perspective, Maṇimēkalai is an example of extreme religious transformation rather than specifically female renunciation. This way of reading Cāttaṉār's text is not gender-specific.

These two perspectives revolve around the image of a religious woman in a Tamil Buddhist text. In the first, the description of Maṇimēkalai's decision to become a nun is interpreted as an example of how a woman goes about renunciation. Thus, the key characteristic in Cāttaṉār's portrayal of her is her gender. In the second, the description of a courtesan's decision to renounce provides a paradigm for male and female renunciation. Thus, the key characteristic in the portrayal is Maṇimēkalai's birth into a community whose occupation encourages craving.[30]

Notes

1. Within this article I have used the standard form of transliteration for Tamil terms, as found in Kamil Zvelebil, *Tamil Literature,* vol. 2, fasc. 1 of *Handbuch Der Orientalistik,* gen. ed. Jan Gonda (Leiden: E. J. Brill, 1975). In the third section of the article, where I deal with Sanskrit and Pali texts, I again use the standard modern system of transliteration as set out respectively in Jan Gonda, *A Concise Elementary Grammar of the Sanskrit Language* (University: University of Alabama Press, 1966), and A. K. Warder, *Introduction to Pali* (London: Routledge and Kegan Paul, 1974).
2. For the earliest printed critical edition of *Maṇimēkalai,* see U. Vē. Cāminātaiyar, ed., *Maṇimēkalai* (Madras: Commercial Press, 1921). A more recent edition that builds upon Cāminātaiyar's work and adds more

commentary on the philosophical chapters near the end of the text is Na. Mu. Vēṅkaṭacāmi Nāṭṭār and Auvai Cu. Turaicāmi Piḷḷai, coms., *Maṇimē-kalai* (Tinnevelly: South India Saiva Siddhanta Works, 1946). At present no complete English translation of *Maṇimēkalai* is available. For a some-what abridged translation, see S. Krishnaswami Aiyangar, *Manimekhalai in Its Historical Setting* (London: Luzac and Co., 1928). For a detailed dis-cussion of the literary background and scholarly evaluation of *Maṇimēka-lai*, see Paula Richman, "Religious Rhetoric in *Maṇimēkalai*," Ph.D. diss., Department of South Asian Languages and Civilizations, University of Chicago, 1983, pp. 1–37.

3. Although scholars have suggested various dates for *Maṇimēkalai*, the sixth century seems most reasonable. See Zvelebil, *Tamil Literature,* p. 115. For a discussion of the issues involved in dating the text see Richman, "Religious Rhetoric," pp. 5–7.

4. Na. Mu. Vēṅkaṭacāmi Nāṭṭār, com., *Cilappatikāram* (Tinnevelly: South India Saiva Siddhanta Works, 1972). The two epics share a set of characters. Maṇimēkalai is the daughter of Kōvalaṉ, the protagonist of *Cilappatikāram*, and a dancing girl.

5. At least two other Buddhist epics did exist at one time. Camaya Tivā-kara Vāmaṉa Muṉivar's commentary on *Nīlakēci* cites a few lines from *Pimpicārakatai*, a Tamil epic concerning Bimbisāra, king of Rājagṛha dur-ing the Buddha's time. The story of another Tamil Buddhist epic, *Kuṇṭa-lakēci*, has also been preserved in the commentary on *Nīlakēci* 176. See Kamil Zvelebil, *Tamil Literature*, vol. 10, fasc. 1 of *A History of Indian Literature* (Weisbaden: Otto Harrasowitz, 1974), p. 142.

6. These minor stories focus upon particular Buddhist virtues, demon-strating their importance by situating their practice in concrete illustra-tions. For an analysis of their role in the epic, see Richman, "Religious Rhetoric," pp. 60–73.

7. Line 97 of the epic's prologue provides a longer name for the text, upon which the theme of this article is based: "The Renunciation of Maṇimēka-lai" (*Maṇimēkalai Turavu*).

8. Kāñcīpuram was a center for the study of Buddhist logic. According to recently uncovered archaeological evidence, Kāviripaṭṭiṉam was an extensive monastic establishment with connections to Southeast Asia.

9. This unusual seat is called the *taruma* (Tamil transliteration of Sanskrit *dharma*) *pīṭikai*, "seat" or "throne." In *Maṇimēkalai*, the seat reveals the events that transpired in one's past births. Scholars believe this throne is the same one described in the *Mahāvaṃsa*. According to the story recorded there, two kinsmen were fighting over the possession of the throne. The Buddha, out of compassion for them, took his alms bowl and went to the scene of the battle. Hovering above the battlefield, he caused darkness to descend and then allowed light to appear once more. This

miracle convinced the two kinsmen to stop fighting. Then the Buddha sat on the throne, and hence it is called the dharma throne. An extremely condensed version of this story is found in *Maṇimēkalai*, chap. 8, lines 44–63.

10. The viewpoints represented in this section include several varieties of Hindu sectarian philosophy as well as Ājīvika, Sāṃkhya, and Vaiśeṣika systems of thought.

11. Several poems describing an ascetic, as understood in classical Indian tradition, appear in the ancient Tamil corpus of poetry. See, for example, Puṟanāṉūṟu 252, entitled "A Hunter Once, Now an Ascetic," and 251, entitled "A Charmer Turned Ascetic," as translated in A. K. Ramanujan, *Poems of Love and War from the Eight Anthologies and the Ten Long Poems of Classical Tamil* (New York: Columbia University Press, 1985), pp. 174–75.

12. Ibid., p. 251.

13. Kenneth Bryant, *Poems to the Child-God: Structures and Strategies in the Poetry of Sūrdās* (Berkeley: University of California Press, 1978), p. 40.

14. Sally Noble, "Landscape, Image, and Song in the *Cilappatikāram*," M.A. paper, University of Chicago, 1981, p. 24.

15. The discussion of Cāttaṉār's use of landscape imagery is limited to the original five landscapes of Tamil poetic convention because the two later situations of love, *kaikkiḷai* and *peruntiṇai,* are not relevant to the discussion at hand.

16. Even *Caṅkam* poets recognized that such phrases were formulaic. See, for example, a *Caṅkam* poem that mocks such formulaic language, in A. K. Ramanujan, *The Interior Landscape: Love Poems from a Classical Tamil Anthology* (Bloomington: Indiana University Press, 1967; reprint, Midland Books, 1975), p. 111.

17. Maṇimēkalai's activities consist of far more than a mere renunciation of her courtesan birth. Her possession of the inexhaustible begging bowl enables her to practice the Buddhist virtues of compassion *(karuṇā)* and generosity *(dāna)* in an active way. With this bowl she travels throughout Tamilnadu feeding hungry people. Thus, her renunciation is only the first step. She goes far beyond mere renunciation; she takes upon herself the role of nurturing unfortunate people of all types. For this reason, the bowl is extremely important in the epic—it almost becomes a character. Chapter 16 provides a biography of the bowl, explaining its origins and history before it came to Maṇimēkalai.

18. J. A. B. van Buitenen, trans., *Tales of Ancient India* (New York: Bantam Books, 1961), pp. 218–58.

19. Vēṅkaṭacāmi Nāṭṭār and Turaicāmi Piḷḷai, *Maṇimēkalai*, p. 210 (chap. 16, lines 9–10).

20. The story of Kōvalan's attraction to Mātavi, which results in the birth of Maṇimēkalai, is told in chapters 3–9 of *Cilappatikāram*.

21. Van Buitenen, *Tales*, p. 224.

22. Vēṅkaṭacāmi Nāṭṭār and Turaicāmi Piḷḷai, *Maṇimēkalai*, p. 241 (chap. 18, lines 15–24).

23. Isaline Blew Horner, *Women under Primitive Buddhism* (London: Routledge and Kegan Paul, 1930; reprint, Delhi: Motilal Banarsidass, 1975), p. 92.

24. Ibid., p. 93.

25. See, for example, Charles S. Prebish, *Buddhist Monastic Discipline: The Sanskrit Prātimokṣa Sūtras of the Mahāsāṃghikas and Mūlasarvāsti-vādins* (University Park: Pennsylvania State University Press, 1975), pp. 50–51, 55.

26. T. W. Rhys Davids and William Stede, *The Pali Text Society's Pali-English Dictionary* (1979), p. 294.

27. Walpola Rahula, *What the Buddha Taught* (New York: Grove Press, 1974), p. 47.

28. Horner, *Women*, p. 90.

29. Ibid., p. 94.

30. Other cases where a woman's experience is interpreted in more than one way, with one interpretation gender-specific and another unmarked with regard to gender, can be found in the Christian tradition. For example the tradition of Mary Magdalene, the repentant prostitute, offers certain parallels. She is an image of devotion for females. But over time she also became the patron saint for all penitents, both male and female. See Victor Saxer, *La culte de Marie Madeleine en Occident des origines à la fin du moyen âge* (Publications de la Société des Fouilles Archaeologiques et des Monuments Historiques de L'Yonne, 1959).

Seven

Gender and Cosmology in Chinese Correlative Thinking
Alison H. Black

The presence of gender in areas of human thought that ostensibly have little or nothing to do with gender is a subject of current interest in feminist writing. One way of posing the question is to ask how far conceptions of gender serve to mirror, or symbolize, already given, universal metaphysical or ontological assumptions. Such is Sherry B. Ortner's approach, which relates the socially constructed distinction between female and male to the more basic distinction between nature and culture.[1] More recently, this approach has been in a sense inverted as the basic assumptions of Western philosophy have themselves been laid open to the charge of being derived from prior gender experience. Thus a newly published symposium of philosophical essays edited by Sandra Harding and Merrill B. Hintikka is appropriately entitled *Discovering Reality: Feminist Perspectives on Epistemology, Metaphysics, Methodology, and Philosophy of Science.*[2] The claim supported in the body of the volume is that these areas of Western thought have

The author wishes to thank other members of the religion faculty seminar at the University of Washington, and especially Caroline Walker Bynum, Stevan Harrell, and Paula Richman, for helpful comment, discussion, and encouragement in the writing of this chapter. An early conversation with Harrell combined with his subsequent seminar presentation (not the one represented in this volume) helped suggest the direction in which this essay should go. The finishing touches were added to the essay while the author was a Fairbank Postdoctoral Fellow at the John King Fairbank East Asia Research Center, Harvard University.

been shaped by "distinctively masculine perspectives on masculine experience."[3] Suggestions are also provided, implicitly and explicitly, on what a more "feminine" version of these disciplines might look like. Thus, for example, masculine bias is detected in the ubiquitous presence of dualism and hierarchy, for instance in such classic distinctions as reason versus appetite and mind versus object, which themselves help generate the (masculine) ideal of scientific objectivity.[4] The presence of gender in these conceptions occurs in at least two ways. It is explicitly present, for example, in Aristotle's treatment of the rational and appetitive natures of men and women respectively, or in the sexual imagery with which Francis Bacon describes the scientific attitude to nature.[5] And several authors of *Discovering Reality* claim that gender is implicitly present in that common philosophical conceptions can be shown to mirror male as distinct from female childhood experience.[6] More congruent with female experience and female perceptions (it is implied) are dynamic and holistic descriptions of reality.[7]

One way of testing the validity and importance of such claims is to look beyond Western to non-Western civilization. In China we are immediately confronted by an ambiguous and perplexing case—judged from the standpoint outlined above. The articulation of philosophical concepts in China was performed by men, as in the West. Yet the substance of these concepts can be seen as providing a "feminine" mirror image to the "masculine" West. This of course would be less of a problem (though still possibly interesting in its own right) if the appearance of femininity arose purely out of the comparison. But the Chinese themselves in at least some cases (notably the Taoists) share this perception of their own philosophical values.[8] And even where (as in the Confucian case) they did not perceive the matter thus, it can be shown that they gave pride of place in their metaphysics to certain values that in fact had more affinity with the female than with the male gender in their own social thinking. Here arises the question of the relevance of gender to Chinese metaphysical discussion. At the metaphysical level, concepts that Westerners, and sometimes Chinese themselves, would identify as feminine in an ordinary social or psychocultural context are either given masculine affinity or transcend the distinction altogether—and it is not always easy to determine which is the case.

Given the explicitly gender-oriented nature of Chinese metaphysics, the diversity of Chinese philosophical opinion on the subject, and the problematical nature of the subject itself, it seems worthwhile to investigate the matter more closely. The focus of investigation will be the metaphysical polarities associated with traditional Chinese cosmology and its religious, ethical, and epistemological implications. If we are confined by the nature of the materials to male perspectives on the subject, at least we need not be confined to one school of thought. It will be instructive to look at Confucianism, Taoism in its classical and religious forms, and the yin-yang cosmology that influenced both Confucianism and religious Taoism. The main focus, however, will be on Confucianism, which in the postclassical period absorbed some features of the other traditions and in addition enjoyed the status of orthodoxy throughout most of that period.

Our source materials are the classics of each tradition, together with later works implicitly or explicitly based on them. The canonical literature of Confucianism and classical Taoism in particular has been scanned systematically for gender-related material. Of central importance are the *Book of Changes* and the *Book of Rites*, which served as generative texts for later cosmological writing. The continuity imposed by the Confucian commentarial tradition in particular justifies the inclusion of sources many centuries apart: themes suggested in the classics were constantly rehearsed and elaborated on thereafter. Furthermore, a process of natural selection leads one to certain texts not because they make the point one wants them to make but because they address the point in a relevant way, and not all texts or authors do this. If somewhat more weight is given in the present instance to the Neo-Confucian interpreters (second millennium A.D.) than to their predecessors, it is because they performed the most sophisticated and explicit integration of ethics and cosmology.[9]

Common to all the traditions is a tendency to dyadic thinking that is particularly marked in China. The language itself is structured in ways that encourage this tendency. Experience is classified in paired concepts that often act as polar opposites. Frequently the concepts also constitute an ordered pair in which one member is more highly valued. Inevitably gender differences found a place in the system. The principle of correlative thinking in which pairs were linked symmetrically with other pairs created chains of meaning in which some links were closer and others looser. The resulting problem for us is to know how to interpret the links: to understand which associations of meaning are relevant on a given occasion.

Our particular problem is to track down the significance of gender within correlative cosmology. The type of cosmology is partly metaphysical and symbolic, dealing with the structure of a cosmos whose inner and outer dimensions are congruent. Our task is to find out how far and in what ways gender was present, both explicitly and implicitly, or how far it was transcended—and how to tell the difference; and to test whether Chinese cosmology supports feminist claims about the relation between gender and world.

Before we can answer any of these questions, we must consider how human gender distinctions were perceived by the writers of our texts.[10] Confucian writings are more explicit in their prescriptions and assumptions about gender in society than are the Taoist texts. Nevertheless it is clear enough that Taoist gender imagery derives much of its significance from commonly held cultural perceptions: that is to say, whatever the private views of Taoist authors on social roles of men and women, and however original their normative assessment, their symbolical use of gender imagery is controlled by socially inherited assumptions and values. (It is unknown whether these assumptions and values were held by all Chinese contemporary with the authors. They may have been held mainly by men, or even mainly by literate men—should any wish to argue the point.)

Basic to the recorded Chinese perceptions of social gender roles is the different biological function of the sexes along with the tendency to define female social roles especially on a biological basis. As child bearer and child nourisher, the woman is inevitably more confined than the man to hearth and home. That she ought in general to be so confined is the clear prescription of the Confucian writers. Hence the female is associated with the private, inner *(nei)* sphere, in contrast to the male, whose business is the public, outer *(wai)* sphere.[11] Maid, wife, mother, or widow, she is either preparing for, experiencing, or mourning the loss of the marriage tie. Role descriptions of men may move beyond the family (e.g., soldier, scholar, official), but women's much more rarely. When women are casually mentioned in these texts it is generally in terms of kinship or marriage ties—as daughters, sisters, wives, and so on. This is as true of the Taoist as of any other texts.

Abstractly considered, domestic confinement might not seem to entail female subservience to the male. (Privacy was a value recommended to emperors as well as to women.) But if there is anything on which Confucian texts are clear it is that the male should be dominant: "When a girl marries, her mother gives her advice, and accompanies her to the door with these cautionary words, 'When you go to your new home, you must be respectful and circumspect. Do not disobey your husband.' It is the way of a wife or concubine to consider obedience and docility the norm" (*Mencius* 3B/2). Even filial piety gives way in the celebrated statement of the *Book of Rites:* "The woman follows [and obeys] the man:—in her youth, she follows her father and elder brother; when married, she follows her husband; when her husband is dead, she follows her son."[12] Of the classical Taoists, Lao Tzu tacitly accepts the principle of female submissiveness in turning it into an illustration of a cosmic value. There is no record what the *Chuang Tzu* of the *Inner Chapters* thought on the subject.[13] The passage in the *T'ien-tao* (Way of Heaven) chapter approving male dominance is too clearly from a different hand.

Reasons for female submission to male are frequently unstated. There was little need for such statement, given the social reality of the Chinese family system with its overarching imperative of patrilineal descent and the continuation of the ancestral sacrifice through the male line. In so far as more philosophical reasons were suggested, the pragmatic argument from superior physical strength would not have appealed to a Confucian or, for different reasons, to a Taoist—although the Confucian might conceivably appeal to the symbolic significance and consequent ethical imperative conveyed by strength.[14] Superior wisdom was for the Confucian a more significant argument. The argument is actually used. To the sentence from the *Book of Rites* quoted above is added the explanation, "'Man' denotes supporter. A man by his Wisdom [*chih*] should [be able to] lead others."[15] Were women perceived as innately less intelligent than men? Wisdom, or knowledge, can after all be acquired, and the man with his free access into public life was in the better position to acquire it. In part the linking of intellect with the male sex may have been the counsel of prudence. A saying current from the later imperial era, "Lack of talent is a virtue in women," recognized the dangers of distracting women from their proper domestic functions in a male-dominated society.[16] The

Book of Odes furnishes a more direct assertion of the unteachability of women: "[D]isorder is not sent down from Heaven; it is produced by women; those who cannot be taught or instructed are women and eunuchs."[17] There is, of course, a context to this petulant remark; the songwriter is thinking particularly of the royal dissipation and consequent neglect of government. But the comparative irrationality of women is suggested more matter-of-factly in a saying attributed to Confucius: "In one's household, it is the women and the small men that are difficult to deal with. If you let them get too close, they become insolent. If you keep them at a distance, they complain."[18]

Allied to the idea of wisdom is that of moral rectitude. The content of understanding for the Confucian was primarily moral. The man is expected to set an example: "If you do not practise the Way yourself, you cannot expect it to be practised even by your own wife and children. If you do not impose work on others in accordance with the Way, you cannot expect obedience even from your own wife and children" (*Mencius* 7B/9). Why the male should ipso facto be better suited to take the lead in the ethical sphere is suggested indirectly in the *Book of Rites,* which contrasts the attitudes of the mother and the father to their children.

> Here now is the affection of a father for his sons;—he loves the worthy among them, and places on a lower level those who do not show ability; but that of a mother for them is such, that while she loves the worthy, she pities those who do not show ability:—the mother deals with them on the ground of affection and not of showing them honour; the father, on the ground of showing them honour and not of affection.[19]

Although the mother's affective behavior betokens a kind of impartiality, in another sense it is based on the partial sentiments she has toward her own children because they are hers. The father's attitude, by contrast, has an objective and impersonal, moral basis. This contrast is mirrored in the repeated association of female with affectivity and male with honor, reverence, or rectitude. As for the children's response:

> The service due to a father is employed in serving a mother, and the love is the same for both. [But] in the sky there are not two suns, nor in a land two kings, nor in a state two rulers, nor in a family two

171

equally honourable:—one [principle] regulates [all] these conditions. Hence, while the father is alive, the sackcloth with even edges is worn [for a mother], [and only] for a year,—showing that there are not [in the family] two equally honourable.[20]

It seems, then, that for sociological and biological reasons the woman is expected to show less discrimination (of the proper sort) than the man. If one omits the value judgment, one may note the similarity of this conclusion to that reached by the feminist philosophers. In the Confucian case, it is not clear whether other innate or metaphysical differences were at issue. But at least biological and social roles were a substantially determining factor, even in the Confucian view of the matter. Also not to be underestimated is the Confucian penchant for hierarchical order: life must be organized, and its organization must be hierarchical. If gender is fed into a classificatory symbol system, it will have to take the shape of the system. But in historical fact and tradition as transmitted by Confucians, for example in the Han collection of female biographies known as the *Lieh-nü chuan,* there were innumerable instances of superior judgment being exercised by women, to the admiration or shame of their male audience. Wives admonished husbands; peasant women remonstrated with rulers; and Mencius was not by a long way the only Confucian whose moral training was attributed to a mother by all accounts neither blind nor doting.[21] Furthermore, even within the classificatory system there is a firm recognition of the need for both "feminine" and "masculine" attributes. Thus the sage-emperor Shun is praised in the *Book of Rites:* "He treated the people as his sons, as if he had been their father and mother. He had a deep and compassionate sympathy for them [like their mother]; he instructed them in loyalty and what was profitable [like their father]. While he showed his affection for them, he also gave them honour; in his natural restfulness, he was reverent; in the terrors of his majesty, he yet was loving."[22]

Implicit in these gender-related Confucian concepts of social role, wisdom, affection, and respect is a distinction resembling that between nature and culture. To be sure, it is a tamed and domesticated nature in so far as it is contained and rendered obedient, but its place is acknowledged. The world of propriety and learning and cultivated judgment is good, but it does not follow that the other is bad. It may at times become so—servants and women may at times be tiresome—but no criticism is voiced against the instinct that prompts the mother to love the dullest of her children. It is the stuff of human nature, even if it must be complemented by educated judgment. Conversely, the values of culture *(wen)* must have a solid basis in nature *(chih:* unadorned substance, plainness).[23] The great fourth-century B.C. Confucian Mencius staked his reputation as a debater on his defense of the naturalness of courtesy, respect, morality, and wisdom. Even Hsun Tzu, further from Rousseau and closer to Hobbes than was Mencius, fully appreciated the emotional significance of ritual.

The assimilation of female to nature and male to culture is more unequivocal in Taoist philosophy, specifically in the *Lao Tzu*. The delicately balanced normative possibilities within each set of gender-related values are exchanged for a simple identification of female with nature and male with culture, and a sweeping rhetorical preference of nature over culture. Each of the gender roles and values discussed above is implicitly acknowledged and explicitly vaunted (in the case of the feminine) or, with qualification, rejected (in the case of the masculine). The woman is hidden, submissive, nurturing, recognizing no distinction. One important modification occurs in Lao Tzu's selective choice of gender imagery. The mother of the Confucian texts is clearly *somebody*'s mother, whose impartial love for her children may be suspected of partiality because they are hers and therefore requires balancing by the father's impartial discrimination. But the mother of the *Lao Tzu* text is already *everybody*'s mother, with a spontaneous and unreflective nurturing relationship to all creatures. The relationship is intimate but impartial; the actual language of affectivity almost absent, if not from the text as a whole, at least from references to the specifically feminine. Another way of putting the matter is to say that the impartiality attributed to the mother is achieved partly through the blurring of the boundary between mother and child; it is really the very young child who is simple, ignorant, and "impartial," depending utterly on what is given— and the mother is seen through the child's eyes.[24]

This Taoist perception of impartiality as a characteristically feminine trait opens up more clearly than in Confucianism the possibility of a revised epistemology on the basis of already existing gender affinities. From the Confucian perspective, feminine as opposed to masculine judgments savor of the partial or subjective as opposed to the impartial or objective. But to the Taoist, the activity of intellectual and ethical discrimination is the opposite of impartial, and it is the woman's undiscriminating and undemanding nurturing activity that wins his approval. What is commonly reckoned as knowledge or wisdom is conventional and often ego based. Notions of "keeping to the role of the female" (*Lao Tzu* 28) or "clinging to the mother" (52) are linked with the refusal to make self-centered discriminations. A kind of wisdom is implied in this apparently "foolish and uncouth" behavior (20): it is holistic and intuitive, linked with the belly rather than the eye (12) and with the uncarved block in its primitive, shapeless simplicity and wholeness (28).

The *Chuang Tzu* offers a comparable example:

> After this [i.e., at the culmination of his Taoist education], Lieh Tzu concluded that he had never really begun to learn anything. He went home and for three years did not go out. He replaced his wife at the stove, fed the pigs as though he were feeding people, and showed no preferences in the things he did. He got rid of the carving and polishing and returned to plainness, letting his body stand alone like a clod. In the midst of entanglement he remained sealed, and in this oneness he ended his life.[25]

A post-Jungian generation would be in immediate sympathy with the Taoists in their classifications according to gender of the two types of knowledge suggested here. What the Chinese, other than the classical Taoists, made of them we shall see shortly. It is worth reiterating that the idealization of "feminine" values in passages such as this does not prove a revolutionary social ethic on the part of the Taoist: although women, rustics, animals, and plants present images of nature as an ideal model, there is at best a deep ambiguity about their worth as compared with the sage (invariably a male, if specified) who has acquired understanding and *returned* to nature.[26]

Gender and Cosmology

Gender is part of the warp and woof of Chinese cosmological thinking, as is illustrated by the treatment of central concepts in the *Book of Changes,* a classic for Confucians and Taoists alike.

There several paired terms are inextricably mixed: Heaven/Earth, Ch'ien/K'un (Creative/Receptive; Heaven/Earth), yang/yin, high/low, hard/soft, male/female. Ch'ien and K'un are the ceaselessly creative agencies of Heaven and Earth. They are the concentrated presence of yang and yin, which in turn denote light and dark, strong and weak, hard and soft, active and passive. The unbroken and broken lines of the images in the *Book of Changes* (——, — —), respectively "hard" and "soft," provide graphic representation of the yang and yin principles. Permutations of these lines yield eight trigrams and sixty-four hexagrams; in each case the pure yang and pure yin images dominate the rest as the Ch'ien (☰, ☰) and K'un(☷, ☷). It must be remembered that yin-yang terminology is always relational. Yang and yin themselves have no fixed meaning, unless one goes back to their early etymological meanings, which included the ideas of light and shade. Metaphysically, they permit a highly flexible organization of the world in overlapping polarities.

Yin-yang symbolism provides a ready device for registering gender as well as other polarities. This is clearly illustrated in passages where the human generative activity provides a symbol for the process of cosmic transformation through the cooperation of Heaven and Earth, or Ch'ien and K'un:

> Ch'ien is Heaven and therefore is called father.
> K'un is Earth and therefore is called mother.[27]

> Heaven and Earth commingle
>   and the myriad things are abundantly transformed.
> Male and female unite their seed
>   and the myriad things are transformed by growth.
>
> (*Great Appendix* B/5)

The same symbolism appears in a much more complicated form in the following passage, worth quoting in extenso for two reasons: first, it says much that is relevant concisely; second, it illustrates the difficulty of distinguishing gender-related from gender-neutral imagery.

> Heaven is honorable, Earth humble:
> Ch'ien and K'un are thereby determined.

Humble and lofty being manifested,
Noble and base take their position.

. . .

In Heaven are constituted the images,
On Earth are constituted physical forms
And so change and transformation are seen.

. . .

The way of Ch'ien constitutes [or brings about] the male,
The way of K'un constitutes [or brings about] the female.
Ch'ien knows the great beginning,
K'un brings things to completion.
Ch'ien knows with ease,
K'un performs with simplicity.

. . .

Ease of knowing encourages familiarity,
Ease of following brings success.
Familiarity enables duration,
Success enables greatness.
Potential for duration is the character of the outstanding man,
Potential for greatness is his field of action.

(*Great Appendix* A/1)

In all three passages, the human generative activity provides part of the symbolism for the process of cosmic transformation. In the third instance, the generative model is suggested or reinforced by a series of polarities: high/low, moving/stilling (or active/passive), hard/soft, beginning/completing. But what are we to make of other metaphors that appear in close proximity and yet are less evidently gender related? What of image/physical form, knowing/completing, knowing/performing, familiarity/success, duration/greatness, character/field of action? The ground here is less firm. For the reader attuned to the resonances of the Chinese terminology, it should be clear that each pair constitutes something like a spiritual/material polarity. The context of the second and third pairs might suggest a connection between knowledge and Ch'ien's maleness and between completing (or performing) and K'un's femaleness. And if one recalls the association of wisdom with the male gender in Confucian social thinking, it is not difficult to imagine that we have here a cosmological reflection of that same view.

The logic is persuasive but not quite conclusive. It could be argued that a principle of knowledge or creative intelligence is a desirable thing to have in one's cosmology, and if such a principle is to be cast in a polar framework then it might very naturally be paired with a principle of concreteness or materiality or physical activity, and it might even more naturally appear in the superior position. In other words, it is not absolutely clear that knowing is here suggested as a specifically masculine activity in contrast with a specifically feminine activity of doing or completing. It could quite conceivably have been introduced in a gender-free context.

Nevertheless, one thing is clear. The presence of the concept of knowledge in such close conjunction with Heaven's masculine attributes ensures that for the reader who remembers this passage the conceptual imagery of cosmic generation is forever haunted by the ascription of intelligence to the male partner, the more particularly as Earth's physical exertions resemble clearly enough the female's nourishing and bringing to birth of the seed engendered. In other words, the link between gender and intelligence has been made, at the cosmic level, and whether accidental or not it will not be easily forgotten.

Gender affinities also seem to be present in other paired ideas in the passage, although they resonate more faintly. Image (*hsiang*) and physical form (*hsing*) suggest degrees of materiality and priority. The images formed in Heaven are, at the most literal level of interpretation, the celestial bodies, which emit light but have little or no material substance, though they could be said to have material essences. According to the *Changes*, they provide models for earthly imitation, partly calendrical but partly archetypal (hence the sun is fire and yang, and the moon is water and yin). Familiarity and success recall the polarity of knowing and doing. Time and space (evoked by duration and greatness) might not seem particularly masculine and feminine in character, yet the link is there. The temporal image is one not of change nor yet of standstill, but of actively maintained duration and constancy, evoking the memory of Heaven with its ceaseless, regular motions ("Heaven moves firmly," in the parlance of the *Changes*), initiating Earth's seasons.[28] The spatial image lurks within the notion of greatness (*ta*), which in Chinese as in English denotes both physical size and moral or abstract superiority. As time is to Heaven, so space is to Earth: "K'un, in its largeness, sustains all things"; "K'un is the storehouse."[29] Character and field of action (Richard Wilhelm's translation of *yeh*: task, vocation) carry a distant echo of the time/space polarity not only because of the way they are introduced here, but through similar treatment elsewhere. We are told, for example, that the "great field of action" of yin and yang refers to the fact of "abundance," and "flourishing character" to that of "daily renovation" (*Great Appendix* A/5). Again, the "field of action" may be "broadened" (A/7). More obviously, the logical priority of character over field of action reinforces the earlier suggestions of priority of immaterial over material.

The passages studied thus reveal a cosmology whose pattern is roughly consistent with that of social gender. This is not to say that gender is the main or only key to such cosmology. And indeed it may be simplistic to assume that even gender values in such writing are confined to what society already (hypothetically, that is) thinks about gender apart from the cosmic setting. Once gender is introduced into cosmology, it not only shapes cosmological thinking but is itself affected by it. The poetic unity of such writing demands it: the images mesh and merge, each sustaining echoes from the others, now near, now far, but never completely beyond hearing. Thus cosmic gender will differ in some respects from its human counterpart—as, for example, in the introduction of notions of time and space. But so far the differences have not appeared irreconcilable or antagonistic.

The Phenomenon of Reversal

In some cases, however, gender concepts at the social level may actually be reversed at the cosmic level. It is this phenomenon of reversal that I now wish specifically to address. I have already shown that in Confucian social thinking the male is aligned with the public sphere, leadership, rationality, and rectitude, and the female with the domestic or private sphere, proper submissiveness and affectivity rather than innate rationality or rectitude. The cosmological passages already scrutinized bear out at least some of these perceptions. But even thus far there are suggestive modifications of social gender stereotypes. These are connected with the polarity (whether gender-inspired or not) of immaterial and material. Materiality is visibility: Earth's operations are abundantly in evidence. To a much greater extent than Ch'ien in this particular model, K'un occupies the public sphere. Again, there may be knowledge in Heaven, but there is energetic action on Earth. This reversal of inner/outer polarity might be interpreted simply as the price of elevating one set of gender images, for example, spiritual/material, over the rest. But the pervasiveness of the inner-outer theme throughout this kind of cosmology seems especially appropriate not just to spiritual/material polarity in general but to the particular rendition of the spiritual, or immaterial, function in Confucian cosmology. This function includes the spectrum of cognitive, affective, conative, and ethical activity as perceived metaphysically in the cosmos. It is in this sphere that there occurs a significant "feminization" of the yang principle, or alternatively a simple transcendence of gender. Intuition and affectivity, in this case, take precedence over rationality and rectitude.

One example is the typical ordering of the two chief ethical virtues of benevolence and righteousness, as the terms *jen* and *i* are frequently translated. *Jen* is humanity or kindness, sharing with both of these English equivalents the dual thought of kinship and kindness (although the former only implicitly and as providing a natural basis for the latter). *I* is rectitude, rightness, or sense of rightness; it adjudicates the application of benevolence. If the concepts of love and rectitude that we have met at the human level were simply transferred to the cosmic level, we might expect that *jen* would be yin and *i* would be yang. The reverse is the case. A striking instance of this appears in the *Book of Rites,* in the chapter on music. The text eulogizes the nature of music by showing its cosmic and human functions in relation to those of ritual (*li*). Not only are *jen* and *i* explicitly drawn into the discussion, but the general language in which the chapter is couched is frequently evocative of the distinction between these two virtues. A few quotations must suffice:

Similarity and union are the aim of music; difference and distinction, that of ceremony. From union comes mutual affection; from difference, mutual respect.[30]

Music comes from within, and ceremonies from without.[31]

Music is [an echo of] the harmony between heaven and earth; ceremonies reflect the orderly distinctions [in the operations of] heaven and

179

earth. From that harmony all things receive their being; to those orderly distinctions they owe the differences between them. Music has its origin from heaven; ceremonies take their form from the appearances of earth.[32]

The processes of growth in spring, and of maturing in summer [suggest the idea of] benevolence; those of in-gathering in autumn and of storing in winter, suggest righteousness. Benevolence is akin to music, and righteousness to ceremonies.[33]

In music we have the expression of feelings which do not admit of any change; in ceremonies that of principles which do not admit of any alteration. Music embraces what all equally share; ceremony distinguishes the things in which men differ.[34]

The blending together without any mutual injuriousness . . . forms the essence of music; and the exhilaration of joy and the glow of affection are its business. Exactitude and correctness, without any inflection or deviation, form the substance of ceremonies, while gravity, respectfulness, and a humble consideration are the rules for their discharge.[35]

To which we may add, from a different chapter: "In affection we have benevolence; in nice distinctions righteousness."[36] The following list may help clarify the associations of ideas in these and other similar passages:

Music	Ceremony
Unity	Diversity
Harmony	Order
Heaven	Earth
Love	Reverence
Feeling	Undeviating principle
Benevolence	Righteousness
Growth	Ingathering and laying in store
Expansive spiritual influences	Retractive spiritual influences
High	Low
Inner	Outer

The alignment of benevolence and righteousness with music and ceremony respectively should occasion no surprise. Some of the reasons given are straightforward. Common to benevolence and music are spontaneity of feeling and a tendency to integration or harmony; righteousness and ceremony, on the other hand, are perceived to mark distinctions based on objective principles, not just on feelings. What is noteworthy is the assimilation of the former set to Heaven and the latter to Earth. In other words, affectivity and subjectivity are associated with the masculine cosmic principle and rectitude and rationality with the feminine— if gender affinities apply. There seem to be two basic reasons for this alignment. One is that music and its correlates clearly reflect the dynamic and expansive activity of yang, an activity that, moreover, is logically prior to the retractive, ordering function of yin. The other reason, which is ultimately related to the first, is that the former set suggests the theme of unity as opposed to diversity. The significance of this theme will be pursued later; suffice it for now to note its relevance to the apparent reversals of gender affinity.

Although the *Book of Changes* is not similarly explicit in its terminology, the generally accepted alignment of *jen* and *i* with yang and yin respectively is clear from commentarial reactions to the following passage: "Of old when the sages made the *Changes,* it was with the intention of following the principles of the nature and destiny of things. In this way they established the way of Heaven as yin and yang, the way of Earth as soft and hard, and the way of man as *jen* and *i*" (*Explanation of the Trigrams* 2). The perfectly normal word order unfortunately suggested in this instance that *jen* was yin and *i* yang. But Chu Hsi, the great twelfth-century Neo-Confucian commentator, rejected this possibility on the grounds that *jen* was primarily outgoing and expansive (*fa-shu*), whereas *i* "gathers in" or "keeps in ward" (*shou-lien*).[37]

Slightly more equivocal is the cosmic status of *jen* and *chih* (wisdom or knowledge). Given the centrality of *jen* and its avowed superiority to wisdom in the Confucian *Analects*, the two seem to fall readily into a yang/yin ordering. For Chang Tsai, writing in the eleventh century, the only important kind of knowledge is that grounded in virtue, and the affective component of virtue takes logical precedence over the rational (for example, "Righteousness is *jen* in action").[38] At the very end of the nineteenth century when beleaguered Confucians were defining the essential core of their tradition, we find T'an Ssu-t'ung even more forcefully denying the validity of knowledge independent of *jen*.[39] But the *Book of Changes* itself provided such an ambivalent interpretation that commentators were driven to most marvellously subtle ways of

181

preserving consistency in the cosmic status of *jen* and wisdom. The matter is raised in the fourth and fifth chapters of the first section of the *Great Appendix*. In a recondite but (to initiates, at least) unmistakable fashion, chapter 4 aligns wisdom (*chih*) with Heaven and *jen* with Earth, and chapter 5 aligns wisdom with yin (cf. Earth) and *jen* with yang (cf. Heaven). Chu Hsi's resolution of the dilemma revolved on a distinction between relative purity or clarity (*ch'ing chu*) and functional order.[40] That is, wisdom as such is clear(-sighted) compared with *jen*, but it can be activated only through *jen*. In other words, wisdom is like yang in its clarity, but *jen* resembles yang in its activity. This solution, which is directly opposed to Chang Tsai's perception of things, may reflect Chu Hsi's unusually rationalistic bias. The consensus of the tradition taken as a whole seems to endorse the primacy of *jen* not merely in function but in essence.

The subject of wisdom and its cosmic ranking falls into better perspective when we look more closely at the concept of cosmic knowledge itself. What must not be missed is the intuitive, a priori element that lies at its core. The predominance of this element is emphasized in a well-known set of commentaries on the *Changes* by the seventeenth-century author Wang Fu-chih: "Heaven's knowledge [or wisdom] develops spontaneously [lit., opens or unfolds of itself]. . . . The clear void does not reflect . . . but possesses its principle naturally. It is a case of knowing 'something out there,' and so how can it be called [ordinary] knowledge?"[41] This characteristic perception of cosmic wisdom must be kept in mind when considering the problem of love and wisdom and their yin-yang affinities. Even if wisdom may on occasion be granted precedence, it contains within it much of what is associated with love: instinct, wholeness, immediacy.

The intuitive basis of cosmic wisdom is conveyed by the use of various pairs of cognitive terms that have this in common: they denote, roughly, the contrast between spirit and intellect, the latter being understood here as reason combined with sense-knowledge. The insistence on the "spiritual" or intuitive aspect of knowledge brings into question the masculine affinities of the Confucian cosmological perspective.

The *Book of Changes* furnishes some examples. Referring to the milfoil stalks and hexagrams used in divination, the *Great Appendix* says, "The virtue of the stalks is that they are round [like Heaven] and spirit-like [*shen*]; the virtue of the diagrams is that they are square [like Earth] and intelligent [*chih*]. . . . Spirit-like, they know the future; intelligent, they store the past" (A/11). A similar but much commoner example is that of *shen-ming*, the "spiritual intelligences" or, better, "spirit and intelligence" that pervade the universe and can be penetrated by the sage. The clearest indication of their yin-yang affinities is in the *Great Appendix* (B/6):

Ch'ien and K'un are the gateway to the Changes.
Ch'ien is yang in nature,
K'un is yin in nature.
Yin and yang unite their virtue,
And hard and soft [lines, or substances]
   acquire form.
Thus are embodied the principles of Heaven and Earth;
Thus can one penetrate the virtues of spirit and
   intelligence [*shen-ming*].

The assumption that spirit and intelligence are ordered on the same lines as the other cosmic polarities named in this passage is confirmed, for example, by the first-century commentator Yang Hsiung in his own *Classic of the Great Mystery*: "Heaven with its motion shows men spirit [*shen*]; Earth with its stability shows men intelligence [*ming*]."[42] Translation is unsatisfactory, but it contrives to suggest the network of ideas that define these two sorts of knowledge. The former is dynamic and a priori, just as Heaven itself (as we know from the *Changes*) anticipates and initiates cosmic change through its "knowledge." The second kind of knowledge in Yang Hsiung's text is communicated visually through Earth's stable spatial properties. It is relevant to notice the composition and meaning of the character *ming* (intelligence) itself: depicting the sun and moon in juxtaposition, it means either visual or mental clarity.

The formal alignment of these two intelligences (the spiritual and the sense-based) with the yang and yin elements in the cosmos, if relevant to gender, suggests a male/female ordering. But in important respects their meanings indicate precisely the opposite. *Shen* invariably carries with it the notion of the incalculable. Like the English term *spirit*, its operations are immediate and intuitive rather than discursive and evidence bound. In the language earlier quoted, it is "round" as opposed to "square"; the metaphor captures its holistic quality just as Lao Tzu's uncarved block and Chuang Tzu's clod captured the same essence in Taoist wisdom. *Ming* on the other hand is closer to understanding rationally based on objective evidence; its distinction-making activity is fittingly expressed in the metaphor of the square, symbolizing the diverse spatial properties of Earth and descriptive of the shape of the hexagrams, whose quantitative aspect enables precise calculation and deduction.

The distinction between these two types of intelligence, the spiritual and intellectual, is significantly similar to that posited by the psychologist Carl Jung between eros and logos, denoting the principles of the female and male psyche respectively. "Eros is an interweaving; logos is differentiating knowledge, clarifying light; eros is relatedness; logos is discrimination and detachment."[43] From the standpoint of Jungian psychology, then, and indeed from a common Western standpoint, the Confucian concept of knowledge in its cosmic setting presents a clear case of femininity in the yang principle itself. Nor is the ascription too farfetched from a Chinese point of view: the Taoists Lao Tzu and Chuang Tzu had each in his own fashion already shown the linkages between common conceptions of femaleness and the concept of intuitive wisdom. The very terminology of Confucian cosmological discourse at this point owed a great deal, one suspects, to the *Chuang Tzu,* for example in its elevation of *shen* over *ming.*[44]

Various instances of apparent gender reversal have been shown to occur in the key concepts of love, rectitude, and wisdom. From some standpoints it seems reasonable to speak of the feminization of the yang principle in the cosmos. But the question remains: is gender really the issue here? So long as we are focusing inquiry on it, we can detect its ramifications and reversals as we have done. But may these not be incidental and even irrelevant to the main thrust of this cosmology? Do not the ambiguities and inconsistencies of gender correlation suggest that gender was not an overriding concern? There may be no ultimate answer to the question. Significance is partly in the eye of the beholder. But we may legitimately pursue the possibility that some of the basic concerns of Chinese metaphysics and cosmology transcend questions of gender.

The Basic Polarity of Chinese Metaphysics

Given the fluidity of gender concepts in any setting beyond the strictly biological, we must ask, Is there any governing factor that lends consistency to the transitions and permutations of gender concepts in Chinese correlative thinking? Can we identify *the* basic polarity, whether it be gender itself or some other sort, that shapes the rest of the system?

It is probably safe to say that the basic polarity is not one of gender. Not only do yin and yang not *mean* "feminine" and "masculine" etymologically or invariably or primarily. Gender in fact depends on too many other concepts in order to develop into something significant itself. (For example, the perception of male/ female as high/low, rational/appetitive, or immaterial/material re-quires that such abstract concepts already exist and count for something in their own right.) At this point, Sherry Ortner's answer to a similar sort of question has considerable relevance to the Chinese case. That answer is expressed in terms of nature/cul-ture, and it could serve to uncover at least some of the workings of Chinese polar logic and its reaction on gender. Another and per-haps ultimately truer way of expressing the central polarity in Chinese thought is in terms of unity/diversity. On one side are clus-tered the values of wholeness, spontaneity, instinct, naturalness, givenness, quietism; on the other those of differentiation, choice, effort, responsibility, artifice, activism.[45]

Unlike the Ortner model, in which culture is valued above na-ture, the Chinese conception assigns ultimate priority to nature interpreted as wholeness. The preeminence of wholeness is mir-rored in the yin-yang symbols of the unbroken and broken line: ⸺, ⸺ ⸺. But immediately we are in the midst of paradox. The definition of yang, symbolized in the drawing of the unbroken line, signals a step away from wholeness. The line has a beginning and an end; it divides an area above and below itself. In other words, yin, the broken line, is already implicit in yang. Unity has been lost in the moment of its definition.[46]

But the paradox is not merely in the symbolism; it lies in the very nature of yin-yang metaphysics as a means of expressing basic Chinese values. For the introduction of yang signifies the beginning of activity and change and the likely loss of naturalness and wholeness. This interpretation is strengthened by what we know of

185

the historical development of yin-yang thinking. Its early textual appearances, in parts of the *Chuang Tzu*, for example, bear witness to its classificatory, ordering function—the creation of minds seeking to articulate and control the world of flux. Such passages, however, are foreign to the general spirit of the book. In one passage the *Chuang Tzu* itself criticizes this use of yin-yang terminology, the culprit being the legendary Taoist Yellow Emperor himself:

> The Yellow Emperor had ruled as Son of Heaven for nineteen years and his commands were heeded throughout the world, when he heard that Master Kuang Ch'eng was living on top of the Mountain of Emptiness and Identity. He therefore went to visit him. "I have heard that you, Sir, have mastered the Perfect Way. May I venture to ask about the essence of the Perfect Way?" he said. ". . . *I would also like to control the yin and yang* in order to insure the growth of all living things. How may this be done?"
> Master Kuang Ch'eng said, "What you say you want to learn about pertains to the true substance of things, but *what you say you want to control pertains to things in their divided state.* Ever since you began to govern the world, rain falls before the cloud vapors have even gathered, the plants and trees shed their leaves before they have even turned yellow, and the light of the sun and moon grows more and more sickly. Shallow and vapid, with the mind of a prattling knave—what good would it do to tell *you* about the Perfect Way?"[47]

It was Chuang Tzu, of course, who seems to have understood better than any of his contemporaries whose writings have come down to us the philosophical problem of articulating unity: that is, of saying it without breaking it. And his social philosophy mirrored as perfectly as any the ideal of primitive simplicity marred by a decline into "civilization."[48]

The activist and non-naturalistic implications of yin-yang symbolism are borne out by its function in other Taoist texts. Here the early philosophical and later religious traditions differ markedly. In Lao Tzu's case, far from seizing on yin as a ready-made symbol of his own "feminine" values, he uses yin-yang terminology *only once* (in chap. 42) and alludes to it on one other occasion (in chap. 10); in both cases (which may be interpolations) priority goes in standard fashion to yang. Religious Taoism, on the other hand, is utterly steeped in yin-yang thinking and aims not at balance but at dominance of yang (whether defined as moral goodness or as the purified yang component of the psyche). It is a system that works in more than one sense against nature, seeking to reverse the process of natural physical, moral, and spiritual degeneration. There can be few stranger phenomena in the history of ideas than the spectacle of un-Taoist Taoism—whether we take the earlier or later form as standard.

The Confucians, who seem to fall somewhere in between, had a problem on their hands. Committed to an anthropogenic world view and to a considerable degree of hierarchic discrimination within the world, they found a use for yin-yang cosmology and its inbuilt male bias. But whatever their views of actual women or supposedly "female" patterns of social activity, their cosmology reflected the priority of natural wholeness and spontaneity, qualities commonly perceived as feminine—by Westerners such as Jung and the feminist writers already mentioned, by Taoists, and to some extent by Confucians themselves.

The embedding of feminine or at any rate holistic values in a yang-oriented philosophy is strikingly suggested in one of the best-loved documents of the Neo-Confucian tradition. This is the inscription Chang Tsai is said to have written on the western window of his classroom:

Heaven [Ch'ien] is my father and Earth [K'un] is my mother, and even such a small creature as I finds an intimate place in their midst.

Therefore that which fills the universe I regard as my body and that which directs the universe I consider as my nature.

All people are my brothers and sisters, and all things are my companions.

The great ruler (the emperor) is the eldest son of my parents (Heaven and Earth), and the great ministers are his stewards. Respect the aged—this is the way to treat them as elders should be treated. The sage identifies his character with that of Heaven and Earth, and the worthy is the most outstanding man. Even those who are tired, infirm, crippled, or sick; those who have no brothers or children, wives or husbands, are all my brothers who are in distress and have no one to turn to.

. . .

In life I follow and serve [Heaven and Earth]. In death I will be at peace.[49]

Chang Tsai's child is at home in the universe that sanctions Confucian ethical values. The motif of filial piety that runs through this short text could have been presented in severer terms, and indeed there are specific allusions to "reverence" and "obedience to the father's command." But what captures the attention above all is the sense of domestic intimacy conveyed through the images of child and cherisher. The male philosopher contemplating the universe has found himself in the unmistakable arena of female, mothering activity.

If we review the various aspects of the transition of gender-related imagery from society to cosmos, the centrality of holistic concerns will become clear. In the case of the Taoists this is unproblematic; they were both explicit and consistent in their endorsement of the principle of oneness and their use of feminine imagery to express the operation of the principle in the cosmos. Yin-yang cosmology likewise endorsed the value of unity even though its assiduous and un–Chuang Tzu-like patronage proved embarrassing to the principle. Classical Confucians were too keenly persuaded of the need for human discrimination and organization in society to risk approving a principle of inchoate and implicit order such as could have been expressed in their own images of femininity. But, as their reversals of gender imagery show, as soon as they engaged in metaphysics and cosmology they paid ultimate tribute to the ideal of spontaneous unity, linking it, however, along with its "feminine" expressions, to images of "masculine" activity such as Heaven and yang. Their holistic commitment may have been influenced by both Taoist and Buddhist philosophy; yet its roots can be clearly enough discerned in the teachings of their own founders.[50]

As far as gender is concerned, we have seen that it is explicitly present in Chinese correlative cosmology, typically in its unreversed and biological form. It is often implicitly present both in its unreversed, biological form and arguably in unexpected extensions of associated meaning. But in some cases there is a notable transference of feminine-related images to masculine-related matrices. It is a moot point whether this should be regarded as producing new and complex forms of cosmic gender or whether the issue of gender is transcended altogether. In the Confucian case, if the most basic value is wholeness in a polarity of whole/divided, for example, then it could be claimed by those who wish to do so that a male philosopher's image of the feminine has been projected onto reality. It is equally possible that the experience of the feminine provided only the occasion for the experience of unity and that the primordial value of unity should not be confused with or at least should not be reduced to the particular gender-related form in which it was (perchance, not necessarily) first discovered. (One might still speak of a "feminization of the cosmos" in the sense that values whose gender affinity happens to be feminine have been attributed to the cosmos, though not necessarily *as* feminine.) The second approach seems more logical, avoiding the danger of circularity. Again, it could be claimed that the image of wholeness has been detached from its feminine moorings and given a "masculine" identity in the cosmos. Against this, it might be argued that such an outright reversal of gender affinity can only mean that gender is irrelevant. It certainly suggests that particular stereotypes of social gender are irrelevant. But it seems that there may still be such a thing as cosmic gender that is almost sui generis, in which a natural logic of cosmic as opposed to human activity (i.e., as perceived in a particular cosmology) produces its own set of associated ideas, these being attached to gender by the same kind of logic though not in the same patterns as hold for social gender and its associated images. Even so, the conclusion surely has to be that not gender itself, but simple duality or polarity, or else the particular polarity of whole/divided, is the basic or underlying principle.

The beginning of this chapter indicated various forms of feminist claims about the relationship of gender to other areas of human experience and activity. The contribution of a Chinese case study is not an unqualified yes or no to these claims. For those who claim that male philosophers produce "masculine" philosophy (rationalistic, dualistic, and hierarchical), Chinese cosmology, Confucian as well as Taoist, is a partial disproof. For those who claim that male-generated concepts of gender have significantly shaped Western philosophy, Chinese metaphysics and cosmology offer some obvious parallels, but also some disconcerting counterexamples. It seems ultimately simpler to assent to one part of Sherry Ortner's thesis and conclude that conceptions of gender are themselves partly shaped by other and perhaps more fundamental categories of thought and experience; Ortner's identification of these as nature and culture is also borne out by the Chinese case, though much of the detail of her argument does not hold true for China.[51]

What is particularly interesting in the case of Confucian cosmology is that when these more ultimate categories were at stake, normal gender alignments went by the board. We may insist that the system shapers were still gender conscious (their favored values generally found their way into the yang category). Or we may insist that yang does not mean male, that unity does not mean female, and that there is no warrant for assuming that gender was always present in the shaping of a cosmological system. The evidence suggests that this is the safer position while simultaneously allowing us to see the indisputable but not so very paradoxical reversal of certain gender-related values when these are transferred from society to cosmos.

Notes

1. Sherry B. Ortner, "Is Female to Male as Nature Is to Culture?" in *Woman, Culture, and Society,* ed. M. Z. Rosaldo and L. Lamphere (Stanford: Stanford University Press, 1974), pp. 67–87.

2. Sandra Harding and Merrill B. Hintikka, eds., *Discovering Reality: Feminist Perspectives on Epistemology, Metaphysics, Methodology, and Philosophy of Science* (Dordrecht, Boston, and London: D. Reidel Publishing Co., 1983).

3. Ibid., p. x.

4. Lynda Lange, "Woman Is Not a Rational Animal: On Aristotle's Biology of Reproduction," in *Discovering Reality,* ed. Harding and Hintikka, pp. 1–15; Elizabeth V. Spelman, "Aristotle and the Politicization of the Soul," in ibid., pp. 17–43; Jane Flax, "Political Philosophy and the Patriarchal Unconscious: A Psychoanalytic Perspective on Epistemology and Metaphysics," in ibid., pp. 245–81; Nancy C. M. Hartsock, "The Feminist Standpoint: Developing the Ground for a Specifically Feminist Historical Materialism," in ibid., pp. 283–310. My highly condensed presentation of selected key themes in this book inevitably obscures the sophistication of much of its writing. Evelyn Fox Keller's "Gender and Science," in ibid., pp. 187–205, for example, presents a critical and qualified version of the relation between masculinity and scientific objectivity.

5. Spelman, "Aristotle"; Keller, "Gender and Science," pp. 190, 203.

6. Keller, "Gender and Science," pp. 196–200; Merrill B. Hintikka and Jaakko Hintikka, "How Can Language Be Sexist?" in *Discovering Reality,* ed. Harding and Hintikka, p. 145; Flax, "Political Philosophy," pp. 245–81; Hartsock, "Feminist Standpoint," pp. 294–98.

7. The implication is made explicit in Hintikka and Hintikka, "How Can Language Be Sexist?" p. 146, and Hartsock, "Feminist Standpoint," pp. 294–95, 298–99.

8. The explicitly feminine values of Taoism have not gone unnoticed by Westerners. They form part of the subject matter of Sandra A. Wawrytko's study, *The Undercurrent of Feminine Philosophy in Eastern and Western Thought* (Washington, D.C.: Press of America, 1976, 1981), originally entitled *The Philosophical Systematization of a 'Feminine' Perspective in Terms of Taoism's "Tao-teh-ching" and the Works of Spinoza.*

9. This raises the question of Buddhist influence on the content of Neo-Confucian thought, since it was under the stimulus of Buddhism and religious Taoism that Confucians of this period developed a serious metaphysics and cosmology. I suspect that the Buddhist influence extended to the treatment of one of the issues handled below (i.e., humanity versus wisdom: compare *karuṇā,* compassion, versus *prajñā,* wisdom); but it is relevant to notice that the Confucian consensus on this issue, if I am correct, points away from Buddhism and the primacy it accords to *prajñā.*

One other methodological point deserves mention. The focus of this essay on key words and phrases within a correlative scheme reflects the nature of Chinese philosophical language. That language is aphoristic rather than discursive, and in consequence a tremendous weight of associative meaning is attached to key terms such as those selected for discussion here. To the modern reader this may produce seemingly arbitrary and eccentric as well as esoteric results. But it is in fact the most concrete way of approaching the very general questions raised. As for the evidence shown and conclusions drawn, they are necessarily limited—as is indicated throughout—but they are sufficiently suggestive to warrant a hearing and perhaps encourage further research and discussion.

10. A useful study is Ch'en Tung-yuan's *Chung-kuo fu-nu sheng-huo shih* (A history of Chinese womanhood) (Shanghai: Commercial Press, 1937).

11. For example, *The Book of Rites* 45/8; trans. James Legge in *Li Ki, Book of Rites,* 2 vols., ed. Ch'u Chai and Winberg Chai (New Hyde Park: University Books, 1967), 2, pp. 432–33, and Mencius 1B/5; trans. D. C. Lau in *Mencius* (Harmondsworth and Baltimore: Penguin Books, 1970). Translations from *Mencius* in this essay are from Lau. Chinese references to the *Rites, Mencius, Analects, Book of Changes, Book of Odes,* and *Chuang Tzu* follow or are consistent with the *Harvard-Yenching Institute Sinological Index Series* (omitting the page numbers), and precede references to translations. Separate numbered references to translations are provided only where these differ from the Chinese numbering. Unless otherwise indicated, translations are my own. For all parentheses within translations I have substituted square brackets except when the translator

used both within the passage quoted. Further additions of my own in square brackets are noted whenever they occur.

12. *Rites* 11/25; Legge, 1, p. 441. This precept was no doubt more honored in the breach than the observance; it was not uniformly supported even in theory.

13. The first seven, or "inner," chapters of the *Chuang Tzu* are generally reckoned by scholars to be the most authentic.

14. *Rites* 11/25; Legge, 1, p. 440.

15. *Rites* 11/25; Legge, 1, p. 441. The insertion [*chih*] is mine.

16. Cf. Li Yu-ning, *Historical Roots of Changes in Women's Status in Modern China*, St. John's Papers in Asian Studies, no. 29 (Jamaica, N.Y.: Center of Asian Studies, St. John's University, [1981?]), p. 3; and Ch'en, *Chung-kuo fu-nu*, p. 13.

17. *Ode* 264; trans. Bernhard Karlgren, in *The Book of Odes* (Stockholm: Museum of Far Eastern Antiquities, 1950).

18. *Analects* 17/24; trans. D. C. Lau in *Confucius: The Analects* (Harmondsworth and New York: Penguin Books, 1979), 17/25.

19. *Rites* 33/11; Legge, 2, p. 341.

20. *Rites* 50/5; Legge, 2, p. 467.

21. *Mencius* 4B/33; *Lieh-nü chuan*, comp. Liu Hsiang, trans. Albert O'Hara, in *The Position of Women in Early China* (Taipei: Mei Ya Publications, Inc., 1971). The biography of Mencius's mother was included in the *Lieh-nü chuan*. Another well-known example was the mother of the eleventh-century Ch'eng brothers who helped to found Neo-Confucianism; see Chu Hsi, ed., *Chin-ssu lu* (Taipei: Taiwan Commercial Press, 1967), pp. 196–97.

22. *Rites* 33/15; Legge, 2, p. 343.

23. Cf. *Analects* 3/8, 6/18, 12/8.

24. *Lao Tzu* 20; trans. D. C. Lau, in *Lao Tzu: Tao Teh Ching* (Harmondsworth and Baltimore: Penguin Books, 1963). Translations from *Lao Tzu* in this essay are from Lau.

25. *Chuang Tzu* 7/29–31; trans. Burton Watson, *The Complete Works of Chuang Tzu* (New York: Columbia University Press, 1968), p. 97. Material in brackets inserted by Alison H. Black.

26. There may be a parallel here to those Christian and Buddhist monks who affected certain "feminine" roles or attitudes without supposing that actual women were their best examplars: see essays by Bynum and Richman in this volume.

27. *Explanation of the Trigrams* 10; cf. ibid., 11.

28. *Changes*, Hsiang Commentary on Ch'ien Hexagram.

29. Ibid., Tuan Commentary on K'un Hexagram, and *Explanation of the Trigrams* 4. Cf. *Changes, Great Appendix* A/5,7. The gender implications

of K'un as the storehouse are brought out by Li Kuang-ti in his Ch'ing compilation of commentaries on the *Changes,* the *Chou I che-chung* (Taipei: Taiwan Commercial Press, 1978), 17/10a.

30. *Rites* 19/1; Legge, 2, p. 98.
31. Ibid.
32. *Rites* 19/4; Legge, 2, p. 100.
33. *Rites* 19/6; Legge, 2, pp. 102–3.
34. *Rites* 19/20; Legge, 2, p. 114.
35. *Rites* 19/4; Legge, 2, p. 101.
36. *Rites* 50/2; Legge, 2, p. 466.
37. Chu Hsi, in *Chou I che-chung,* ed. Li Kuang-ti, 17/5b. Cf. the identification of *jen* with spring and *i* with autumn in Shao Yung, *Huang-chi ching-shih shu Ssu-pu pei-yao (SPPY)* ed., 7B/16b. Wang Fu-chih of the seventeenth century comments on the confusion and hair-splitting evasions of the commentators, whom he characteristically sees as too rigid in their demand for order. See Wang Fu-chih, *Chang Tsai Cheng-meng chu* (Commentary on Chang Tsai's *Cheng-meng*) in his *Ch'uan-shan i-shu* (Shanghai: Tai-p'ing yang Bookstore, 1933), 5/6b. Chang Tsai's text reflects the yang classification of *jen* over *i*'s yin. See, for example, 6a. In fact the reversal of love and rectitude is by no means unequivocal. For example, as indicated earlier, even at the human level the father is supposed to be loved as much as the mother. Again, since rectitude (like propriety or ceremony, with which it is closely associated) connotes the mutually entailed notions of authority and submission, in some contexts the female rather than the male would be readily suggested. The instability of yin-yang ordering is also suggested in the alignment of music with feeling and of ceremonies with principles (*li*); in other contexts principles and feelings would usually be interpreted as yang and yin respectively. These qualifications are significant as reminders of the essential fluidity of yin-yang polarity, although they do not seriously affect the main argument.
38. Chang Tsai, in Wang Fu-chih, *Chang Tsai cheng-meng chu,* 5/6a.
39. T'an Ssu-t'ung, *Jen-hsueh,* in his *T'an Liu-yang ch'üan-chi* (Taipei: Chung-hua Bookstore, 1962), A/5b–6a. For translation see Wing-tsit Chan, *A Source Book in Chinese Philosophy* (Princeton: Princeton University Press, 1963), p. 739.
40. Chu Hsi, in *Chou I che-chung,* ed. Li Kuang-ti, 13/24a. The alignment of wisdom with yin and *jen* with yang in the *Great Appendix* A/5 is accomplished partly through the seasonal imagery that commentators discern in the passage. See *Chou I che-chung,* 13/25a–26a, comments by Chu Hsi, Wu Teng, and Yü Yen. See also Hu Ping-wen's first comment on p. 26a. For further evidence of seasonal identifications of *jen* and wisdom, see Shao

Yung, *Huang-chi ching-shih shu* 7B/16b, where *jen* is assigned to spring and wisdom to winter.

41. Wang Fu-chih, *Chou I wai-chuan,* in *Ch'uan-shan i-shu,* 5/1a.

42. Yang Hsiung, *T'ai-hsuan ching,* SPPY ed., 7/7b.

43. Carl Jung, *The Secret of the Golden Flower: A Chinese Book of Life,* rev. ed., trans. and explained by Richard Wilhelm (New York and London: Harcourt Brace Jovanovich, 1962), p. 118. It is ironical that Jung wrote these words with a misunderstanding of their application to Chinese conceptions of the psyche. In relating logos and eros respectively to the yang and yin aspects of the soul, *hun* and *p'o* (which are directly linked with the *shen* and *ming* cosmic intelligences), he was misled by the formal correspondences of the Chinese system, presumably too by his readiness to perceive resemblances to his own system, and perhaps most fundamentally by historical and pervasive Western assumptions about the mind and its faculties. For the connection between the Chinese concepts just mentioned, see, for example, Tai Chen's *Yuan-shan,* in *Tai Chen's Inquiry into Goodness,* trans. with Chinese text by Ch'eng Chung-ying (Honolulu: East-West Center Press, 1970), B/11, tr. pp. 96–97.

44. Explicitly stated in *Chuang Tzu* 32/51.

45. Cf. Tai Chen's observation that polar terms such as benevolence and righteousness (*jen-i*) or wisdom and benevolence (*chih-jen*) connoted a combination of life-process (*sheng-sheng*) and articulate order (*t'iao-li*). Tai Chen, *Meng Tzu tzu-i,* in his *Tai Chen chi* (Shanghai: Shang-hai ku-chi ch'u-pan she, 1980), p. 317.

46. See Alison H. Black, *Man and Nature in the Philosophical Thought of Wang Fu-chih* (Seattle: University of Washington Press, 1986), chap. 2, for a discussion of this paradox and its treatment by Chinese cosmologists and for further information on yin-yang cosmology in general.

47. *Chuang Tzu* 11/28–33; Watson, pp. 118–19. Italics mine, except in last sentence.

48. For example, *Chuang Tzu* 14/64–74; 16/4–11; Watson, pp. 164–65, 172–73. On the articulation of unity, see *Chuang Tzu* 2/52–54; Watson, p. 43.

49. Chang Tsai's so-called Western Inscription, in *Chang-tzu cheng-meng chu,* ed. Wang, 9/2a–4b; trans. Wing-tsit Chan, in *A Source Book in Chinese Philosophy* (Princeton, N.J.: Princeton University Press, 1963, 1969), pp. 497–98. Material in first two square brackets inserted by me.

50. Cf., for example, Confucius's insistence that a connecting thread ran through all his teachings, Mencius's emphasis on the universality of human nature and the unity of man and Heaven, and Hsun Tzu's conception of the Way that embraced all differences.

51. Ortner's claim that culture is valued over nature is untrue for the

Taoists and only partly true for the Confucians. Her claim that maleness is valued over femaleness holds for the formal Confucian attitude but clearly not for the Taoist. And her claim that female is aligned with nature and male with culture, though true for the Taoist and also for Confucian social theory, is not particularly true for Confucian metaphysics and cosmology.

Eight

Uses of Gender Imagery in Ancient Gnostic Texts
Michael A. Williams

Today, applications of the labels gnosticism or Gnostic (from the Greek *gnōsis,* "knowledge") include an array of both past and present phenomena, and often phenomena that otherwise are not ordinarily associated—Marxism and Christian Science, for example.[1] But when I refer to ancient gnosticism, I am using *gnosticism* in the more classical sense which the term has had since being coined in the eighteenth century by scholarship dealing with religion in the ancient world. That is, I am using *gnosticism* as an umbrella designation for a certain general type of religious expression that seems to have flourished in a particularly visible way in the Roman Empire during the second, third, and fourth centuries of the Common Era.[2] By *ancient gnosticism* we are not referring to a single sect or religious organization, with one founder, or even to one founding community. Instead, we are speaking about a large number of often quite separate communities, individual teachers, prophets, and other leaders. For instance, many Gnostics were decidedly Christian Gnostics, whereas others show no obvious connection with any form of ancient Christianity.

Two general sorts of interrelationship among these various groups have justified their common classification in past scholar-

I wish to acknowledge the helpful criticism of earlier drafts of this chapter, that I received from all three of the volume editors, Caroline Walker Bynum, Stevan Harrell, and Paula Richman. They bear no responsibility for any unremedied weaknesses, but deserve considerable credit for many improvements.

ship as Gnostic. There is first of all a phenomenological pattern, involving such elements as the assertion that the god(s) or power(s) responsible for creating and managing the cosmos must be identified as distinct from, and inferior to, a higher God; or, the importance that Gnostics tended to give to *gnosis*—that is, a heavenly, revealed knowledge—in their teachings about salvation from this inferior, created cosmos.[3] A second sort of interrelationship among ancient Gnostic sources involves definite historical connections that we know existed: cases where one Gnostic teacher had studied under another, or where the two were even blood relatives, or instances where Gnostic writers who are anonymous to us were obviously either borrowing from one another or from common sources.[4]

On the one hand, such justifications for speaking of gnosticism as a category within ancient religion remain at least generally convincing. However, we are at the same time constantly refining our awareness of the genuine variety represented by what we call gnosticism. This is of course true of modern research on religions in the Greco-Roman world in general: Even such traditions as ancient Judaism and Christianity, which one might have visualized as fairly homogeneous, are today known to have been remarkably variegated.[5] So too for a category such as gnosticism, there are topics on which it is both possible and important to emphasize how ancient Gnostics could differ from one another.

One such topic is gender imagery. Much of modern scholarship about gender imagery in gnosticism has focused particularly on what is perceived to have been an unusually prominent role given by Gnostics to the female gender.[6] We will see examples of this in some of the Gnostic material discussed later. Female divinities were of course not unusual in the mythology of the ancient world. But most Gnostic sources that have survived represent forms of Jewish or Christian gnosticism, and their uses of female imagery are indeed often in striking contrast to what is normally encountered in more "orthodox" forms of Judaism or Christianity. Due especially to enhanced sensitivities of the most recent generation of scholarship to the correlation between androcentric religious symbolism and social dominance by males, there has been interest in the possibility that Gnostic mythology was making a statement rejecting traditional forms of androcentrism and asserting the equality of female and male, women and men.[7] No clear consensus has emerged on this question. Some have maintained that, in spite of the more visible role of the female in Gnostic mythology, this mythology nevertheless continues to subordinate the female to the male, and thus, "Gnostic dualism shares the patriarchal paradigm of Western culture."[8]

A fundamental mistake in much of what has been written on gnosticism and gender has been the tendency to speak as though there were a single Gnostic perspective in this area. Even in more recent works, it has been all too tempting to lapse into generalized statements about "the Gnostic myth of the female,"[9] or "the gnostic pattern" in the use of gender imagery,[10] or how "Gnosticism . . . employed the categories of 'male' and 'female.'"[11] Such generalizations are attempted not because these scholars are unaware of some diversity on this topic in Gnostic sources, but because they are evidently more impressed by how much of a common perspective on gender they find among Gnostic writings. To be sure, there are topics in gnosticism about which we can generalize, but perspective on gender is not one of them.

I propose to illustrate the diversity of which I speak by looking closely at three Gnostic sources. Two of these texts, the *Gospel of Philip* and the *Hypostasis of the Archons,* are found together in the same manuscript: they are the third and fourth tractates, respectively, in Codex II of the Nag Hammadi Library, a collection of twelve books, plus pages from a thirteenth, that were discovered in about 1945 near Nag Hammadi, Egypt.[12] The books date from the fourth century C.E. and are written in the Coptic language, but in almost all instances the writings found in them seem to be translations of works originally composed in Greek. The dates for the original versions of the *Gospel of Philip* and the *Hypostasis of the Archons* are uncertain, but probably fall somewhere from about 150 C.E. to about 300 C.E. The authors of these two texts are not known to us by name: the *Hypostasis* is anonymous, and the only obvious reason some scribe applied the *Gospel of Philip* to the other text is that in the middle of the work there is a quotation of one brief saying of "Philip the apostle" (*Gos. Phil.* 73, 8–15). Therefore we are not certain of the gender of the author in either case. The other Gnostic source I will discuss is one for which we do not have the original work; we have only a summary, given by an opponent. In a heresiological writing thought by some to come from the pen of the Roman Christian Hippolytus (early third century C.E.), we find a summary and criticism of a document that, we are told, was titled *Baruch* and was composed by a Gnostic named Justin.[13] In spite of the disadvantage of having only second-hand access to this work, I have included a discussion of it here because of interesting points of comparison that exist between it and the other two Gnostic writings.

These three Gnostic works illustrate three different perspectives on gender. It is not simply a matter of, say, one text treating femaleness more "positively" or "negatively" than another text. Rather, there are "qualitative" differences in the ways these three authors experienced gender itself. In both *Baruch* and the *Gospel of Philip,* images relating to union and separation of male and female are central to the organization of experience. Yet the two texts differ fundamentally: in *Baruch,* existence in this world is experienced as the union of male and female, a union that must be broken in order to achieve transcendence; in the *Gospel of Philip* it is precisely transcendence that is experienced as the union of male and female. Also, in each case we find a different "quality" in the way gender relationships are experienced: in *Baruch,* the relationship of male to female is above all a voluntary contractual relationship between parties, ordered by a well-intended system of mutual responsibilities, but with all the attendant potential for violation and disappointment. In the *Gospel of Philip* the relation of male to female is much more like the relation between two oppositely charged particles, which are dangerously unstable until properly paired. And finally, if these first two texts represent examples—contrasting examples—of the organization of experience in gender categories, the *Hypostasis of the Archons* is a case in which a Gnostic document's fairly rich store of male and female mythological images does not seem to make a point about gender at all.

Justin's *Baruch*

Justin claimed that all things began from three unbegotten principles, two male and one female. The highest of these was male and is called "the Good one" (Greek: *ho agathos*), reminiscent of the philosophical notion of the Absolute Good (*to agathon auto*) in Platonic tradition (e.g., Plato, *Republic* 7.540a). The second male principle is called Elohim, a Hebrew plural (lit., "gods"), commonly encountered in Jewish scripture as one of the designations for the single "God" of Israel (e.g., Exod. 3:1). The female principle is called Edem, which is of course the name of the location of Paradise in Genesis 2:8ff. The entire myth is constructed around the relationships among these three and the various ways in which these relationships are mirrored in cosmic experience. Edem is described as having a body whose upper half is in the form of a maiden and whose lower half is in the form of a serpent. Neither Elohim nor Edem had foreknowledge, and therefore Elohim's desire for Edem led to their union. From the union, twelve paternal and twelve maternal angels were produced, and these constitute the trees of Paradise.

The angels of Elohim created the first man, Adam, as a sort of stamp or seal (*sphragis*), a love token that, as an eternal (*aiōnion*) symbol, would forever call to mind the marriage of Elohim and Edem. Adam was created from the finest earth—that is, from the humanlike and civilized portions of Edem, not from the animal portions—and into Adam were placed soul (*psychē*) from Edem and spirit (*pneuma*) from Elohim. This distinction between spirit, soul, and material body in the human being appears frequently in the literature of the day, with *soul* sometimes designating, as it does in *Baruch,* a level of the self less sublime than one's spirit and involved most of all with "lower" forms of self-expression—mere animation, emotions, and so forth, as opposed to abstract thought or contemplation (of which the spirit is capable). Eve then came into being, "just as Moses wrote," as an eternal image, symbol and seal of Eden (5.26.9), and she too received a soul from Edem and a spirit from Elohim. Adam and Eve were then told to increase and multiply.

In short, the picture the myth presents thus far is one of heartfelt love between Elohim and Edem, for which the created humans stand as symbols at two levels: individually by each possessing both soul and spirit, and together by their relationship as husband and wife. The description at this point portrays a positive relationship of happy devotion. An aside by Justin here links the myth to marriage customs of the day: in her love, Edem brought to Elohim all her power, establishing a "divine and paternal law" of the dowry that was to be followed in marriages ever since (5.26.10).

However, this pleasant scene turns sour in the latter portion of the myth. The trouble is initiated by the male partner, Elohim. After creating the world, Elohim wished to survey his work from a more lofty vantage point to insure that there were no defects. Thus, Elohim ascended, taking his twelve angels with him, leaving Edem and her angels behind, since, being earth, such ascensions were not to her liking. But once Elohim had reached the highest part of heaven, he saw a light, the light of the Good one, that was still more transcendent than anything Elohim had created. He asked for entrance into the higher realm, was admitted, and was shown the wonder of that place, and then was seated at the right hand of the Good one. Elohim's next thought was for his spirit, still bound within the humans in the world below, and he asked permission to destroy the world so as to free his spirit. But, we are told, the Good one would never have allowed such an evil act. Instead, Edem was to be allowed to have the creation for as long as she desired. But she had lost Elohim forever (5.26.18).

This abandonment of Edem by Elohim becomes the central paradigm in *Baruch*. The interesting thing about the motif is the ambivalence with which it is charged. On the one hand, as we will see, the abandonment of Edem and the ascent to the Good one form the paradigm for ultimate salvation. On the other hand, this act of abandonment is described negatively as the violation of the previous vows that Elohim had made to Edem. Because of the pain she feels at Elohim's abandonment, Edem in turn commands one of her angels, Babel (= Aphrodite), to introduce adulteries and divorces among human beings so that the spirit of Elohim still dwelling in humans might suffer the same anguish that Edem was experiencing. Hence, Justin says that both evil and good spring from a common origin—the actions of Elohim (5.26.23f.).

One of the twelve paternal angels of Elohim operates throughout the text, descending into the world to bring knowledge to Elohim's spirit in humans. This angel, Baruch, is said to have spoken in Paradise to Adam and Eve, urging them to eat from all the trees of Paradise except the tree of the knowledge of good and evil, which Justin also allegorically identifies with one of the maternal angels, Naas (which in Hebrew means "serpent"). However, Naas deceived the first couple. Baruch spoke through Moses, but Naas distorted the commands. Baruch spoke through the prophets, and even through the Greek hero Heracles, but all these also were led astray. The final messenger through whom Baruch spoke was Jesus, who, when Naas was unable to seduce him, was caused by Naas to be crucified. At Jesus' death, he left the psychic (soul) and earthly portions behind. Justin understands the words from the cross, "Woman, you have your son" (cf. John 19:26), to be addressed to Edem and to be referring to the abandoned body and soul. Jesus' spirit ascended to the Good one.

In the mythology in *Baruch,* gender distinction is explicit and prominent from the very beginning. The description of the two male principles and the one female principle clearly implies that the latter is the least transcendent of the three. In the creation of the humans, she contributes the earth from which the bodies are formed, and she contributes the soul, while the highest element of the human, the spirit, comes from Elohim. The goal mapped out by the text is for the human spirit to leave behind its body and soul and ascend to the Good one. Yet this mythology is not sharply dualistic, for one is immediately struck by the sympathetic fashion in which Edem is treated. The ascent of the spirit in this text is not described with metaphors of the gleeful or scornful "rejection of the female," but rather with the sober and wrenchingly ambivalent metaphor of marital separation.[14]

Marital unfaithfulness or outright abandonment of one's mate was of course not a religious metaphor new with Justin. It is in fact a widely encountered theme in Gnostic sources, among other places. Yet the theme is employed in diverse ways. For example, *Baruch* stands out from almost all Gnostic texts in assigning the initiative toward separation to the *male* partner. Several Gnostic sources give a mythological account of the origin of the world in which the process of cosmic creation is initiated by the action of a female figure, Wisdom, who desires to act on her own, without her male consort.[15] And while in some Gnostic texts the separation of female consort from male is experienced as a problem to be overcome, in *Baruch* the separation of male from female is a problem only in the limited sense that it is not yet complete (Elohim's spirit remains within humans); ultimately the problem is overcome not by the reunion of male and female but by their complete separation.

However, Justin does not seem to have advocated the segregation of men from women. By contrast with many Gnostic texts, *Baruch* does not reject marriage as a social institution, nor does it reject sexual activity in marriage. When Adam and Eve are told to "increase and multiply," there is no indication that Justin understood this in any other than the traditional biblical sense—to reproduce physically. The only sexuality that receives a specifically negative valuation in the text involves acts traditionally considered immoral, such as adultery. Eve's eating from the tree is described as an act of adultery between Naas and Eve, an act that was "against the Law" (5.26.23); similarly Naas is said to have used Adam sexually and thereby to have introduced the unlawful act of pederasty into the world.[16]

What we know of *Baruch* in fact suggests that its mythology was intended to offer mythic support for and depth to the institution of marriage. Justin saw condensed in the contractual marriage commitments of men and women a direct reflection of the structure of the cosmos itself. In Justin's view, the constitution of the cosmos, like marriage, involves an arrangement between two parties for mutual benefit. Yet at the same time, in the marriage contract's vulnerability to violation, Justin seems to have found an equally direct reflection of how tentative the commitment to the cosmic order not only is, but ought to be. Violations (adulteries, divorces, etc.) of the correct and beneficial relationship of male to female *within* the cosmic order were, for Justin, dark reminders that union of male and female could not point *beyond* the cosmos, to perfection or transcendence.

Therefore, Elohim's desertion of Edem, not his marriage with her, is the paradigm for initiation into the mysteries that transcend the cosmos. There seems to have been some kind of formal rite involved in this initiation. The readers of *Baruch* were evidently called upon to swear an oath in which they vowed to preserve with secrecy the mysteries revealed in *Baruch* and not to turn back from the Good one to creation (5.27.1–2). Following this, there was some kind of baptismal experience, although it is not clear whether it included a physical washing or was instead a completely spiritualized mystic rite (5.27.2). Just exactly what the life of the initiate, turned toward the Good one rather than toward creation, would have looked like is not certain. But it does not seem to have involved any type of ascetic rejection of marriage and sexuality. Indeed, when Adam and Eve are in Paradise, they are told to avoid only the tree of the knowledge of good and evil (= Naas); on the other hand they are explicitly told to eat of all the other eleven trees, "that is, to *obey* the other eleven angels of Edem; for the eleven do have passions, but they do not have transgression— while Naas does have transgression" (5.26.22). Therefore, turning

203

to the Good one would not seem to have included a renunciation of passion per se, but only a turning away from transgressions such as adultery.

The desertion of the female by the male in this initiation rite referred to the separation of the male (spirit) from the female (soul and body) portions of the individual. This ritual celebration of the separation of these elements anticipated the ascent of one's spirit at death. Our text explicitly points out that both men and women have the female as well as the male elements: "the soul is Edem and the spirit is Elohim, both being in all humans, both females and males" (5.26.25). Both women and men, therefore, underwent an initiation, which was structured in gender categories (abandonment of the female by the male), but in which the sexuality of the initiates was irrelevant.

In sum, Justin employed the union of male and female as the preeminent symbol for existence in this world and the separation of male from female as the symbol for redemption from the world. Each has its own time, according to Justin. Union of male spirit and female soul in the human being is not a union that is inherently evil, nor is its correlate, the social institution of marriage. That Justin did not see in earthly marriage and intercourse a zone of "defilement" as did many Gnostic writers, is indicated by statements such as: "to the present day, women bring a dowry to their husbands after the model of that first marriage (between Elohim and Edem), thus obeying a divine and paternal law which originated with Elohim and Edem" (5.26.10). This union and the created world in which it took place originated from the "mutual satisfaction of Elohim and Edem" (5.26.18); therefore there is something fundamentally good about it. More precisely, we might say there is something fundamentally "lawful" about it, for Justin seems to have underscored the correspondence of the male and female union to "law."[17] Unlike some Gnostic texts, *Baruch* did not intend to undercut the traditional law (above all, the Jewish Torah) by disclosing that it was actually the product of inferior archons. It is not law, but disobedience of the law, that Justin criticizes. The paradigmatic act of Elohim's abandonment of Edem is itself analyzed in legal terms: Elohim's spirit, left dwelling within humans, receives its punishment because Elohim "abandoned his spouse, contrary to the contracts [*kata tas sunthekas*] which he had made" (5.26.21).

But Elohim's disobedience is a special case precisely because it is at the same time a transcending of the realm within which the marriage law is valid. Ascension beyond the material world involves a transcendence that the male-female union does not express. Indeed, it involves a transcendence in which the female plays no role whatsoever, since both Elohim and the Good one are male principles. There is no primal androgynous relationship between Elohim and Edem that must be restored or protected. Edem is distinct from Elohim; she is not his alter ego.

Gospel of Philip

The *Gospel of Philip* is not in the form of a continuous mythic narrative, but instead consists of a meandering series of theological statements covering a variety of subjects. However, the collection manifests some theological coherence. Many scholars have seen in the text some form of Valentinian Gnostic Christianity—that is, a gnosticism deriving from the Christian Gnostic teacher Valentinus (fl. ca. 150 C.E.) or one of his several students.[18] There has been a special interest in what the *Gospel of Philip* has to say about sacraments, since the text seems to name five sacraments—baptism, eucharist, chrism (i.e., anointing), redemption, and the bridal chamber—and devotes considerable space to discussions of the bridal chamber and, to a lesser extent, baptism and chrism.[19]

Even before the discovery of the *Gospel of Philip,* we knew of the image of the bridal chamber in a sacramental context—for example, in a report that the second-century writer Irenaeus gives us about rites performed by certain Valentinians (*Adv. haer.* 1.21.3). Yet nowhere did we have the kind of extensive discussion of this image by Gnostics themselves, such as we now find in the *Gospel of Philip.* This text has invested much in the symbolism of marriage, just as Justin did in *Baruch.* But the contrasts between these two sources, in their perspectives on marriage and on male and female in general, are striking.

We saw that in *Baruch* the symbolism of marriage was not cut loose from social reality; rather it was anchored in the literal pairing of man and woman as husband and wife. The same is true of the *Gospel of Philip,* for the "mystery of marriage" about which this work speaks was acted out concretely by couples who were living together. However, the marriages into which men and women

Gnostics were urged to enter were "spiritual marriages," that is, marriages in which couples lived together without sexual intercourse.[20] We know that this kind of marriage was in fact attempted by a variety of Christians in antiquity and not just by Valentinian Gnostics.[21] That some Valentinians advocated this practice is reported by the bishop Irenaeus, who, in a section where he describes Valentinian teaching, says that some of these persons pretend to live with one another merely as "brother" and "sister." Irenaeus is skeptical about this, however, since he claims that too often the "sister" somehow becomes pregnant (*Adv. haer.* 1.6.3).

Even if Irenaeus is not trading in sheer gossip here and did know of cases where the flesh had proved weak, the teaching about the mystery of marriage in the *Gospel of Philip* lends support to the view that certain Gnostics were sincere in their attempts at spiritual marriages. The author of the *Gospel of Philip* contrasts the "marriage of defilement" (i.e., ordinary marriages, in which there is intercourse) with the "undefiled marriage," which is "genuine, not fleshy" (82, 4–8). The "bridal chamber" about which the text has so much to say is described as something "not for the beasts, nor is it for the slaves, nor is it for the defiled women; but rather it is for free men and virgins" (69, 1–4). The "perfect" (i.e., Gnostics bound in spiritual marriages) are said to produce immortal offspring, not like the mortal offspring of Adam. The begetting involved is not natural or sexual, rather, "It is through a kiss that the perfect conceive and beget; because of this we ourselves kiss one another, conceiving by means of the grace that is in one another" (59, 2–6).

One passage in particular reveals much about this text's rationale for the importance of cohabitation, even though the "defilement" of sexual intercourse is to have no part in this undefiled marriage. We are told (65, 1–26) that unclean spirits roam the cosmos and that these include both male and female spirits. Male unclean spirits cohabit with human souls that live in female forms, while female unclean spirits mingle with souls that dwell in male bodies. The attacks by these incubi and succubi are portrayed vividly:[22]

> When the ignorant women [spirits] see a male sitting alone, they rush upon him and sport with him and defile him. Similarly, when ignorant men [spirits] see beautiful woman sitting alone, they persuade her

and force her, desiring to defile her. But when they see the husband and his wife sitting beside one another, the women cannot come in to the male, nor can the males come in to the female. Thus, if the image [*eikōn*] and the angel are united with one another, neither can any dare to come in to the male or the female. (65, 12–26)

I have suggested by parenthetical additions that the author is speaking directly of attacks by the spirits. Perhaps another possibility is that the sexual attacks described here refer to seduction and rape as in ordinary human society, and that these only illustrate by analogy the attacks by unclean spirits.

In any case, the point of the passage as a whole is clear: The unclean spirits that roam the cosmos are gender-charged, not gender-neutral, and not androgynous. These spirits are capable of attaching themselves to souls and defiling them, a fate the soul can avoid only by "receiving a male or a female power—namely, the bridegroom and the bride; one receives [the power] from the imaged bridal chamber" (65, 9–12). Whatever else it involved, this bridal chamber ritual was understood to balance the "gender-charge" that any human possesses by virtue of being man or woman and thus to eliminate vulnerability to defiling assaults from highly gender-charged unclean spirits.

However, the balancing of gender-charge through a marital (but nonsexual) pairing with a Gnostic of the opposite sex is actually only one axis of the ritual. The other, the vertical axis, is referred to in the passage quoted earlier about the union of image and angel (cf. 58, 10–14). Other Valentinian sources report the notion that corresponding to the company of Gnostics on earth (the images), there exists a company of undescended angelic counterparts. There is some diversity among the sources, but most speak of an expected union of Gnostics with their angels. However, the angels usually are said to play the male role of bridegroom, while the Gnostics are the female brides.[23]

Therefore, the remarkable thing about our passage in the *Gospel of Philip* is that rather than asserting that all Gnostics (men and women) are "females" who must be united as brides with their angelic bridegrooms, this text places far more weight on the actual physical sex of a Gnostic: For a Gnostic man there is a female angelic power with whom he must be united, and this "vertical" union coincides with his "horizontal" ritual pairing with a Gnostic woman. For a Gnostic woman there is union with a male angelic power, mirrored in the ritual marriage to a Gnostic man. Also this text contrasts with the perspective of Justin, who evidently saw one's sexual identity as irrelevant to the "gender structure" of transcendence (i.e., male abandoning and transcending the female), since for both men and women the ascent from this world involved one's male spirit abandoning one's female elements. In the *Gospel of Philip* we are not able to say that one's sexual identity is irrelevant to the gendered-structured mechanisms of transcendence. At the same time, the author seems to have a notion of a gender identity (I have been calling this a gender charge) that encompasses more characteristics than simply one or the other set of sexual organs, since the "vertical" union with an angelic power of the opposite gender is not a sexual union.

To be sure, certain passages in the *Gospel of Philip* seem at first to represent contradictions to the gender pattern I have just described. In one section, the author, perhaps drawing on popular theory,[24] suggests that if a woman has her mind on her adulterous lover while she is making love with her own husband, then any child resulting from that intercourse will resemble the lover, not the husband. So also, the author warns, those who dwell with the Son of God ought to love him and not the world so that their "offspring" will resemble the Lord and not the world (78, 12–24). The Gnostics play the role of bride in this metaphor. Yet the assignment of gender here seems to be completely a function of the metaphor at hand, whose real point is love of the Divine; therefore this passage hardly weakens the force of the earlier references to male and female unclean spirits attacking their gender opposites among human beings.

The contrast we have seen thus far between the *Gospel of Philip* and *Baruch* can be summarized as follows: Both texts give considerable significance to earthly marriages between men and women, and yet they do this with completely different understandings of both the nature of the marriages and their significance. The marriage condoned in *Baruch* is primarily a legal relationship epitomizing the contractual protection of social order and therefore by definition confined to the realm (the earth) in which such law plays a useful role. The undefiled marriage praised in the *Gospel of Philip* is primarily a matter of neutralizing otherwise dangerous polarities.

The *Gospel of Philip* traces the original separation of male from female to the story of Adam and Eve. If from Justin's perspective the story of the creation of Adam and Eve was about the union of male and female, the author of the *Gospel of Philip* is struck by the division in gender: "When Eve was in Adam, death did not exist; when she separated from him, death came into being" (68, 22–24). Death will be no more when Adam and Eve are reunited (68, 25f.).

> If the female had not separated from the male, she would not have died with the male. His separation became the beginning of death. Therefore, Christ came in order to correct the separation that existed from the beginning, and to unite the two once again, and give life to those who died from the separation and unite them. Now the woman unites with her husband in the bridal chamber, and those who have united in the bridal chamber will no longer be separated. For this reason Eve separated from Adam, since she did not unite with him in the bridal chamber. (70, 9–22)

The allusions in such passages are to the notion, of which we have many versions in antiquity, that Adam was androgynous when first created.[25] This notion was completely absent in *Baruch*. And even though we will encounter a similar fundamental tradition in the third Gnostic writing to be examined, its functions there are quite different.

The reunification expressed in the bridal chamber mirrors a reunification of male and female in the divine realm. We must not too facilely read into the *Gospel of Philip* Valentinian mythology familiar to us from other sources, especially because there is not always unanimity among such sources themselves. However, the *Gospel of Philip* knows and alludes to myths about Wisdom. In most Valentinian sources, Wisdom is one of the several divine entities that, as a group, constitute the full reality (Greek: *Pleroma*) of God, the Father of All. In Valentinian sources, these entities typically are grouped in male-female pairs, or syzygies. And the problem described by Valentinian myths is normally precipitated by Wisdom acting "alone," without her consort. The fruit born of this individual act is the creator (demiurge) and creation. The problem usually is resolved through ultimate reunification of Wisdom with her male consort, and the arrival of Jesus is understood as the most immanent manifestation of this male consort.[26]

The *Gospel of Philip*, in apparent agreement with some such

Wisdom myth, sees in Christ the one who has come "to correct the separation" (see quotation of 70, 9–22 given earlier). The correction of the separation is seen first in Christ's own birth and then also in his pairing with Mary Magdalene. In an enigmatic passage, the *Gospel of Philip* says that the "Father of All united with the virgin who came down," in a union taking place in the "great bridal chamber," and from this union the body of Christ came forth (71, 3–15). Mary the mother of Christ is earlier called the "virgin whom no power defiled" (55, 27), an epithet that we find applied to another female figure, Norea, in the *Hypostasis of the Archons*. In both cases, the implied contrast seems to be with the fleshly Eve who was sexually defiled by the cosmic archons or angels, according to various Gnostic as well as (Jewish and Christian) non-Gnostic traditions.[27] The *Gospel of Philip* has such a tradition in mind when elsewhere (61, 5–12) it says that the murderer (Cain) who killed his brother was begotten in adultery, since he was a child of the serpent (not of Adam). Therefore, the separation of male and female, which led to defilement, began to be reversed when Christ was born from an undefiled union of male (the Father) and female (the virgin).

This text also sees the mystery of reunification of male and female in the relationship between Christ and Mary Magdalene, whom the writing calls (in 59, 9; 63, 33) Christ's "companion" (Greek: *koinōnos*). The author draws attention to the fact that there were three Marys in Christ's life (59, 6–11), his mother, her sister, and Mary Magdalene (cf. John 19:25); the author could be suggesting that allegorically these represent different levels of the marriage between Christ and consort. Another passage (63, 32–36), in speaking of Christ's special love for Mary Magdalene, apparently (the manuscript is fragmentary here) refers to Christ's practice of kissing this Mary—which, as I mentioned earlier, is the manner in which the "perfect" beget spiritual (rather than sexually produced) offspring (59, 2–6).

Thus, the *Gospel of Philip* sees male and female in sharply defined terms of separation/reunification. Separation is the problem, reunification the solution. Separation is death, reunification life. While androgyny played no role at all in *Baruch*, it is central in the *Gospel of Philip*. On the other hand, by contrast with the next text to be discussed, the *Gospel of Philip* knows nothing of androgyny among the archons or cosmic powers. Indeed, for humans vulnerability to "defilement" results from the uninitiated male or female human (prior to the bridal chamber) carrying an unstable male or female gender-charge, which attracts, like so many flies, unclean cosmic powers, who themselves carry unbalanced gender-charges. In the *Hypostasis of the Archons*, gender separation and reunification play no important role, and androgyny has quite a different function.

Hypostasis of the Archons

The *Hypostasis of the Archons* may use mythological traditions from Jewish gnosis, but in its present form it is a Christian Gnostic product; it begins with a reference to the declaration by the "great apostle" that "our struggle is not against flesh and blood" but rather against the cosmic powers of archons (cf. Eph. 6:12). The author claims to be writing the text in answer to inquiries about the hypostasis ("nature," or perhaps here "reality") of these archons.

The tractate contains continuous mythic narrative, unlike the *Gospel of Philip*, although the order of the material is curious: not until the latter half of the text is the actual origin of the archons described, in a sort of visionary flashback. For our purposes, it may be best to begin there (94, 1ff.).

The transcendent realm is referred to as Incorruptibility, or the place where Incorruptibility dwells. We are abruptly introduced to "Wisdom, who is called Faith," presumably an entity belonging to the realm of Incorruptibility:

> Wisdom, who is called "Faith," wanted to make something on her own, without her consort, and her work became the heavenly images. There is a curtain existing between the things above and the realms below. A shadow came into being beneath the curtain. That shadow became matter, and that shadow was cast apart. Its [or her—i.e., Wisdom's?] product became a work in matter, like an aborted fetus. It took shape from the shadow and became an arrogant beast, resembling a lion. (94, 5–16)

This arrogant, beastly figure is the chief archon of the cosmos and is usually called Ialdabaoth.[28] Ialdabaoth, we are told (94, 17), was androgynous. When he (grammatically, the male gender is used of Ialdabaoth in the Coptic text) awoke and looked around at the

realm in which he existed, he boasted, in his arrogance and ignorance, that he alone was God. A divine voice from the transcendent realm announced to him that he was wrong; when in response
he asked to be shown what could have existed before him, Wisdom
stretched forth her finger and sent light into Matter. Nothing more
is said about this light in this part of the *Hypostasis*, but perhaps it
is intended to allude to the divine involvement in the creation of
humans—events covered in the earlier part of the work, which I
will discuss later. Ialdabaoth then created for himself a great realm
and seven androgynous offspring.

Once again Ialdabaoth belched forth his boast that he was God
of Everything. This time the correction came from Life (Greek:
Zoe), who is daughter of Wisdom. Already in Jewish wisdom
speculation, Wisdom had often been closely connected or even
identified with Life (e.g., Prov. 8:35). Life breathed into Ialdabaoth's face, and this breath of Life—that is, the power of the Holy
Spirit—became a fiery angel who bound Ialdabaoth and cast him
into Tartaros.

Watching all of this was one of Ialdabaoth's offspring, Sabaoth
(the name is of course one of the frequent biblical epithets of God:
"Lord *of hosts*," here "of the powers"). Sabaoth was sufficiently
impressed that he "repented and condemned his father [i.e.,
Ialdabaoth] and his mother, Matter. He loathed her [Matter],
but he sang praises up to Wisdom and to her daughter, Life" (95,
15–18). As a reward, Wisdom and Life snatched up Sabaoth and
enthroned him in the seventh heaven, just below the curtain;
Wisdom seated Life at Sabaoth's right hand in order to "instruct"
him about things in the eighth heaven, while on his left hand
Wisdom placed the Angel of Wrath. Ialdabaoth, beholding
Sabaoth's good fortune, was filled with Envy, which itself became
an androgynous entity that engendered Death, which in turn
engendered many offspring, "and all the heavens of Chaos became
full of their numbers" (96, 10f.). This account of the origin and
nature of the archons then concludes with the remark that all these
things happened by the will of the Father of All.

A few observations must be made about the use of gender-
related imagery in this portion of the narrative. In spite of the fact
that we see several male and female images here, the account of
the origin of the archons and their realm is not structured in terms
of gender. For example, we do not find here what we found in

Baruch, namely, that Spirit is to Matter (and Soul) as Male is to Female. To be sure Matter is called the "mother" of Sabaoth, yet Sabaoth's "father" is not a spiritual being, but Ialdabaoth. And on the other hand, the grammatically female beings Wisdom and Life are spiritual. The real contrast the author is attempting to set forth is that between the spiritual and material realms, but there seems to be no attempt to correlate this in any consistent way with gender categories.

The author does not seem so interested in Wisdom as female, but rather in Wisdom as divine fashioner, revealer, begetter of Life. By contrast, in several other Gnostic texts that also have some form of Wisdom myth, we do find Wisdom's femaleness brought into bold relief. We find texts that portray Wisdom giving birth to a daughter who is a kind of "lower Wisdom," and who then can be described as having "no father nor male consort" and as being "a female from a female." Or elsewhere we can find Wisdom's product, produced without her male consort, referred to as a "weak and female fruit" since it was without form.[29] But this kind of explicit gender marking is not applied to Wisdom in the *Hypostasis.* It is a methodological mistake to assume that, simply because gender was an explicit interest in other Gnostic texts that used similar mythology, this author is interested in making a point about the gender of Wisdom.

The author also is not so much interested in Life as female, but rather in Life as the offspring of Wisdom and in Life as teacher (here, of Sabaoth). This last connection actually involves a Semitic pun on the Aramaic words for "to live" (*ḥayā'*) and "to instruct" (*ḥawā'*).[30] Jewish wisdom tradition already knew how to speak metaphorically of Wisdom sitting by the throne of God (e.g., Wisdom of Solomon 9:4), although there Wisdom presumably was not teaching God about a higher heaven. In the *Hypostasis of the Archons,* as Frank Fallon has shown, the story of the enthronement of Sabaoth may legitimate the revelation of the God who revealed himself in Jewish scripture.[31] This God's revelation contains truth, since he is receiving instruction from Life, offspring of heavenly Wisdom. This God is therefore not entirely evil, as is his father Ialdabaoth, because Sabaoth has "repented." The reader will recall a similar motif in Justin's *Baruch,* where the male Elohim also "repented" and turned away from the female Edem. There the motif was distinctly organized in gender categories, in a way that is not the case in the *Hypostasis*. Sabaoth condemns both his father, Ialdabaoth, and his mother, Matter, and turns to Wisdom and Life.

We now turn back to the first half of the *Hypostasis of the Archons*, to the Adam and Eve narrative. What we find in this section confirms that although the author uses gender-related images, he or she is not trying to make a statement about the social or religious meaning of gender. The real distinction the author makes is between beings that have spirit (*pneumatikoi*) and those that have only soul (*psychikoi*) and/or flesh (*sarkikoi*). The former need fear no threat from the latter—such is the message of comfort conveyed by this text to readers, who are presumed to be spiritual.

This message is declared first through an account of the creation of Adam and Eve. The cosmic archons, beings that are only psychical, behold, in the waters below, the image cast by divine (spiritual) Incorruptibility. In their ignorance, they attempt to capture this divine being. They fashion, from earthly matter, a human who resembles their own bodies. Possibly this first-created human was androgynous, but the papyrus page is damaged just at this point, and the precise wording of a remark about the gender of the archons' bodies is not certain. (As we have seen, the author states later in the text that archons are androgynous.) They breathe soul into this material human, but the creature is still unable to stand erect since it lacks spirit (which the archons cannot supply).

The Spirit, seeing the soul-endowed human below, descends and comes to dwell within him. Recalling the wording of Genesis 2:18–20, where Greek versions speak of God's supplying a "helper" (*boēthos*) for Adam, the *Hypostasis* describes this descent of the Spirit as a "voice" that came forth from Incorruptibility as a "help" (*boētheia*) for Adam. With the reception of the Spirit, Adam then has all three of the components that so much of ancient anthropology assumed: spirit, soul, and flesh. The spiritual component, however, gives Adam clear superiority over his own archontic creators. They command him not to eat of the tree of knowledge, although the very form of their command is providentially directed by the Father above, so as to guarantee that Adam will later disobey it.

The archons, attempting to incapacitate their creature, put him to sleep; during this sleep (= the sleep of ignorance) they "opened his side [or rib—Coptic *spir*] like a living woman" (89, 7f.).

Whether they actually know what they are doing in this operation, or are only clumsily trying some crude experimental surgery to cripple the human, is not clear. The woman, however, now has not only flesh and soul, but all of the spirit that was in Adam. The archons then patch up Adam's side with some extra flesh. Immediately the narrative describes the waking of Adam (who is now no longer spiritual) by the "spiritual woman." As Adam awakes and beholds her, he says, "It is you who have given me life. You will be called 'Mother of the Living' [cf. Gen 3:20]—for she is my mother; she is the physician and the woman and the one who has given birth" (89, 14–17). Punning on the name of Eve is present already in the text of Genesis 3:20, where the play is on the Hebrew words for Eve (*Ḥawwāh*) and living (*ḥaweh*). The text of the *Hypostasis* contains evidence that such punning continued in Jewish tradition, for Eve's connection with certain titles and roles in this text is at least in part built on a series of Aramaic puns, now no longer any more visible in our Coptic text than they are in an English translation of it. The name of Eve (*Ḥawwāh*) is similar to the Aramaic words for physician or midwife (*ḥayyətā*), serpent (*ḥewəyā*), and instructor (*ḥawaəyā*).[32] We will see the relevance of these last two puns below.

Because of certain similarities between the account of Adam and Eve here and the way in which the Adam and Eve tradition is used in the *Gospel of Philip*, it might have been tempting initially to see in the two texts roughly the same perspective on gender, and basically the same employment of the Adam and Eve tradition, in order to express this perspective.[33] After all, the extraction of the woman from Adam in the *Hypostatis of the Archons* means Adam's loss of spirit. And in one place the *Gospel of Philip* also refers to the spirit given to Adam as "his mother" (*Gos. Phil.* 70, 24f.). Yet the differences are important: the *Gospel of Philip* saw in the appearance of Eve a gender separation producing death. It was the unequivocally negative moment, correctable only through reunification of male and female. Here in the *Hypostasis*, the moment of Eve's appearance has an unmistakably positive flavor. It is a moment of revelation. To be sure, the archons have deprived Adam of the Spirit for the time being, yet the event is not narrated with despair or melancholy, for the Spirit has in fact not gone far.

At the sight of the woman, the archons become sexually aroused, and they attempt to rape her. Since the archons are supposedly androgynous in this text, one might wonder why they should be sexually attracted to the female Eve, but not also to Adam. However, this only illustrates how the concerns of this author for the Adam and Eve story, and this author's perspective on gender in general, differ from what was seen in the *Gospel of Philip*. The androgyny of the archons in the *Hypostasis* is contrasted with what we found in the *Gospel of Philip*, where the author spoke of the cosmos as a place swarming with male or female spirits, not androgynous beings. In the *Hypostasis*, the androgyny of the archons is clearly not intended to symbolize their perfection. The only obvious function of androgyny in the case of these creatures is to account for how they multiplied. It is not because they carry some unbalanced male or female gender-charges that they are nuisances or threats to humans, according to the *Hypostasis of the Archons*. It is not their gender that accounts for their attack on Eve, but rather the fact that they are nonspiritual and are attacking spirit. But because they are only physical beings, they are entirely unsuccessful in this. When they attempt to rape the spiritual woman, she only laughs at their stupidity and blindness; then she quickly turns into a tree, leaving behind only her shadowy image for the archons to "defile with pollution" (89, 27–29). This shadowy image presumably refers to the fleshly Eve. That the spiritual female being becomes a tree may be a version of an earlier Jewish legend; the tree of knowledge is the likely reference, as we will see.[34] We saw the theme of the defilement of Eve by the powers (also probably inherited by our author from Jewish tradition) both in *Baruch* and in the *Gospel of Philip*. But in both those instances the emphasis was on the act as adultery, the adultery of Eve with Naas (in *Baruch*) or the serpent (in *Gos. Phil.*). What is interesting about the version in the *Hypostasis* is that here the story is really one of escape rather than defilement.

The reader's growing sense that the archons are fighting a losing battle is only confirmed in the continuation of the narrative. We are told that the "Spiritual One [female: *tipneumatikē*] came into the serpent, the Instructor" [male: *preftamo*] (89, 31f.). The Serpent-Instructor then approached the human couple and informed them that eating from the tree of knowledge would not be fatal, but illuminating. After this instruction, the "Instructor [female: *treftamo*] was taken away from the serpent, and she left it by itself as a thing of the earth" (90, 11f.).[35] Curiously, we are not informed just where she went this time, but we may not be wrong in assuming that she went back into the tree of knowledge. This would seem to fit best the logic of the myth, since when the "fleshly woman" then took of the fruit of the tree and gave some also to her husband, the "physical ones [i.e., Adam and Eve,] ate, and their imperfection became evident in their ignorance, and they recognized that they were naked of the spiritual, and they took fig leaves and bound them around their loins" (90, 15–19). The archons discovered the violation of their command, cursed Adam, Eve, and the serpent, cast Adam and Eve out of Paradise, and loaded them down with distractions and a life of toil, "so that they would have no leisure to devote themselves to the Holy Spirit" (91, 10f.).

We are then told about the children of Adam and Eve. The story of Cain and Abel follows closely the biblical narrative, without any startling inversions or extensive gnosticizing midrash. Seth's birth is mentioned briefly. But the real child prodigy to whom Eve gives birth is her daughter Norea, after whose birth Eve proclaims, "'He [God? Adam?] has begotten on me a virgin as a help [*boētheia*] for many generations of humankind.' She is the virgin whom the powers did not defile" (91, 35–92, 3). We hear that following the birth of Norea, "humankind began to multiply and improve," and in reaction the archons decide to bring the flood. However, one of the archons—not named here, but probably Sabaoth, who in this text symbolizes the inferior, Jewish revelation—tries to avert humanity's complete destruction by telling Noah to build the ark. When Norea tries to climb aboard the ark, Noah refuses to admit her and Norea then incinerates the ark with her breath. Noah builds a second ark, and that is the last we hear of him. As Layton has pointed out, Noah's resistance symbolizes ignorance of the fact that Norea is the true instrument of salvation.[36] The final episode involving Norea is the attempt by the archons to rape her, as they had done with Eve. But when they try to convince Norea to cooperate by telling her how willing a lover her mother Eve had been, Norea scoffs at their pitiful ignorance of what had really happened and tells them it was not her mother whom they had known: "For I am not from you, but rather it is from above that I have come" (92, 25f.).

For the reader who has been following the narrative in the *Hypostasis* with a copy of Genesis alongside, this virgin Norea comes as a bolt out of the blue. Yet she is not a complete invention of Gnostic mythology, but rather an inheritance, as Birger Pearson has shown, from Jewish Haggadic traditions about a woman named Na⁵amah, who appears variously as the wife or twin sister of Seth; or Noah's wife, who in some traditions tries to prevent the building of the ark; or a Cainite woman (cf. Gen 4:22) who goes about naked and seduces angels.³⁷

However, in our text Norea is not a naughty lady but a heroine. Like the spiritual "help" that first descended to dwell in Adam, so Norea is the spiritual "help for generations of humankind." Indeed, we are to understand that she is that same spiritual, instructing presence, the "virgin whom the powers did not defile," neither in their first attempt with Eve nor later in the generations after the flood. During the attempted rape of Norea, she "calls out" for deliverance from above. Her call is answered by an angel named Eleleth, who appears to her in a vision and reveals the story of the origin of the archons (which I summarized earlier), assuring her of the invulnerability of both herself and her offspring.

In the *Gospel of Philip,* the Adam and Eve story was of the fall of humans from androgyny into death. The focus was on the moment of separation itself, and the almost moralistic wording implies that Eve might have avoided the tragedy: "If the female had not separated from the male, she would not die with the male" (*Gos. Phil.* 70, 9–11). Although in the *Gospel of Philip* we had no continuous narrative of the Paradise events, it was obvious that the author saw nothing positive in the activity that followed the separation of male from female. Eve committed adultery with the serpent, who in the *Gospel of Philip* was an entirely evil figure (61, 4012). Adam, for his part, is blamed for having eaten of the wrong tree in the Garden, the one that produces beasts (tree of knowledge) rather than the one that produces humans (tree of life): Adam became a beast and begot beasts (71, 22–26)—that is, sexual reproduction was introduced. Hence, this tree brought only death (74, 1–12).

The purpose of the Adam and Eve story in the *Hypostasis of the Archons* is completely different. Eve appears in a moment when Adam speaks of Life and not Death. The rape of Eve by the archons is not blamed on her in this text, and in reality it is a story of escape. The serpent is not evil, but even serves as a vessel for the revelation. The eating from the tree of knowledge is a divinely ordained and orchestrated event. The generations of humans after

218

this first couple do not inherit the consequences of a fall, but rather the divine "help" of Norea. The entire story is one of providential protection. We are given no reason to anticipate a reentry of Eve into Adam. We hear nothing about a reunification of male and female.

In summary, it is questionable that the author of the *Hypostasis* was trying to make some point about the religious significance of gender. We do not encounter the religious problem defined in terms of the separation of male and female, as was the case in the *Gospel of Philip*. Nor do we find the sort of gender organization that we saw in *Baruch:* Spirit : Male : : Soul : Female. In the *Hypostasis* the account of Eve's emergence from Adam might have tempted us to think of the opposite association: Spirit : Female : : Soul : Male. Yet when we look at the tractate as a whole, this hardly works since in the spiritual realm the author assigns the pre-eminent place to the "Father of All" (86, 21; 87, 22; 88, 34, etc.) Admittedly, the revealing agent in the *Hypostasis* seems exceptionally female, by comparison with what is found in more "orthodox" Christian or Jewish texts of the period. Above all, the positive role of the spiritual Eve stands in sharp contrast with the tendency of much of ancient Christian and Jewish exegesis to locate blame for the first sin with Eve.[38] Since the blame placed on Eve was often used as the religious justification for the social subordination of women, it is only natural to ask whether the positive role of the spiritual Eve in the *Hypostasis* is some kind of answer to this, that is, a mythic justification for an enhanced social status for women. At the very least we must recognize that the more misogynistic use of the Adam and Eve story will certainly have found little encouragement from this text. Nevertheless, it is not clear that Eve's prominence and more positive role in the *Hypostasis* has been prompted by anything more than the biblical Eve's close connection with knowledge *(gnōsis)*. The author of the *Hypostasis* sees gnosis as salvific and, to express this, has interpreted the story of the tree of gnosis as a revelatory event, not as a sin. Therefore, it is not so surprising to find correspondingly positive roles for both Eve and the serpent. Each of the three cases— Eve as help/instructor, Norea as help, and Life as instructor of Sabaoth—indeed makes a "statement," but not about gender. The Life/Sabaoth story establishes the legitimacy (but, the limited legitimacy) of Jewish revelation. The choosing of Norea as a spiritual heroine also involves a revaluation of Jewish tradition. And the role of Eve and the serpent in connection with the tree of knowledge is a statement about knowledge, not necessarily about femaleness.

Moreover, much of the apparently "female" character of the revealing Spirit seems to have emerged in the first place in an exegetical tradition of wordplays and other associations: Spirit is connected with Life; Spirit gives Life to Adam, therefore is Adam's "Mother"; a word for Life is similar to the name of Eve, whom Genesis had called "Mother of the living"; Wisdom (grammatically female) is connected with Life (grammatically female); a word for Life is similar to a word for Instruction, is similar to a word for serpent, is similar to the name of Eve; Eve and the serpent are both connected with the tree of knowledge (= Wisdom or Instruction); the solution for Ignorance is the "help" *(boētheia)* afforded by Instruction or Knowledge, and scripture had called Eve man's "helper" *(boēthos* in Greek versions of Gen. 3:20). That these kinds of associations link so much of the "female" imagery of the text gives us reason to doubt that the author is doing anything more than picking exegetical "targets of opportunity" in an effort to underscore the salvific effect of spiritual wisdom.

Conclusion

We have seen considerable variety in the gender imagery among even these three Gnostic sources.[39] I have been primarily interested in what I call "qualitative" differences in the ways these writings employ gender imagery. The *Hypostasis of the Archons* probably does not differ that much from the other two texts as far as the sheer quantity of male and female images on its pages. Yet in qualitative terms there is a world of difference because the author of the *Hypostasis* is not setting forth maleness and femaleness as basic categories in terms of which human experience and ultimate concerns are organized. Such a text may have little or nothing to tell us about what its author understood by femaleness per se or maleness per se, or the author's experience of or aspirations for the respective socializations of men and women. In brief, one might say that here was an author whose perspective on gender was not at all focused.

By contrast, *Baruch* and the *Gospel of Philip* reveal sharply focused, yet also differing, perspectives. In *Baruch,* we find an organization of experience and ultimate concerns in gender categories. The most intriguing aspect of this organization is the way the gender categories function to convey an ambivalence toward life in the cosmos: life in the cosmos is fundamentally good, and its order is distilled in the symbol of the contracts between male and female in marriage. The union of male and female thus serves as the primary symbol for ordered existence in this world, and instabilities that threaten this union (such as divorces, adulteries, etc.) are negatively valued. The union also expresses psychological experience, that the self has both a "higher" element (spirit) and a "lower" element (soul), and that the marriage of these in the self is somehow good. But there is more to be hoped for, beyond the order (and disorder) of this cosmos, and for this only the image of the separation of the male from the female will suffice. The *Gospel of Philip* also organizes in terms of gender, but here the gender imagery serves to articulate a precisely *non*ambivalent attitude toward the cosmos. Defiled marriage is contrasted with undefiled marriage. Transcendence is a union of male and female that is precisely threatened by life in this cosmos, where separation from the true union is sustained by deception through illicit and impure imitations (defiled marriages, attacks from incubi and succubi).

The existence of such different perspectives essentially rules out the usefulness of generalizations about the "Gnostic pattern" in the use of male and female imagery or the "Gnostic attitude" toward the relationship between women and men, and so forth. There is no single pattern in the use of the imagery. And the use of the imagery does not always tell us anything about the relationships between Gnostic men and women; when it does, it does not always tell us the same thing.

Notes

1. For gnosticism used with reference to modern political phenomena such as Marxism, see Eric Voegelin, *The New Science of Politics* (Chicago: University of Chicago Press, 1952); idem, *Science, Politics, and Gnosticism* (Chicago: Henry Regnery, 1968); on Voegelin's concept of gnosticism, see Eugene Webb, *Eric Voegelin: Philosopher of History* (Seattle and London: University of Washington Press, 1981), pp. 196–207; Gregor

Sebba, "History, Modernity, and Gnosticism," in *The Philosophy of Order: Essays on History, Consciousness, and Politics*, ed. Peter J. Opitz and Gregor Sebba (Stuttgart: Klett-Cotta, 1981), pp. 190–241. In the early versions of his typology of sectarian movements, Bryan Wilson used the category Gnostic to designate a type that included Christian Science; see his "An Analysis of Sect Development," *American Sociological Review* 24 (1959):3–15.

2. See Hans Jonas, *The Gnostic Religion* (Boston: Beacon, 1970); Kurt Rudolph, *Gnosis: The Nature and History of Gnosticism* (New York: Harper and Row, 1983); R. van den Broek, "The Present State of Gnostic Studies," *Vigiliae Christianae* 37 (1983):41–71.

3. See Jonas, *Gnostic Religion,* and Rudolph, *Gnosis.*

4. Gnostic teachers such as Ptolemaeus and Heracleon were at least developing the ideas of the teacher Valentinus, if they had not in fact studied directly with him (see Rudolph, *Gnosis,* pp. 318–24); the Gnostic teacher Isidore is referred to once as the "legitimate [*gnēsios*] child and disciple of Basilides" (Hippolytus, *Ref.* 7.20.1), which might indicate that Isidore was a natural son (but cf. Rudolph, *Gnosis,* p. 312).

5. On diversity even in the earliest stages of Christianity, see James M. Robinson and Helmut Koester, *Trajectories through Early Christianity* (Philadelphia: Fortress, 1971); on diversity in Second Temple Judaism, see, for example, Michael E. Stone, *Scriptures, Sects, and Visions: A Profile of Judaism from Ezra to the Jewish Revolts* (Philadelphia: Fortress, 1980).

6. E.g., Elaine Pagels, *The Gnostic Gospels* (New York: Vintage Books, 1979), pp. 57–83; Raoul Mortley, *Womanhood: The Feminine in Ancient Hellenism, Gnosticism, Christianity, and Islam* (Sydney: Delacroix, 1981), esp. pp. 55–67; Elizabeth Schüssler Fiorenza, *In Memory of Her: A Feminist Theological Reconstruction of Christian Origins* (New York: Crossroad, 1983), esp. pp. 270–79; R. Joseph Hoffmann, *"De Statu Feminarum:* The Correlation between Gnostic Theory and Social Practice," *Eglise et Théologie* 14 (1983):293–304; and see the extensive collection of papers from the November 19–25, 1985 Claremont/Anaheim conference on this theme, in: *Images of the Feminine in Gnosticism,* ed. Karen King, Studies in Antiquity and Christianity 3 (Philadelphia: Fortress forthcoming).

7. E.g., Pagels, *Gnostic Gospels,* p. 79.

8. Schüssler Fiorenza, *Memory,* p. 274; cf. Hoffmann, *"Feminarum,"* pp. 303f.

9. Mortley, *Womanhood,* p. 64.

10. Pagels, *Gnostic Gospels,* pp. 79–81.

11. Schüssler Fiorenza, *Memory,* p. 274.

12. For preliminary English translations of the tractates in the Nag Ham-

madi collection and a general introduction to the texts, see James M. Robinson, ed., *The Nag Hammadi Library in English* (New York: Harper and Row, 1977). The critical editions of the tractates, with the final revisions of these English translations, are appearing in the Nag Hammadi Studies Series, published by E. J. Brill, although as of this writing, the edition of Codex II has not yet appeared. Available for some years now have been the English translation and commentary by R. McL. Wilson of *The Gospel of Philip* (New York: Harper and Row; London: A. R. Mowbray, 1962), as well as the editions of the text, with translation and commentary, by W. C. Till, *Das Evangelium nach Philippos,* Patristische Texte und Studien 2 (Berlin: De Gruyter, 1963), and J.-E. Ménard, *L-'Evangile selon Philippe: Introduction, texte, traduction, commentaire* (Paris: Letouzey et Ané, 1967). For the *Hypostasis* there is Roger A. Bullard, *The Hypostasis of the Archons: The Coptic Text with Translation and Commentary,* Patristische Texte und Studien 10 (Berlin: De Gruyter, 1970); the splendid introduction, text, English translation, and commentary by Bentley Layton, "The Hypostasis of the Archons," *Harvard Theological Review* 67 (1974):351–425 and 69 (1976):31–101; and Bernard Barc, *L'Hypostase des Archons: Traité gnostique sur l'origine de l'homme, du monde et des archontes (NH II, 4);* Michel Roberge, *Norea (NH IX, 2),* Bibliothèque copte de Nag Hammadi, Section: "Textes," 5 (Québec: Presses de l'Université Laval, 1980).

Unlike most of the other Nag Hammadi manuscripts, Codex II contains no page numbers provided by the ancient scribes. Two photographic facsimiles have been published, with two different systems of pagination. In my citation of the *Gospel of Philip* and the *Hypostasis of the Archons,* I give the page and line number(s) according to what is now the standard system of pagination, from *The Facsimile Edition of the Nag Hammadi Codices,* published under the auspices of the Department of Antiquities of the Arab Republic of Egypt, in conjunction with UNESCO, Codex II (Leiden: E. J. Brill, 1974).

13. For the text see Paul Wendland, ed., *Hippolytus Werke; Dritter Band: Refutatio omnium haeresium,* Die griechischen christlichen Schriftsteller der ersten drei Jahrhunderte 26 (Leipzig: Hinrichs, 1916); for an English translation, see Werner Foerster, ed., *Gnosis: A Selection of Gnostic Texts,* English trans. edited by R. McL. Wilson (Oxford: Oxford University Press, 1972), 1:48–58. See also the introduction to Justin's *Baruch* by Rudolph, *Gnosis,* pp. 144–47, who refers to it as "one of the most original and probably also the oldest testimonies to Gnosis" (p. 145).

14. On the generally sympathetic fashion in which Edem is treated, cf. R. van den Broeck, "The Shape of Edem According to Justin the Gnostic," *Vigiliae Christianae* 27 (1973):35–45, esp. 40f. Unfortunately, the interesting article by Jorunn Jacobsen Buckley, "Transcendence and Sexuality in

The Book Baruch," History of Religions *24 (1985):328–44, did not become available to me until this present study was completed. Buckley also is struck by a "mood of strong ambivalence" (p. 338) in *Baruch,* and in fact, her analysis would find an even sharper, more excruciating form of ambivalence. In her view, *Baruch*'s central religious mystery was that both earthly sexual power and spiritual transcendence had a common origin in the Good one, and thus Justin was saying that "the goal of life is both here on earth and up above with 'the Good'" (p. 341). The mythology therefore portrays the human condition as a conflict between two choices: "either to remain ruled by the life of the earth, the procreative forces, or to ascend, like Elohim. In either case, one loses something" (p. 342). Equating the second choice, ascension, with the ritual initiation into Justin's mysteries, Buckley imagines potential initiates to have been vulnerable to "acute anxiety about the decision to join in the mystery," since after turning away from a life which included sexual procreation there was the "chance that one might regret one's membership or even become an apostate" (p. 337). However, I disagree with Buckley's apparent assumption that the ritual initiation of which the text speaks required the rejection of marriage and procreation which (as Buckley rightly emphasizes) Justin clearly viewed as good. That indeed would set up an impossible choice, more impossible than what Justin actually had in mind. For, as I will argue later, the abandonment of Eden by Elohim is the model for the separation of spirit from soul and body (at death), not for the adoption of a celibate lifestyle while still in the world. The gender imagery expresses an ambivalence, not between sexually procreative and ascetic lifestyles, but between the fundamental goodness of life in this world and the higher good that can be experienced only when the body is left behind.

15. E.g., Irenaeus, *Adv. haer.* 1.2.2f.; and in the following writings in the Nag Hammadi collection: *Apocryphon of John* II 9, 30–33; *The Sophia of Jesus Christ* III 112, 17; *A Valentinian Exposition* 34, 25–34; 36, 35–38; and cf. also *The Exegesis on the Soul* 137, 1–11.

16. R. M. Grant, *Gnosticism and Early Christianity,* rev. ed. (New York: Harper and Row, 1966), p. 23, makes essentially the same observation about the positive role of marriage in *Baruch;* so also van den Broeck, "Shape of Eden," pp. 40f., 43. On adultery, see G. Delling, *s.v.* "Ehebruch," in *Reallexikon für Antike und Christentum,* ed. Theodor Klauser, Band IV (Stuttgart: Hiersemann, 1959); on pederasty as a traditional target of condemnation, see Robin Scroggs, *The New Testament and Homosexuality* (Philadelphia: Fortress, 1983), and the sources and literature cited there. With regard to my overall point about Justin's legal-contractual perspective on the male-female relationship in marriage, in marriage contracts from Greco-Roman Egypt an interdiction against the husband having relations with another man is often included; see Claude

Vatin, *Recherches sur le mariage et la condition de la femme mariée a l'époque Hellénistique,* Bibliothèque des Ecoles Françaises d'Athènes et de Rome 216 (Paris: E. de Boccard, 1970), p. 201.

17. Cf. van den Broeck, "Shape of Eden," pp. 40f. Ernest Haenchen, "Das Buch Baruch," *Zeitschrift für Theologie und Kirche* 50 (1953):157, overstated, I think, the degree of world rejection in *Baruch.* Haenchen suggested that Justin viewed the cosmos as evil *(böse)* now, although this condition had developed only after the ascent of Elohim. Justin was demanding, Haenchen argued, that the world itself be left behind, although "how this unworldly [*weltlose*] existence within the world was supposed, in practical terms, to be lived out, is not indicated in Hippolytus' excerpts from the *Book of Baruch.*" Admittedly, we do not have a very clear picture of this, but we do know more about at least one dimension of this lived-out existence—the positive role of marriage—than Haenchen seems to allow. Justin seems to have referred to the created order as "bad" or "wicked" (*ponēra*—5.26.26; 5.27.3), and hence he views the cosmos as flawed. But even though it is flawed by unlawful or sinful forces and elements, it is a realm in which a legitimate, "lawful" order is still present, and therefore a "lawful" pattern of life is possible.

18. Cf. R. McL. Wilson, "Philip, Gospel of," in *The Interpreter's Dictionary of the Bible,* supp. vol., ed. K. Crim (Nashville: Abingdon, 1976), pp. 664–65; on Valentinianism, see Rudolph, *Gnosis,* pp. 318–25, *passim.*

19. E. Segelberg, "The Coptic-Gnostic Gospel According to Philip and Its Sacramental System," *Numen* 7 (1960):189–200; R. M. Grant, "The Mystery of Marriage in the Gospel of Philip," *Vigiliae Christianae* 15 (1961):129–40; D. H. Tripp, "The 'Sacramental System' of the Gospel of Philip," in *Studia Patristica,* vol. 17 in three parts, ed. E. A. Livingstone (Oxford: Pergamon, 1982), pt. 1, pp. 251–60; Jorunn Jacobson Buckley, "A Cult-Mystery in *The Gospel of Philip," Journal of Biblical Literature* 99 (1980):569–81.

20. *Contra* Grant, "Mystery of Marriage," p. 135: "The Gnostic, who is 'from above,' experiences love and expresses it in sexual union. The non-Gnostic, who is 'from below,' experiences nothing but lust"; cf. Elaine H. Pagels, "Adam and Eve, Christ and the Church: A Survey of Second Century Controversies concerning Marriage," in *The New Testament and Gnosis: Essays in Honour of Robert McL. Wilson,* ed. A. H. B. Logan and A. J. M. Wedderburn (Edinburgh: T. and T. Clark, 1983), esp. pp. 166–70, who also interprets the "undefiled marriage" of the *Gospel of Philip* as a marriage between Gnostics that includes actual sexual union, but one that is now consecrated because the partners, as initiated Gnostics, enjoy a condition of "spiritual, psychic, and bodily integration" (p. 169).

21. See Hans Achelis, *Virgines subintroductae: Ein Beitrag zum VII.*

Kapitel des 1 Korintherbriefs (Leipzig: Hinrichs, 1902); Pierre de La-briolle, "La mariage spiritual dans l'antiquité chrétienne," *Revue Histori-que* 137 (1921):204–25; Jo Ann McNamara, *A New Song: Celibate Women in the First Three Christian Centuries* (New York: Haworth, 1983), pp. 112–14.

22. Cf. Gilles Quispel, "Genius and Spirit," in *Essays on Nag Hammadi Texts in Honour of Pahor Labib*, Nag Hammadi Studies 6, ed. Martin Krause (Leiden: Brill, 1975), pp. 164f. Consciousness of being vulnerable to sexual exploitation by demons was of course not uncommon in late antiquity. In the fourth century, for example, Epiphanius of Salamis (*Panarion* 26.13.4f.) claims that certain Gnostics taught that when Elijah ascended to heaven, he was actually dragged back down into the world by a female demon, who claimed to be the mother of children by Elijah. When the bewildered Elijah asked how this could be, since he had lived a celibate life, the female demon announced that she had received the semen of Elijah that once had been emitted in a wet dream; cf. *Historia Lausiaca* 23.

23. For example, Clement Alex., *Exc. Theod.* 21.1; 53.3; Iren. *Adv. haer.* 1.7.1; 1.13.6.

24. Cf. Grant, "Mystery of Marriage," p. 135.

25. See Wayne Meeks, "The Image of the Androgyne: Some Uses of a Symbol in Earliest Christianity," *History of Religions* 13 (1974):183–89.

26. See George W. MacRae, "The Jewish Background of the Gnostic Sophia Myth," *Novum Testamentum* 12 (1970):86–101; G. C. Stead, "The Valentinian Myth of Sophia," *Journal of Theological Studies,* n.s., 20 (1969):75–104.

27. See Birger A. Pearson, "Jewish Haggadic Traditions in *The Testimony of Truth* from Nag Hammadi (CG IX, *3*)," in *Ex Orbe Religionum: Studia Geo Widengren,* Pars Prior, supp. to *Numen* 21 (Leiden: Brill, 1972), p. 467.

28. The origin and meaning of the name Ialdabaoth is obscure, but may derive from *yld,* "child," and *baoth,* which may be a version of the ancient Semitic root for Chaos. If Ialdabaoth means "son of Chaos," then the myth of this archon's origin from chaos (*Hyp. Arch.* 94, 4–95, 11) may be a Gnostic development of an ancient Canaanite cosmological myth; see Francis T. Fallon, *The Enthronement of Sabaoth: Jewish Elements in Gnostic Creation Myths,* Nag Hammadi Studies 10 (Leiden: Brill, 1978), pp. 29–34. In this writing Ialdabaoth also has the names Sakla (Aramaic: fool), and Samael (a frequent name in Jewish literature for the devil or an evil angel).

29. E.g., Hippolytus, *Ref.* 6.30.6–8; Iren. *Adv. haer.* 1.2.2–4; *Exc. Theod.* 68; *First Apocalypse of James* 35, 10–14.

30. Fallon, *Enthronement of Sabaoth,* p. 61.

31. Ibid., p. 68.
32. Layton, "Hypostasis," 1976, pp. 55f.
33. So Bullard, *Hypostasis,* pp. 77f.
34. Cf. Stephen Gero, "The Seduction of Eve and the Trees of Paradise—A Note on a Gnostic Myth," *Harvard Theological Review* 71 (1978):299–301.
35. The way the grammatical gender of the Coptic noun *reftamo,* "Instructor," shifts back and forth from female to male in this passage suggests that it is really instruction *qua* instruction, not instruction as female or male, that is of interest to the author. Instruction simply assumes the gender of the figure who, at a given moment in the narrative, happens to be doing the instructing.
36. Layton, "Hypostasis," 1976, p. 62, n. 99.
37. Birger Pearson, "The Figure of Norea in Gnostic Literature," in *Proceedings of the International Colloquium on Gnosticism, Stockholm, August 20–25, 1973,* Kungl. Vitterhets Historie och Antikvitets Akademien, Filologisk-filosofiska serien 17 (Stockholm: Almquist and Wiksell; Leiden: Brill, 1977), pp. 143–52.
38. 1 Tim. 2:13–15; Tertullian, *On the Dress of Women* 1.1.1; John Chrysostom, *Homily 9 on 1 Timothy,* and so forth.
39. Since the completion of this study, I have discussed a more extensive sampling of this variety in "Variety in Gnostic Perspectives on Gender," in King, *Images of the Feminine in Gnosticism.*

Part 3
Gender as Point-of-View

Nine

Images of Gender in the Poetry of Krishna
John Stratton Hawley

Of all the gender-related imagery to appear in the literature of religion, the most striking is perhaps the motif of sex reversal, since it
seems to take for granted the notion that gender itself is invested
with religious meaning. And it would be hard to imagine a more
vivid and influential example of sex reversal in religious creativity
than is provided by the worship of Krishna. From the twelfth century onward in North India, one finds poet after poet writing from
the point of view of one of the simple young women (*gopīs*) who
herd cows along the banks of the River Jumna in the pastoral Braj
region south of Delhi, the area that Krishna chose for his earthly
home.[1] In the theology and devotional literature of Braj, anyone
who would gain access to the intimate presence of Krishna has no
other option but to become as one of the *gopīs*, for it was with them
that this God of Love danced his *rās* dance in the forest on moonlit
nights, multiplying himself so that each of his rustic consorts felt
the full pleasure of union with him.[2]

Most of the poetry and all of the theology describing this miraculous union of human and divine have been fashioned by men. For
them, to assume the role of a *gopī* as a technique for gaining access
to Krishna is to undergo a social devaluation in two ways. First,
they must shed the pretensions of learning, literacy, and caste to

The author is indebted to Paula Richman, Laura Shapiro, Linda Hess, and
Karine Schomer for helpful comments on the style and substance of the
prose sections of this chapter, and to Mark Juergensmeyer for coaxing
the verse translations into their present form.

231

become cowherds; second, they must leave behind their maleness—in Indian society a superior social station—and become
women. Vaishnava theologians have generally agreed, moreover,
that men suffer yet another loss when they recognize this female
identity within themselves. As *gopīs* they are not Krishna's
wives—a socially acceptable role—but women who are tied to him
by an illicit liaison (*parakīyā*).[3] Most of the *gopīs* who are attracted
to Krishna, it is said, already have husbands, whom they leave behind when they hear his call. In doing so they abandon the measure
of status that society has accorded them, all of it conferred through
marriage. To become one of Krishna's *gopīs*, then, is to become
not merely a low-caste, rural person and a woman but an adulter-
ess as well—or at best an unmarried young girl living a life that in
worldy terms must be seen as irredeemably profligate. When one
recognizes that one is a *gopī* in relation to Krishna—for these
cowherd women symbolize the soul in relation to God—one embraces, in the religious realm, not only humility but social opprobrium as well.

So much seems clear, at least, when it is men who assume the
gopīs' role. One might well ask, however, what is implied when a
woman takes on this persona, and that is the subject of the present
essay. One of the great poet-saints of North India—Mīrā Bāī—is
indeed a woman, and in singing her praises to Krishna she makes
use not only of essentially the same genres of religious poetry as do
her male counterparts, but substantially the same vocabulary of
religious imagery as well. Hence she seems a good test case for seeing whether, other things being equal, a North Indian woman
would put the same construction upon a given set of gender-related
religious images as would a man.[4]

Tradition holds that Mīrā was a woman of princely status living
in sixteenth-century Rajasthan; she is easily the most influential
female poet of North India. If one were to seek a male poet against
whose religious imagery hers could fairly be compared, one might
well turn to Sūr Dās, an equally important and nearly con-
temporaneous poet who also composed in the Krishnaite mode.
Tradition locates Sūr in Braj rather than neighboring Rajasthan,
but many of the manuscripts upon which the Sūr tradition is based
were preserved in Rajasthani libraries; Mīrā, for her part, is said to
have traveled to Braj. In many of the poems that have come down

to us, furthermore, she composes in roughly the same dialect of Hindi that Sūr uses.[5]

Two important matters divide the poets, however, and these should be noted at the outset. First, and perhaps less important, Mīrā's poems tend to be closer to a folk idiom than Sūr's, though he is often praised above other male poets for his success at evoking common speech. In Mīrā's poetry, for instance, one hears much more of the repetitive style that characterizes women's folk songs of Rajasthan and Braj than one does in Sūr. This is not entirely unexpected in poetry attributed to a woman, but it is worth keeping in mind. Tradition sometimes portrays Sūr as a far more learned person than Mīrā was, but there is no evidence in the poetry itself that he had first-hand access to the high Sanskritic tradition. This note of doubt is strengthened by the widespread tradition that he was blind, since blindness would have impeded his study of the requisite texts. Mīrā, furthermore, is traditionally said to have been of royal blood, whereas Sūr was not, so perhaps their positions are not so disparate as at first they seem.

The second point of difference between Sūr and Mīrā is more consequential, namely, that the traditions that come down to us under these two poets' names have markedly different shapes. For Sūr we have a vast body of literature collected in multitudinous manuscripts, the oldest of which dates back to the sixteenth century. For Mīrā, by contrast, we have almost nothing that can be dated as early as the sixteenth or seventeenth century. Not a single independent collection of her poems has survived from that early period, and even in anthologies of the time one finds only the rarest poem attributed to Mīrā. As if in response to this situation, until recently almost no work has been done on the manuscript tradition associated with Mīrā, whereas Sūr's poetry has occasioned considerable scholarly activity over the last fifty years. Similarly, the most widely available edition of poems attributed to Mīrā, that of Paraśurām Caturvedī, contains only about two hundred entries, whereas the standard edition of compositions attributed to Sūr has some five thousand.[6] In the cause of fair comparison one could reduce that number to several hundred by considering only those poems of Sūr that appear in the old manuscripts of his *Sūr Sāgar* (Sūr's Ocean); but that would introduce a more serious imbalance, since at least in the current state of scholarship one could not turn to similarly venerable manuscripts comprising poems that bear Mīrā's name.

I will adopt, therefore, a "modified Vulgate" approach, using the standard editions of both poets as my basic text, but making reference, where it seems helpful, to editions that are more rigorously critical. In Sūr's case this is a substantial body of material.[7] In Mīrā's case there is less, though one has the use of a volume recently published by the Rajasthan Oriental Research Institute in which over two hundred poems found in various Rajasthani manuscripts are added to the corpus already accessible in print and some manuscript variants are listed for poems already published.[8] The size of our two "Vulgates" still differs enormously, as does our knowledge of when individual poems were first included in the two corpuses. Even so, these Vulgate texts yield valuable information about the sort of poetry thought appropriate to a woman's perspective on Krishna as against a man's, and significant enough differences appear between the two collections to make the comparison worthwhile, even in such gross terms.

It ought be made clear at the outset that we know literally nothing with certainty about two historical beings named Mīrā and Sūr. What we have instead are two cumulative bodies of poetry and two hagiographical traditions that accompany them. When we speak here of Mīrā and Sūr, then, we merely accept the collective designation for the poems that have been attributed to each over the course of time. It is possible that some of the poems of "Mīrā" were composed by men or that some of those attributed to "Sūr" first emerged from the lips of women, since both sexes sing both sets of poems. Even so, I prefer to dispense with the quotation marks and treat these collective poetic personalities as if they were real historical beings.

Such an approach has more than the advantage of grammatical simplicity. It introduces the two poetic traditions as they are perceived by Indians themselves, who think of Mīrā and Sūr as two definite persons. However, these two are important to Hindus less as historical beings than as figures whose characteristic perspectives, as revealed in their poetry, found resonance in the experience of other people. For this reason the Mīrā and Sūr traditions could be amplified over the course of time without any feeling of dishonesty. In a way, then, Mīrā and Sūr as collective personalities tell us more about perceptions of gender in North Indian society than a corpus of "authentic" works could do. While both sexes respond to the poetry of both traditions, women show a special affection for the songs of Mīrā. On the basis of the poetry itself, there seems good reason to believe that many of the poets who used Mīrā's name—in addition to Mīrā herself, if there ever was such a person—were women, as were a great many in their audience; those who announced their poems as Sūr's were for the most part men.[9]

The *Gopī* Persona

In the oldest surviving hagiographical account of Mīrā there is a story, repeated many times since, to the effect that Mīrā once undertook a trip from her home in the west of Rajasthan to Brindavan, the town in Braj that was established at the beginning of the sixteenth century to commemorate the site where Krishna first danced his *rās* dance with the *gopīs*.[10] One of the most important personages in Brindavan was Jīv Gosvāmī, the priest in Brindavan's largest temple and the town's most influential theologian at the time. The story goes that Mīrā desired to have an audience with Jīv, and the request was certainly not an audacious one, since she herself had garnered quite a reputation in devotional circles. Though married at a young age into a kingly Rajput family, she always refused to accept her wedded state, insisting that she had been married from youth to Krishna. As her "family" she adopted the traveling singers and ascetics who made Krishna the focus of their musical devotions; indeed, she regarded anyone who praised Krishna and joined her ecstatic musical salon as one of her own. This enraged her family, who tried to poison her, but Mīrā survived her trials miraculously unscathed, and her reputation spread far and wide.

Jīv, then, should have had every motive for wanting to make Mīrā's acquaintance. But he would not. The reason he offered was that, to avoid temptations of the flesh, he had taken a vow never to have concourse with a woman. Undaunted by this rebuff, Mīrā returned a message in which she reminded the great theologian of one of the most basic tenets of the faith. In Brindavan, she said, there is only one male, Krishna; in his presence all of humanity is reduced to womanhood. It is a commonplace in the history of religions that a theological appreciation of the power of the feminine does not necessarily lead to a positive evaluation of real women, and perhaps the conceptual and practical arenas are rightly kept separate; but in this case, we are told, Jīv saw the point and acceded to Mīrā's request.

To appreciate the full force of this story, one must understand that Jīv stood at the culmination of a long tradition of devotional thought that had arisen in Bengal and come to fruition in Braj. In this Gauḍīya tradition even more than in many other branches of Vaishnava theology it was felt that to become a woman before Krishna was the apex and aim of the spiritual life. Hence a great deal was at stake when Jīv responded to Mīrā's initiative. In religious terms, at least, he was not a man like other men. He was spiritually female, and one might think that he would have welcomed the company of a great female devotee. His initial reaction to her request, however, seems to indicate that his understanding of what was involved in adopting the *gopīs'* path was quite different from Mīrā's. To her it seemed obvious that their common acceptance of a single gender role as required by religion drew them together; to him it did not. It is to get at this fundamental difference of opinion that we shall be comparing Mīrā's poetic utterances with those of the male poet Sūr. Was her understanding of what it meant to embrace spiritual womanhood different from his? When the two of them spoke as *gopīs*, did they do so in the same way?

The answer is yes and no. On the one hand, we can reel off a whole series of motifs and perspectives that are shared by Sūr and Mīrā when they speak in the voice of one of Krishna's *gopīs*. On the other hand, something about Mīrā's relation to this *gopī* persona is characteristically different from Sūr's, and that casts things in quite a different light. It has to do primarily with the fact that she requires no imaginative change of sex to become a *gopī*.

The similarities between Mīrā and Sūr as spokespersons for Krishna's *gopīs* are legion. Both of them, as *gopīs* singing songs of their beloved, make reference to a wide range of activities characterizing Krishna's sojourn in Braj—from the mischievous pranks of his carefree childhood to his sad and irrevocable departure for Mathura. In collections both of Mīrā's poetry and of Sūr's there are reports of how Krishna stole the *gopīs'* butter and curds as they took them to market (*dān līlā*); how he made off with their clothes as they bathed (*cīr haran līlā*); how he played the festive game of *holī* with them and in particular with Rādhā, his favorite among the *gopīs* ; how he stole away their hearts and left the *gopīs* longing for his presence; how he was fetched by a messenger from the evil king Kaṃsa and taken off to Mathura; and how, finally, he sent back another messenger to persuade the *gopīs* that they need not pine after him in his absence, since with a little yogic concentration they could discover him in their hearts.

Both Mīrā and Sūr tell these incidents from the perspective of the women who experienced them, and they often use the same specific stances, even the same figures of speech, to do so. Both poets speak, as *gopīs*, of having been auctioned off to Krishna for no price whatever.[11] Both reproduce a tête-à-tête between one *gopī* and a companion in which the speaker complains about how Krishna's flute has totally deprived her of her wits.[12] Both poets, as *gopīs*, dwell on the fact that they have been dyed in Krishna's dark color and cannot be bleached back to normalcy (the word "Krishna" means black, and his title Śyām indicates a dusky hue).[13] Both bewail the loss of their decorum and social standing, using phrases such as *lok lāj* (modesty before the world) with clichélike frequency.[14] And both show how fully they have made imaginative entry into the world of Braj through poems such as those in which the speaker urges Krishna to awaken from his slumbers.[15]

Yet this catalog of consonances is not the whole story.[16] One can also locate differences in how these two poets take on the *gopīs'* perspective, and some of them do seem to follow from the fact that in this world Mīrā shares the *gopīs'* gender and Sūr does not. For example, Mīrā imports into the *gopīs'* charmed realm a mention of the festival of Gaurī Pūjā, which is widely celebrated by the women of Rajasthan;[17] she also introduces the "songs of the twelve months" (*bārahmāsā*) that are so prominent in the women's songs of her native region.[18] In a distinctly female style of speech, she sometimes spices the *gopīs'* discourse with complaints about tensions between various women in the family—a kind of complaint that is frequent in women's folk songs and appears in the poetry of female devotees elsewhere in the subcontinent.[19]

It is not impossible for male poets to reproduce these women's concerns as they compose in the *gopī* persona,[20] but there is little of this in Sūr. His eye is more firmly fixed on the position of the *gopīs* in relation to Krishna, something that takes place entirely outside of family boundaries; hence he is less apt to evoke the tensions they experience in relation to their in-laws. Instead of family arguments, he stresses the jealousies that arise between one *gopī* and another insofar as they are rivals for Krishna's affections—a new sort of "family." In particular one hears a great deal in the *Sūr Sāgar* about the rivalry between the *gopīs* and the female who stands in some ways closest to Krishna—Muralī, his flute.[21] Mīrā has less to say about Muralī; sometimes she does not even bother to give the flute her proper name.[22] Instead of dwelling on the rivalry and jealousy that are prescribed as a poetic conceit in the literature of Krishna, she emphasizes the political maneuvers and internecine jealousies that arise so typically between women in joint families and are the basis in real life for Sūr's imagined conflicts. The struggles Mīrā records seem matters of personal experience, though they too had doubtless come to serve as the occasion for an important aspect of women's folk literature by the time Mīrā's poems were composed. There is much about domestic tensions in Rajasthani women's songs, and Mīrā transfers elements of this material into the domestic experience of the Braj women she describes.

This sort of cleavage between Sūr and Mīrā points to the central difference in their appropriation of the *gopīs'* role. Mīrā's entry into the specific dramatic imagery of Krishna's world is less clearly marked as a jump of the imagination. The distance between her own life and the life of the *gopīs* through whom she speaks is not so noticeable as in Sūr's case.[23] To this extent Mīrā appears to be a good example of the "natural devotee" to whom A. K. Ramanujan alludes in contrasting the devotional roles of women and low-caste people with those assumed by their male or high-caste counterparts.[24] Because women are not among Hinduism's "twice born"—because society does not give them a second, cultural birth to complement the one nature has provided—they do not need to renounce their identities in the same measure that men do. They are perceived in Hindu tradition as already close to the intimacy and naturalness of spirit that it is the purpose of *bhakti* (loving devotion) to cultivate.

In Mīrā's poetry one can see this convergence of profane and religious experience in several ways. Consider, for example, the following composition, in which Mīrā addresses the god Rām, whose mythology is distinct from but closely associated with that of Krishna. The genre in which she speaks, usually called petitionary (*vinaya*), is customarily taken to represent the voice of the poet herself rather than that of any persona. What is important in *vinaya* poems of this sort is that the God being addressed, whether under the name of Krishna or Rām, is known as the savior of the fallen (*patit-pāvan*) and is called to uphold his reputation. The poet makes this challenge or plea by citing one or more occasions on which the Lord has shown mercy to others and argues, at least by implication, that the author of the poem is no less in need of divine succor than those unfortunates and reprobates. Mīrā reminds Rām of what he did when he encountered a poor outcaste Bhīl woman:

> The Bhīl woman tasted them, plum after plum,
>   and finally found one she could offer him.
> What kind of genteel breeding was this?
>   And hers was no ravishing beauty;
> Her family was poor, her caste quite low,
>   her clothes a matter of rags,
> Yet Rām took that fruit—that touched, spoiled fruit—
>   for he knew that it stood for her love.
> This was a woman who loved the taste of love,
>   and Rām knows no high, no low.
> What sort of Veda could she ever have learned?
>   But quick as a flash she sped to heaven,
> Mounting her chariot to swing on a swing
>   suspended on nothing but God.
> You are the Lord who cares for the fallen;
>   rescue whoever loves as she did:
> Let Mīrā, your servant, safely cross over,
>   a cowherding Gokul girl.[25]

Sūr also makes use of this petitionary genre. He is characteristically more lavish in his self-deprecation than Mīrā—in other poems he actually spells out his various sins—but the point is essentially the same:

> I, only I, am best at being worst, Lord.
> It's me! The others are powerless to match me.
>   I set the pace, forging onward, alone.
> All those other sinners are a flock of amateurs,
>   but I have practiced every day since birth,

And look: you've abandoned me, rescuing the rest!
How can I cause life's stabbing pain to cease?
You've favored the vulture, the hunter, tyrant, whore,
and cast me aside, most worthless of them all.
Quick save me, says Sūr, I'm dying of shame:
who ever was finer at failure than I?[26]

Two differences between Mīrā's poem and Sūr's are important
for our purposes. First, Mīrā has obviously selected a female figure
against whom to compare her state, rather than one of the males to
whom Sūr makes usual, if by no means exclusive, reference (here,
in the penultimate verse). Mīrā refers to Śabarī, a woman whose
gift of half-eaten fruit was accepted by Rām, contrary to all Hindu
dietary sensibilities. This attention to another woman on Mīrā's
part is no isolated instance. In similar catalogs of persons whom the
Lord has rescued she makes what is by comparison to Sūr Dās or a
host of other male poets a clearly disproportionate reference to
women. In Sūr one hears about the needy of both sexes, though
the women seem comfortably outnumbered by men—hunters and
kings, the Pāṇḍav brothers, Jaṭāyu the vulture, Vibhīṣan the peni-
tent brother of demonic Rāvaṇ, and above all Ajāmil the repro-
bate Brahmin. Mīrā refers to both sexes too, but sometimes singles
out certain female figures in Vaishnava mythology for special attention: the courtesan,[27] the hunchback,[28] Draupadī,[29] Ahilyā,[30] a
figure called Karamā Bāī who never once appears in the *Sūr Sāgar*
despite its size,[31] and, of course, Śabarī.[32] Obviously Mīrā identifies
particularly with women, whereas Sūr does not.

The second difference between these two poems jumps less
quickly to the eye, but is no less significant. It pertains to their contrasting conclusions. Sūr's stays firmly within the *vinaya* genre: he
brings the poem to a close by speaking for himself. With Mīrā,
however, it is not so clear that she speaks only for herself. Though
she does make use of her own signature, as Sūr does, and though
she follows it with a verb (*tarai*) that would most naturally be taken
to refer to herself ("Let Mīrā, your servant, safely cross over"),
the poem concludes with the reference "a cowherding Gokul girl,"
which transports us to the region where Krishna dwelt and to the
cowherding (*ahīr*) community of which he was a part.

Mīrā gives us no syntactic means for separating her own love
from her mention of this *gopī;* the two are most easily construed in

an appositional sense. At some level, it seems, Mīrā is a *gopī*, for in a poem of this genre there is no other reason for expecting a milkmaid to appear.[33] To solve the anomaly, one translator renders the last half-line as follows: "And I was a cowherd-maiden at Gokul / In a former birth."[34] This does indeed remove the problem, but only at the price of importing an explanation that the text does not offer. In the original there is no mention of such a "former birth"; Mīrā and the *gopī* are simply juxtaposed, as if either of them—or both together—could have been the person pleading for help and salvation.

One senses something similar in regard to poems that celebrate the joys of union with Krishna. Both in the *Sūr Sāgar* and in Mīrā's verse such poems are far less frequent than poems bemoaning the pain of being separated from the great Lover. In both corpuses such poems of longing (*viraha*) can sometimes be read as having been voiced either by one of the *gopīs*—that is, someone within the narrative realm of Krishna—or by the poet who stands outside it. But poems of union do not have this potential ambivalence. In the *Sūr Sāgar* the poet seems to understand that his only means for attaining union with Krishna is his imaginative access to Krishna's world; only as a *gopī* can he claim such joy. Indeed, when he describes the union as an act of marriage, he steps back further still. He does not describe a marriage between Krishna and the *gopī* whose voice he shares, but a wedding between Krishna and Rādhā, the preeminent maiden among the *gopīs* and Krishna's favorite. He celebrates this consummation through the eyes of one of the lesser, anonymous *gopīs* on the scene.[35]

Mīrā's situation is quite different. In a much quoted poem, she proclaims that she herself has been joined to Krishna in matrimonial union, thus placing herself on a par with and perhaps in the same world as the *gopīs*:

Sister, I had a dream that I wed
  the Lord of those who live in need:
Five hundred sixty thousand people came
  and the Lord of Braj was the groom.
    In dream they set up a wedding pavilion;
    In dream he grasped my hand;
    In dream he led me around the wedding fire
    And I became unshakably his bride.

Mīrā's been granted her mountain-lifting Lord:
from living past lives, a prize.[36]

Of course, Mīrā's depiction of her union with Krishna as a dream-marriage signals a certain distance between the profane realm and the realm in which total knowledge of Krishna is possible. But whatever that gap, it is Mīrā herself who bridges it, thereby gaining direct access to Krishna's presence. Or so this poem and others like it have always been interpreted.[37] They are understood as Mīrā's personal confessions, as indications that her intimacy with Krishna is no less vivid than the *gopīs'*, and on that account Mīrā has at times been celebrated as a consort to Krishna in roughly the same sense that the *gopīs* are.[38]

Another expression of the proximity that exists between Mīrā's world and the one she discovers through the *gopīs* comes from what might seem an unexpected quarter. Sūr is famous for the poems in which he takes the role of Krishna's foster mother Yaśodā (or, sometimes, his biological mother Devakī) and delights in the this-worldly details of the divine child's infancy—his crawling, his first teeth, the first time he eats food that is too heavily spiced, and so on, at great length. In Mīrā's poetry there is not a word of all this. One might think that to be a woman would be to take natural pleasure in Krishna's early childhood, but evidently not. We can only speculate as to the reason for this omission in Mīrā's poetry. Perhaps because she rejected family ties and had no children of her own she did not relish the maternal identity as an approach to Krishna; or perhaps tradition disallowed such moods in its passionate, virginal portrait of her. Whatever the case, the identification between Mīrā's experience and that of Krishna's *gopī* lovers (as against other women in his world who could feel maternal emotions toward him—his mother, older women) was too strong to permit the introduction of such maternal poems into the corpus.

If we look back over what we have seen about contrasts between Mīrā and Sūr, it appears that Mīrā's womanhood—whether real or ascribed—conditions her access to her religious world in important ways. On the one hand, her womanhood intensifies; on the other, it constricts. When Mīrā speaks of experiences in the *gopīs'* lives that tradition recognizes as having been hers as well, she scarcely senses any membrane separating the two, with the result that the two strengthen and reinforce one another. By the same token she seems to refrain from exploring the maternal aspect of the Braj women's experience, since it is not her own. Sūr, by contrast, shows a greater fidelity to dramatic circumstance and a great catholicity in exploring the female realm of which he speaks. As Ramanujan's hypothesis would predict, then, Mīrā's womanhood strengthens the ties between the human world and the divine, while blurring the distinction between them. When the poet either is or is assumed to be a male imagining himself to be religiously female, it is much easier to maintain a sense of clarity about the boundaries that separate the profane and sacred worlds. If the poet's voice is that of a woman, such crisp distinctions tend to wash away.

The Yogi and the Yoginī

On the basis of what we have surveyed so far, Mīrā's gender seems to give her a simpler, more direct access to the world of Krishna than is possible for Sūr. One would certainly expect just that on the basis of men's evaluations of women in India. Women, on the whole, are understood by men to be the simpler sex, and that is in large part what makes the *gopīs'* role such a religiously appealing one: their love for Krishna is wholehearted, unarguable, unshakable. To underline this laudable simplicity, Sūr sometimes delights in comparing the *gopīs'* way of approaching their Lord with the machinations that yogis undergo to achieve essentially the same goal of religious realization. Yogis must steel themselves to leave home in order to adopt a life of wandering that will make it possible for them to concentrate on their ascetic practices, but for the *gopīs* such acts of self-abnegation come entirely without effort: on them, domestic attachments have no effect. As love-struck girls, they are everything that yogis are not, yet they succeed at winning what the yogis strive so fruitlessly to attain. They manifest naturally the abstracted states that yogis go to such lengths to cultivate—sleeplessness, fixity of gaze, inattention to dress, tangled locks, and a great store of interior heat. In the *gopīs'* case, this fire is stoked not by yogic discipline but by separation from Krishna, who soon departs from their midst; yet one of the terms by which that separation is familiarly designated, *viyoga,* makes it perfectly clear that the comparison is intentional.[39]

It is of the essence in Sūr's poetry that the *gopīs* make no attempt to cultivate these fruits of yogic practice. Theirs is a woman's yoga—the "unyoga" of love—and they have no need to ape the religious pretensions of men. For Sūr the *gopīs* manifest ideal religious behavior—crucially, without intending to do so. The sole object of their attention is Krishna, and its sole vehicle their love. It is critical that no attention be paid to the cultural artifacts of religion—the rituals and theologies, the regimens of meditation. In the realm of faith, these *gopīs* are noble savages; they are presented as dichotomously different from the world of learning and spiritual effort that one sees epitomized in Ūdho, the male messenger whom the departed Krishna sends from Mathura to persuade the *gopīs* of the virtues of the yogic life. His efforts are in vain. These women have no interest in discovering Krishna within themselves, having known him in the flesh, and they argue back forthrightly. There can be no accommodation between these women and Ūdho because they are already what he would have them be, but in a form that he, with his religiously distorted vision, cannot see.

Since Mīrā shares the *gopīs'* gender, we might expect that her aversion to religious constructs such as yoga would be even stronger than the one Sūr expresses through his *gopīs*. We might anticipate, too, that Mīrā would underscore even more than Sūr the simplicity of the *gopīs'* love, together with its specifically feminine connotations. The reverse, however, is true. Not only does Mīrā refrain from ridiculing the role of a yogi, as represented in the figure of Ūdho, but she addresses Krishna himself as a yogi, something unheard of in the *Sūr Sāgar*.[40] Far from eschewing the yogic path, in fact, she asserts that she has adopted it as her own.[41]

Before we venture an interpretation as to why this is so, let us set out the contrast between Sūr's and Mīrā's perspectives on yoga in greater detail. First, Mīrā's poetry frequently mentions the features that Sūr so often treats as a sort of yoga manqué. Mīrā refers often, for instance, to the sleeplessness that the *gopīs* experience in Krishna's absence, but nowhere does she hold it up with amusement and approval as a natural analogue to the yogi's attempt at wakefulness.[42] The stylized contrast between the characteristic religious behavior of the two sexes is much less clearly drawn in Mīrā than in Sūr.

In a similar fashion Mīrā occasionally mentions the specific accoutrements that single out yogis from the mass—the ashes they wear to signify the death of any attachment to the flesh, the little bag they carry to conceal their meditation beads, or the rough woolen cloth they often fasten about their necks.[43] But again there is a difference. Whereas Sūr sees the equivalent to yogic poses and implements in the *gopīs'* strained behavior and love-disheveled garb,[44] Mīrā is apt to announce (probably on behalf of the *gopī* for whom she is speaking, though perhaps for herself as well) that she can do without yogic excesses.[45] Alternatively, she may claim that she has tried to learn ascetic practices, though without success, or that she will try again.[46] Yoga exerts a strong pull for her, since her lover is such a wanderer himself and since he seems with such inveterate resolution to withhold himself from her, as a yogi might.

This portrayal of Krishna as a yogi is entirely foreign to the spirit of the *Sūr Sāgar*. Sūr's *gopīs* know there is nothing truthful about the yogic image that Krishna tries to project to cover up his absence from them. They know he is off having fun with the women of Mathura, and they are not about to be deceived by any yogic instruction that Ūdho might have to offer in his stead. They vent their feelings in words such as the following:

> Those Mathura people, they're rife with vice,
> My friend: they've taken our beautiful Śyām,
>   and the fast, jaded ways they've taught him!
> Ūdho, they say, has arrived in our midst
>   to peddle his yoga to poor young maidens;
> His postures, dispassion, his eyes turned within—
>   how can they shorten our distance from Śyām?
> We may be just herders, but this much we know:
>   Śyām's coupled in passion to a hunchback girl!
> What kind of doctor, says Sūr, is this,
>   who has no idea what true illness is?[47]

Mīrā's attitude to yoga is quite different. She is entirely unconcerned with the task of making yoga appear false wherever it intrudes into Krishna's world, hence the yogic dimension of Ūdho's personality is so unimportant as almost to vanish from sight. Mīrā's *gopīs* perceive him not as a teacher of some grand metaphysics but as a simple courier who can carry their message of pain and longing to the lover they have lost.[48] In Mīrā's poetry Krishna too is unburdened of the charge that he dissimulates by

245

preaching yoga, with the result that Mīrā is at liberty to address him as a yogi without suggesting any pejorative connotation. She calls upon him as a yogi because his silence,[49] absence,[50] and apparent remoteness from human contact[51] mark him as an ascetic. Even when she pleads with him in the simple language of a village girl to "come to my house," she sometimes addresses her call to a yogi.[52] And she carries the figure further still. If Krishna the yogi comes to her and then threatens to depart again, she vows that she will immolate herself to become the ash with which he may smear his peripatetic body.[53] Or again, she may announce that she will herself become an ascetic—a female yogi, a *yoginī*—and go in search of him. In the poem that follows she reports that urge to a female companion:

> Oh, the yogi—
>   my friend, that clever one
>   whose mind is on Siva and the Snake,
>   that all-knowing yogi—tell him this:
>
> "I'm not staying here, not staying where
>   the land's grown strange without my dear,
> But coming home, coming to where your place is;
>   take me, guard me with your guardian mercy,
>   please.
> I'll take up your yogic garb—
>   your prayer beads,
>   earrings,
>   begging-bowl skull,
>   tattered yogic cloth—
>   I'll take them all
> And search through the world as a yogi does
>   with you—yogi and yogini, side by side.
>
> My loved one, the rains have come,
>   and you promised that when they did, you'd come too.
> And now the days have gone: I've counted them
>   one by one on the folds of my fingers
>   till the lines at the joints have blurred
> And on account of my love I've grown pale,
>   my youth grown yellow as with age.
>
> Singing of Rām
>   your servant Mīrā

has offered you an offering:
her body and her mind."[54]

Perhaps the most complex and interesting expressions of this yogic line of thought are those in which Mīrā imagines herself as both Krishna's bride and in some sense his *yoginī*. With one breath she announces that if it please him she will garb herself in the red wedding sari and part her hair with the special wedding jewels; in the next breath she says that she is ready to don the ocher robes of a yogi and leave her hair untended if that be his will instead. Again she seems to speak to a friend:

Go to where my loved one lives,
  go where he lives and tell him
  If he says so, I'll color my sari red;
  If he says so, I'll wear the godly yellow garb;
  If he says so, I'll drape the part in my hair
    with pearls;
  If he says so, I'll let my hair grow wild.
The clever mountain-lifter, Mīrā's Lord:
  listen to the praises of that king.[55]

Both these images—of marriage and of yoga—are inadmissible from Sūr's point of view. The women he idealizes and whose religious role he desires to assume are definitely not tied to Krishna by bonds of marriage, though an exception is made for Rādhā, as we have seen, in a dozen poems that were included in the *Sūr Sāgar* at a relatively late date.[56] Sūr's *gopīs* mirror the life of a yogi only through ironic contrast. They come to Krishna in a state of praiseworthy naturalness that would be debased by either form of structural identity, whether domestic or antidomestic.

The difference between Sūr and Mīrā on the subject of marriage goes even further. Mīrā is not content merely to flee from the conjugal fate to which tradition assigns her—marriage to a *rāṇā*, to royalty; she positively insists on being married to Krishna instead.[57] Evidently she has no interest in affirming through an illicit affair the "natural" womanhood that male poets find so admirable in the religious sphere. Instead she insists upon institutionalizing her defiance of convention by claiming a conjugal bond with Krishna that will challenge and degrade the earthly marriage that she

247

scorns.[58] To men there is a transcendent dimension—or rather, a holy immanence—in the *gopīs'* untrammeled love for Krishna, a love that exists outside of or in spite of any socially sanctioned bond. But to Mīrā, a woman, such transcendence requires an image or institution to give it shape. Only thus can it be clear how her religious vocation contrasts with and goes beyond her given, apparent condition.

Mīrā is so absorbed by the matter of marriage that she sometimes seems to ignore distinctions that are usually made in the mythology of Krishna between his "legitimate" wives—those affirmed in public ceremony: Satyabhāmā and Rukmiṇī—and those that are united to him in a less formal marital bond. Rādhā is apparently among the latter and so, surprisingly, is the hunchback Kubjā, whom Mīrā seems to understand as having been Krishna's queen during the period when he ruled Mathura. Mīrā joins her own name to the list, or pleads with Krishna that it be so joined.[59] Sometimes it seems she does so by invoking a form of marriage that society no longer condones, one that has an ancient pedigree and that somehow accords with the heroic image of Rajput women. For Mīrā speaks of having chosen Krishna as her bridegroom, as if to recall the time when Indian princesses did indeed choose their mates by the *svayamvar* rite rather than by accepting the candidate society designated for them.[60] Still other times Mīrā reaches beyond marriage as commonly defined by settling on a deeper, subtler, more expansive definition of the institution. She interprets the manifestations of her separation from Krishna as its sacraments: the painful heat of his absence becomes her nuptial fire. And often, as in the poem that follows, she envisions her marriage to Krishna as one that has priority over any that a single lifespan could conjure:

> I have talked to you, talked,
>   dark lifter of mountains,
> About this old love—
>   birth after birth's worth.
> Don't go, don't,
>   lifter of mountains
> Let me offer a sacrifice—myself—
>   to your beloved,
>   beautiful face.

Come, here in the courtyard,
dark Lord:
The women are singing auspicious wedding songs,
My eyes have fashioned
an altar of pearl tears,
And here is the sacrifice:
the body and mind of
Mīrā,
the servant who clings to your feet,
through life after life,
a virginal harvest for you to reap.[61]

In regard to both yoga and marriage, then, rather than abandoning institutions altogether, Mīrā seems in her religious imagination to forge institutions that will suit her. The latter course perhaps works as a statement of religious antistructure for men, who hold the reins in this world, but it cannot serve the same end for women, who are the subjects of such controls rather than their creators. For women as well as for men, the intense identifications of religion challenge the rules that society establishes. Yet Mīrā's images of escape do not call structure itself into question; rather they set up contrary structures to fend off what society demands.

One final matter needs to be addressed, namely, whose yoga and whose marriage are we talking about? The *gopīs*' or Mīrā's? In a certain sense it is easiest to say that when we speak of such things we must be talking of Mīrā herself, as projected by the poets writing in her name. After all, there is nothing in the dramatic setting of the poems that forces us to conclude that the voice we hear belongs to one of the *gopīs*; and the poems that concern Satyabhāmā and Rukmiṇī can only with difficulty be construed as the milkmaids' speech, since they imply a knowledge of the life Krishna adopted in Dvaraka, some time after he had left Braj behind. Furthermore, if the *gopīs* had spoken as positively of yoga and marriage as Mīrā does, they would have defied what the dominant tradition took to be their position in regard to both.

Yet it is possible that Mīrā did not accept such clear conventions about who the *gopīs* were and when a poet was or was not speaking on their behalf. In Sūr a distinct boundary exists between petitionary poems, in which the poet speaks for himself, and narrative poems, which are composed in such a way that they could have been spoken by someone on the scene, most often the *gopīs*. But when the poet's own voice is already female, there is less impetus to keep the two genres apart. If this sometimes means that the personality of the *gopīs* is imported into the poet's own world, as in the poem about the Bhīl woman that we quoted above, then there is no reason to think that the reverse could not also happen—even if the dominant tradition, the men's tradition, forbade it. Not only could the *gopīs*' experience illuminate Mīrā's, but hers could shape theirs as well, enabling them to speak at times of yoga and marriage. Or to be more precise, in Mīrā's poetry the two realms—the near-at-hand and the imagined—are all but indistinguishable. Thus in Mīrā's poetry more than in Sūr's, the line containing the poet's signature can be read either as expressing something about the poet or as saying something about the persona through whom the poet speaks.

This confusion of realms is a notable phenomenon, and Mīrā sometimes reports that the world did indeed take note of it, calling her crazy.[62] But in a sense the world had it coming. As the story concerning Jīv Gosvāmī shows, its spokesmen, in the process of projecting a "natural" image of womanhood onto the *gopīs*, had neglected real women. When Mīrā rejoined these two, building implicit bridges between the *gopīs*' world and her own, she necessarily complicated men's image of life in Krishna's bucolic, antistructural realm. She inserted competing structures there: marriage to Krishna and the sharing of a yogic state with him. In envisioning a marriage to Krishna, she doubly defied the male view of things: not only did she reject conjugal bonds at the mundane level where they were expected, but she embraced them at the divine level, where they were not. Furthermore, in accepting the womanhood that men projected onto the *gopīs*, she did so in a different spirit than was intended. To her the *gopīs*' freedom became a license to literary and devotional creativity. In her hands the clear definitions that mediate between Sūr's *gopīs* and the males they encounter, both Krishna and Ūdho, come tumbling down, and new categories—new visions of domesticity and renunciation—arise in their place.

Notes

1. To represent the sounds of Hindi, as opposed to Sanskrit, the standard system for transliterating Devanagari script into roman has been somewhat modified here. In Hindi the neutral vowel often occurs in a position in the word that renders it silent; when this happens, it is omitted in transliteration. The nasalization of vowels is uniformly indicated by a tilde.

2. For a brief consideration of theological issues involved in the experience of the *rās* dance, together with a dramatic representation of it, see J. S. Hawley, *At Play with Krishna: Pilgrimage Dramas from Brindavan* (Princeton: Princeton University Press, 1981), pp. 155–226.

3. There is a minority opinion on this point, in which an attempt has been made to justify a marital relationship between Krishna and the *gopīs*. It has force particularly in regard to Krishna's favorite among the *gopīs*, Rādhā, but even there it remains distinctly the minority position. See J. S. Hawley and Donna M. Wulff, eds., *The Divine Consort: Rādhā and the Goddesses of India* (Berkeley: Graduate Theological Union, 1982), pp. 53, 58–62, 82.

4. Scholarly attention to Mīrā Bāī in European languages has been meager in relation to her stature in Hindi literature and hagiography; translations are somewhat more plentiful. The following are among the principal works in English: Bankey Behari, *Bhakta Mira* (Bombay: Bharatiya Vidya Bhavan, 1961); S. M. Pandey, "Mīrābāī and Her Contributions to the Bhakti Movement," *History of Religions* 5.1 (1965): 54–73; Herman Goetz, *Mira Bai: Her Life and Times* (Bombay: Bharatiya Vidya Bhavan, 1966); Usha S. Nilsson, *Mira Bai* (New Delhi: Sahitya Akademi, 1969); Shreeprakash Kurl, *The Devotional Poems of Mirabai* (Calcutta: Writers Workshop, 1973); Baldoon Dinghra, *Songs of Meera: Lyrics in Ecstasy* (New Delhi: Orient Paperbacks, 1977); V. K. Sethi, *Mira, The Divine Lover* (Beas, Punjab: Radha Soami Satsang Beas, 1979); A. J. Alston, *The Devotional Poems of Mīrābāī* (Delhi: Motilal Banarsidass, 1980); and J. S. Hawley, "Morality beyond Morality in Three Hindu Saints," in *Saints and Virtues*, ed. Hawley (Berkeley: University of California Press, 1987).

5. The literature on Sūr in European languages may be surveyed in the bibliography of J. S. Hawley, *Sūr Dās: Poet, Singer, Saint* (Seattle: University of Washington Press, 1984). The most important single work in English to date is that of Kenneth E. Bryant, *Poems to the Child-God: Structures and Strategies in the Poetry of Sūrdās* (Berkeley: University of California Press, 1978).

6. Paraśurām Caturvedī, ed., *Mīrābāī kī Padāvalī* (Prayāg: Hindī Sāhitya Sammelan, 1973); Jagannāthdās 'Ratnākar,' et al., *Sūr Sāgar*, 2 vols. (Varanasi: Kāśī Nāgarīpracāriṇī Sabhā, 1972, 1976). These editions are hereinafter cited by the abbreviations *P* and *S* respectively.

7. Such materials are listed in J. S. Hawley, *Krishna, the Butter Thief* (Princeton: Princeton University Press, 1983), p. 104, n. 13. A critical edition based on the oldest manuscripts of the *Sūr Sāgar*, with annotation and translation, is now being prepared by Kenneth E. Bryant and myself in cooperation with Vidyut Aklujkar, Mandakranta Bose, and Thomas B. Ridgeway.

8. Kalyāṇsiṃh Śekhāvat, ed., *Mīrā-Bṛhatpadāvalī*, vol. 2 (Jodhpur: Rajasthan Oriental Research Institute, 1975). (Hereinafter cited as *B*.) This volume is published in a format that suggests it is the second volume of a work already in print. The first volume in the set, however, is of a very different sort. It contains a series of poems attributed to Mīrā that were collected from various places by Harinārāyan Śarmā and published posthumously in 1968. (Hereinafter cited as *H*.) Śarmā's sources and editorial methods are not entirely known. Śekhāvat's study is much more useful from a critical point of view; still, the oldest dated manuscripts he was able to find go back only to the latter half of the eighteenth century (v.s. 1826, 1834, and 1836; i.e., A.D. 1769, 1777, and 1779). See Śekhāvat, *Mīrā*, pp. 4, 6.

In citations that follow, verse numbers in *B* and *H*, as in *S*, refer to actual lines of print on the page, including the title line, rather than reproducing the numbers assigned in *B* and *H* themselves.

9. The concept of the "Sūr tradition" was first suggested by Bryant (*Child-God*, pp. xi–xiii). A gender analysis of present-day audiences for poems attributed to women as against men has not yet, to my knowledge, been undertaken in North India. It would obviously contribute to the present discussion, as would the development of sophisticated techniques for assessing whether in the past poems might characteristically have been sung by or to women rather than men, or vice versa. An indication of the direction in which such studies should move is provided by Milton Singer, "The Rādhā-Krishna *Bhajanas* of Madras City," in *Krishna: Myths, Rites, and Attitudes,* ed. Singer (Chicago: University of Chicago Press, 1966), pp. 90–138. Fragmentary indications of the attraction of women to songs of Mīrā appear in various places, for example, in Monika Thiel-Horstmann, "The *Bhajan* Repertoire of the Present-Day Dādūpanth," in *Bhakti in Current Research, 1979–1982,* ed. Thiel-Horstmann (Berlin: Dietrich Reimer Verlag, 1983), pp. 395–96.

10. Priyā Dās, *Bhaktirasabodhinī* Commentary on Nābhājī's *Bhaktamāl* (Lucknow: Tejkumar Press, 1969), p. 721. For a more extended account of the *Bhaktamal*'s portrait of Mīrā, see J. S. Hawley, "The Music in Faith and Morality," *Journal of the American Academy of Religion* 52.2 (1984): 243–62; and "Morality beyond Morality."

11. *P* 58.7; *B* 61.3; *H* 30.5, 264.5; *S* 1621.8, 1652.2. Here and in what follows citations are meant to be illustrative rather than exhaustive.

12. *P* 167.2; *S* 1269.2. Mīrā's *gopī* also speaks of the maddening effect of the flute (*P* 167.1). Poems in the same vein by Krishna Dās and Raskhān, both males, are translated in Hawley, *At Play with Krishna*, pp. 115–20.

13. *P* 19.1, 23.1, 25.1, 37.1, 40.9, 66.7, 106.6; cf. *H* 493.1; *S* 332.8, 2276.5–6, 4144.4, 4346.2.

14. E.g., *P* 172.5; *B* 85.3, 98.2, 148.1; *H* 494.4; *S* 2490.3, 4182.4.

15. *P* 165.1, 165.4; *S* 820–27, 1021–23, 1803, appendix 245. A sample of this genre is translated in Hawley, *Butter Thief*, p. 194.

16. Such a catalog could be amplified by reference to literary genres and motifs shared by Mīrā and Sūr that do not concern poems composed as if they had been uttered from within Krishna's narrative universe. In compositions that would normally be assigned to various aspects of the *vinaya* genre, both poets speak of the importance of the Name of God (*P* 140.1–8, 199.1, 200.1–2; *B* 131.8; *S* 68.4, 279.8, 351.5, 352.12), of the preciousness of human birth (*P* 196. 1–4; *S* 68.8), and of beating the annunciatory drum (*P* 35.6, 58.2, 59.4; *S* 233.6, 235.3); both indulge in self-denigration to the glory of God (*P* 158, 159; *B* 4; *S* 77, 103, 131–51); both use nautical imagery to speak of crossing the "sea of existence" (*P* 196. 5–6, cf. *B* 99; *S* 68.6, 99.2); and so forth.

17. *P* 145.1. Cf. L. Winifred Bryce, *Women's Folk-Songs of Rajputana* (Delhi: Government of India, 1964), pp. 33–34.

18. *P* 115. For a discussion of literature relating to this folk genre, see J. S. Hawley, "*Yoga* and *Viyoga*: Simple Religion in Hinduism," *Harvard Theological Review* 74.1 (1981):16, n. 27.

19. E.g., *P* 169.6. Cf. Bryce, *Folk-Songs*, pp. 118–19; Nilsson, *Mira Bai*, p. 9. An interesting comparison can be seen in the poetry of Mahādē-viyakka, a female saint from South India, as translated by A. K. Ramanujan, *Speaking of Śiva* (Baltimore: Penguin, 1973), p. 141. In Rajasthani women's songs, complaints can also be directed against male in-laws, as one can see in Ann Grodzins Gold, *Village Families in Story and Song: An Approach through Women's Oral Tradition in Rajasthan* (Chicago: South Asia Language and Area Center, University of Chicago, 1982), pp. 87, 88, 91. See also Susan Wadley, "Women in the Hindu Tradition," in *Women in India: Two Perspectives*, ed. Doranne Jacobson and Susan Wadley (New Delhi: Manohar, 1977), p. 120.

20. E.g., the Bengali poet Balarām Dās, as translated in Edward C. Dimock, Jr., and Denise Levertov, *In Praise of Krishna* (Garden City, N.Y.: Doubleday, 1967), p. 33.

21. Several examples of the genre are translated in Bryant, *Child-God*, pp. 196–98, and the *Sūr Sāgar* contains a great many more, grouped in the section numbered *S* 1835–1947. In certain poems the *gopīs* explicitly designate Muralī as a disruptive co-wife (e.g., *S* 1839.6, 1858.1, cf. 1832.4); in others, one hears the tone of contest and resentment in a more general

way. Finally, there is a group of poems in which Muralī is permitted to respond to the *gopīs*' broadsides (*S* 1948–56).

22. E.g., *B* 72.

23. This is not to say that Mīrā senses no distance at all; sometimes, for example, she speaks of Krishna's having manifested himself to her in dream rather than in waking consciousness (*P* 27.1–4, 43.4, 75.2).

24. A. K. Ramanujan, "On Women Saints," in *The Divine Consort,* ed. Hawley and Wulff, pp. 316, 324.

25. *P* 186. The Bhīls are a tribal group living in southwestern Rajasthan. They are traditionally looked down upon as being outside the caste structure of Hindi society.

26. *S* 138, critically edited as explained in Hawley, *Sūr Dās,* pp. 199–200.

27. *P* 134.3, 140.4.

28. *P* 134.5; *B* 37, 41, 42, 130.2.

29. *P* 131.3, 137.4. Also Bankey Behari, *Bhakta Mira,* p. 78.

30. *P* 137.6.

31. *P* 139.5.

32. *P* 134.5, 139.4; *B* 128.2.

33. The converse is not the case. Even in poems spoken through one of the persons in Krishna's world, the poet's signature customarily appears. It usually conveys the simple sense "Mīrā says," but the verb is normally omitted, with the result that stronger bonds can also be implied between the poet's name and the rest of her discourse. I have discussed this in relation to Sūr in *Butter Thief,* pp. 118–21.

34. Alston, *Devotional Poems,* p. 112. In doing so, Alston adopts the suggestion made in the commentary appended to the Hindi text. See Caturvedī, *Mīrābāī,* p. 194.

35. The "marriage" poems in the *Sūr Sāgar* are collected in the section numbered *S* 1689–1702; it is notable that as a group they have only the scantiest support in the old manuscripts. The marriage being celebrated is Krishna's rās līlā.

36. *P* 27. Perhaps the dream referred to in *P* 75.2 is the same.

37. In regard to *P* 27, see Pandey, "Mīrābāī," pp. 71–72. In regard to other poems, see Pandey, "Mīrābāī," pp. 68–69; Nilsson, *Mira Bai,* p. 31; and Bankey Behari, *Bhakta Mira,* pp. 61, 139. A particularly unambiguous affirmation of union with Krishna is *P* 150; cf. also *P* 201.5.

38. Darshan Singh, personal communication, Mar. 1, 1984.

39. All this is laid out in greater detail in Hawley, *"Yoga* and *Viyoga."* The Krishnaite setting is not the only one in which women's powers are compared with those manifested by yogis, however. See, for example, Sheryl B. Daniel, "Marriage in Tamil Culture: The Problem of Conflicting 'Models,' " in *The Powers of Tamil Women,* ed. Susan B. Wadley (Syra-

cuse: Maxwell School of Citizenship and Public Affairs, Syracuse University, 1980), pp. 78–80.

40. *P* 44.1, 46.1, 55.1–3, 58.1, 97.1, 98.1, 188.1. Cf. third-person references in *P* 53.1, 54.1–3, 57.1, 117.1–2. Mīrā's use of the title *yogī* to describe Krishna has caused considerable consternation among traditional critics, some of whom have suggested that poems in which such language occurs should be expunged as inauthentic. Aspects of this discussion are reviewed in Śekhāvat, *Mīrā,* pp. 17–19; Sékhāvat presents his own analysis on pp. 19–42.

41. *P* 68.1–4, 188.1–3.

42. *P* 74.1–2, 75.1, 86.1, 87.1–2, 92.1, 102.1, 107.3, 126.1.

43. *P* 58.5, 98.2, 188.3.

44. E.g., *S* 4184, 4225, 4237. A translation and discussion of the first of these can be found in Hawley, "*Yoga* and *Viyoga,*" pp. 12–14.

45. *P* 58.5.

46. *P* 49.3, 117.5–6, 188.2–3 (understanding *baiṭho* as equivalent to *baiṭhyau* and construing it in the first person, to accord with the apparent sense of 188.1; cf., however, 55.2).

47. *S* 4208. A number of sarcastic songs about Krishna's attachment to the hunchback Kubjā (*B* 37, 41, 42) are also attributed to Mīrā, but never to refute the suggestion that Krishna has become a yogi.

48. *P* 183–85; *B* 18, 27–30.

49. *P* 58.5.

50. *P* 44.3, 54.2, 55.1, 117.3.

51. *P* 58.2 and the motif of friendlessness in *P* 53.2, 55.4, and 57.2.

52. *P* 98.1, cf. 116.1. In a number of other poems no explicit mention is made of Krishna's wandering yogi qualities, yet such a peripatetic nature seems to be implied by the use of the same "come to my house" formula. E.g., *P* 109.1, 112.1, 114.1, 120.1, 147.1, 150.1.

53. *P* 46.3. *B* 74 records a different version of the same poem. In another poem, however, Mīrā seemingly takes the opposite tack, and the more frequent one in the literature of *bhakti:* she ridicules any adoption of yogic practice, including specifically the practice of suicide in Benares (*P* 195).

54. *P* 117. Cf. *P* 49.1–3, 68.3; *B* 85.5–7, 149.1–4. One variant of *P* 117 is provided by Paraśurām Caturvedī himself (*Mīrābāī,* pp. 134–35), and another appears as *B* 62. I have translated the version preferred by Caturvedī with a single exception: the substitution of *jag* for *jug* in verse 6. The earrings (*mudarā*) mentioned among the paraphernalia listed in verse 4 imply that the *yoginī* is pictured as a member of the Nāth sect. In this poem, particularly in the final verse, it is difficult to know whether to translate in the second or third person; the original often does not force one to choose.

55. *P* 153. Cf. also *P* 32. The motif of incipient marriage and incipient yoga are connected by the theme of virginity, which finds expression in *P* 51.6 and 77.12.

56. See note 34 above; also Hawley and Wulff, *Divine Consort,* p. 53.

57. *P* 26.7–13, 27.1–4, 32.5, 39.5, 51.4–6, 141.3, 150.3–4, 154.9, 201.3–4.

58. It is perhaps her conjugal image of Krishna that is responsible for her preference for the title *giridhar,* "Lifter of the Mountain," in addressing him. In the poetry of Sūr, by contrast, this title, together with the protective role it connotes, is pushed far to the background or even referred to in ironic terms.

59. *B* 130.1–2, 151.1–6, 152.5–6, cf. 128.4. On Kubjā as queen (*paṭarāṇī*), see *B* 37.3, 41.5.

60. Especially *P* 201.3–4.

61. *P* 51. Indian weddings typically take place in the inner courtyard of the bride's house to the accompaniment of traditional songs of auspiciousness that are sung by women of the household. The ceremony revolves around a low altar (here called *cauk*) that honors various gods and a fire into which Vedic sacrificial offerings are made.

62. *P* 99.4, 130.2.

Ten

"...And Woman His Humanity": Female Imagery in the Religious Writing of the Later Middle Ages
Caroline Walker Bynum

Introduction

The misogyny of the later Middle Ages is well known. Not merely a defensive reaction on the part of men who were in fact socially, economically, and politically dominant, it was fully articulated in theological, philosophical, and scientific theory that was centuries old.[1] *Male* and *female* were contrasted and asymmetrically valued as intellect/body, active/passive, rational/irrational, reason/emotion, self-control/lust, judgment/mercy, and order/disorder. In the devotional writing of the later Middle Ages, they were even contrasted in the image of God—Father or Bridegroom—and soul (*anima*)—child or bride. Although noblewomen managed property while their husbands were away on crusade and middle-class women ran businesses and formed guilds in towns, there was little positive discussion of the role of mother or wife.[2] When devotional writers mentioned marriage and motherhood, it was by and large to warn against the horrors that accompanied them; when secular literature commented on women's roles, it was chiefly to romanti-

The author would like to thank members of the University of Washington faculty seminar, especially Stevan Harrell and John S. Hawley, for their perceptive comments. She owes special gratitude for trenchant criticism to Judith Van Herik. Where possible, medieval works are cited in English translations. Many of the points treated here are dealt with at greater length in Caroline Walker Bynum, *Holy Feast and Holy Fast: The Religious Significance of Food to Medieval Women* (Berkeley: University of California Press, 1986), chaps. 3, 9, 10.

cize adultery by aristocratic ladies or to mock the sexual appetites of peasant or middle-class wives and girls. Even the folk rituals of town and countryside suggested an identification of woman with the disorderly.[3] And as sex ratios and life expectancies altered in favor of women, the size of dowries went steadily up; the birth of a daughter sometimes seemed an extraordinary piece of ill luck.

Historians, whether they have found such misogyny titillating or horrifying, have in general assumed that medieval women internalized it. Much recent interpretation of later medieval religion, for example, has seen misogyny as a causal factor not only in the persecution of women as witches, heretics, or eccentric mystics, but also in women's own religious behavior. Such interpretation has argued that women—seeing themselves as "lust" or "emotionality" or "disorder"—castigated their flesh for its fleshly desires and were sometimes driven to hysteria by the notion that they remained sexual by definition even if their bodies were anesthetized by self-abnegation.[4] Assuming that women's religiosity was fundamentally shaped by the misogyny their clerical advisers so often articulated, historians have suggested that chastity was the central religious issue for women and that Mary, God's ever-virgin mother, was the dominant symbol. Behind such suggestions lies an even more basic assumption—that is, that the image of woman in the later Middle Ages is primarily an aspect of, and an influence on, the history of women.

But, if we look carefully at what medieval religious people wrote, how they worshiped, and how they behaved, their notions about gender seem vastly more complex than recent attention to the misogynist tradition would suggest. In the period from the twelfth to the fifteenth century, in contrast to the early Middle Ages, positive female figures and feminine metaphors took a significant place in spirituality alongside both positive male figures and misogynist images of women. Devotion to the Virgin and to women saints increased; the proportion of women among the newly canonized rose sharply; heretical movements occasionally claimed female clergy or a female god; female erotic experience, childbirth, and marriage became major metaphors for spiritual advance, for service of neighbor, and for union with the divine.[5]

Such ideas and images were not, however, created by or especially attractive to women. As Simon Roisin has demonstrated, the Virgin Mary appeared more often to men than to women in northern European visions.[6] The recent quantitative study of 864 saints by Weinstein and Bell establishes conclusively that the devotion to the human Christ was a "female" theme in a way devotion to Mary was not.[7] Moreover, the fullest elaboration of the notion that Mary is a model for women or the notion that women are models for each other was found in biographies written by men (for example, those of Clare of Assisi and Columba of Rieti). Where we can compare the biographer's perspective with that of the subject (as we can in the case of Clare), we find that the woman herself tended to ignore the female model to discuss instead the imitation of Christ.[8] The idea of Jesus as mother was first elaborated by male devotional writers. In addition, women writers had no monopoly of homey, domestic metaphors. Christ or the soul as seamstress, washer-woman, serving maid, and so forth appeared in the writings of, for example, Marguerite of Oingt, the Helfta nuns, Henry Suso, Richard Rolle, and the monk of Farne.[9]

There was, in the later Middle Ages, no clear association of ordinary women and men with saints of their own sex. Some female saints performed miracles predominantly for women, but so did some male saints.[10] Some shrines dedicated to male saints had predominantly female clientele and vice versa.[11] Since women's visits to shrines were frequently on behalf of sick children, they quite naturally responded to the particular curative powers of the saint (for example, for sore throats, eye disease, etc.) rather than to his or her gender. Indeed certain male religious leaders and writers (for example, Richard Rolle, Henry Suso, John Tauler) acquired circles of female followers, and certain religious women had mostly male followers. Sometimes, when their adherents were in fact of both sexes, women in their exhortations focused on those whom they described as "sons."[12]

Women did not, moreover, develop a religious subculture moti-vated by the need to counter the stereotype of woman as fleshly, weak, irrational, and disorderly. Throughout the period, women's religiosity overlapped in characteristics with men's. For both sexes, asceticism, mysticism, evangelism, eucharistic piety, and devotion to the human Christ increased.[13]

Women's spirituality did have distinctive emphases. Penitential asceticism was more prominent in women's religiosity, particularly in the form of food deprivation, self-inflicted suffering, and an interpretation of illness as religious experience. The religious authority and significance of holy women for others in the society (both male and female) lay more centrally in their charismatic, especially their prophetic, gifts, whereas male saints often owed their power to ecclesiastical or even secular office.[14] The life pattern of holy women showed less adolescent crisis, more childhood vocation, than that of men. Those women whose biographies are recorded are frequently said to have found their vocation before the age of seven or, much later, in widowhood, whereas adolescent conversion is the predominant pattern for males. Of 646 male saints studied by Weinstein and Bell, 357 (or 55 percent) converted as teenagers and only 96 (or 15 percent) as children; of 172 female saints, 55 (or 31 percent) converted as children and 58 (or 34 percent) as adolescents.[15] As I have argued elsewhere, women's stories are less frequently told as stories of crisis and change, regardless of the sex of the narrator, and women writers seem less interested in stories of conversion than in stories of constant and courageous suffering.[16] But there is still little reason to feel that these distinctive themes of women's religiosity were primarily an effort by women to counter the notion that they were lustful and weak. The immediate religious motive was, as it was for men, desire to imitate Jesus.

In fact, religious women paid surprisingly little attention to their supposed incapacity. Although told by the theological tradition that, qua women, they were not created in God's image, women writers ignored the warning. Creation in the image of God and return to his likeness were reiterated and significant themes in their spirituality.[17] For example, when Douceline of Marseille asked herself, "What is the soul?" she answered confidently, "It is the mirror of divine majesty; in it God has put his seal." The nun Mechtild of Hackeborn saw herself in a vision, resting on Christ's breast and receiving the "word and works of his holy humanity" from his own hands. "Incorporated in Christ and liquefied in divine love," she then received "the imprint of resemblance [to God] like a seal in wax." On another occasion, she was reassured by a vision that the married are not further from Christ than virgins because the "Word is made flesh."[18] Becoming one with God in mystical union was a more frequent aspect of women's devotional life than of men's in the thirteenth and fourteenth centuries. Francis of Assisi received the marks of Christ's Passion from a seraph, but such gifts came more frequently to women. And in the later thirteenth century the nun Lukardis of Oberweimar appeared to a monk in a vision as Christ on the cross, with two thieves—one male and one female—crucified on either side.[19] The religious history of the later Middle Ages, characterized by the appearance of new quasi-religious roles for women and for the married, does not support the argument that women shaped their self-conception either in conformity with or in opposition to the misogynist image of Eve, symbol of female sinfulness and sexuality.

Both men and women were aware of the misogynist tradition, with its interwoven and mutually reinforcing notions of woman's physiological, ontological, and functional inferiority. The first great woman theologian, Hildegard of Bingen, both used and argued against the idea that woman is to man as flesh is to spirit; she supported the denial of ordination to women, arguing that woman's role as bride of Christ (i.e., mystic) was complementary to the priesthood.[20] Women such as many of the Italian tertiaries or northern beguines, who remained in the world and were dominated not only by male confessors but by male adherents as well, sometimes spoke of women as weak and urged both women and men to "virility."[21] Women visionaries sometimes expressed resentment, wonder, or fear at the male monopoly of priesthood. Male biographers enjoyed pointing out the weakness—moral and physical—of their female subjects, particularly in order to castigate male readers who, by their own failure and worldliness, allowed the "inferior sex" to reach greater heights of spiritual achievement.[22] Asymmetrical valuing of the genders and some association of male with spiritual and rational, female with fleshly and irrational, was seldom completely absent from medieval gender imagery. But if we take our stand with male and female religious writers respectively, and chart the differences in their use of gender-related notions, we find not only that men and women use the image of woman differently but that it is not simply misogyny in either usage. Moreover, we find that it is a more articulated, self-conscious notion in men's religiosity than in women's. Women say less about gender, make less use of dichotomous gender images, speak less of gender reversal, and place more emphasis on interior motivation and continuity of self. Men use more dichotomous images, are more concerned to define "the female" as both positive and negative, and speak more often of reversal and conversion. A careful and comparative reading of texts by male and female

authors from the twelfth to the fifteenth century thus suggests that
it is men who develop conceptions of gender, whereas women
develop conceptions of humanity. My purpose in this chapter is,
first, to demonstrate that this is so and, second, to suggest some
reasons why.

To demonstrate the difference in male and female perspectives,
I shall explore a variety of female images in late medieval spiritual
writing, taking care to locate the particular images in the clusters of
other images among which they appear. So as not to prejudice my
conclusions by my initial choice of texts, I shall compare those
male and female writers who are, on the surface, most similar.
After all, to compare the university-trained Thomas Aquinas or
Meister Eckhart with a virtually illiterate Italian nun or tertiary
would reveal differences in educational background and philosophical sources so vast that differences owing to gender or social
experience could never be determined. Not only do I limit myself
to comparable genres by male and female authors (vision collections, saints' lives, and devotional texts); I also limit myself to
those male writers whose spirituality is most "affective"—that is,
to those male writers who, in style of religious life and in style of
devotion, come closest to the piety of twelfth-, thirteenth-, and
fourteenth-century women. I concentrate here therefore on men
such as Bernard of Clairvaux, Francis of Assisi, Richard Rolle,
and Henry Suso, whose spirituality has been called "emotional,"
"lyrical," and "nuptial," and on men such as Thomas of Cantimpré,
James of Vitry, and John Tauler, who cultivated and were
influenced by female followers. If these men give to images drawn
from gender a significantly different meaning from that given by
women writers, the difference is likely to stem at least in part from
the gender of the author.[23] Let me begin, then, with a topic I have
treated before: maternal images for the deity.[24]

Female Images for God

When we look at medieval devotional writing, we note at once that
God is described in both masculine and feminine terms. To the traditional and dominant description of God as Father and Christ as
Son, central to the Christian belief in a personal God, devotional
and occasionally even theological writers added the idea of the
motherhood of Christ (and more occasionally of the Holy Spirit).

In general, the image of the motherhood of Christ expressed three
aspects of Christian belief about Christ's role in the economy of
salvation: Christ's sacrificial death on the cross, which generated
redemption, was described as a mother giving birth; Christ's love
for the soul was described as the unquestioning pity and tenderness
of a mother for her child; Christ's feeding of the soul with himself
(his body and blood) in the eucharist was described as a mother
nursing her baby. In general also we can say that, between the
twelfth and the fourteenth century, the use of these images became
"darker"; suffering was increasingly stressed. Death on the cross
as birthpangs and feeding with the blood from Christ's wound
tended to replace images of conception, gestation, and lactation
when Christ's motherhood was elaborated in prayer, sermon, and
vision. Within this broad pattern, in which both theology and chronology help account for the specific use of images, we find that men
and women differ in their use of the idea of Christ's motherhood.
The difference is not merely that *mother* has one set of connotations to women and another set to men; it is also that, in male and
female writing, *mother* occurs among a different group of images.

To male writers (such as Bernard of Clairvaux, Aelred of
Rievaulx, the monk of Farne, Francis of Assisi, and Henry Suso),
mothering meant not only nurturing but also an affectivity that was
needed to complement authority. Aelred of Rievaulx, describing
the crucifix (a new devotional object in twelfth-century monasteries), emphasized motherhood as union, tenderness, nurture, and
nourishment: "On your altar let it be enough for you to have a representation of our Savior hanging on the cross; that will bring
before your mind his Passion for you to imitate, his outspread arms
will invite you to embrace him, his naked breasts will feed you with
the milk of sweetness to console you."[25] Two hundred years later,
the anonymous monk of Farne wrote in a similar vein, although the
food was now blood rather than milk: "Little ones . . . run and
throw themselves into their mothers' arms. . . . Christ our Lord
does the same with men. He stretches out his hands to embrace us,
bows down his head to kiss us, and opens his side to give us suck;
and though it is blood he offers us to suck we believe that it is
health-giving and *sweeter than honey and the honey-comb*" (Ps.
18:11).[26] Repeatedly in such texts, mothering meant security, compassion, nurture, whereas fathering or fatherhood meant authority, instruction, and discipline. Guerric of Igny wrote in a sermon

263

for SS. Peter and Paul's Day (and it is significant that the context in which the image occurs is a discussion of the authority of apostles and preachers): "The Bridegroom [Christ] . . . has breasts, lest he should be lacking any one of all duties and titles of loving kindness. He is a father in virtue of natural creation . . . and also in virtue of the authority with which he instructs. He is a mother, too, in the mildness of his affection, and a nurse."[27]

Christ's affectivity as a complement to authority was often connected by male writers with their own roles as abbots or preachers. Commenting on Song of Songs 1:1–2, the Cistercian abbot Bernard of Clairvaux associated nursing with Christ the Bridegroom, but moved swiftly to the issue of clerical or monastic authority:

> She [the bride, i.e., the soul] would seem to say to the bridegroom [Christ]: "What wonder if I presume to ask you for this favor since your breasts have given me such overwhelming joy?" . . . When she said, then, "Your breasts are better than wine," she meant: "The richness of grace that flows from your breasts contributes far more to my spiritual progress than the biting reprimands of superiors." . . . how many [superiors] there are today who reveal their lack of the requisite capabilities. . . . They display an insatiable passion for gain. . . . Neither the peril of souls nor their salvation gives them any concern. They are certainly devoid of the maternal instinct. . . . There is no pretense about a true mother; the breasts she displays are full for the taking. She knows how to *rejoice with those who rejoice,* and to be sad with those who sorrow [Rom. 12:15], pressing the milk of encouragement without intermission from the breast of joyful sympathy, the milk of consolation from the breast of compassion.[28]

Moreover, Bernard applied such analysis explicitly to himself. To a delinquent monk he wrote: "And I have said this, my son, . . . to help you as a loving father. . . . I begot you in religion by word and example. I nourished you with milk. . . . You too were torn from my breast, cut from my womb. My heart cannot forget you."[29] Male writers thus linked their own "motherhood" (i.e., nurturing) with that of Christ and explored, through these images, their own ambivalence about the exercise of authority and, at a deeper level, about the growing power of the clergy.

In contrast, women writers (such as Marguerite of Oingt, Hadewijch, the nuns of Helfta, and Catherine of Siena) did not associate mothering so exclusively with nurturing and affectivity, nor did they use *mother* and *father* as paired and contradictory descriptions. To Mechtild of Hackeborn, for example, Christ as spouse and father is both merciful and judgmental, tender and severe.[30] Gertrude of Helfta uses androgynous imagery to describe God, Jesus, Mary, and John the Evangelist as emperors, queens, soldiers, fathers, mothers, nurses, and friends. To Gertrude, Christ's fatherhood includes loving, cuddling, feeding from his breast, and teaching the baby soul its letters; Christ's motherhood includes protecting the soul during a storm at sea, clothing it with fine dresses, punishing it, denying it jewels and ornaments, refusing it affection so that it learns patience, and frightening it with ugly faces or masks.[31] Not only are characteristics we would call affective and merciful, judgmental and authoritarian, respectively, distributed randomly between father and mother, but the sets are not usually discussed together or as complements to each other. In the letters and visions of the thirteenth-century Flemish writer Hadewijch, for example, motherhood (usually her own spiritual motherhood) means disciplining as well as loving. In only one letter does Hadewijch identify maternal with loving and paternal with discipline, speak of the two as complements, and apply the description to Christ. The wording of this particular text, unlike the others, turns out to be borrowed from William of St. Thierry, a twelfth-century monk and abbot deeply influenced by Bernard of Clairvaux.[32]

Women writers did not ordinarily use the image of Jesus as mother in a context that associated it with their own leadership roles or with leadership in general—either as critique or as complement. Women writers simply projected themselves into the role of child vis-à-vis mother Jesus, whereas men sometimes drew an analogy between God's motherhood and their own. Moreover, in women's visions and writing, the image does not seem to refer or relate to women's social roles. If any male/female contrast is implied, it is one of biological roles—a contrast between begetting and conceiving, perhaps, but not one between authority and love. By and large, women seem to move from images of lactation or giving birth directly to theological matters, such as eucharist and redemption. The idea of Christ's motherhood becomes either a way of referring to the fact that Christians eat and drink Jesus or a metaphor for Christ's suffering on the cross, which gives birth to the world.

Lutgard of Aywières, for example, had visions of nursing from Christ's side, which occurred at crucial points in her own life.[33] Angela of Foligno and Catherine of Siena were nursed by Christ, and Angela saw him place the heads of her spiritual sons in his wound to drink.[34] Aldobrandesca of Siena tasted a drop of blood from Christ's side and, in memory of this, had a picture of the Virgin Mary painted, holding Christ in her arms and drinking from his wound.[35] The Carthusian prioress Marguerite of Oingt spoke thus of mother Jesus:

> My sweet Lord, I gave up for you my father and my mother and my brothers and all the wealth of the world. . . . You know, my sweet Lord, that if I had a thousand worlds and could bend them all to my will, I would give them all up for you . . . for you are the life of my soul. Nor do I have father or mother besides you nor do I wish to have. For are you not my mother and more than my mother? The mother who bore me labored in delivering me for one day or one night but you, my sweet and lovely Lord, labored for me for more than thirty years. Ah, my sweet and lovely Lord, with what love you labored for me and bore me through your whole life. But when the time approached for you to be delivered, your labor pains were so great that your holy sweat was like great drops of blood that came out from your body and fell on the earth. . . . Ah! Sweet Lord Jesus Christ, who ever saw a mother suffer such a birth! For when the hour of your delivery came you were placed on the hard bed of the cross . . . and your nerves and all your veins were broken. And truly it is no surprise that your veins burst when in one day you gave birth to the whole world.[36]

Although fourteenth-century male writers such as Richard Rolle and the monk of Farne also emphasized the crucifixion as birthing more than did twelfth-century male writers, the fullest development of a theology of motherhood as creation and redemption is by an English anchoress of the late fourteenth century, Julian of Norwich, in whose hands it became a solution to the problem of evil. Unlike earlier women, Julian saw motherhood as the completion of fatherhood, but her theological position went well beyond all earlier formulations, male and female. To Julian, God's motherhood, expressed in Christ, is not merely love and mercy, not merely redemption through the sacrifice of the cross, but a taking on of our physical humanity in the Incarnation, as a mother gives herself to the fetus she bears.

I saw and understood that the high might of the Trinity is our Father, and the deep wisdom of the Trinity is our Mother, and the great love of the Trinity is our Lord; and all these we have in nature and in our substantial creation. And furthermore I saw that the second person, who is our Mother, substantially the same beloved person, has now become our mother sensually because we are double by God's creating, that is to say substantial and sensual. Our substance is the higher part, which we have in our Father, God almighty; and the second person of the Trinity is our Mother in nature in our substantial creation, in whom we are founded and rooted, and he is our Mother of mercy in taking our sensuality. And so our Mother is working on us in various ways, in whom our parts are kept undivided; for in our Mother Christ we profit and increase, and in mercy he reforms and restores us, and by the power of his Passion, his death and his Resurrection he unites us to our substance. So our Mother works in mercy on all his beloved children who are docile and obedient to him.[37]

Moreover, Julian sees discipline, judgment, and wisdom as part of mothering. Elsewhere she writes:

The mother can give her child to suck of her milk, but our precious Mother Jesus can feed us with himself, and does, most courteously and most tenderly, with the blessed sacrament, which is the precious food of true life. . . . The mother can lay her child tenderly to breast, but our tender Mother Jesus can lead us easily into his blessed breast through his sweet open side, and show us there a part of the godhead. . . . And always as the child grows in age and in stature, [the mother] acts differently, but she does not change her love. And when it is even older, she allows it to be chastised to destroy its faults, so as to make the child receive virtues and grace.[38]

Use of the theme of mother Jesus in late medieval writing is clearly conditioned by the tenets of Christian theology, by recognition of male/female biological differences, and by the misogynist definition of women as weak. Within these constraints, however, men and women used the image in complex and different ways. Men were more apt to pair mothering with fathering. They saw motherhood as a social role and a set of personal characteristics (especially tenderness and emotionality), contrasted to male authority and power. Women were less likely to pair motherhood with fatherhood or to define motherhood as a given set of personal characteristics. To them, mothering was associated most clearly with eating and feeding, and with *passio* (suffering, which was in some sense childbirth). This difference in use of the theme of mother Jesus takes on deeper significance when we move from gender-related images of God to gender-related images of the soul. For the dominant religious image of the self in the late Middle Ages was female; the soul was woman or bride (or sometimes child). Not surprisingly, this image expressed very different meanings in the hands of male and female authors.

Images of the Soul

When male writers used female images of the soul, they sometimes simply slipped into the metaphor in order to express the "child-like" or "womanly" dependence of the good Christian on a power-ful, "fatherly" God. But they also expressed something more complicated: conversion or renunciation. When describing the self, as when describing God, male writers made more frequent use than did women writers of male/female as a contrasting pair. Moreover, men often called attention to their adoption of the oppo-site gender as self-description. In other words, men saw male and female as contrasting sets of values or behaviors and used gender reversal as an image of their exchange of ordinary (male) for extra-ordinary (female) status.

Sometimes men used *woman* as a term of opprobrium and accused themselves (as did Helinand of Froidmont) of being weak—even menstruating—women.[39] More frequently, however, their description of themselves as "weak women" expressed some-thing positive: their desire to reject the world, to become the meek who inherit the earth. Bernard of Clairvaux wrote that monks were women, whereas bishops were men.[40] In the words of his male biographer, Francis of Assisi not only married Lady Poverty, he was Lady Poverty.[41] In the biographies and writing of some male religious leaders (often those whose own mothers deeply in-fluenced their lives), we find not just elaboration of the notion of the soul as bride; we also find consistent avoidance of male imagery for the self.[42] Henry Suso, for example, when offered the role of knight in a vision, debated with himself over the appropriateness of the image. But he happily adopted as self-description the image of a maiden picking roses, a baby being nursed, or a mother nursing, and he explicitly identified himself with his own mother's religiosity.[43] When Richard Rolle converted to the hermit's life, he horrified his father by making a habit from two of his sister's dresses.[44]

Indeed male appropriation of the notion of woman as weak sometimes became a claim to superior lowliness. Women, whose lives were in fact characterized by more virulent asceticism than men's and who might have been presumed to need such asceticism to purge their greater physicality, were advised by Suso and Abelard, among others, that theirs should be the way of moderation.[45] When male writers took femaleness as an image to describe their renunciation of the world, they sometimes said explicitly that women were too weak to be women. They sometimes implied that their own role reversal—that is, their appropriation of or choice for lowliness—was a superior "femaleness" to the femaleness of women, which was not chosen. Suso, for example, occasionally suggested that the tears and suffering of real women were whining, whereas men's austerities were imitation of Christ.[46]

Thus, to men, woman was a marked category, an exception to the generalization homo, a reversal of ordinary condition. "To become woman" was an obvious image of renunciation and conversion. Moreover, as I have argued elsewhere, male writers assumed that women would undergo reversals too.[47] Male biographers not only labeled women as weak far more frequently than women described themselves in such terms, they also told women's stories as stories of radical conversion and urged women to become virile, masculine, in rising to God. Late medieval men, like those of the patristic period, were titillated and made anxious by stories (some of which they clearly fabricated) of women masquerading as men in order to enter monasteries.[48] Male biographers (who also, somewhat inconsistently, advised women to choose female models) felt that saintly women must be elevated or authenticated by male qualities. For example, when Raymond of Capua worried about the authenticity of Catherine of Siena's visions, he received a vision from God in which Catherine's face changed into the face of a bearded man. (Raymond understood the bearded man to be Christ.)[49]

But women themselves did not, by and large, see woman as a marked category, nor did they worry about themselves as exceptions or special cases of the general category humanity. Women did not assume that their religious progress involved "becoming male."

Women, of course, described themselves in female images. Moreover, religious women—whether nuns, beguines, tertiaries, or lay women without ostensible affiliation to any order—adopted practices (such as fasting, chastity, white garments, uncontrolled weeping) that distinguished them from those in worldly roles. But female writers often seem, by *woman,* to have meant human being. And conversion or reversal was a less central theme in women's spirituality than in men's.

Women sheltered by special religious status, especially those raised in convents, rarely spoke of female weakness as a bar to theological expression or religious practice. Gertrude of Helfta and Mechtild of Hackeborn, for example, did not speak of themselves as weak. And Julian of Norwich eliminated her one reference to woman's intellectual inferiority between the first and second recensions of her famous *Showings.*[50] Even ordinary housewives could be forthright and fierce in defending their religious inspiration. Margery Kempe's spirited assertion of her right to point out clerical failings is well known.

> Then the Archbishop said to her: "I am evil informed of thee. I hear it said that thou art a right wicked woman."
> And she answered back: "I also hear it said that ye are a wicked man. And if ye be as wicked as men say, ye shall never come to Heaven, unless ye amend whilst ye be here."
> . . .
> "Ah! Sir," said the clerks, "here wot we well that she hath a devil within her, for she speaketh of the Gospel."
> As quickly as possible, a great clerk brough forth a book and laid Saint Paul, for his part, against her, that no woman should preach.
> She answering thereto said: "I preach not, sir; I come into no pulpit. I use but communication and good words, and that I will do while I live."[51]

Female authors who discuss woman as a social category—a gender contrasted to and weaker than maleness—are usually women such as Mechtild of Magdeburg, Catherine of Siena, and Angela of Foligno, who remained in the world, experienced lengthy struggle with family over vocation, and had predominantly male followers.[52]

When describing self as when describing God, women used imagery more androgynously than did men. It is true that women described their souls as female, and such imagery sometimes enabled them to release highly erotic energy toward God. Margery Kempe, for example, cuddled with Christ in bed and clearly saw herself as a woman responding to a male Jesus.[53] Marguerite of Oingt wrote thus of her meditation on the crucifixion:

> And when I see that the evil crowd has left, I approach and take out the nails and then I carry him on my shoulders down from the cross and put him between the arms of my heart. . . . And in the evening, when I go to bed, I in spirit put him in my bed and I kiss his tender hands and his feet so cruelly pierced for my sins. And I lean over that glorious side pierced for me.[54]

Hadewijch, in a eucharistic vision of particular beauty, described mystical union in words that suggest orgasm.

> Then he gave himself to me in the shape of the sacrament, in its outward form, as the custom is; and then he gave me to drink from the chalice. . . . After that he came himself to me, took me entirely in his arms, and pressed me to him; and all my members felt his in full felicity, in accordance with the desire of my heart and my humanity. So I was outwardly satisfied and fully transported. And then, for a short while, I had the strength to bear this; but soon, after a short time, I lost that manly beauty outwardly in the sight of his form. I saw him completely come to nought and so fade and all at once dissolve that I could no longer recognize or perceive him outside me, and I could no longer distinguish him within me. Then it was to me as if we were one without difference.[55]

But, as even these examples make clear, women did not have a strong sense of binary opposites grouped around the male/female contrast. They did not associate specific personality characteristics or roles—such as authority, rationality, nurture, emotion—with one or the other sex. Although they made use of the conventions of vernacular love poetry to write of themselves as brides, they also slipped easily into male imagery where no reversal or even gender-specific meaning was implied. Hadewijch saw the soul sometimes as a knight seeking his lady, sometimes as a bride reaching her lover. To Julian of Norwich, the soul that is saved and cared for by mother God is a genderless "child." (The pronoun *it* rather than *he* or *she* is used in the Middle English.)

A sharply defined sense of the male as superior was unimportant in women's writings and visions. Although women in the early church sometimes had visions in which they acquired spiritual maleness, this motif drops out of late medieval visions.[56] In the later Middle Ages, women (like Joan of Arc) cross-dressed in order to change social roles, but not as symbols of spiritual advance. Hildegard of Bingen actually dressed her nuns in bridal dresses when they went forward to communion.[57] Despite God's revelation to Raymond of Capua that a male authority lay behind Catherine's visions, Catherine herself received a different message. She had thought since childhood that she ought to put on male attire in order to entitle her to the role of preacher and prophet. But God sent a revelation that he "who has created both sexes and all sorts of men . . . who can create an angel as easily as an ant" would send her to preach and teach *as a woman* in order to shame immoral men.[58] Although women who influenced or directed men sometimes urged those men to be virile rather than womanly, I know of only a few cases where a woman urged a woman to maleness.[59] Indeed, women such as Margery Kempe, Lutgard of Aywières, Ida of Louvain, or Agnes of Montepulciano, who received visions of Jesus as bridegroom or as suckling child, were implicitly responding to their own gender as a positive route to union with God.[60]

The issue of actual and metaphorical cross-dressing is worth pursuing a little further. Natalie Davis has demonstrated the prevalence of role inversion generally in the calendrical rituals of medieval and early modern peasants and townspeople; in such festivals and carnivals—by definition infrequent and unusual events—men aped women as children aped the powerful, providing an expression of and escape valve for psychological discomfort and social discontent. But, as Vern Bullough has shown, cross-dressing by males (outside a ritual context) was extremely rare in the Middle Ages because such acts represented decline in status.[61] Actual cross-dressing by lay women, even by women who gave it some religious significance, was fairly common. Joan of Arc was unusual in donning male clothes to lead an army, but a number of cases are recorded of women who put on male clothing to travel—especially on pilgrimage—or to run away from home. Their cross-dressing was a mechanism to aid in role change or a real disguise to gain the physical protection offered by superior status. In short, cross-dressing and role reversal were more common among women than men and less disturbing to them. Such inversions (both women masquerading as men and men cross-dressing or reversing gender) were far more disturbing possibilities, and thus more heightened and powerful symbols, to men. It does not seem surprising, therefore, that religious men spoke of their renunciation of the world as adopting another gender, as the cross-dressing they seldom in fact did. On the other hand, women, who more commonly put on male dress in the world in order to accomplish certain goals (occasionally even religious goals, like Joan's), did not in the safety of the cloister or anchorhold use "acquiring maleness" as a symbol or metaphor with any spiritual content.

The male writer who saw his soul as a bride of God or his religious role as womanly submission and humility was conscious of using an image of reversal. He sought reversal because reversal and renunciation were at the heart of a religion whose dominant symbol is the cross—life achieved through death. When a woman writer (often but not always a virgin) spoke of herself as either a bride or a knight, each image was in a sense a reversal. But neither was as highly charged as the notion of the male as bride or woman, for neither expressed renunciation. Because women were women, they could not embrace the female as a symbol of renunciation. Because society was male-dominated, they could not embrace the male as a symbol of renunciation. To become male was elevation, not renunciation, and elevation was a less significant reversal given the values at the core of medieval Christianity. Thus women did not in their writings play with male and female oppositions; they did not tell their own stories or the stories of other women as reversals or conversions. They did, however, explore and play in very complicated ways with what femaleness meant in the theological tradition—that is, with physicality.

Women's Concern with Physicality

From Hildegard of Bingen and Elisabeth of Schönau to Catherine of Siena and Julian of Norwich, women theologians in the later Middle Ages saw woman as the symbol of humanity, where humanity was understood as physicality. To Elisabeth of Schönau, the humanity of Christ appeared in a vision as a female virgin;[62] to Hildegard of Bingen, Christ's humanity was to Christ's divinity as woman is to man, and *mulier* represented humankind, fallen in Eve, restored in *ecclesia* and Maria. Hildegard wrote explicitly in the *Liber divinorum operum* the words I have taken as the theme of this essay: "Man . . . signifies the divinity of the Son of God and woman his humanity."[63] Moreover, to Mechtild of Magdeburg and Catherine of Siena, Mary was the source and container of Christ's physicality; the flesh Christ put on was in some sense female, because it was his mother's.[64] And to Julian of Norwich, God was mother exactly in that our humanity with its full sensuality was not merely loved and saved but even given being by and from him.

> For in the same time that God joined himself to our body in the maiden's womb, he took our soul, which is sensual, and in taking it, having enclosed us all in himself, he united it to our substance. In this union he was perfect man, for Christ, having joined in himself every man who will be saved, is perfect man.
>
> So our Lady is our mother, in whom we are all enclosed and born of her in Christ, for she who is mother of our saviour is mother of all who are saved in our saviour; and our saviour is our true Mother, in whom we are endlessly born and out of whom we shall never come.[65]

Thus *female* was not to women writers primarily paired with *male* as contrasting image. The one woman theologian (Hildegard of Bingen) who did discuss the two genders directly stressed complementarity.[66] The woman writer's sense of herself as female was less a sense of herself as evil or as not male than a sense of herself as physical. And women saw the humanity-physicality that linked them to Christ as in continuity with, rather than reversal from, their own ordinary experience of physical and social vulnerability. Women, of course, sought to leave the world, as did men, and they marked themselves off from their worldly sisters by renouncing such things as jewels, cosmetics, soft beds, gaiety, food, husbands, lovers, children, and parents. But they spoke of their union with Christ in images that continued ordinary female roles (bride, child, mother) and stereotypical female behavior (vulnerability, illness, bleeding). Thus women reached God not by reversing what they were but by sinking more fully into it. In fact and in image, suffering (both self-inflicted and involuntary) and food (both eucharist and fasting) were women's most characteristic ways of attaining God.[67] For example, not only was blood (blood as food) Catherine of Siena's most frequent image; her most frequent description of loving one's neighbor was "eating souls on the table of the cross," and her most characteristic practice was fasting. Her vision of marriage to Christ, which her male biographer described as performed with a golden ring, was described by Catherine herself as involving a ring of skin. The context of her letters makes it clear that she saw herself as married with Christ's foreskin—a graphic indication of the centrality for her of humanness as physicality.[68]

Late medieval spirituality abounds in examples of women emphasizing their physicality in order to join with Christ. Ida of Louvain in the thirteenth century and Dorothy of Montau in the fourteenth experienced mystical pregnancy as a preparation for or a result of the eucharist.[69] The vast majority of stigmatics were women, and the reception of stigmata (bearing the marks of Christ's physical body in one's own physicality) was frequently the result of communion—of eating physical elements that literally *were* the similarly marked body of Christ.[70] It is against this background that we must place the little-noticed fact that eating is a far more central image to late medieval women than to men. Hadewijch wrote, of encounter with God:

In the anguish of the repose of the madness of love,
. . .

The heart of each devours the other's heart.
. . .

As he who is Love itself showed us
When he gave us himself to eat
. . .

. . . love's most intimate union
Is through eating, tasting, and seeing interiorly.
He eats us; we think we eat him,
And we do eat him, of that we can be certain.
But because he remains so undevoured
. . .

Each of us remains uneaten by him
. . .

As soon as Love thus touches the soul,
She eats its flesh and drinks its blood.[71]

While penitential asceticism and devotion to the human Christ
are found in male lives also, they are more prominent themes in
women's religiosity. Indeed, women, only about 18 percent of
medieval saints, were an absolute majority (53 percent) of those
whose saintliness was based on debilitating illness.[72] Mary of
Oignies and Villana de' Botti refused prayers for relief of sickness;
Gertrude of Helfta embraced headaches as a source of grace;
Beatrice of Nazareth, who desired the torments of illness, was
healed almost against her wishes; Margaret of Ypres so desired to
join with Christ's suffering that she prayed for her illness to last
beyond the grave. Dauphine of Puimichel even suggested that if
people know how useful diseases were for self-discipline, they
would purchase them in the marketplace.[73] Julian of Norwich
asked for and received the grace of literal *imitatio Christi,* of dying
with Jesus in anguish that became unspeakable joy. She wrote:

> This revelation was made to a simple, unlettered creature, living in
> this mortal flesh, the year of our Lord one thousand, three hundred and
> seventy-three, on the thirteenth day of May; and before this the crea-
> ture had desired three graces by the gift of God. The first was recollec-
> tion of the Passion. The second was bodily sickness. The third was to
> have, of God's gift, three wounds. . . .
>
> And when I was thirty and a half years old, God sent me a bodily
> sickness in which I lay for three days and three nights, and on the third
> night I received all the rites of Holy Church, and did not expect to live
> until day. . . .
>
> After this the upper part of my body began to die, until I could
> scarcely feel anything. My greatest pain was my shortness of breath and
> the ebbing of my life. Then truly I believed that I was at the point of
> death. And suddenly at that moment all my pain was taken from me,
> and I was as sound, particularly in the upper part of my body, as ever I
> was before. I was astonished by this sudden change, for it seemed to me
> that it was by God's secret doing and not natural. . . .
>
> Then suddenly it came into my mind that I ought to wish for the
> second wound as a gift and a grace from our Lord, that my body might
> be filled full of recollection and feeling of his blessed Passion, as I had
> prayed before, for I wished that his pains might be my pains, with com-
> passion which would lead to longing for God. . . .
>
> And at this, suddenly I saw the red blood running down from under

276

the crown, hot and flowing freely and copiously, a living stream, just as it was at the time when the crown of thorns was pressed on his blessed head. I perceived, truly and powerfully, that it was he who just so, both God and man, himself suffered for me, who showed it to me without any intermediary.

And in the same revelation, suddenly the Trinity filled my heart full of the greatest joy. . . . And I said: Blessed be the Lord! This I said with a reverent intention and in a loud voice, and I was greatly astonished by this wonder and marvel, that he who is so to be revered and feared would be so familiar with a sinful creature living in this wretched flesh.[74]

Conclusions and Explanations

Medieval men and women looked at and used gender-related notions very differently. Male writers saw the genders as dichotomous. They stressed male as power, judgment, discipline, and reason, female as weakness, mercy, lust, and unreason. They applied female images to themselves to express world denial, and the world they renounced was predominantly the world of wealth and power. Women writers used imagery more androgynously. Personal and social characteristics were more often shared by the two genders in women's writings. The female was a less marked category; it was more often simply a symbol of an almost genderless self. When women did give the female content taken from the traditional idea of asymmetrical genders, they saw it as physical and bodily. And this physicality was seen as useful in joining with a human Christ. Women's religiosity was less characterized by conversion and inversion; their sense of self and of Christ as physical stressed continuity between their social and biological experience, on the one hand, and the experience of encounter with God, on the other.

Why then do men and women use gender imagery so differently in the religious writing of the later Middle Ages? The reasons undoubtedly lie in part in the nature of medieval society. For example, men renounced power and wealth, whereas women renounced food, because these were aspects of experience that the two sexes respectively controlled.[75] But men's renunciations were more radical breaks with previous life, whereas women's fasting and illness in certain ways enhanced their sense of being bodies and being vulnerable. For this contrast, there are social reasons

277

also. As I pointed out above, men frequently changed roles as adolescents; women who took on specialized religious roles often found their vocations in childhood. Thus men underwent conversions and inverted previous roles more frequently than did women. This was undoubtedly because medieval men had greater ability than women to determine the shape of their lives. For example, Mary of Oignies and Clare of Assisi, wishing to renounce property, were virtually forced to retain income and servants; women such as Margaret of Cortona, Umiliana Cerchi, and Angela of Foligno had to wait for the death of husbands or lovers before espousing chastity.[76] As Weinstein and Bell note:

> Men may have been slower to recognize a call to the holy life, but once called they progressed steadily to ever higher plateaus of heroic virtue. Women were inspired earlier, but their quest for spiritual perfection was less regular. Not only did they encounter obstacles in the form of angry parents and a distrusting world, but they were more likely to judge themselves harshly, to condemn their own backsliding.[77]

Indeed there may be psychological as well as social reasons for the differing male and female patterns. In any society where child rearing is done predominantly by women, young men are forced to undergo more fundamental reversals in self-conception than women, who grow up to be "like" the mother who is their first love. One need not invoke ideas as complicated and problematic as the Oedipus complex to suggest that, since male maturation involved breaking with mother and mother's world, medieval males were more used than females to seeing self as defined by conversion, reversal, and renunciation.[78] Moreover, as Weinstein and Bell point out, male saints tended to see sin as a response to an external stimulus. By contrast, in the lives of female saints, sin "usually appears to arise from the depths of woman herself."[79] Such evidence suggests that women had a greater sense of interior motivation and of continuity of self, although the evidence may merely show that male biographers were more likely to blame male sins on forces outside men's control.

Such explanations relate the differing perceptions characteristic of men and women to their differing social and psychological experiences. And there is an even simpler—and equally convincing—explanation that relates male and female perspectives to women's experience of constricted opportunities. It may be that, in any patriarchal society, men will stress gender differences because such an emphasis consolidates their advantage. Women, on the other hand, unable to propose their experience as dominant and unwilling to accept it as exceptional, will quite naturally couch their perceptions in terms of an androgynous humanity.[80]

Such an explanation does not, however, quite capture the meaning of *humanity* to religious women. To them, humanity was, as Mechtild of Hackeborn said, the "Word made flesh." Behind medieval women's concern with physicality lay the doctrine of the Incarnation. To understand male and female perspectives fully, we must thus turn to the religious context of behavior and ideas.

In the dominant theological tradition inherited by the later Middle Ages, *male* and *female* were contrasted and asymmetrically valued as soul and body. Such values suggested that men were like God in a sense women could never achieve, that women ought to sluff off femaleness in rising to meet the divine. In early Christianity we find some use of imagery that suggests that both men and women felt this way about gender, and writing by men in the later Middle Ages sometimes implied that women's spiritual advance was advance toward maleness—that is, toward rationality and self-control.[81] Women in the late Middle Ages seem, however, to have abandoned this concept; and, for men as well, the notion of woman's irrationality and disorder became in some ways positive—an image of mercy and meekness.

The positive image of woman in the later Middle Ages must be understood against the background of the fierce world-denial that characterized the period. As social and religious roles proliferated with bewildering rapidity in the twelfth century, the rhetoric of reversal and renunciation grew more strident. Since religious conversion meant the reversal of all earthly values, men enthusiastically adopted images of themselves as women—that is, powerless, poor, irrational, without influence or authority. If God was male and the soul was other than God, woman was a natural image both for what God redeemed and for what the powerful, successful male became when he renounced the world. In revering female saints, worshiping the Virgin Mary, attracting female followers, holding up saintly women as a reproach to worldly prelates, and describing themselves as women and fools, medieval men were in one sense ignoring the negative side of the earlier medieval image of woman. But in another sense, asymmetry was implicit in the very notion of the reversal.

Such gender images were, in any case, as problematic to religious women as the notion of woman as lust. If reversal and renunciation were the heart of religious dedication, women, who were already inferior, did not have much to offer. Moreover, neither maleness nor femaleness could serve for them as an image of renunciation.

Women thus asserted and embraced their humanity. They asserted it because traditional dichotomous images of woman and man opposed humanity-physicality-woman to divinity-rationality-man. Women stressed their humanity and Jesus' because tradition had accustomed them to associate humanity with the female. But humanity is not, in the final analysis, a gender-related image. Humanity is genderless. To medieval women humanity was, most basically, not femaleness but physicality, the flesh of the "Word made flesh." It was the ultimate negative—the otherness from God that the God-man redeemed by taking it into himself. Images of male and female alike were insipid and unimportant in the blinding light of the ultimate asymmetry between God and creation.

If religious women spoke less frequently in gender terms than did religious men, it is because they understood that "man . . . signifies the divinity of the Son of God and woman his humanity." And they understood that both equations were metaphorical. But, given the ultimate dichotomy of God and creation, the first was only metaphorical. Man was not divinity. The second was in some sense, however, literally true.

Notes

1. Julia O'Faolain and Lauro Martines, eds., *Not in God's Image* (New York: Harper and Row, 1973); Vern L. Bullough, "Medieval Medical and Scientific Views of Women," *Viator* 4 (1973):487–93; Eleanor C. McLaughlin, "Equality of Souls, Inequality of Sexes: Women in Medieval Theology," in *Religion and Sexism: Images of Women in the Jewish and Christian Traditions,* ed. Rosemary Ruether (New York: Simon and Schuster, 1974), pp. 213–66; Marie-Thérèse d'Alverny, "Comment les théologiens et les philosophes voient la femme?" *La femme dans les civilisations*

des Xe–XIIIe siècles: Actes du colloque tenu à Poitiers les 23–25 septembre 1976, Cahiers de civilisation médiévale 20 (1977):105–29.

2. David Herlihy, "Women in Medieval Society," reprinted in *The Social History of Italy and Western Europe 700–1500,* Variorum Reprints (London, 1978).

3. Natalie Z. Davis, *Society and Culture in Early Modern France* (Stanford: Stanford University Press, 1975), pp. 124–31.

4. André Vauchez, *La sainteté en Occident aux derniers siècles du moyen âge d'après les procès de canonisation et les documents hagiographiques,* Bibliothèque des Ecoles Françaises d'Athènes et de Rome 241 (Rome: Ecole Française de Rome, 1981), pp. 427–35; Donald Weinstein and Rudolph M. Bell, *Saints and Society: The Two Worlds of Western Christendom, 1000 to 1700* (Chicago: University of Chicago Press, 1983), *passim,* especially p. 87; Elizabeth Petroff, *Consolation of the Blessed* (New York: Alta Gaia Society, 1979). For an interesting recent example of this interpretation, see Hope P. Weissman, "Margery Kempe in Jerusalem: *Hysteria Compassio* in the Late Middle Ages," in *Acts of Interpretation: The Text in its Context, 700–1600: Essays . . . in Honor of E. Talbot Donaldson,* ed. M. J. Carruthers and E. D. Kirk (Norman, Okla.: Pilgrim Books, 1982), pp. 201–17.

5. Caroline Walker Bynum, *Jesus as Mother: Studies in the Spirituality of the High Middle Ages* (Berkeley and Los Angeles: University of California Press, 1982), pp. 135–46; Joan M. Ferrante, *Woman as Image in Medieval Literature from the Twelfth Century to Dante* (New York: Columbia University Press, 1975); Vauchez, *La sainteté en Occident;* Weinstein and Bell, *Saints and Society;* Jane Tibbets Schulenburg, "Sexism and the Celestial Gynaeceum from 500 to 1200," *Journal of Medieval History* 4 (1978):117–33; Stephen E. Wessley, "The Thirteenth-Century Guglielmites: Salvation through Women," in *Medieval Women: Dedicated and Presented to Professor Rosalind M. T. Hill,* ed. Derek Baker, Studies in Church History: Subsidia 1 (Oxford: Basil Blackwell, 1978), pp. 289–303; Marjorie Reeves, *The Influence of Prophecy in the Later Middle Ages* (Oxford: Oxford University Press, 1969), pp. 248–50.

6. Simone Roisin, *L'hagiographie cistercienne dans le diocèse de Liège au XIIIe siècle* (Louvain: Bibliothèque de l'Université, 1947), pp. 108, 111–13.

7. See Weinstein and Bell, *Saints and Society,* tables on pp. 123–37. According to Weinstein and Bell, women (who represented about 18 percent of the saints canonized or revered between 1000 and 1700) accounted for about half of the saints who were especially devoted to Jesus. They represented only about a third of the saints characterized by devotion to Mary, however. Since women's piety was more affective than men's, we

expect devotion to all members of the holy family to be disproportionately represented in their spirituality. Such affectivity perhaps accounts for their devotion to Mary, which may have nothing to do with Mary's gender (although it may).

8. See life of Columba of Rieti, *Acta sanctorum* [hereafter *AASS*], ed. the Bollandists, May, vol. 5 (1866):149–226; and cf. Thomas of Celano's life of Clare with Clare's own writings in *Legenda sanctae Clarae virginis,* ed. Francesco Pennacchi, Società internazionale di studi Francescani in Assisi (Assisi: Tipografia metastasio, 1910).

9. Bynum, *Jesus as Mother,* pp. 110–69.

10. Douceline of Marseille and Umiliana Cerchi performed miracles predominantly for women; so did Richard Rolle and Henry Suso. See Claude Carozzi, "Douceline et les autres," in *La religion populaire en Languedoc du XIIIe siècle à la moitié du XIV siècle,* Cahiers de Fanjeaux 11 (Toulouse: Edouard Privat, 1976), pp. 251–67; Weinstein and Bell, *Saints and Society,* p. 53; and the office of Richard Rolle, translated from the York Breviary, in Richard Rolle, *The Fire of Love or Melody of Love and the Mending of Life . . . translated by Richard Misyn,* ed. and trans. Frances M. M. Comper (London: Methuen, 1914), pp. xlv–lxii. On Suso, see nn. 43, 45, and 46 below.

11. Ronald C. Finucane, *Miracles and Pilgrims: Popular Beliefs in Medieval England* (Totowa, N.J.: Rowman and Littlefield, 1977).

12. This is true of Catherine of Siena, Angela of Foligno, and Margaret of Cortona; see life of Catherine, *AASS,* Apr., vol. 3 (1866):862–967; life of Angela, *AASS,* Jan., vol. 1 (1863):186–234; life of Margaret, *AASS,* Feb., vol. 3 (1865):302–63.

13. Weinstein and Bell, *Saints and Society,* pp. 220–38. And see Peter Dinzelbacher, "Europäische Frauenmystik des Mittelalters. Ein Überblick," in *Frauenmystik im Mittelalter,* ed. Peter Dinzelbacher and Dieter R. Bauer, Wissenschaftliche Studientagung der Akademie der Diözese Rottenburg-Stuttgart 22.–25. Februar 1984 in Weingarten (Ostfildern: Schwabenverlag, 1985), pp. 11–23.

14. Weinstein and Bell, *Saints and Society,* pp. 228–32; Bynum, *Jesus as Mother,* pp. 247–62.

15. Derived from Weinstein and Bell, *Saints and Society,* tables on pp. 123–37. Peter Dinzelbacher, *Vision und Visionsliteratur im Mittelalter* (Stuttgart: Anton Hiersemann, 1981), p. 229, sums up differences between early medieval visions characteristic of men and later visions characteristic of women in a way that underlines this point. Women's visions were expected and sought for; men's occurred suddenly. Women's visions confirmed them in an already chosen way of life; men's marked the onset of a new life.

16. Caroline Walker Bynum, "Women's Stories, Women's Symbols: A

Critique of Victor Turner's Theory of Liminality," in *Anthropology and the Study of Religion*, ed. Frank Reynolds and Robert Moore (Chicago: Center for the Scientific Study of Religion, 1984), pp. 105–25.

17. For example, *Vita Beatricis: De Autobiografie van de Z. Beatrijs van Tienen O. Cist. 1200–1268*, ed. L. Reypens (Antwerp: Ruusbroec-Genootschap, 1964), pp. 71, 99–100, 110–11; *Les oeuvres de Marguerite d'Oingt*, ed. and trans. Antonin Duraffour, P. Gardette, and P. Durdilly, Publications de l'institut de linguistique romane de Lyon 21 (Paris: Société d'Edition "Les belles lettres," 1965), pp. 73, 101; and see Bynum, *Jesus as Mother*, pp. 136, 170–262. For the negative idea, see O'Faolain and Martines, *Not in God's Image*, which sometimes misleads by quoting out of context.

18. *La vie de sainte Douceline, fondatrice des béguines de Marseille*, ed. J.-H. Albanés (Marseille: E. Camoin, 1897), p. 91. And on Mechtild of Hackeborn see Bynum, *Jesus as Mother*, pp. 210, 215.

19. Herbert Grundmann, "Die Frauen und die Literatur im Mittelalter: Ein Beitrag zur Frage nach der Entstehung des Schrifttums in der Volkssprache," *Archiv für Kulturgeschichte* 26 (1936):129–61; Simone Roisin, "L'efflorescense cistercienne et le courant féminin de piété au XIIIe siècle," *Revue d'histoire ecclésiastique* 39 (1943):342–78; Bynum, *Jesus as Mother*, pp. 170–74; n. 70 below; and Life of Lukardis of Oberweimar, *Analecta Bollandiana* 18 (1899):340–41.

20. Bynum, *Jesus as Mother*, pp. 91–92, 141–42.

21. Ibid., pp. 235–47. See *Lettres de sainte Catherine de Sienne*, trans. E. Cartier, 4 vols., Bibliothèque Dominicaine, 2d ed. (Paris: Editions P. Téquin, 1886), letter 147, p. 907, and letter 268, p. 1380, where Catherine calls weakness "female" and urges "virility." Peter Dronke, *Women Writers of the Middle Ages: A Critical Study of Texts from Perpetua (+203) to Marguerite Porete (+1310)* (Cambridge: Cambridge University Press, 1984) argues throughout that the topos of the "poor little woman" was often used by women writers as an ironic and assertive statement of female ability.

22. Bynum, *Jesus as Mother*, pp. 203–9, 221, 259–61, and idem, "Critique of Turner." For women who felt vulnerable before the control over the eucharist that priests exercised, see life of Ida of Louvain, *AASS*, Apr., vol. 2 (1865):164–65, and life of Margaret of Cortona, *AASS*, Feb., vol. 3:311, 316, and 339–44. Catherine of Siena venerated priests for their ability to consecrate the eucharist.

23. On the various types of spiritual literature produced in the Middle Ages and the major writers, the best discussion is still Jean Leclercq, François Vandenbroucke, and Louis Bouyer, *La spiritualité du moyen âge* (Paris: Aubier, 1961), which is vol. 2 of *Histoire de la spiritualité chrétienne*, ed. Bouyer, Leclercq, Vandenbroucke, and Cognet.

24. Bynum, *Jesus as Mother*, pp. 110–69. See also André Cabassut, "Une dévotion médiévale peu connue: La dévotion à 'Jésus Notre Mère,'" *Mélanges Marcel Viller, Revue d'ascétique et de mystique* 25 (1949):234–45; Eleanor C. McLaughlin, "'Christ My Mother': Feminine Naming and Metaphor in Medieval Spirituality," *Nashota Review* 15 (1975):228–48; and Valerie Lagorio, "Variations on the Theme of God's Motherhood in Medieval English Mystical and Devotional Writings," *Studia mystica* 8 (1985):15–37.

25. *The Works of Aelred of Rievaulx*, 1: *Treatises and Pastoral Prayer*, trans. M. P. Mcpherson, Cistercian Fathers Series 2 (Spencer, Mass.: Cistercian Publications, 1971), p. 73.

26. *The Monk of Farne: The Meditations of a Fourteenth-Century Monk*, trans. a Benedictine nun of Stanbrook, Benedictine Studies 1 (Baltimore: Helicon Press, 1961), p. 64.

27. Second sermon for SS. Peter and Paul, c. 2, in *Liturgical Sermons*, 2 vols., trans. the monks of Mount St. Bernard Abbey, Cistercian Fathers Series 8, 32 (Spencer, Mass.: Cistercian Publications, 1970–1971), 2:155.

28. Sermons 9 and 10, in *The Works of Bernard of Clairvaux*, 2: *On the Song of Songs*, 1, trans. Kilian Walsh, Cistercian Fathers Series 4 (Spencer, Mass.: Cistercian Publications, 1971), pp. 57–58, 62–63.

29. *The Letters of St. Bernard of Clairvaux*, trans. Bruno Scott James (London: Burns, Oates, 1953), pp. 3, 7, with my changes. For other examples of male usage, see Bynum, *Jesus as Mother*, pp. 113–54.

30. Ibid., pp. 211–15.

31. Ibid., pp. 186–96, especially nn. 47 and 48. For other examples of androgynous imagery in women's lives, see Petroff, *Consolation*, pp. 66–78, and n. 58 below.

32. *Hadewijch: The Complete Works*, trans. Columba Hart (New York: Paulist Press, 1980), p. 16, n. 57, and p. 87; cf. pp. 47, 114, 119.

33. Life of Lutgard, *AASS*, June, vol. 4 (1867):189–210, esp. pp. 191–93.

34. Life of Angela, *AASS*, Jan., vol. 1:189, 206; life of Catherine, *AASS*, Apr., vol. 3:903.

35. Life of Alda or Aldobrandesca of Siena, *AASS*, Apr., vol. 3 (1866):471–76, written in the sixteenth century.

36. *Oeuvres de Marguerite d'Oingt*, pp. 77–79.

37. *Julian of Norwich: Showings*, trans. Edmund Colledge and James Walsh (New York: Paulist Press, 1978), long text, c. 58, p. 294. On Julian, see Brant Pelphrey, *Love Was His Meaning: The Theology and Mysticism of Julian of Norwich*, Salzburg Studies in English Literature: Elizabethan and Renaissance Studies 92.4 (Salzburg: Institut für Anglistik und Amerikanistik, Universität Salzburg, 1982). When Julian says we are "substantial and sensual," she means (roughly translated) that we are "soul and body." It is worth noting that the pronouns that refer to mother Jesus

remain male in the original Middle English, thus enhancing the androgyny of Julian's image of Jesus.

38. Julian, *Showings,* long text, c. 60, pp. 298–99.

39. Helinand of Froidmont, sermon 27, in *Patrologiae cursus completus: Series latina* [hereafter *PL*], ed. J.-P. Migne, 221 vols. (Paris, 1841–1864), 212: col. 622B; see also sermon 20, cols. 646–52.

40. Bynum, *Jesus as Mother,* p. 128, n. 63.

41. Bonaventure, The Life of Francis, in *Bonaventure: The Soul's Journey into God,* trans. E. Cousins (New York: Paulist Press, 1978), pp. 204–6, 243, 251–52, 257, 278.

42. On Bernard's female image of himself, see Bynum, *Jesus as Mother,* pp. 115–18. Hester Gelber of the Stanford University Department of Religion is studying this theme in Francis of Assisi. On Suso and Rolle, see below nn. 43, 44. For saints influenced by their mothers, see Weinstein and Bell, *Saints and Society,* p. 23.

43. *The Exemplar: Life and Writings of Blessed Henry Suso, O.P.: Complete Edition based on Manuscripts,* trans. Sister M. Ann Edwards, 2 vols. (Dubuque: Priory Press, 1962), 1:xxxviii, 12, 45–46, 51–52, 54.

44. See office for Rolle in Rolle, *Fire or Melody.*

45. Suso, *Exemplar,* 1:xxxiv–xxxv, 95–98, 103–6; for assessments of Abelard's attitudes toward women, see Robert Javelet, *Image et ressemblance au douzième siècle, de saint Anselme à Alain de Lille,* 2 vols. (Paris: Letouzey et Ané, 1967), 1:241–42; Mary M. McLaughlin, "Peter Abelard and the Dignity of Women: Twelfth-Century 'Feminism' in Theory and Practice," in *Pierre Abélard, Pierre le Vénérable: Les courants philosophiques, littéraires et artistiques en Occident au milieu du XIIe siècle,* Colloques internationaux du Centre National de la Recherche Scientifique 546 (Paris: Editions du Centre National de la Recherche Scientifique, 1975), pp. 282–333.

46. Suso, *Exemplar,* 1:103–6. Another woman-oriented Dominican of the fourteenth century was similarly critical of the penitential asceticism and eucharistic devotion that he correctly saw as characteristic of women: see John Tauler, *Spiritual Conferences,* ed. and trans. E. Colledge and Sister M. Jane (St. Louis: Herder, 1961), sermon xxxiii, pp. 269–76.

47. Bynum, "Critique of Turner." Tauler, *Spiritual Conferences,* p. 274, urges women not to be "womanly."

48. John Anson, "The Female Transvestite in Early Monasticism: The Origin and Development of a Motif," *Viator* 5 (1974):1–32.

49. Raymond of Capua, life of Catherine, *AASS,* Apr., vol. 3:892.

50. Bynum, *Jesus as Mother,* pp. 208–9, 226–27; Julian, *Showings,* short text, c. 6, p. 135, deleted in long text.

51. *The Book of Margery Kempe,* trans. W. Butler-Bowdon (New York: Devin-Adair Co., 1944), c. 52, pp. 110–15.

52. See Bynum, *Jesus as Mother*, pp. 240–47, and idem, "Critique of Turner."

53. *Book of Margery Kempe*, pp. 22–23, 74–77.

54. *Oeuvres de Marguerite d'Oingt*, p. 139.

55. *Hadewijch*, pp. 280–81.

56. Jo Ann McNamara, "Sexual Equality and the Cult of Virginity in Early Christian Thought," *Feminist Studies* 3.3/4 (1976):145–58.

57. Letter 116, from Abbess T[engswich] of Andernach to Hildegard, *PL* 197:col. 336C.

58. *AASS*, Apr., vol. 3:884. Catherine's own images for herself are female and for Christ androgynous. Her Christ is bridegroom and mother: see Catherine of Siena, *The Dialogue*, trans. Suzanne Noffke (New York: Paulist Press, 1980).

59. See n. 21 above.

60. Caroline Walker Bynum, "Women Mystics and Eucharistic Devotion in the Thirteenth Century," *Women's Studies* 11 (1984):209–10, nn. 40–44.

61. Davis, *Society and Culture*, cc. 4 and 5, pp. 97–151; Vern L. Bullough, "Transvestites in the Middle Ages," *American Journal of Sociology* 79 (1974):1381–94. See also Anson, "Female Transvestite," and Bynum, "Critique of Turner."

62. *Die Visionen der hl. Elisabeth und die Schriften der Aebte Ekbert und Emecho von Schönau*, ed. F. W. E. Roth (Brünn: "Studien aus dem Benedictiner- und Cistercienser-Orden," 1884), p. 60.

63. Hildegard of Bingen, *Liber divinorum operum*, *PL* 197:col. 885. See also, idem, *Liber vitae meritorum*, ed. J.-B. Pitra, *Analecta sacra* 8 (Monte Cassino, 1882; reprint, Farnborough: Gregg Press, 1966), p. 158; and idem, *Scivias*, ed. Adelgundis Führkötter and A. Carlevaris, Corpus christianorum: Continuatio medievalis 43, 2 vols. (Turnhout: Brepols, 1978), 1:225–306, esp. p. 231 and plate 15.

64. On Mechtild, see Bynum, *Jesus as Mother*, pp. 229, 233–34, 244. And see Catherine, *Lettres*, letter 196, p. 1098. For Catherine, unlike Mechtild and Hildegard, humanity is more frequently Adam—i.e., a male image (see ibid., p. 319).

65. Julian, *Showings*, long text, c. 57, p. 292.

66. Hildegard, *Scivias*, 1:19–21, 147–48, 290–91.

67. Bynum, "Eucharistic Devotion."

68. See Catherine, *Lettres*, letter 36, pp. 316–17; letter 198, pp. 1112–13; letter 231, p. 1234; letter 322, p. 1538. And see Robert Fawtier and Louis Canet, *La double expérience de Catherine Benincasa (Sainte Catherine de Sienne)*, Bibliothèque des Idées (Paris: Librairie Gallimard, 1948), pp. 245–46.

69. Life of Ida of Louvain, *AASS*, Apr., vol. 2:165, 166–67. On Dorothy, see Richard Kieckhefer, *Unquiet Souls: Fourteenth-Century Saints and*

Their Religious Milieu (Chicago: University of Chicago Press, 1985), pp. 22–33. *Hadewijch,* pp. 345–49, works out an extended allegory of the soul pregnant with Christ.

70. On stigmata, see E. Amann, "Stigmatisation," in *Dictionnaire de théologie catholique,* 15 vols. (Paris, 1909–1950), 14.2:cols. 2616–24; Vauchez, *La sainteté en Occident,* pp. 514–18; and Bynum, "Eucharistic Devotion."

71. *Hadewijch,* pp. 353–55. Bynum, *Holy Feast and Holy Fast,* explores this theme more fully.

72. Weinstein and Bell, *Saints and Society,* p. 235. See also Ernst Benz, *Die Vision: Erfahrungsformen und Bilderwelt* (Stuttgart: Ernst Klett Verlag, 1969), pp. 17–34.

73. Life of Mary of Oignies, *AASS,* June, vol. 5 (1867):552; *Beatrijs van Tienen,* p. 64; life of Margaret of Ypres, ed. G. G. Meersseman, "Frères prêcheurs et mouvement dévot en Flandre au XIIIe siècle," *Archivum Fratrum Praedicatorum* 18 (1948):125–26. On Gertrude, see Bynum, *Jesus as Mother,* pp. 192 and 253, n. 295. On Villana de' Botti and Dauphine of Puimichel, see Kieckhefer, *Unquiet Souls,* p. 57.

74. Julian, *Showings,* long text, cc. 2, 3, and 4, pp. 177–81.

75. For the prominence of poverty as a theme in male spirituality, see Lester K. Little, *Religious Poverty and the Profit Economy in Medieval Europe* (Ithaca, N.Y.: Cornell University Press, 1978). There is some evidence that food is a theme in women's piety cross-culturally; see Bynum, "Eucharistic Devotion," esp. nn. 85, 93; Jack Goody, *Cooking, Cuisine and Class: A Study in Comparative Sociology* (Cambridge: Cambridge University Press, 1982), p. 193; and Peggy Reeves Sanday, *Female Power and Male Dominance: On the Origins of Sexual Inequality* (Cambridge: Cambridge University Press, 1981), pp. 76–77.

76. Brenda Bolton, "*Vitae Matrum:* A Further Aspect of the *Frauenfrage,*" in *Medieval Women,* ed. Baker, pp. 253–73; Rosalind B. Brooke and Christopher N. L. Brooke, "St. Clare," in ibid., pp. 275–87; Weinstein and Bell, *Saints and Society,* pp. 88–97; and Bynum, "Critique of Turner."

77. Weinstein and Bell, *Saints and Society,* p. 235. Pelphrey, *Love Was His Meaning,* suggests that Julian of Norwich saw sin as a painful and necessary part of being human and that her theory of union with God did not involve "stages" the soul "passed beyond" but rather a continuity of self, a becoming fully human with Jesus. This reading of Julian would make her *Showings* a more conceptually and theologically subtle statement of the kind of "continuity" I find in other women's writing from the period.

78. Nancy Chodorow, *The Reproduction of Mothering: Psychoanalysis and the Sociology of Gender* (Berkeley and Los Angeles: University of California Press, 1978). A. K. Ramanujan, "On Women Saints," in *The Divine Consort: Rādhā and the Goddesses of India,* ed. J. S. Hawley and

287

D. M. Wulff (Berkeley: Graduate Theological Union, 1982), pp. 316–24, applies these ideas to Indian saints. See Bynum, "Critique of Turner," nn. 72, 89, for differences and similarities in the Indian and Western usages. See also chap. 1, n. 23.

79. Weinstein and Bell, *Saints and Society,* pp. 235–36.

80. This suggestion runs counter to the literature that argues that women need, and tend to create, female images; see, for example, Elaine Pagels, "What Became of God the Mother?" *Signs* 2 (1976):293–303, and Carol P. Christ, "Heretics and Outsiders: The Struggle over Female Power in Western Religion," *Soundings* 61.3, *Dilemmas of Pluralism* (1978):260–80. See also chap. 1, nn. 1, 2, 13, 15.

81. See above, nn. 21, 46, 47, 56.

Eleven

Male and Female Perspectives on a Psychoanalytic Myth
John E. Toews

In the context of an analysis of the universal structures of Oedipus myths, Claude Lévi-Strauss stated that "not only Sophocles, but Freud himself should be included among the recorded versions of the Oedipus myth, on a par with earlier or seemingly more 'authentic' versions."[1] In this chapter I will pursue Lévi-Strauss's suggestion that Freud's apparently demythologizing interpretation of the Sophoclean dramatization of the Oedipus legend is itself a dramatic text and form of authentic modern myth. Freudian oedipal theory can be considered a mythic text in the sense that it provides not only a critical analysis of the human production of manifest, illusory meaning, but also a positive construction and symbolization of the hidden, true meaning of human experience. It constitutes a narrative account, a story, in terms of both personal and collective history, of the primal genesis and universal structures of human experience as nature remade in culture. The verification of the truth of this story ultimately remains dependent not on the marshaling of empirical data or on logical incontrovertibility, but on the act of mutual recognition whereby one person discovers an adequate symbolization of his or her life story in the story of another.

Viewing Freudian oedipal theory as a mythic text raises, in a specific and acute fashion, the question of the experiential appropriation of psychoanalytic theory. For what particular types of experience did this story provide a satisfactory, meaningful symbolization? In what ways did the story change as it was appropriated from different perspectives? These questions can be approached in a wide variety of ways: issues of cultural context, religious and political affiliation, ethnicity, class, profession, and generation are all obviously relevant to an exploration of the formation and reception of the Freudian perspective on human experience. In this chapter, however, I would like to focus on one of the most pervasive, elusive, and controversial of the existential determinants of perspectival variance in theoretical construction and symbolic appropriation—gender. In what ways could Freud's oedipal story be described as a male myth? How were the modifications, elaborations, and criticisms of oedipal theory, which emerged during the process of its appropriation by Freud's male and female disciples during the 1920s, influenced by gender perspective?

Two complicating and potentially distracting factors in my analysis should be mentioned at the outset. First, Freud himself was a major participant in the debates over oedipal theory within the psychoanalytic movement during the 1920s, and he modified and elaborated his views at the same time his followers were modifying and elaborating them in often very different ways. Second, a major focus of Freud's revisions and elaborations concerned the relationship between oedipal conflicts and the process of gender differentiation—a central issue in the disagreements among his disciples. This last factor might be especially distracting because I do not intend to give an account of female critiques of Freud's theories of femininity. Instead, my focus will be on the ways in which gender perspective influenced interpretations of oedipal theory in general, including, but not restricted to, the story of the human cultural production of gender difference. For this reason I have chosen to concentrate my analysis primarily on the early work of Melanie Klein, rather than on the more narrowly focused writings of female psychoanalysts of female psychology such as Karen Horney or Helene Deutsch. The central question in my investigation is not whether gender perspective influenced interpretations of Freud's theory of gender, but whether gender perspective produced differing versions of the archetypal masterplot, the general mythical frame, in which Freud's accounts of gender differentiation were articulated.

Freud's Oedipus Myth

Freud first articulated his distinctive version of the Oedipus story in the midst of his self-analysis in the fall of 1897. At the most obvious level the story universalized the repressed history of the unconscious desires that had come to the surface as Freud worked through the impact of his father's death. On October 15, 1897, Freud wrote to his friend Wilhelm Fliess:

> Being entirely honest with oneself is a good exercise. Only one idea of general value has occurred to me. I have found love of the mother and jealousy of the father in my own case too, and now believe it to be a general phenomenon of early childhood. . . . If that is the case, the gripping power of *Oedipus Rex,* in spite of all the objections to the inexorable fate that the story presupposes, becomes intelligible, and one can understand why later fate dramas were such failures. Our feelings rise against any arbitrary individual fate such as shown in the *Ahnfrau,* etc., but the Greek myth seizes on a compulsion which everyone recognizes, because he has felt traces of it in himself. Every member of the audience was once a budding Oedipus in phantasy, and this dream-fulfillment played out in reality causes everyone to recoil in horror, with the full measure of repression which separates his infantile from his present state.[2]

We know, from Ernest Jones's report, that Freud had identified himself in fantasy with Sophocles' Oedipus—the heroic adult Oedipus who divined the riddle of the Sphinx and saved the people of Thebes—at an earlier moment in his life, when he first committed himself to the vocation of a scientific investigator during his student years.[3] During Freud's personal and theoretical crisis of the late 1890s, from which emerged the fundamental principles of psychoanalysis, this imaginative identification gained a new dimension. In Sophocles' dramatization of the Oedipus story Freud now discerned an objectification of the meaning and source of the riddle of our common tragic human fate. In the first published account of the psychoanalytic meaning of the Oedipus myth in *The Interpretation of Dreams* (1900), both aspects of Freud's identification with Oedipus were prominently displayed. On the one hand, the story of Oedipus was so universally compelling because "it might have been ours"; it showed us the "fulfillment of our own childhood wishes." On the other hand, Sophocles' account of Oedipus' struggle to overcome the forces of repression and grasp the meaning of his destiny was compared to the "work of the psychoanalyst."[4]

In Freud's interpretation of the Sophoclean tragedy, therefore, the Oedipus story is both the story of our tragic fate as creatures determined by unconscious childhood desire and the story of the recognition and acceptance of that fate in self-conscious knowledge. From this perspective Freud criticized all modern attempts to re-create the Oedipus story in terms of divine will and human impotence as inauthentic theological rationalizations. "The attempt to harmonize divine omnipotence with human responsibility must naturally fail," Freud insisted, "with this subject matter just as with any other."[5] The Freudian Oedipus myth was a story of the disabused recognition of human destiny as determined by the unconscious impulses of "nature," as an immanent, self-imposed suffering.

Freud's earliest formulation of psychoanalytic oedipal theory already displayed a number of its distinctive permanent elements. First, the reality reference of Freud's Oedipus story is to the inner, psychic reality of unconscious desire.[6] The events of the story constitute objectifications of unconscious wishes; they are productions of fantasy rather than reproductions of memory. In the historical formation of psychoanalysis the Oedipus myth replaced the rejected "fairy tale" of infantile parental seduction in which the reality reference of the story was to actual, external, objective events.[7] Although Freud never entirely denied the significance of external events in the process of psychic formation, after 1897 he definitely relegated such events to the status of "accidental" factors that could not explain the universal aspects of human destiny.[8] We were not all sexually abused by our parents, but everyone was once a "budding Oedipus in his phantasy." The Oedipus story was thus a story of the individual's ultimate, though unconscious, responsibility for, or at least complicity in, his or her own history. The temporal reference of Freud's Oedipus myth has two dimensions. Whereas the seduction story had clearly referred to past traumas, the Oedipus story referred both to the originating moment when incestuous infantile desire instigated the conflicts that determined human destiny and to the eternal present in which those conflicts continued to operate in a repressed, unconscious fashion.

Second, Freud's earliest versions of oedipal theory revealed that he understood the Oedipus story as a triangular family romance, constituted by the complex of relationships between child, mother, and father. Moreover, this romance was written from the perspective of the child as son, whose incestuous desire instigated its relationships. In the intrapsychic world of the son's unconscious fantasy, the mother was the primal object of desire and the father the possessor of that object, who had to be removed or destroyed for gratification to be achieved. Although Freud was certainly aware that parental desires and preferences could awaken and direct oedipal feelings, he insisted that the "spontaneous nature of the Oedipus complex in children cannot be seriously shaken even by this factor."[9] Many later commentators have noted that the Freudian account of the Oedipus story reveals a peculiarly selective reading of Sophocles' text. Laius is absolved of his crimes. The sins of the father have been displaced by the guilt of the son.[10] But if Freud ignored the acts of the parents, and especially the father, in the production of the oedipal relationship, he certainly did not ignore the significance of the father's position. He assumed that infantile sexual desire was formed within the context of a universal patriarchal order in which the father was the legitimate owner of the maternal object, represented the ethical and political authority that judged the son's natural desire as a transgression, and thus produced filial anxiety, guilt, and renunciation. "The father is the oldest, first, and for children only authority," he wrote in 1900, "and from his autocratic power the other social authorities have developed in the course of human civilization."[11]

Freud's reformulation of the Oedipus story assumed the perspective of the son in a patriarchal order, but it was not simply "*about* the paternally socialized son."[12] As he applied and amplified his theory after 1900, Freud became increasingly convinced that his insight into the oedipal origins of the conflicts in his own life history provided him with a theoretical base for unraveling the hidden meaning of all variants of the human fate. The riddles of everyday life, the puzzling variations of sexual orientation and character type, the enigmatic qualities of works of artistic and scientific genius—all surrendered their secrets to the same master key. As Freud expanded the scope of his investigations and elaborated his conceptual formulations, it became evident that the unconscious dynamics of oedipal relations constituted the epochal and problematic mediating link between nature and culture. For Freud the Oedipus story became the story of cultural formation in the psyche, of "enculturation." In *Totem and Taboo* (1912–1913) Freud consciously articulated the implications of his position by constructing his famous anthropological parable of the actual historical emergence of human culture from a prehistorical oedipal conflict.[13]

Freud never relinquished his claims about the universality and epochal importance of unconscious oedipal conflicts. During the 1920s he toyed with the possibility that the Oedipus story might be merely a subplot in the larger cosmic story of the conflict between Eros and Death, but such speculations remained peripheral to Freud's main concern, which was the riddle of human existence, rather than the mystery of being as such. In one of his last writings he asserted that "if psychoanalysis could boast of no other achievement than the discovery of the repressed Oedipus complex, that alone would give it a claim to be counted among the precious new acquisitions of mankind."[14] If Freud did not waver in his insistence on the primary importance of oedipal dynamics in human cultural formation, however, he did modify his account of the oedipal story in a number of significant ways during the immediate postwar years. These revisions were a part of the general theoretical reorientation from which emerged the concept of a primal aggressive or "death" drive and the structural model of the psyche (id, ego, superego).

As Freud reconstructed his Oedipus story, he focused particularly on the ways in which the superego was formed through an internalization of oedipal relations, through complicated processes of introjection of and identification with the feared and loved parental objects. The superego, Freud claimed, was the "heir" of the Oedipus complex.[15] He had been aware for some time that gender orientation was also a product of the Oedipus complex, but before the 1920s he had conceived the cultural production of gender difference in symmetrical terms. As late as 1923 he noted that despite the enormous complexities introduced into oedipal relations by individual bisexuality and instinctual ambivalence, the production of masculine and feminine identities proceeded in "precisely analogous" ways. In the same work, however, Freud also implicitly argued that such symmetrical development of maternal and paternal superegos simply could not be correct because of the father's preeminent role in thwarting the gratification of all oedipal wishes. The superego in both boys and girls was described as a substitute for the father. The moral, suprapersonal dimension of psychic life was defined as a male achievement, "transmitted to women by cross-inheritance."[16] The implication was that the production of male and female superegos in the Oedipus crisis was not symmetrical at all, that women were not just differently encultured, but less encultured, than men. This implication was made explicit in Freud's papers of 1924–1925.

Freud's recognition of asymmetry in the Oedipal stories of men and women was tied to the discovery of the importance of the prehistorical, pre-oedipal stage of human development, the primal dependence of children of both sexes on the mother.[17] As they made the critical transition from narcissism to social individuation and object relations, boys and girls both "naturally" chose the mother as their first love object. Moreover, at this crucial moment of original object choice, the libidinal organization and ego identity of both boys and girls were focused on the active, penetrating, aggressive, phallic, "masculine" genital organ—the penis or clitoris. "With their entry into the phallic phase," Freud claimed, "the differences between the sexes are completely eclipsed by their agreements. We are now obliged to recognize that the little girl is a little man."[18] For the male child, entry into the classic constellation of oedipal conflicts was relatively unproblematic. He simply transformed his pre-oedipal maternal attachment into an active desire for genital possession of the mother as love object, and thus perceived the father as both model and rival. For the girl, however, this entry was more complicated. In order to take her father as love object and view her mother as model and rival, she had to break her pre-oedipal attachments, recognize that her clitoris was not a real penis (i.e., accept the "fact" of castration), renounce her active sexual aims, and assume a passive, receptive stance toward the paternal figure. The trauma of this radical renunciation and reversal produced inevitable scars—penis envy, a tendency toward frigidity, a sense of inferiority, contempt for her own sex. Only by accepting this humiliation as her biological and social fate could the little girl enter into oedipal relations with her parents and become a "little woman": "She gives up her wish for a penis and puts in place of it a wish for a child: and with this purpose in view she takes her father as love-object. Her mother becomes the object

295

of her jealousy. The girl has turned into a little woman."[19] In Freud's view the little girl established her feminine identity within the oedipal situation—as the object of paternal love and as future mother.

The little boy's Oedipus story was rather different. His recognition of anatomical genital difference produced a fear rather than an acceptance of castration. His incestuous and parricidal desires were not produced by, but forced into repression or "dissolution" by, the castration complex. He maintained his penis and masculine identity by transcending the familial oedipal triangle, replacing it with the father-dominated superego, and entering the "processes that are designed to make the individual find a place in the cultural community."[20]

This construction of asymmetrical Oedipus stories had significant social and cultural implications. As Freud noted, the "Oedipus complex . . . is such an important thing that the manner in which one enters and leaves it cannot be without its effects." Fear of castration drove the penis-possessing boy from the world of infantile familial dependencies into the more impersonal, internalized dependencies of the world of culture. For girls, however,

the motive for the demolition of the Oedipus complex is lacking. Castration has already had its effect, which was to force the child into the situation of the Oedipus complex. Thus the Oedipus complex escapes the fate which it meets with in boys: it may be slowly abandoned or dealt with by repression, or its effects may persist far into women's normal mental life. I cannot evade the notion . . . that for women the level of what is ethically normal is different from what it is in men. Their superego is never so inexorable, so impersonal, so independent of its emotional origins as we require it to be in men. Character traits which critics of every epoch have brought up against women—that they show less sense of justice than men, that they are less ready to submit to the great exigencies of life, that they are more often influenced in their judgements by feelings of affection and hostility—all these would be amply accounted for by the modification in the formation of their superego which we have inferred above.[21]

As this passage indicates, Freud's analysis of the production of gender difference in the Oedipus complex amounted to a critique of femininity, in which masculine development served as the human and cultural norm.[22] It was not just that the process whereby women were made in culture gave them a qualitatively different orientation toward morality, rationality, and sociocultural necessity; it stalled their development in the transition from nature to culture and thus made them quantitatively less moral, less rational, less ready to submit to the "great exigencies of life."

The critique of femininity that emerged in Freud's analysis of gender differentiation made explicit a crucial element that had been implicit in the psychoanalytic version of the Oedipus story from the beginning. The Freudian Oedipus myth was a story of the human struggle for emancipation, first from nature and then from the culturally produced constraints—"illusions"—that mediated the original break with nature. The Freudian critique of femininity was an analysis of failed emancipation, of incomplete detachment from the prehistorical mother/child dyad, of the inability to move beyond dependence on protective father figures. Freud's ideal Oedipus became the master of his fate, the possessor of his own story, by courageously recognizing and rejecting the redemptive illusions produced by his unconscious wishes to submerge his individuality in the prehistorical mother/child symbiosis and to find consolation in the protective arms of a loving, all-powerful father. Both illusions were "feminine." Oedipus achieved autonomy and mastery by repudiating the feminine, as object and as model, by renouncing instinctual gratification and the illusions of consolatory or escapist cultural meaning. Yet Freud had many female patients and disciples who also found their story in the psychoanalytic Oedipus myth of the universal human fate. How was this possible? Did the story change as they made it their own?

Melanie Klein's Revision of Freud's Oedipus Myth

When Melanie Klein published *The Psychoanalysis of Children* in 1932, she presented her work on the theoretical and practical implications of child analysis as a mere extension and "full confirmation of the knowledge Freud has gained from the analysis of adults." Her contributions, she insisted, did not deviate in any respect from the Freudian framework; she had merely tried to "add a few more stones to the growing edifice" that Freud himself had raised on secure foundations. Klein also expressed her fundamental agreement with, and profound dependence on, the work of three of Freud's most loyal and influential disciples of an older

generation—Sandor Ferenczi, Karl Abraham, and Ernest Jones—
who guided, encouraged, and supported her in her applications of
Freud's techniques and theories to the psyches of young children.
Ferenczi had initiated her into the "real essence and meaning" of
psychoanalysis and inspired her with the confidence she needed to
begin a career in the relatively unexplored field of child analysis.
Abraham had recognized the legitimacy and importance of her
earliest work, and she viewed her results as "a natural development of his own discoveries." Jones, finally, had given her his
"whole-hearted support" at a difficult time and opened the doors
for a career in England. Moreover, his own studies in early sexual
development agreed with hers "in all essential points."[23] Such pro-
testations of unswerving loyalty to the tenets and proponents of
psychoanalytic orthodoxy, however, could be viewed as defensive
and repressive postures, burying latent rebellion under manifest
submission. For in the twelve years of psychoanalytic practice,
research, and writing that preceded and led up to *The Psychoanalysis of Children*, Klein had not just been adding a few stones to
some outlying wings of the Freudian edifice; she had been rear-
ranging its foundations and rewriting its fundamental myth.

To comprehend the purposes and perspectives that informed
Klein's revisions of oedipal theory, one must go back to her early
work as a psychoanalytic student and apprentice in the years
between 1919 and 1924. Her first paper, delivered as a lecture to
the Psychoanalytic Society in Budapest in 1919, was animated by
an intense confidence in the liberating power of psychoanalytically
directing child-rearing and early education. "We can spare the
child unnecessary repression," she proclaimed, "by freeing—and
first and foremost in ourselves—the whole wide sphere of sexuality
from the dense veils of secrecy, falsehood and danger spun by a
hypocritical civilization upon an affective and uninformed foundation." Klein's attack in this early essay on the "superfluous suffering" produced by "unnecessary repression" was inspired by a
vision of the child as an innocent Oedipus in whom the natural evolution of infantile impulse into intellectual curiosity, independence, and the power to recognize and creatively manipulate reality was thwarted by the withholding of information and parentally
encouraged submission to the "authority principle." The barriers
preventing full actualization of human intellectual powers appeared as external, unnatural, unjust, and arbitrary prohibitions.[24]

Although Klein never lost her pedagogical zeal and practical optimism, by the time she published her first essay in 1921 she had made significant revisions in her story of human destiny. Criticism by her psychoanalytic mentors and the deepening of her own personal analysis led her to recognize that a significant portion of the inhibition and repression of the child's intellectual power and creative independence was spontaneous, self-imposed. Childhood inhibitions and repressions arose from the need to avoid the anxiety connected to the fulfillment of unconscious desires.[25] By 1923 Klein had begun to develop a more orthodox psychoanalytic position focused on the problems and potentialities of the sublimation of the unconscious incestuous and parricidal impulses of the Oedipus complex. She now viewed the child's anxiety as caused by fear of the imagined consequence of the fulfillment of oedipal desires—castration. Certain activities and interests were repressed or inhibited because of their "sexual-symbolic" significance as images of oedipal desire. In a wide-ranging essay titled "The Role of the School in the Libidinal Development of the Child," Klein attempted to demonstrate that

> the fundamental activities exercised in school are channels for the flow of libido and . . . by this means the component instincts achieve sublimation under the supremacy of the genitals. This libidinal cathexis, however, is carried over from the most elementary studies—reading, writing and arithmetic—to wider efforts and interests based on these, so that the foundations of later inhibitions—of vocational inhibitions as well—is to be found in the frequently evanescent ones concerned with the earliest studies. The inhibitions of these earliest studies, however, are built upon play inhibitions, so that in the end we can see all the later inhibitions, so significant for life and development, evolving from the earliest play inhibitions.[26]

The therapeutic implication Klein drew from this analysis was that children should be encouraged to symbolize their unconscious desires in fantasy and play in completely uninhibited fashion. In this way their anxieties could be released and worked through, opening paths to creative sublimation rather than excessive inhibition or neurotic symptom formation.

In 1923 one could have legitimately claimed that Melanie Klein was a loyal worker in Freud's vineyard. She had focused her theoretical interests on an area that Freud had treated in a cursory manner—the mechanics of sublimation—and her practical efforts on an equally neglected area—child analysis. But the framework in which her theory and practice were articulated seemed strictly Freudian. She viewed the young child as dominated by desires arising from the unconscious dynamics of the oedipal situation, in which the oral and anal components of libido were organized under the primacy of genital desires directed toward parental figures. Moreover, she clearly accepted the view that the masculine (active and penetrating) and the feminine (passive and receptive) orientations were primarily determined by relations to the father.[27] To be sure, her continuing optimism regarding the trajectory of the oedipal story and her focus on the positive aspects of childhood fantasy and symbolization in the education toward autonomy and reality gave her work a distinctive quality. But it was only after a new series of traumatizing and liberating crises—the final collapse of her marriage, the death of her mentor and personal analyst, Karl Abraham, and the emigration to a new country and culture—that the distinctive emphases of her perspective were transformed into a new perspective.

Klein's revision of Freudian oedipal theory in the years between 1926 and 1932 had a paradoxical quality because it was connected to an intensification of commitment to certain fundamental Freudian positions and especially to some of the new directions in Freud's thought after 1920. She was one of the few analysts who completely accepted and appropriated the theory of a primal aggressive "death" drive and made it the center of her clinical interpretation. As Ernest Jones noted years later, in her instinct theory Klein was more loyal to Freud than most of the analysts who accused her of heresy.[28] Klein also followed Freud in his new focus on the processes of internalization of infantile object relations, which determined the formation of the superego. Finally, she shared with Freud, and especially with her personal mentor Karl Abraham, an increasing consciousness of the importance of the so-called pregenital (oral and anal) organizations of infantile sexuality in the formation of neurosis and character structure.

Moreover, Klein continued to believe, in agreement with Freud, that infantile relations to mother and father figures determined "all subsequent relations in life," that the unconscious dynamics of the oedipal crisis inaugurated and structured the process of the enculturation of primitive natural being and thus revealed the inner meaning of the human fate:

> Psychoanalysis has shown that the Oedipus Complex plays the largest part in the entire development of the personality, as much in persons who will become normal as in those who will become neurotic. Psychoanalytic work has demonstrated more and more that the whole of character formation too is derived from Oedipus development, that all shades of character, from the slightly neurotic to the criminalistic are determined by it.[29]

Like Freud, Klein believed that oedipal relations were produced by the unconscious wishes and fantasies of the child, not by the wishes, fantasies, or actions of the parents. Her Oedipus as well was the inaugurator of his or her own history and thus ultimately responsible for achieving mastery of it. Klein thus assumed the perspective of the child, although the sex of her child was often not as obvious or as theoretically significant as Freud's identification of *child* and *son*.

Klein's most obvious deviation from the Freudian oedipal story lay in her timing of its origins. The constellation of oedipal relations—desire for possession of the parent of the opposite sex, rivalry with the parent of the same sex—Klein claimed, was set in motion during the first year of life by the oral deprivations and frustrations of the weaning process. Since she continued to believe that oedipal conflicts marked the epochal transition from nature to culture and thus determined the human fate, pushing back the date of the onset of these conflicts meant that the formation of the superego through the internalization of parental objects, the transcendence of primary narcissism in the shift to object-relations and recognition of "reality," the beginnings of anxiety, guilt, self-punishment, and neurosis, the origins of socialization, morality, and gender identity, could also be traced back into what had previously been defined as the pre-oedipal, prehistorical period. What Freud had perceived as the originating moment of oedipal relations—the genital or phallic organization of the child's desire in relation to parental objects—appeared to Klein as a late "reaction formation" in the process of enculturation: "The analysis of little children . . . if it is carried far enough gives a very clear picture of the enormous complexity of development which we find even in very little ones and shows that children at the age of, say, three years, just because they are already so much the products of civilization, have gone and are going through, severe conflicts."[30] The three-year-old Oedipus had already left behind it the "most important" part of its development. Its orientation to the world was already culturally formed through repressions and feelings of guilt.

Within the framework of orthodox psychoanalytic theory, Klein's chronology of oedipal relations had pushed their origins back into the oral phase in the organization of sexual desire. The child's relations to parental objects, and thus ultimately to all subsequent objects, were formed at the primal level by fantasies of oral gratification and aggression, as relations of sucking, devouring, biting, and tearing. Although Klein certainly exploited to its fullest extent the claim that the onset of oedipal conflicts coincided with the oral phase of libidinal development, she rejected any rigid separation of libidinal phases and criticized the hierarchical evaluation that defined oral and anal desire as pregenital. "I do not think a sharp distinction can be made between the early stages of oedipal conflict and the later ones," she claimed.[31] Genital impulses were associated with oral and anal impulses from the very beginning of oedipal relations, and their later development never lost the traces of this primal association. One of the apparent implications of this view was a conception of early enculturation marked by much greater continuity and duration than Freud had envisioned.

This appearance of evolutionary continuity rather than revolutionary discontinuity in the transition from nature to culture, however, can be misleading. Klein did not deny, but, if anything, exaggerated, the Freudian vision of a radical disjuncture between primitive desire and the requirements of civilized life. "The primitive part of the personality," she noted, "entirely contradicts the cultured part of the personality, which is the one that actually engenders repression."[32] Oedipus' entry into the human world was traumatic. In the first years of its life, Klein claimed, the child "goes through an immeasurable degree of suffering."[33] In her view, there were no prehistorical stages to prepare the way for cultural entry. The child was enmeshed in the conflicts and pains of human destiny from the moment it encountered the otherness of the object, the reality of deprivation, at its mother's breast.

Klein's conception of the traumatic character of cultural entry was grounded in her belief in the primacy of the aggressive destructive instincts. "My whole argument," she admitted in 1930, "depends on the fact that the Oedipus conflict begins at the period when sadism predominates."[34] It was not incestuous love, but hatred of the withdrawn maternal breast, that brought on the Oedipus conflicts and fueled their early development. The original experience of deprivation aroused innate destructive impulses and produced unconscious fantasies of uninhibited oral aggression. Since the hated object was invested, through a primitive act of a projective identification, with all of the destructive tendencies directed against it, these primal aggressive fantasies produced an intense fear of persecution, which in turn led to an increase of sadistic and destructive wishes against the threatening object. Aggression was redirected inward as the fantasized persecuting objects were introjected by the weak childhood ego in an attempt to master the uncontrollable impulses of the id and avoid the anxiety produced by externally directed aggression. Fear of self-destruction by the sadistic internalized objects, however, led to their expulsion once again into the external world, and so on, in an apparently endless torturous cycle of aggression, fear, anxiety, and renewed aggression.[35] Even analysts experienced in the world of unconscious fantasy found this vision of the psychic world of the budding Oedipus offensive. As Klein admitted: "The idea of an infant of from six to twelve months trying to destroy its mother by every method at the disposal of its sadistic tendencies—with its teeth, nails, excreta, with the whole of its body, transformed in imagination into all kinds of dangerous weapons—presents a horrifying not to say unbelievable picture to our minds."[36]

For Klein, however, the discovery of the horrifying inner world of unconscious childhood fantasy had important theoretical and practical implications. It demonstrated first of all that infantile desire did not first enter into relations with objects or others in the genital phase of incestuous love and rivalry, but was object related from the moment it encountered the reality of externality or otherness in the experience of deprivation. The early history of Oedipus' desire was situated in a world and only emerged together with that world. Initially, to be sure, the world experienced by the child was a fantasy world, a world produced by its flight from a hated and feared reality, a mirror of its own instinctual life. "In the earliest reality of the child," Klein stated, "it is no exaggeration to say that the world is a breast and a belly which is filled with dangerous objects, dangerous because of the child's own impulse to attack them."[37] The creation of this fantasy world of internal and external relations to significant parental objects was an initial attempt to master, know, and manipulate the real world that had induced its production.

The second major theoretical claim that Klein grounded in her analysis of the child's fantasy world concerned the formation of the superego. In Freud's view the superego was formed as an internalized precipitate of the parental objects of oedipal love and aggression. In Klein's view the internalization or introjection of parental objects for purposes of binding oedipal desire began during the very first stages of oedipal relations, that is, under the sadistic sway of oral and anal aggression. The early superego was as cruel and sadistic as the fantasized parental objects that it represented. The oedipal child's entry into the moral, social, and cultural world was marked by submission to an internal master as vicious as the destructive impulses it had to subdue.[38]

Klein's description of the traumatic nature of the budding Oedipus' introduction to its human fate raises the obvious question: How will the weak and suffering ego of the young child ever gain mastery over this fate, control its aggressive drives, reduce the anxiety and guilt they produce, and thus mitigate the sadistic severity of its superego? One part of her answer is simply that in the normal process of development beyond the early oral and anal sadistic phases, the child gains experiences of the real world, especially of the real nature of the parental objects, which significantly reduce its primitive persecutory fears, allay its anxiety and guilt, and thus release the flow of positive libido with which the ego can form an alliance against the powers of self- and world destruction. Under favorable conditions, Oedipus simply grows up. The second part of her answer focuses on the therapeutic value of psychoanalytic knowledge of repressed unconscious fantasies and conflicts in liberating the ego from the burdensome baggage of its traumatic beginnings. There are, however, three distinctive elements in Klein's conception of the "passing" or "dissolution" of the Oedipus complex. The first is her emphasis on the need for acts of restitution and atonement in the achievement of ego strength, intellectual objectivity and independence, and sustained creative energy. To free itself from its debilitating sense of guilt, Oedipus must repair the damage it had unconsciously perpetrated on itself and especially on its imagined parental objects.[39] Second, Klein placed an extraordinary importance on the role of uninhibited play and fantasy and on the ability to act out, symbolize, and objectify unconscious impulses and anxieties in the achievement of freedom and knowledge.[40] Imaginative objectification of unconscious inner reality allowed the child to recognize and deal with his unconscious aggressions, fears, and anxieties and thus provided the "foundation of adaptation to external reality."[41] Oedipus must recognize and master its inner demons before it can hope to achieve mastery over its external fate. Finally, Klein continued to express her original optimism in the prophylactic power of psychoanalysis. The analyst need not rest content with providing adults with a liberating knowledge of their fate, but could intervene in the psyches of children going through the conflicts of the oedipal crisis and thus, perhaps, change the apparently tragic trajectory of human destiny. If child analysis would become "as much a part of every person's upbringing as school education is now," she wrote in 1933, then the "hostile attitude, springing from fear and suspicion which is latent more or less strongly in each human being . . . will give way to kindlier and more trustful feelings toward his fellowmen and people may inhabit the world together in greater peace and goodwill than they do now."[42] Oedipus could not only appropriate its own past, but make its own future.

Freud's account of the resolution and transcendence of oedipal conflicts, we noted above, was ultimately formulated in gender-differentiated terms. Klein also reconstructed the story of the human fate as the story of the boy and the story of the girl, but in ways that diverged sharply from Freud's views. A detailed account of Klein's complex analyses of male and female development cannot be given here, but I will point out some of their salient characteristics. First, by extending the Oedipus complex back to the moment of original oral frustration at the mother's breast, and emphasizing the critical importance of primal aggression in its formation, Klein undermined two of the foundations of Freud's conception of asymmetrical gender production. Boys and girls experienced deprivation with equal intensity, responded with equal ferocity, and were burdened with equal anxiety and guilt. Gender differences were thus not aligned with stages or extent of enculturation. Children of both sexes were socialized and moralized with equal intensity; their superegos were equally severe. If anything, Klein claimed, the receptive structure of the female genitals gave the girl stronger introjective tendencies and thus a more powerful and extensive superego than the boy.[43] Moreover, since the entry into culture took place under the sway of oral and anal sadism, it was the mother, rather than the father, who was the primary agent of enculturation. She was the first "castrator."[44] The child's relations to the mother were not pre-oedipal and prehistorical, but oedipal and historical. Nevertheless, Klein tended to emphasize the importance of the combined parents as opponents and objects of the child's aggressive drives. The mother was desired and feared in part because she was imagined to possess the paternal penis in her belly. Second, Klein emphasized the positive aspects of feminine genital anatomy in unconscious childhood fantasies. Little girls were not imagined to be, either by themselves or by little boys, simply castrated males. The little girl, she claimed, was "brought under the sway of her Oedipus impulses not indirectly, through her masculine tendencies and her penis-envy, but directly, as a result of her dominant feminine instinctual components." Unconscious knowledge of the vagina was evident in the earliest childhood fantasies. Although Klein agreed with Freud that the little girl wanted a penis and hated her mother for not giving her one, in her interpretation the penis that the little girl wanted was the penis of her father, and it was desired in a distinctly feminine, receptive, incorporative fashion.[45]

Third, although Klein recognized that anatomical difference had psychical consequences in differences of ethical and cultural orientation and achievement, she did not describe these differences in terms of unequal value, of less and more. The powerful introjective and projective tendencies that developed from the female's psychic reaction to the hidden, interior position of her genitals tended to produce a strong sense of duty, an ability to renounce self "for the sake of other people," as well as intense concern for the empirical particularity of external reality. Female ethical orientation and intellectual achievement might be distinctively "feminine," but the capacity for cultural sublimation of natural impulse was as strong in women as in men.[46]

Finally, Klein's account of gender development presented a vision of the human ideal for both sexes that emphasized the psychical consequences of Freud's doctrine of biological bisexuality. Both boys and girls experienced a negative as well as positive version of the Oedipus complex, but the achievement of mature heterosexuality in Klein's view did not imply either a repudiation of femininity by the boy or a rejection of masculinity by the girl. For example, the boy's early feminine phase of identification with his mother, in which he introjected the father's penis as a love object and desired to have children by the father, allowed him to comprehend the woman's "tendency to introject and preserve what she loves" as well as her desire for a love object that would re-create her experience of bountiful maternal love. "Thus and only thus," Klein claimed, "by sublimating his feminine instinctual components and surmounting his feelings of envy, hatred and anxiety towards his mother, will he be able to consolidate his heterosexual position in the stage of genital supremacy."[47]

This vision of the consolidation of gender identity as an affirmative recognition of, and reconciliation with, the other, both within oneself and in the world, represents an important implicit theme in Klein's revision of the Freudian oedipal myth. Freud, we noted, turned the Oedipus story into a story of the struggle for autonomy. In Klein's writings this struggle is certainly present, but it is always combined with and made dependent on a desire for restitution and reconciliation. If Oedipus is to truly become the master of its own destiny, it must learn to join its destiny to the fate of the other and to the fate of the "world." In her conclusion of an analysis of the sexual development of the girl, Klein stated:

> if her restitutive mechanisms have been successfully established she will not only be in harmony with the external world, but . . . she will be at one with her internal world and with herself. If her menacing imagos fade into the background and her kindly father-imago and mother-imago emerge to act in friendly co-operation and give her a guarantee of peace and security within her own body, she can work out her feminine and masculine components under the auspices of her introjected parents, and she will have secured a basis in herself for the full development of a harmonious personality.[48]

307

It would be tempting simply to derive the differences between Kleinian and Freudian versions of the Oedipus story from differences in gender perspective. Such a derivation could take a number of forms. One might, for example, focus on Klein's construction of parallel yet different histories of feminine and masculine development. The significance of her female perspective in this context would consist of her rejection of Freud's inflation of the male story into a universal human myth and his consequent critical judgment of female development as a failure of full participation in the human fate. Klein's contribution to psychoanalytic oedipal theory could then be seen as the addition of a positive female myth to Freud's male myth. The result would be a human story composed of two stories of equal value and validity. What such an interpretation ignores, however, is the fact that Klein accepted the gender-transcendent universality of the Oedipus story, but changed its plot and structure. To grasp this second, deeper level of Klein's revision one might take recourse to an analysis of the distinctively "feminine" nature of some of the fundamental conceptions that undergird her Oedipus story—the primary role of the mother as agent of instinctual renunciation and enculturation, oral frustration as the primal source of love and hate, maturation as an atonement of aggression through restitution and reconciliation, the object-related character of all desire, the importance of fantasy and symbolization in the education to reality, the androgynous component in successful achievement of gender identity, and so on. But on what basis could these conceptions be defined as distinctively feminine? Surely we do not want to return to some kind of metaphysical notion of woman's eternal nature. Yet how can we avoid such regression without arguing in circles?

A convincing definition of *the* feminine perspective on anything is probably impossible, but the problem can be formulated in more manageable terms. In what ways, if any, did Melanie Klein's Oedipus story express the experience of at least certain groups of women in a particular time and place? This is also, of course, the way in which the problem of Freud's "masculine" perspective should be approached. To define Freud's psychology as masculine in some universal sense is as unhelpful and misleading as seeing it as an expression of his Jewish "nature." The issue that should and can be addressed is the ways in which his particular historical experience as a male or as a Jew formed his theoretical and practical vision.[49] Even within these limitations, however, the task of defining male and female perspectives remains immense, and I can only suggest a few directions that might be taken. Our first task must be to compare Klein's perspective on Oedipus with those of her contemporary female and male analysts. Among the female analysts, Helene Deutsch and Karen Horney seem obvious choices. Both were members of Klein's generation; both made the psychoanalytic theories of the psychosexual development of gender, and especially feminine gender, the focus of their research and writing; and both expressed a therapeutic optimism comparable to Klein's as they launched their psychoanalytic careers after the war.[50] Yet, on the surface at least, the oedipal theories of Deutsch and Horney diverged sharply from each other as well as from that of Klein.

Over the years Helene Deutsch gained the reputation of being one of Freud's most loyal and devoted disciples. One consequence of this reputation is that her work on feminine psychology has been the constant object of feminist attacks, which accuse her of simply subordinating woman's experience to Freud's masculine perspective and incorporating the female story into Freud's male oedipal myth. Most of this criticism has been directed at Deutsch's *The Psychology of Women,* published in 1944, but the general outlines of her position were already evident in a book and a number of articles published in the 1920s.[51]

In Deutsch's account, the little girl's human fate is determined by a prolonged struggle to overcome her masculine strivings for active penetration and domination of the world in order to recover her "natural" feminine identity as passive sexual partner and self-denying mother. The critical originating point of this story occurs in the phallic phase of libidinal development. Incipient tendencies toward a passive, receptive mode of sexual gratification in the pre-oedipal period are overwhelmed and repressed by the concentration of libidinal energy on the "masculine" clitoris. The little girl enters the world of oedipal object relations with a false conception of her identity and suffers the consequences of this illusion. To realize her true feminine identity she must renounce her illusory masculinity and discover her vagina as an authentic organ of gratification and as the real representative of her ego. This goal can be attained only with external help: the discovery of the vagina occurs "through being masochistically subjugated by the penis." The act of coitus restores the woman to herself in the act of merger with the other: "Coitus signifies for the woman a restoring of that first relation of the human being with the outside world, in which the object is orally incorporated, introjected; that is to say, it restores that condition of perfect unity of being and harmony in which the distinction between subject and object was annuled."[52] The revelatory act of coitus leads to the experiences of conception, pregnancy, parturition, lactation, and child nurture, in which the woman actualizes her feminine identity in the biological, social, and moral orders.

Deutsch's story diverges sharply (especially in its biologistic emphasis) from the oedipal theories of both Freud and Klein. What is important for our theme, however, is the way in which it agrees with Klein against Freud. First, it replaces Freud's identification of the male and human story with a "parallel and equal, yet different" theory. Although Deutsch generally agreed with Freud's descriptions of the nature of femininity, she infused these descriptions with positive moral value and emphasized the primary, natural sources of feminine social and ethical orientations. Her women were not castrated males; they lived their own stories. Second, like Klein, Deutsch extended the process of enculturation into a lengthy, complex evolution patterned on a model of alienation and return in which the reconstruction of a broken unity was the primary task and goal. Third, the most striking parallel in Klein's and Deutsch's oedipal stories is their common emphasis on reparation, restitution, and reconciliation. Oedipus' task was to heal the rift that marked the entry into the world of culture. It is noteworthy that Deutsch defined the oedipal tasks of both men *and* women in terms of a quest to overcome the anxiety and insecurity of isolation from the world of "objects" and attain the "bliss of the primal state."[53] For both Klein and Deutsch, autonomy and self-mastery were inextricably linked to a recognition of interdependence and mutuality. Unlike Klein, however, Deutsch believed that achievement of the desired unity entailed a repudiation of the other within oneself—of femininity for men, of masculinity for women.

The theory of the oedipal production of gender differences developed by Karen Horney during the 1920s diverged from the positions of Klein and Deutsch in two significant respects. Horney directly attacked Freudian oedipal theory as a masculine myth that expressed unconscious male envy and fear of women. She also claimed that this myth helped maintain and rationalize the actual "social subordination of women."[54] Despite her self-conscious feminism and sociological emphasis, however, Horney agreed with Klein and Deutsch on the three central issues mentioned above. She articulated a "parallel and equal, yet different" theory that not only stressed the autonomous and thus "natural" sources of femminine sexuality and feminine forms of enculturation and sublimation, but also unveiled the self-deceptions and repressed dependencies of masculine development. She described the dynamics of oedipal relations as a prolonged process of enculturation, originating in "pre-oedipal" conflicts and extending beyond puberty. Finally, Horney defined the resolution of Oedipal conflicts not in terms of detachment, autonomy, and the acceptance of tragedy, but in terms of reconciliation, interdependence, and the possibilities of fulfillment. Her studies of masculine and feminine psychology during the 1920s culminated in discussions of the possibility of authentic mutuality in marriage.[55]

Before we proceed to consolidate these three points into a unified feminine perspective, however, a different kind of comparison—with the contemporary work of male analysts—is obviously necessary. Implicit and explicit dissatisfaction with Freud's version of the Oedipus story was also present among male psychoanalysts during the 1920s.[56] The shift in perspective of one prominent psychoanalytic pioneer and member of Freud's inner circle—Ernest Jones—is of special interest.

In an important series of conference papers and lectures delivered between 1926 and 1935, Jones summarized and consolidated the revisions of psychoanalytic oedipal theory proposed by Klein, Horney, Deutsch, and other female analysts and defended them against the orthodox positions of what he called the "Viennese School." He rejected Freud's claim that the phallic phase inaugurated oedipal conflicts and thus determined their consequences and resolutions. The classical oedipal constellation of incestuous desire and fear of retaliation, he insisted, began at the moment of oral frustration and developed in a parallel fashion in children of both sexes. The penis envy and penis narcissism of the phallic phase were simply reaction formations produced by the anxieties of already well-developed oedipal conflicts. The superego was not a product of castration fear, but of the primal anxiety and

311

fear of destruction that emerged from early oral, anal, and genital fantasies of incestuous object choice. Like Klein, Jones came to view Oedipus' story as a long struggle in education to reality instigated by primal deprivation and fear of destruction. The phallic phase was a mere episode in this story.[57]

One implication that Jones drew from this revised Oedipus story was that it recognized the independent reality of a distinctively feminine sexuality. Feminine gender, he noted, "develops progressively from the promptings of an instinctual constitution. . . . In short, I do not see woman—in the way feminists do—as un homme manqué, as a permanently disappointed creature struggling to console herself with secondary substitutes alien to her nature. The ultimate question is whether a woman is born or made."[58] The parenthetical attack on feminists and insinuations of biological destiny in this quotation should make us pause and examine what conclusions Jones actually drew from his acceptance of a "parallel and equal, yet different" theory of gender production. Two of his claims are particularly revealing. First, he stated that "for obvious psychological reasons," woman "is much more dependent on her partner for gratification than is the male." The "promptings of her instinctual constitution" led the female to depend much more on the willingness and moral approbation of her partner than the male, who experienced this kind of dependence only in relations with other "authoritative" males, that is, father figures. The biological "fact" of female dependence had important ethical implications. For the girl, fear of destruction was focused on withdrawal of the male, on abandonment and separation. The boy on the other hand, envisioned death as the active destruction of his potency. Despite his recognition of the mother's early role in inducing instinctual frustration and renunciation, Jones ultimately reinstated the father as the primary source of renunciation and the defining authority in the formation of the superego. "It is well known," he wrote, "that the morality of the world is essentially a male creation and . . . that the moral ideals of women are mainly copied from men."[59]

In the final analysis, therefore, Jones could not accept the third element that the positions of Klein, Deutsch, and Horney had in common—the emphasis on reconciliation and reciprocity. For Jones, the Oedipus story, even after the inclusion of a feminine subplot, still culminated in correlated relations of domination and submission—penis over vagina, male over female, culture over na-ture. It is interesting that Jones rejected the particular element in Klein's theory of the Oedipus complex that transformed it into a vision of the human fate which contradicted his own—the primacy of the destructive aggressive drives.[60] By integrating Freud's theory of primal aggression into her extended conception of the Oedipus complex, Klein created a story of man and woman's common complex assumption of their cultured humanity through a mastery of primitive impulse, anxiety, and guilt. The human fate and hu-man tasks of both sexes were determined by their original destruc-tive response to the frustration of deprivation and separation. The devastation and suffering produced by the initial relations of domi-nation and fear had to be repaired and allayed before a genuine inner and outer mastery of the human fate could be achieved. Rec-onciliation and reciprocity were the conditions of autonomy. By rejecting Klein's vision of the origins of the human fate, Jones radi-cally changed its end, reinstituting the alliance between autonomy and domination which she had opposed.

The essence of the distinctively feminine perspective on the psy-choanalytic Oedipus myth during the immediate postwar period thus appears to be centered on reconciliation and reciprocity. Freud's reconception of the Oedipus myth, as we have seen, was focused on the issues of detachment and emancipation from both maternal prehistory and paternal culture. There can be no doubt that many of the women who joined the early psychoanalytic movement found in this myth a representation of their own eman-cipatory struggles and hopes. Klein, Horney, and Deutsch were members of the pioneer generation of university-educated profes-sional women in central Europe. During the 1920s, however, they were struggling not only with the detachment from parental figures as they established themselves in their new careers, but also with marital tensions and child-rearing difficulties.[61] The early female psychoanalysts lived in the zone of tension between the spheres that Freud and other male analysts defined in terms of asymmetri-cally valued and progressively ordered oppositions. It is clearly in the complex conflicts of this historical situation that we must seek for the experiential origins of their distinctive vision of our common fate and future possibilities.

However, the value of a comparative, phenomenological de-scription of female appropriations of psychoanalysis' founding myth need not be confined to its role as a prolegomena to future investigations of cause and psychosocial origin; it can also contribute to an understanding of the ways in which so-called theoretical models function in modern intellectual subcultures like the psychoanalytic movement. It is clearly inadequate to view psychoanalytic oedipal theory as a rigidly structured model that imprisoned its users in an order of univocal meanings. Freud's rewriting of the Oedipus legend constituted a multivalent mythical narrative that opened up the possibility of a variety of psychic appropriations and actualizations. The mere fact of women's participation in the language and practices of the psychoanalytic movement did not necessarily imply the subjugation of their thought and experience to the perspective of the "other." Viewing Freudian oedipal theory as not only moral prescription or scientific description, but as a symbolic, mythical narrative open to both feminine and masculine actualizations, could lead to new ways of thinking through gender construction and gender perspective in psychoanalysis. Without rejecting the critical insight that men and women are made in culture in unequally valued ways, the time has come to pay closer attention to the ways in which they also have made, and continue to make, themselves.

Notes

1. Claude Lévi-Strauss, "The Structural Study of Myth," in *Structural Anthropology,* trans. Claire Jacobson and Brooke Schoepf (Garden City, N.Y.: Anchor Books, 1967), p. 213.
2. Sigmund Freud, *The Origins of Psychoanalysis: Letters to Wilhelm Fliess, Drafts and Notes: 1887–1902,* ed. Marie Bonaparte, Anna Freud, and Ernst Kris (New York: Basic Books, 1954), p. 223.
3. Ernst Jones, *The Life and Work of Sigmund Freud,* 3 vols. (New York: Basic Books, 1953–1957), 2:14.
4. Sigmund Freud, *The Interpretation of Dreams* (1900), in *The Standard Edition of the Complete Works of Sigmund Freud,* trans. and ed. James Strachey, 24 vols. (London: Hogarth Press, 1953–1974), 4:262–63. Cited hereafter as *SE.*
5. Ibid., p. 264.
6. Sigmund Freud, *On the History of the Psycho-Analytic Movement* (1914), in *SE,* 14:16–18.

7. Sigmund Freud, "The Aetiology of Hysteria" (1896), in *SE*, 3:203. Freud had described the theory to Fliess in January 1896 as a "Christmas Fairy Tale." Cf. Freud, *Origins*, p. 146.

8. Sigmund Freud, "My Views on the Part Played by Sexuality in the Aetiology of Neuroses" (1906), in *SE*, 7:275ff.

9. Sigmund Freud, *Introductory Lectures on Psychoanalysis* (1916–1917), in *SE* 16:333.

10. For an extended recent discussion of this issue see Marie Balmary, *Psychoanalyzing Psychoanalysis: Freud and the Hidden Fault of the Father*, trans. Ned Lukacher (Baltimore and London: Johns Hopkins University Press, 1982), esp. pp. 7–24.

11. Sigmund Freud, *The Interpretation of Dreams* (1900), in *SE*, 4:217.

12. Judith Van Herik, *Freud on Femininity and Faith* (Berkeley and Los Angeles: University of California Press, 1982), p. 55.

13. Sigmund Freud, *Totem and Taboo* (1913), in *SE*, 13:156.

14. Sigmund Freud, *An Outline of Psychoanalysis* (1938), in *SE*, 23:192–93.

15. Sigmund Freud, *The Ego and the Id* (1923), in *SE*, 19:36.

16. Ibid., p. 37.

17. In 1931, Freud compared the discovery of the pre-oedipal mother to the discovery of the Minoan-Mycenaean civilization behind that of classical Greece. Cf. Sigmund Freud, "Female Sexuality" (1931), in *SE*, 21:226.

18. Sigmund Freud, *New Introductory Lectures on Psychoanalysis* (1933), in *SE*, 22:118.

19. Sigmund Freud, "Some Physical Consequences of the Anatomical Distinction between the Sexes" (1925), in *SE*, 19:256.

20. Freud, "Female Sexuality," p. 229.

21. Freud, "Some Psychical Consequences," pp. 257–58.

22. This point is explored in great detail in Van Herik, *Freud on Femininity and Faith*, pp. 135ff.

23. Melanie Klein, "Preface to the First Edition" (1932), in Klein, *The Psychoanalysis of Children*, trans. Alex Strachey (New York: Grove Press, 1960), pp. 7–9.

24. Melanie Klein, "The Influence of Sexual Enlightenment and Relaxation of Authority on the Intellectual Development of Children" (1919), published as part 1 of "The Development of a Child" (1921), in Klein, *Contributions to Psycho-Analysis 1921–1945* (London: Hogarth Press, 1948), pp. 13, 14, 35.

25. Melanie Klein, "Early Analysis" (1921), published as part 2 of "The Development of a Child" (1921), in *Contributions*, pp. 42–43, 62–63.

26. Melanie Klein, "The Role of the School in the Libidinal Development of the Child" (1923), in *Contributions*, p. 82.

27. Ibid., pp. 69, 83–85.

28. Ernest Jones, "Introduction" (1948), in Klein, *Contributions,* pp. 10–11.

29. Melanie Klein, "Criminal Tendencies in Normal Children" (1927), in *Contributions,* pp. 188, 186.

30. Melanie Klein, "Symposium on Child-Analysis" (1927), in *Contributions,* p. 168.

31. Klein, *Psycho-Analysis of Children,* p. 192.

32. Klein, "Criminal Tendencies in Normal Children," p. 185.

33. Ibid., p. 189.

34. Melanie Klein, "The Importance of Symbol-Formation in the Development of the Ego" (1930), in *Contributions,* p. 236.

35. Klein, *Psycho-Analysis of Children,* pp. 179–209.

36. Ibid., p. 187.

37. Melanie Klein, "The Psychotherapy of the Psychoses" (1930), in *Contributions,* p. 251.

38. Klein, *Psycho-Analysis of Children,* p. 198.

39. Ibid., pp. 298–301, 336–38.

40. Klein, "Symposium on Child-Analysis," p. 160.

41. Klein, *Psycho-Analysis of Children,* p. 311, n. 1.

42. Melanie Klein, "The Early Development of Conscience in the Child" (1933), in *Contributions,* p. 277.

43. Klein, *Psycho-Analysis of Children,* pp. 316–17.

44. Melanie Klein, "Early Stages of the Oedipus Conflict" (1928), in *Contributions,* p. 206.

45. Klein, *Psycho-Analysis of Children,* pp. 270–71.

46. Ibid., pp. 319–20.

47. Ibid., pp. 339–40.

48. Ibid., pp. 322–23.

49. For a recent study of Freud's historical experience as a Jew, see Dennis Klein, *Jewish Origins of the Psychoanalytic Movement* (New York: Praeger, 1981). Freud's historical experience as a male has hardly been addressed in the literature.

50. Paul Roazen, "Introduction," to Helene Deutsch, "Two Cases of Induced Insanity," *International Journal of Psycho-Analysis* 62 (1981):140–41; Helene Deutsch, *Confrontations with Myself* (New York: W. W. Norton, 1973), pp. 148–71; Jack L. Rubins, *Karen Horney: Gentle Rebel of Psychoanalysis* (New York: Dial Press, 1978), pp. 53–55.

51. See especially Deutsch's article "The Psychology of Women in Relation to the Functions of Reproduction," *International Journal of Psycho-Analysis* 6 (1925):405–18, which summarizes the positions of her book *Psychoanalyse der weiblichen Sexualfunktionen* (Leipzig, Wien, Zürich: Internationaler Psychoanalytischer Verlag, 1925).

52. Deutsch, "Psychology of Women," p. 409.

53. Ibid., pp. 410–11.

54. Karen Horney, "The Flight from Womanhood: The Masculinity-Complex in Women as Viewed by Men and Women" (1926), in Horney, *Feminine Psychology,* ed. Harold Kelman (New York: W. W. Norton, 1967), p. 70.

55. See especially Horney's essays "The Problem of the Monogamous Ideal" (1928); "The Distrust between the Sexes" (1930); and "Problems of Marriage" (1932), in *Feminine Psychology.*

56. See, for example, Otto Rank's subordination of oedipal relations to primary mother/child relations in his *The Trauma of Birth,* originally published in 1924.

57. Ernest Jones, "The Early Development of Female Sexuality" (1927); "The Phallic Phase" (1932); and "Early Female Sexuality" (1935), in Jones, *Papers on Psycho-Analysis,* 5th ed. (Baltimore: Williams and Wilkens, 1949), pp. 438–95.

58. Jones, "Early Female Sexuality," p. 495.

59. Jones, "Early Development of Female Sexuality," pp. 441–42.

60. Jones, "Introduction," in Klein, *Contributions,* p. 12.

61. Hanna Segal, *Melanie Klein* (New York: Viking Press, 1979), pp. 19–27; Deutsch, *Confrontations with Myself,* pp. 115–27; Rubins, *Horney,* pp. 56–89.

Contributors

ALISON H. BLACK is Johnston Visiting Professor of Philosophy at Whitman College. She is the author of *Man and Nature in the Philosophical Thought of Wang Fu-chih (1619–92)*, scheduled for publication in 1986 by the University of Washington Press.

CAROLINE WALKER BYNUM is Professor of History at the University of Washington. She is the author of *Docere Verbo et Exemplo: An Aspect of Twelfth-Century Spirituality* (1979) and *Jesus as Mother: Studies in the Spirituality of the High Middle Ages* (1982). Her forthcoming book, *Holy Feast and Holy Fast* (University of California Press, 1986), is a study of the religious significance of food to medieval women. Recent articles include "Women Mystics and Eucharistic Devotion," *Women's Studies* 11 (1984), pp. 179–214, which won the Berkshire prize in 1985.

STEVAN HARRELL is Associate Professor of Anthropology and International Studies at the University of Washington. He is author of *Ploughshare Village: Culture and Context in Taiwan* (1982). His articles on Chinese folk religion cover such topics as change in the nature of local cults, ancestor worship, the idea of the soul, individual differences in belief and practice, and the relationship between the idea of fate and the entrepreneurial ethic.

JOHN STRATTON HAWLEY, formerly of the Department of Asian Languages and Literature at the University of Washington, is now Professor of Religion at Barnard College, Columbia University. He has written *At Play with Krishna* (with Shrivatsa Goswami, 1981), *Krishna, the Butter Thief* (1983), and *Sūr Dās* (1984), and has edited a volume of essays entitled *The Divine Consort: Rādhā and the Goddesses of India* (with Donna M. Wulff, 1982).

319

LAAL JAMZADEH is a Ph.D. candidate at Harvard University in the department of Near Eastern Languages and Civilizations. She is now working on her dissertation "101 Names of God in Zoroastrianism." This article is based on her paper, "Ceremonial Use of Food in Zoroastrianism," presented at the Middle Eastern Studies Association meeting in Seattle, Washington, in November 1982.

CHARLES F. KEYES is Professor and Chairman of the Department of Anthropology at the University of Washington. He is the author of *The Golden Peninsula: Culture and Adaptation in Mainland Southeast Asia* (1977, revised edition in process) and *Thailand: Buddhist Kingdom as Modern Nation-State* (1986). He is also editor of *Ethnic Identity and Adaptation: The Karen on the Thai Frontier with Burma* (1979), *Ethnic Change* (1981), *Karma: An Anthropological Inquiry* (1983), and *Reshaping Local Worlds: Rural Education and Cultural Change in Southeast Asia* (forthcoming). Among his most recent articles are "Mother or Mistress but Never a Monk: Culture of Gender and Rural Women in Buddhist Thailand" in the *American Ethnologist* (1983) and "The Interpretive Basis of Depression" in *Culture and Depression: Studies in the Anthropology and Cross Cultural Psychiatry of Affect and Disorder,* ed. by Arthur Kleinman and Byron J. Good (1985).

MARGARET MILLS received her Ph.D. in Folklore and Near Eastern Languages and Culture from Harvard University in 1978. She presently teaches in the Folklore Department at the University of Pennsylvania and continues research and publication mainly on oral narrative traditions in Persian languages from Afghanistan.

PAULA RICHMAN is Assistant Professor of Religion at Oberlin College. Her publications include "Sources and Strategies for the Study of Women in India" (with Michael Fisher), *Journal of Ethnic Studies* (1980) and "Framed Narrative and the Dramatized Audience in a Tamil Buddhist Epic," *Asian Folklore Studies* (1984). She is currently completing a book on religious rhetoric in *Maṇimēkalai.*

JOHN E. TOEWS is Associate Professor of History at the University of Washington and a MacArthur Fellow. He is the author of *Hegelianism: The Path Toward Dialectical Humanism, 1805–1841* (1981). He is concurrently working on a study of the collapse of philosophical humanism in the 1840s and a book on the early years of the Psychoanalytic Movement.

CAROLYN M. WALLACE received her Ph.D. in Anthropology from the University of Washington in 1982. This article is based in part on her dissertation, *Daughters of God: Meanings of Womanhood in the Church of*

Jesus Christ of Latter-day Saints. She is currently engaged in further re-search on the LDS Church.

MICHAEL A. WILLIAMS is Associate Professor and chairman of the Comparative Religion Program in the Jackson School of International Studies at the University of Washington. He is the author of *The Immovable Race: A Gnostic Designation and the Theme of Stability in Late Antiquity* (1985) and editor of *Charisma and Sacred Biography* (1982). Among his recent articles is "Variety in Gnostic Perspectives on Gender," to appear in *Images of the Feminine in Gnosticism,* ed. Karen King.

Index